Bonfire of the Humanities

BONFIRE
OF THE
HUMANITIES

Rescuing the Classics in an
Impoverished Age

જી

Victor Davis Hanson
John Heath
Bruce S. Thornton

ISI BOOKS
WILMINGTON, DELAWARE
2001

Cataloging-in-Publication Data:

Hanson, Victor Davis.
    Bonfire of the humanities : rescuing the classics in an impoverished age / by Victor Davis Hanson, John Heath, and Bruce S. Thornton. — 1st ed. — Wilmington, Del. : ISI Books, 2001.

    p.   ; cm.

ISBN 1-882926-54-4
    1. Education, Humanistic — United States. 2. Classical education — United States. I. Heath, John. II. Thornton, Bruce S. III. Title.

LC1011 .H36 2001   00-106783
378.01/2—DC21   CIP

Published in the United States by:

    ISI Books
    Post Office Box 4431
    Wilmington, DE 19807-0431

Manufactured in the United States of America

CONTENTS

ACKNOWLEDGMENTS

THE authors wish to thank Jeffrey O. Nelson, Brooke Haas, and Jeremy Beer of ISI Books for their support. We thank too Herb Golder and Nicholas Poburko of *Arion: A Journal of Humanities and the Classics,* where versions of chapters 1, 3, 4, 5, and 7 first appeared, for permission to reprint them here. Chapter 2 first appeared in *Echos du Monde Classique/Classical Views,* chapter 6 in *Classical World,* and chapter 8 in the *Intercollegiate Review.* They are reprinted here, in slightly revised form, by permission. Finally, we appreciate all our classics colleagues across the country who have had the courage to laugh out loud at seeing the emperor strutting down the street buck naked.

ACADEMIC POPULISM AND THE ASSAULT ON THE CLASSICS

THE American university is in trouble, and classics, once the foundation of higher learning in the liberal arts, is nearly moribund. The study of ancient Greek and Latin language and civilization has been immolated in various bonfires lit by any number of modern Savonarolas, the ideologues of the multicultural and postmodern Left who wish to destroy the beauty and brilliance they cannot acknowledge or appreciate.

Of course, this ideological fanaticism—frequently documented and deplored—is not the whole story of why classics is in such dire straits. Much of what is wrong about American life—its utilitarianism, crass materialism, and consumerism—has also contributed to the erosion of the university and the lost primacy of classical studies. Yet this contemporary assault has not come completely from outside the university. Rather, the American professor and the culture of the American campus deserve much of the blame as well, for those who knew better adopted the very values that would feed rather than resist this national pathology.

In short, we believe that there is a direct connection between the increasing failure of our students and the enormous rate of publication in the humanities in journals and academic presses—most of it read by very few, and written primarily to advance careers rather than knowledge or ideas. We believe that our students sense that many of their professors are hypocrites who berate them about race, gender, and class, and then live lives as separate from the underprivileged as those whom they castigate. And we believe that too often these professors lie to our students, citing the evils of capitalism but not the one hundred million killed by communism in this century; decrying the evils of Western culture, while failing to mention the lives that are saved and enriched when societies adopt the constitutional government, capitalism, freedom, and rationalism derived solely from the Western tradition; and denigrating the Greeks as racists and sexists, but ignoring that theirs was the only culture in the ancient world in which the condition of foreigners and women was under constant public discussion.

As we attempt to demonstrate in these essays, today's classics professor is deemed successful to the degree he professes a life he does not live—and does so through travel, a comfortable salary, a convenient orthodox ideology, and the avoidance of undergraduates. Of course, other critics share our skepticism over the dubious aspects of feminist theory, the unworkable quotas of affirmative action, and the nihilism of postmodernism. But they often do so for reasons quite *different* from our own, which admittedly more narrowly center on rather basic concerns: Do professors teach? Can others read what they write? Are they interested in expanding their field and arguing for its relevance to the people outside the academy?

Our approach can perhaps be termed "academic populism." American populism was always basically a pragmatic movement, a concrete attempt to address the inequities created by the power of capital and the wide disparity between those who produce and those who profit from their labor. It was never a means of income redistribution or a comprehensive utopian or socialist scheme to address the very foundation of American social and cultural exploitation. It was a modest and focused effort to bring a fair return for a good product.

So too with academic populism and its concern with teaching loads, fair compensation, the dearth of tenure-track jobs, the abuse of part-time faculty, the neglect of undergraduate teaching, and the explosion of esoteric academic publication at a time when its readership is lower than ever. Behind our criticism of contemporary academic fads and trends lie these more mundane concerns.

Throughout this book a common theme is the absurdity of the well-heeled and tenured railing from comfortable enclaves about abstract -ologies and -isms when concrete problems in their own immediate midst—a dying field, an uninterested public, poorly prepared students, unemployed Ph.D.'s, and exploited part-time and adjunct lecturers—receive little concern. And, frankly, we are also quite tired of reading about the unfairness of American life from professors who are among the most comfortable in our country—lifetime jobs, secure suburban existences, frequent travel, summers off, ten hours or so a week in class—thanks precisely to the system of democratic capitalism which they so frequently assail in the abstract.

The hypocrisy, then, of the contemporary academic is a common theme throughout these essays and reviews. Academic populism argues that the campus humanities department is a very poor place to rail against racial discrimination, economic inequity, and the elitism of American culture. For such stalwart critics we suggest that a sojourn in Bakersfield, Mendota, or Compton would provide more opportunity for upper-class revolutionaries to implement their calls for social change than would La Jolla, Santa Cruz, or Palo Alto.

Nineteenth-century distinctions between Progressives and Populists are also of value when entrenched critics such as classicists Peter Green and David Konstan, in not-so-subtle attempts to lampoon our calls for more teaching, clearer writing, and greater concern for the public at large, deride our arguments as "populist," "evangelical," or even "sleazy." Populists in the 1890s were similarly stereotyped, called "Uncle Hayseed" because of their identity with the working class and their antagonism towards an unimaginative corporate oligarchy. We are not, then, academic progressives, who wish to entertain a particular type of revisionist scholarship—one for the most part that seeks to redress the supposed failings of prior positivist historical and philological research with special emphases on gender, race, and class—and all the other cutting-edge ideologies that aim to provide a theoretical basis to rectify the supposed social and cultural pathologies of contemporary society.

Nor are we rightists yearning for the elite university of the traditional and privileged who are to learn about and then operate within High Culture. In fact, ideology in and of itself is of little interest to us; the inclusion of the American people in the university and the academic industry of publication most surely are. We care very little whether a scholar makes the argument that women were oppressed or liberated in ancient Greece, whether Athens was a murderous imperial power or a beacon of hope for the exploited, or whether Alexander was a drunken thug or an emissary of Western civilization. And we certainly care little whether a scholar is female, Mexican-American, or an ex-army officer from Utah. Rather, we care a great deal about whether scholars' ideas are expressed clearly, are the results of empirical and honest research, are supported by the evidence, are formulated in the pursuit of truth, and are the dividends of hours of give-and-take between teachers and undergraduates.

Nor are we anti-intellectuals who call for excessively burdensome instructional loads or a rejection of research altogether—a common reductionist criticism, when in the past we have called for teaching, say, three classes rather than one a semester, for teaching *without* rather than *with* graders, or for meeting *with* rather than lecturing *at* undergraduates. All three of us have found it manageable to publish scholarly articles, academic books, and nonfiction literature for the general public while teaching more than two courses a semester and maintaining some semblance of family and community life. Interaction with townspeople, spouses, children, and students is critical to research. They are the canaries in the mine, reminding the detached scholar that he is suffocating and will soon expire if he does not leave the rarified and deadening atmosphere of his own particular shaft to breathe fresh air with his students and readers. Aeschylus, Socrates, Thucydides, Plato, Aristotle, and Archimedes were men of action, whose lives were one with those of their peers and whose work was a product of a continual—and often dangerous—plunge into the mêlée.

So by use of the term "academic populism" we wish to concentrate on the methodology of research and the manner in which professors live their lives, teach their students, and present their knowledge—and, above all, the degree of consistency between their advocacy and their behavior. Populism was inspired by the discrepancy between the ideals preached by America's leaders in both parties and the actual practices of those in power. Every essay in this collection makes the latter point—that it is hard to believe most academics' purported radicalism when they enjoy an existence about which most Americans can only dream.

In these essays we agitate for an academic ethos that is both pragmatic and egalitarian, an alternative to the therapeutic, multicultural, and postmodern Left and the corporate, vocational, and utilitarian Right—enemies both of broad, accessible liberal education. The six-figure salaries of the university administrators who teach not at all, in order to oversee distance-learning programs or corporate internships, seem not all that different from those of grandees in humanities departments who likewise develop new strategies to turn the university into something other than a disinterested pursuer of the truth—and to avoid teaching undergraduates in the process. It is no accident that both the high-flying campus administrator and the academic grandee ultimately justify their compensation and avoidance of undergraduates by comparison to the corporate world: "I oversee a budget as large as that of a CEO," the overpaid president huffs; "My ideas are surely as important to society as those of the president of a corporation," the postmodernist pedant whines. Academic populism, like its political progenitor, is a third party likely to irritate both the conservative and the liberal, but at times and for unanticipated reasons to find support in both quarters as well.

As these essays show, we do not like most postmodern research, not merely because it is anti-empirical, logically incoherent, and tritely nihilistic, but ultimately because it is usually jargon-ridden, antihumanist, antiliberal, and inaccessible to our students and the public at large—and has become a method of subsidy for professors by excusing them from teaching those who pay their salaries. All research need not be immediately utilitarian in the facile sense, but there is no reason why a researcher in the humanities should not be able to transmit his ideas to the student and public at large. To the extent that he cannot or does not, we deem him a failure. Brain surgeons and engineers employ a technical vocabulary and engage in nearly incomprehensible specialized research so that people's tumors can be removed and rivers can be bridged; textual critics and postmodern theorists on campus employ a commensurate level of abstraction that ensures students cannot be taught and the public remains ignorant of the classical cultures.

Classicists should *not* boast of their obscurity. Classicists should *not* declare that professors should "fight for more research time" in order to publish on "women's roles or slavery or sexuality in antiquity." Classicists should *not* scoff that the profession does not need "the pose of middle-class populism" or "good citizenship and chumminess, to the point of opening our homes to calls at all hours from students." And classicists should surely *not* whine that "deans and college presidents and legislators (with the collaboration of a certain number of faculty members) at more and more colleges and universities are trying to increase teaching loads and take away time from research."[1]

Classicists like these reveal two general truths about the prevailing contemporary academic ethos, particularly that of *soi-disant* academic progressivism: its disdain for "the newly empowered middle class," and its disturbing tendency to be disingenuous when it is a matter of money. The very organization that David Konstan previously served as president, the American Philological Association, in fact, once wrote to its membership that it should adopt Konstan's despised "pose of middle-class populism"—when the government threatened to cut off National Endowment for the Humanities (NEH) grants for faculty leaves: "*Use simple language.* Critics have often charged that NEH money supports elitist scholars. Thus it is important not to use technical words or high theory.... Observers believe that the 104th Congress is populist-minded. In demonstrating to your representatives the impact of the NEH in your district, highlight traditionally populist concerns such as equal access and participation by the many, not the few" (emphasis in original).

Populism is bad when it is a matter of questioning obscure research, cushy perks, and the avoidance of teaching; populism is good when money and prestige are involved. Indeed, one of our most severe critics, Peter Green, approximately thirty years ago, when he was outside the mainstream American academic establishment, flayed classics on precisely the grounds that it was elitist and its careerist ethos had killed the entire field: "There is some difficulty in countering the charge that classical studies are 'dead,'" Green the maverick concluded (*Essays in Antiquity*, 20). Yet three decades and an endowed professorship later, this same Peter Green barked that our advocacy of academic populism was the "the kind of antiestablishment diatribe that tends to surface every thirty years or so"—and he went on to worry terribly that we have gained fame and fortune from our "populist" writings.

Perhaps the most central claim of academic populism—the one that has bothered classicists such as Konstan and Green the most and remains the least frequently mentioned—is that the engine driving the demise of classics is careerism, *not* ideology. Most of the silly prose of the new generation of postmodernists, gender-studies devotees, and multiculturalists would never have been tolerated if classicists were not more interested in promoting their careers than in pursuing the truth about the Greeks. The more tiny the idea, the more obscure the allusions, the more likely no one has ever thought such a vision of the Greeks possible (and for good reason), the more conferences, colloquia, and chat rooms—the better for one's career.

Most of these authors, of course, do not believe their own postmodern tenets. They criticize capitalism because it pays financial dividends. As Thornton and Heath point out in chapters 1 and 2 in their reviews of the work of Martha Nussbaum, and Hanson in his examination of the personal voice theory school (chapter 4), none wish to share their salaries with the dispossessed or live among the muscular classes. They advocate multiculturalism, as Heath notes of current humanities research in chapter 6, because it promotes them out of the classroom and away from the lowly undergraduates—the very people their curriculum is supposed to liberate.

They say there are no facts, but are outraged when their research is criticized—as Hanson and Heath can attest from the shrill attacks on *Who Killed Homer?* They pile up the frequent-flier mileage on gravity-defying jets that whisk them to the latest conference on the social construction and relativism of the scientific method. They hate the West, but demand the freedom of speech, material prosperity, lack of religious interference, respect for diversity, and competitive merit-based rewards that the West alone ensures, as Thornton notes in his description of the twilight of the professors (see chapter 8). They insist that nothing can be known, that knowledge is a mere construct of unreliable language, that linear thinking is phallocentric, imperialistic, and oppressive, and then, without a hint of irony, write heavily footnoted book after book to tell us so (on this point, see especially chapter 5). They say that truth is relative, yet condemn opposing theories as less valid than their own.

They reject "narrow" disciplines in favor of "inclusive" cultural studies—and then rigorously exclude anything that does not support their tendentious political agenda. They denounce an imagined world governed exclusively by issues of power even as they spend their time handing out *curricula vitae*, applying for the next job, and running for office in professional organizations. They proclaim the death of the author, and then sign their names to their books and wear nametags at the convention. They advocate the overthrow of hierarchical privilege while clutching desperately an outdated system of tenure that guarantees their own power and privilege. They insist that facts are not discovered and that history is invented, yet publish professionally sponsored personal-voice narratives of their own real and painfully formative tenure humiliations. They decry culturally imposed hierarchies as they scramble up the career ladder of the corporate academy. They profess radical skepticism in their scholarship but use inductive logic to plan every second of their personal and professional lives: what car to buy, what neighborhood to live in, what schools to send their children to, what articles to write and classes to teach (and not to teach).

The contradictions of the medieval Church or eighteenth-century French letters do not match the hypocrisy of contemporary American academic culture. Indeed, we believe that American academic culture is one of the most glaring failures and embarrassments of modern society itself.

Academics of the present generation do not generally like to be told that they do not teach many undergraduates—and that they should; that they should write for broader audiences in clear English—and that they often don't; that they should be upset that they teach little and get paid lots, while the adjuncts and part-timers in their midst teach lots and get paid little; and that they should be populist rather than elitist in their approach to formal learning. Instead, the usual alleged culprit for the fall of the humanities in general and classics in particular is the bogeyman of the "modern world": video games, television, utilitarian college administrators, the crassness of popular American culture, or even populist criticism from folks like us! In short, anything other than the professors themselves.

When we look to the behavior of prominent academics, the usual apologies of hardship are proffered: tutorials are demanding work; phone calls, meetings, and peer review are exhausting activities that are not appreciated by ignorant outsiders; teaching quality, not quantity, is what counts; cutting-edge research is difficult, time-consuming, and has revitalized the field; "folksy" lecturing and "pop platitudes" are no substitute for the intellectual rigor that can bloom only when fertilized by fellowship, grant, and conference. Just as the modern, urban academic has trouble appreciating the vanished agrarian world, so too he finds it difficult to embrace a populist agenda so hostile to these rites of passage of the careerist professor.

But why should we anchor academic populism in classics, purportedly the most elite of all the humanistic disciplines? Of course, the study of classical antiquity is what we three were trained in and know best—and thus we see first-hand how it suffers from careerism. And Greek and Latin are not English composition or Psychology I, but instead rather difficult pursuits, often without institutional support, that require advocacy and missionary zeal to survive, and thus can least afford poor or indifferent teaching.

But even more importantly, classicists should be populist for reasons other than self-interest. The dominant and most influential ethos of the Greeks was neither aristocratic nor socialistic but rather egalitarian, an agrarian-based vision that demanded equal places in the land, electoral process, and fighting ranks for as many citizens as possible, a vision that antedated even Athenian democracy and was part of the evolving Greek idea of equality and freedom at the very beginning of the city-state. The classical world was, of course, a ranked, hierarchical society, whose citizens' prosperity often depended on the brutal exploitation of slave labor and at times of the free poor and foreigners, depending on the constitution, physical setting, and culture of the particular *polis* involved. But given the status of politics elsewhere in the Mediterranean at the time, we must emphasize just how singular the anti-aristocratic ethos was in Greece. Indeed, it is quite unmatched by anything in Egyptian, Persian, or Northern European tribal culture, literature, or philosophy.

Greek authors of the upper classes were not themselves uniformly aristocratic. Many were often quite suspicious of wealth and privilege, as the pronouncements of Archilochus, Euripides, and Phocylides attest, and the careers of Aeschylus, Socrates, and Thucydides prove. From what little we know of broad-based oligarchic constitutions outside of democratic Athens such as that at Thebes, perhaps a quarter to half of the male adult resident population enjoyed full citizenship rights. In the *chôra* of Attica as many as 20,000 families had title to plots of roughly similar size. Modern scholars often have envisioned a fourth to a third of polis residents owning two-thirds of the land surrounding their communities—a far cry from, say, Bautista's Cuba or California at the millennium, where 5 percent of the landowners possess over 90 percent of the land.

Thus the uniqueness of a viable middle stratum of citizen—although with clear disdain for the poor, and often owning slaves—remains a valid generalization about Greek society. The record of Hellenic land tenure and constitutional clauses about property qualifications suggests something larger than a narrow class of citizen participants in most *poleis*; there are numerous anti-aristocratic Greek authors, and even rightists such as the Old Oligarch, Plato, and Aristotle assume a body of both pragmatic and philosophical thinkers hostile to their often elitist views. The discovery of freedom by the Greeks was not perfect upon inception, but inaugurated an evolving process whose ultimate ends even now we have not yet reached.

Consequently, we must be populist in a practical way to save classics, but we also must be populist in a larger sense because the Greeks themselves were populist—*hoi mesoi* (middle guys), *autourgoi* (yeomen), *geôrgoi* (farmers), *politai* (citizens), *hoi polloi* (most of the people), *ho dêmos* (the people)—in a way unknown in other ancient Mediterranean cultures. Classical antiquity is at the heart of Western civilization, and Western civilization—democracy, capitalism, individualism, middle-class empowerment—for better or worse is increasingly at the heart of world civilization. Whether we like it or not, the world is becoming more populist, more Greek, if you will, at precisely the time the stewards of Hellenism have betrayed their stewardship. And so we offer these essays and reviews in the hope that the entire ethos of the contemporary academic will be dismantled before it dismantles public support for the university and higher learning itself.

PART I

WHAT WE SHOULD NOT BE AND NOT DO

CHAPTER I

⤸

BRUCE S. THORNTON

CULTIVATING SOPHISTRY

The rise of multiculturalism in the academy has created a dilemma for many faculty and scholars. Those honest enough to
think through the implications of identity politics realize that it
is inimical to the fundamental assumptions of liberal democracy:
that autonomous, rational individuals are the loci of nonnego-
tiable rights more essential than the accidents of race or ethnicity,
and that government exists first to protect the rights of those
individuals. In contrast, identity politics asserts that race or "culture" (usually vaguely or tendentiously defined) constitutes the
basis for public treatment: membership in certain groups (those
considered victims of historical oppression and exclusion) *ipso
facto* entitles one to special consideration by public institutions.

Yet, at the same time, multiculturalism and its twin, "diversity," constitute the dominant orthodoxy on campus, in the media, and in government: hence, public obeisance to it is necessary
for the ambitious. The grant, the promotion, the prize, the next
rung of the employment ladder are all more accessible to those
who at least publicly can mouth the pieties of multiculturalism.
Therein lies the dilemma.

Martha Nussbaum's *Cultivating Humanity*, the subject of the review-essays that follow, represents a sophistic (in the worse sense) attempt to resolve this dilemma. Nussbaum's career, like Bill Clinton's, is a masterpiece of "triangulation": she has attacked the loonier excesses of postmodernism that trouble the editors of organs of middle-brow intellectual orthodoxy such as the *New York Review of Books* and the *New York Times Book Review*, yet at the same time has distanced herself from the so-called "conservative" intellectual bogeys represented by, *inter alia*, Allan Bloom. She has also championed tony liberal causes like gay rights, even giving (what some have argued was perjurous) testimony in the court challenge to Colorado's Amendment 2.[1] And, like Clinton's, her triangulation has worked: she is a darling of the *New York Times* and now holds a prestigious chair at the University of Chicago.

꒳

For in my sight, the villain with a crafty tongue incurs a most heavy retribution: he boasts that his words will cloak deceit decently, and boldly pursues his wicked end: yet in fact he is not so very wise.
                                        Medea 580–83, trans. D. L. Page

IN *Cultivating Humanity*, Martha Nussbaum tries to make a liberal-democratic silk purse out of the sow's ear of multicultural identity-politics. Despite numerous commentaries from across the political spectrum that have demonstrated the anti-Enlightenment, antihumanist assumptions of multicultural ideology,[2] Nussbaum asks us to dismiss all this work as a distorted picture that "bears little resemblance to the daily reality of higher education in America" (2), one motivated by the usual pop-psyche suspects, "anxiety and resentment" (21), on the part of a blinkered, conservative establishment jealously guarding its traditional prerogatives. Yet the only counterevidence Nussbaum presents is anecdotal in the worst sense: her own subjective and biased accounts of her experiences in the classrooms of people she knows and "trusts" (x). This un-Socratic reliance on impressionistic "opinion" rather than on knowledge does not bode well for the soundness of Nussbaum's argument.

Just as troubling is Nussbaum's un-Socratic failure to examine carefully the concept of multiculturalism. Her implied definition is the standard pragmatic one repeated by the popular press and educrats alike: "Today's teachers are shaping future citizens in an age of cultural diversity and increasing internationalization. Our country is inescapably plural." Hence we must understand different cultures "if our economy is to remain vital and effective solutions to pressing human problems are to be found" (6). This is the establishment version of multi-cult, and as such is dismissed by true believers as "corporate multiculturalism," the ideology "of a centrist academy and multinational corporations that take themselves to be committed to the broad tenets of philosophical liberalism."[3] Most multiculturalists reject this definition because it insidiously universalizes Western ideology in order to strengthen the West's pernicious hegemony: "This view often collapses into an ethnocentric and oppressively universalistic humanism in which the legitimating norms which govern the substance of citizenship are identified most strongly with Anglo-American cultural-political communities."[4] Nussbaum's version of multi-cult, then, is one its own theorists reject as inauthentic, which again raises the issue of just how accurate it is.

Other problems, however, lurk about this concept, problems an old-fashioned Socratic examination of terms could bring to the surface. First, two issues are confused by Nussbaum: the need of businessmen and government officials to know something about the foreign countries they deal with, an issue as old as Ambrose's advice *Si fueris Romae, Romano vivito more*; and the problem of what constitutes the "cultures" of American minorities or women or homosexuals. As for the first, I can't imagine any corporate hegemon who wouldn't agree that a knowledge of, say, Asian custom and protocol makes good business sense. The second is more complicated, demanding a discussion of "culture" that Nussbaum never undertakes.

In what sense do middle-class white women, for example, have a "culture" different from their fathers' or husbands'? And even in the case of American-born minorities, how much of their identities derives from a non-Western "culture" that is presumably so "other" from American culture? Leaving aside for the moment the diversity ignored by labels like "African-American" or "Hispanic," how much does Africa (ignoring again the variety of societies, dialects, religions, etc., subsumed under that vast noun) really account for American black identity, given that the slave trade was ended in 1808, and so African culture among the slaves could not be renewed and kept alive by fresh captives? How do, say, Mexican-Americans—who typically speak languages like Spanish and English and worship as Catholics— become non-Western "others"? They can't all have descended from the Aztecs, precious few of whom were left alive by the Spaniards. They are at least as likely to have as antecedents the Tlascalans who helped Cortes destroy the Aztecs.

In addition to indulging the gross simplifications and distortions lurking within the "culture" half of "multiculturalism," Nussbaum ignores the role of American popular culture in shaping the identities of American students whatever their backgrounds. Russell Jacoby has pointed out how the chimera of "cultural difference" hides the commonality created by consumerism and popular culture:

> The issue is how different these "cultures" are from each other and the dominant American culture. Do they constitute distinct structures of work, living and beliefs? In their dress, activities, religion, and desires these cultures are becoming more alike. Only in the current ideological climate is this news or heresy.... America's multiple cultures exist within a single consumer society. Professional sports, Hollywood movies, automobiles, designer clothes,

namebrand sneakers, television and videos, commercial music and CDs: these pervade America's multiculturalism.... The multiple cultures define themselves by their preferences within a consumer society, not by a rejection of it.[5]

So the issue is infinitely more complex than evidenced in Nussbaum's Diversity Industry boilerplate. Given the kinds of pop-culture-laden lives our students live, the ethnic "culture" they encounter in a university course is likely to be an ideologically loaded fantasy concocted by academics, though one replete with potential for career and resumé aggrandizement.

Multiculturalism, then, is not about teaching authentic "cultures" in the framework of liberal Enlightenment tolerance. Rather, at the heart of multiculturalism is an antiliberal identity-politics Nussbaum correctly deplores (7, 12, 67). Multiculturalists themselves are up front about the obsession with group identity: "Much of the utopian project of multiculturalism," the Chicago Cultural Studies Group writes, "lies in the notion that it will allow intellectual work to be the expression and medium of identity."[6] One of the classic essays discussing the philosophical assumptions of multiculturalism is Charles Taylor's "The Politics of Recognition," which he defines precisely in opposition to the liberal politics of universalism:

> With the politics of equal dignity, what is established is meant to be universally the same, an identical basket of rights and immunities; with the politics of difference, what we are asked to recognize is the unique identity of this individual group, their distinctness from everyone else. The idea is that it is precisely this distinctness that has been ignored, glossed over, assimilated to a dominant majority identity. And this assimilation is the cardinal sin against the ideal of authenticity.[7]

Moreover, the universal political procedures of liberalism in this view are, as we have already seen, highly suspect: "The claim is that the supposedly neutral set of difference-blind principles of the politics of equal dignity is in fact a reflection of one hegemonic culture. As it turns out, then, only the minority or suppressed cultures are being forced to take alien form.... [B]lind liberalisms are themselves the reflection of particular cultures.... [T]he very idea of such a liberalism may be a kind of pragmatic contradiction, a particularism masquerading as the universal."[8] As Taylor suggests, this concern with group identity necessarily militates against the universal human nature that underwrites liberalism and its notion of human rights. And we shouldn't forget that ideologies of group identity have some unsavory bedfellows: "Like the racists before them," Alain Finkielkraut writes, "contemporary fanatics of cultural identity confine individuals to their group of origin. Like them, they carry differences to the absolute extreme, and in the name of the multiplicity of specific causalities destroy any possibility of a natural or cultural community among peoples."[9]

Multi-cult, then, is not really about just tolerating diversity within the big tent of liberalism. Rather, it is a form of history as therapeutic melodrama: it provides victim-narratives that bolster the self-esteem of those groups who have been designated as "others" oppressed by Western science, capitalism, political ideology, and so on. As such its roots—ironically, given its anti-Western bias—lie in that nineteenth-century Teutonic fit of anti-Enlightenment pique that found expression in, *inter alia*, Germanic romantic nationalism.[10] Just as Germans resented the cool Gallic "universal man" for ignoring what was distinctly vital about the unique *Volk*, so today's multiculturalists define their identities in opposition to a soulless Western culture and its destructive values of rationalism and individualism and materialism. These anti-Enlightenment, identity-politics roots of multiculturalism seriously challenge Nussbaum's attempt to sugarcoat it as an expression of universal liberalism.

In fact, Nussbaum herself occasionally lapses into the questionable assumptions of identity politics. Consider the following statement explaining the presumed alienation of pre-multiculturalism black students from the masterpieces of Western culture, an alienation she implies was corrected by ethnic-studies courses: "In short, for a black student being asked to study the great books was not like being asked to do so for a white student. For the latter, it was an initiation into the elite stratum of one's own world. For the former, it was like going to a debutante party in whiteface and knowing that one wasn't on the invitation list" (159). And the "price of admittance" to the great tradition required black students to "repudiate their origins and to avow the superior value of European civilization" (151). These statements make sense only in terms of a simplistic racialist view of culture that sees it as somehow biologically linked to race. Consider all the identity-politics assumptions in Nussbaum's statement, leaving aside the marvelous variety ignored by the catch-all phrase "great books," and the implication that they are mere hosts for uniform totalizing ideologies. The first is that if you are white you immediately feel some mystic kinship with Homer and Shakespeare. Presumably, Caucasians have a "great books" gene that can overcome the limitations of economic class and ignorance. Maybe in Nussbaum's privileged "elite stratum" reading Homer is an initiation into a world recognizable because one's upbringing has been surrounded by the art and literature of high culture, but for many so-called "white" people who lack such cultural advantages, the only Homer they know is surnamed Simpson. Or does Nussbaum believe that a poor-white Appalachian by nature has some racial affinity with a Mediterranean Greek? Nussbaum's unacknowledged class biases are particularly glaring coming from someone so conspicuously concerned about the excluded "other."

The second assumption is that black American "culture" is "African" and hence so completely different from American culture and its European antecedents that any black student would find them at some level incomprehensible. This, as I have mentioned, is simply untrue. Black "culture" is American, and no matter how many African folkways managed to survive and influence three centuries of black (and white) life in America, black identity at its core is Western; just consider the important role Christianity has played in black life. Astonishingly, Nussbaum twenty pages later admits as much and contradicts this assumption of the great books' alien irrelevance for blacks when she quotes a famous passage from Du Bois in which he speaks of reading great literature as "cross[ing] the color line." Nussbaum's gloss—nearly identical, by the way, to Allan Bloom's earlier one on the same passage—is that "the world of the mind is common to all. To judge that truth, logic, and literature written by whites are all inappropriate objects of study for the African-American is to yield to the feudal society of 'knightly America,' which made Truth and Beauty off-limits to all but an elite" (177-78). Amen, but you're not likely to hear such sentiments in the multiculturalist classroom that Nussbaum champions.

Nussbaum, however, apparently believes that contemporary multiculturalism facilitates a Du Bois-like understanding of the Western tradition on the part of blacks by somehow making that tradition "relevant" or by linking it to a self-esteem-boosting recognition of black "culture." But who today argues that Western culture is inappropriate for black students, that it is a hegemonic imposition of alien values? Certainly not traditionalists, who believe exactly as Nussbaum does about what Bloom calls the "common transcultural humanity" exemplified in Du Bois's statement.[11] No, one is more likely to find the rejection of "white culture" in the classrooms of the multiculturalist, who subscribes to an identity politics that Nussbaum implies was forced on black students in the past. On the contrary, it is the contemporary multiculturalist who is partially responsible for keeping today's black students away from the great works of a tradition that, as Du Bois recognized without the benefit of multi-cult guidance, is their birthright as much as it is anyone's.[12]

Nussbaum herself, however, provides us with the clue to understanding her confusion. She pauses from her argument to confess that all her knowledge of black American life is second-hand, since she wasn't allowed to play with blacks when she was a child, and as a professor has had few black students or colleagues (151–52). That lack of first-hand experience is exactly why Nussbaum is so vulnerable to the definitions of "black identity" or "black culture" created by self-selected race tribunes who have an institutional and professional stake in controlling the "race dialogue" and exploiting the privilege, segregation, and guilt of the white academic. Unlike Nussbaum, I grew up in rural Fresno County where the majority comprised poor and working-class blacks and Mexicans; I *lived* the diversity that to Nussbaum is a mere abstraction or collection of exotic lifestyle accessories. That experience is precisely why I reject most of what academics have to say about race—it usually trades in stereotypes and generalizations that simply don't reflect what I learned day-by-day from the unique individuals with whom I walked to school, worked, fought, danced, and made out: that race is an illusion, and that people have to be taken on their merits, one at a time. In other words, I learned through experience the fundamental truth of Enlightenment liberalism: it is the individual heart and mind that counts, not the group. And that knowledge is reinforced for me every semester, since again, unlike Nussbaum, I teach the "great books" in an institution in which half the students are minorities. I have never once noticed receptivity to Socrates or Homer conditioned by race or gender or anything other than the inclination and mind of the individual.[13]

Another confusion that results from Nussbaum's failure to scrutinize Socratically the concept of multiculturalism concerns the issue of cultural relativism. Most multiculturalists would agree with the proto-fascist philosopher Joseph de Maistre, who rejected Enlightenment universalism: "In the course of my life I have seen Frenchmen, Italians, Russians, etc.... But as for *man*, I declare that I have never met him in my life; if he exists, he is unknown to me."[14] So too modern multiculturalists, as we have seen above, are cultural determinists who distrust any pretensions to universalism, all values and identities ultimately reflecting contingent, specific circumstances. Hence no culture or values are more "true" or "better" than any other; indeed, no standard exists by which we can judge another culture, since any standard ultimately is fixed in a particular time and place and thus serves particular power interests. The logical result must be cultural relativism, though multi-cult aficionados are notoriously inconsistent in this regard: the West can be wantonly criticized, almost always, of course, on the basis of principles invented by the West, and always from the material safety and abundance of the West.

As a liberal, Nussbaum necessarily must reject the idea that one cannot criticize other cultures: "Confrontation with the different in no way entails that there are no cross-cultural moral standards and that the only norms are set by each local tradition" (33). Self-criticism, she says later, "does not entail suspending criticism about practices and beliefs of non-Western cultures or portraying them as free from domination or misrepresentation" (116). Obviously, but the question begged is where does this historically contingent "standard" come from? Why is it privileged over others? What is the basis of the criticism? That standard or basis will involve principles and ethical assumptions that have specific origins, growth, and development. Freedom, for example, for Nussbaum provides a basis for criticizing cultural practices: "Tolerant people usually do not tolerate everything: where real harm to others is present, their interest in the protection of liberty will require them to draw a line" (136). But where does the idea of freedom come from? Who first identified it as an abstract good to be pursued? The Greeks, of course, are the first people to record a self-consciousness about the concept of freedom that none of their contemporary cultures possessed. What is the word for "freedom" or "free citizen" in Persian or Egyptian?[15] If Nussbaum is going to trump cultural practices with the standard of freedom, then she necessarily is assenting to the belief that the West invented a superior ideal that should apply to *all* peoples everywhere, regardless of their ethnicity or race or culture—precisely the belief of the so-called traditionalists who want the Western tradition to take priority in the curriculum because in it are embodied those universal ideals like freedom or a critical consciousness that, if globally endorsed, could allow people, as Nussbaum herself puts it, "to take charge of their own thought and to conduct a critical examination of their own society's norms and traditions" (30). But aren't those "norms and traditions" precisely what is *celebrated* in the multicultural classroom?

Nussbaum's anxious concern to avoid any hurtful hierarchies and to give every culture its due leads her to further confusion on the issue of cultural relativism. Consider the following: "If we have in mind a general shared goal but, like the Stoics, acknowledge that our students approach the goal from many different starting points, we will naturally conclude that many different curricular approaches are required" (32). Once more, where does the "shared goal" come from? Why is it chosen over others? And more important, what if the "starting point" conflicts with the "shared goal"? If the starting point, say, is a belief in the subordination of women as enforced by purdah, what possible "curricular approach" will get to that liberal goal that does not at some point require the critical rejection of the "starting point," as well as an assertion that it is flawed or simply wrong and perforce inferior? Ultimately, the Western notion of innate rights that cannot be compromised because of gender will trump the "starting point"— and once more we are back to the traditionalist view that is anathema in the typical multicultural classroom.

Over and over Nussbaum's attempt to eat her multicultural cake and have it too confuses her argument. She asserts, remarkably, that "any and every human tradition is a tradition of reason, and the transition from these more ordinary and intracultural exercises to a more global exercise of critical argument need not be an abrupt transition" (63). I'd like to know how human sacrifice, female infanticide, cannibalism, slavery, suttee, clitoridectomies, female foot-binding, torture, apartheid, and witch burning are "traditions of reason." Nor do all the cultures that practice those abominations practice as well a "critical argument" based on reason and the assumption of innate rights possessed by all humans, a criticism that ultimately can dispel the superstitions of tradition and liberate people from such horrors. That critical tradition arose in the West, was used in the West to end its own irrational oppressive customs, and from there spread to the whole world, so that now attacks on traditional cruelties and oppression are based on Western assumptions of human rights. That's why a model of the Statue of Liberty was erected in Tiananmen Square; that's why indigenous critics of their own culture's crimes seek refuge, support, and aid from the West.

Nussbaum's attempt to honor simultaneously multicultural difference and liberal universalism culminates in her assertion that the West *didn't* alone invent these notions of human rights and tolerance and rationalism and individualism, but rather all these can be found in other traditions as well (139–43). Such a remarkable argument requires a lot of sophistic tweaking of terms and rhetorical hedging: "Once we spell the ideas out, asking what it means to say human beings have a right and on what basis they are taken to have these rights, we will find that many cultures have at least some of the elements that are involved in the various different views of rights that we inherit from the Enlightenment" (141). Notice the loophole of "at least some of the elements": of course "some of the elements" of just about anything can be found probably everywhere, given the variety of human behavior and societies; but the point avoided is that only in the West did the elements cohere into a system of abstract *concepts* that could be the subject matter of a *rational* intellectual (as opposed to religious) tradition, and hence develop, be refined, and ultimately culminate in the Enlightenment. It was in the West that these rights became ideals and goods to be consciously pursued, rather than remaining accidental "elements" subject to the contingencies of time and place and power and superstition. That's why the West developed a vocabulary for these concepts, and other traditions didn't; that's why the Enlightenment happened in Europe instead of in China or India; that's why the "other" is becoming more Western rather than the Westerner becoming more "other." Likewise with individualism and the rest: practices and behaviors and sentiments that *look* like these ideals no doubt occurred accidentally, but the trick for humans has been to identify these ideals as goods to be consciously pursued and liberated from both the whim of individuals with power and from the vagaries of chance and time. There's a world of difference between the *de facto* freedom of the savage Scythian and the *de jure* freedom celebrated in Herodotus; a palace coup against the Pharaoh is very different from a city-state's creation of democratic institutions.

Nussbaum's confusion on this score is obvious in her attempt to attribute the invention of religious tolerance to the third-century B.C. Indian king Ashoka: "What we take to be a crucial aspect of the Enlightenment turns up in India, well before any Western thinker dreamed of it, as a humane response to the fact of religious pluralism" (143). Yet Nussbaum fudges several issues in making this claim. First is the possibility that Stoic ideas of tolerance influenced Ashoka, given that there were cultural and diplomatic contacts between Mauryan India and the Hellenic world since the time of Ashoka's grandfather Chandragupta.[16] Next, Nussbaum ignores the distinction between a philosophy, like Buddhism, that is deeply embedded in a religious worldview with soteriological and theological implications, and a secular philosophy that grounds ideals not in the supernatural or the mystical but mainly in reason and argument, a reason possessed by every human being, not just the divinely sanctioned priest or king or believer. And third, practices endorsed by men of power because such practices reinforce public order and facilitate their rule must be distinguished from practices resulting from rational *principles* viewed as valid apart from any political power or individual man. The former will last only as long as the individual ruler and be dependent on his whims, which is why, despite Ashoka's tolerance, the caste system exists in India today and religious violence flourishes; the latter can transcend particular times and places and ethnicities and become part of a developing tradition available to reformers, just as the Enlightenment ideal of human rights, though violated by American institutionalized racism, was nonetheless available to Martin Luther King to justify the civil rights movement.

Contrary to Nussbaum, it is the West alone that invented the idea her own book celebrates: the rational individual who should be free to choose apart from the accidental constraints of race or national origins, and who possesses certain inalienable rights that should demand our respect regardless of gender, race, religion, or culture. This vision of human identity had its beginnings in ancient Athens and Jerusalem, and over the centuries its slow, painful development has been repeatedly betrayed by those in the West who should have known better. But despite that betrayal, it is the West that has identified those universal human evils like slavery or racism or sexism *as* evils to be rejected and combated; it is the West that has discovered and nourished the idea of natural rights inherent in *all* humans simply because they are human and not because they are members of some clan or tribe or sect. And despite that betrayal, that ideal of freedom for the individual has survived, and today this vision of human rights represents the best hope that all humans, Western or not, have for creating societies in which freedom, justice, and respect for individuals take precedence over the appetites or whims or superstitions of various elites. In this sense most of the world is either Western or trying to become Western; for as Jacques Ellul, no cheerleader of the

West, has put it, non-Western societies have "inherited the consciousness of and desire for freedom. Everything they do today and everything they seek is an expression of what the western world has taught
them."[17] And those parts of the world that brutally repress the freedom of the individual are those, like Bosnia and Rwanda, that are
riven by an ethnic particularism too often found in the multicultural
classroom.

Nussbaum's muddled concept of multiculturalism is the
Tweedledum of her argument; the Tweedledee is the traditionalist
straw man. This ragged scarecrow is the favorite bogey of the
postmodern philosopher and multicultural apologist alike, a caricature that feeds the self-serving illusion that antitraditionalist professors are embattled, cutting-edge minorities fighting a powerful establishment anxiously bent on repressing the "other" and protecting its
power and privilege: "In our own society, traditionalists frequently
resist the idea that we should cultivate our perceptions of the human
through confrontation with cultures and groups that we have traditionally regarded as unequal. Defenders of the older idea of a
gentleman's education urge that our colleges and universities focus
on acculturation to what is great and fine in our own tradition, rather
than on Socratic and universalistic goals" (294). "Traditionally regarded as unequal," the adverb recalling its cognate "traditionalists,"
is a sly slur, implying that anybody who criticizes multiculturalism is
committed to inequality. Likewise with "gentleman's education,"
which suggests a philistine elite concerned only with cultural gate
keeping. But the big lie is the contrast of "our tradition" and traditionalists with "Socratic and universalistic goals." I'll get to that false
Socratic analogy later. For now, let's look more closely at this assumed Western tradition of jealous exclusion of the "other."

Anyone casually familiar with Western history knows that it invented the idea of diversity, not to mention cultural relativism. Starting with the Greeks (as Nussbaum herself notes, 53–60), no other

culture has left a more extensive record of fascination with other peoples, partly because of geography, partly because of the critical curiosity that has typified the Western mind. In fact, no other world culture has been as receptive to the "other" as the West, no other people less resistant to the stranger and more voracious at appropriating everything from technology to fashion. Closer to home, how else can one explain the remarkable influence that black people—despised and legally excluded for centuries—have had on American culture, if not partly by this tradition of curiosity about different people and cultures? How did such a presumably exclusionary humanities professoriate come to make classics out of the works of Du Bois and Ellison and Wright,[18] not to mention numerous other Third World writers who were translated and taught and studied before the multiculturalists came along?[19]

Western intellectuals have always sought out the cultural productions of other peoples, from Chinese novels in Goethe's time to African masks in D. H. Lawrence's. When Matthew Arnold defined "true criticism," he asserted that it "obeys an instinct prompting it to try to know the best that is known and thought in the world, irrespectively of practice, politics, and everything of the kind; and to value knowledge and thought as they approach this best, without the intrusion of any other considerations whatever." Hence, Arnold went on, "The English critic of literature...must dwell much on foreign thought, and with particular heed on any part of it which, while significant and fruitful in itself, is for any reason specially likely to escape him."[20] These are hardly the sentiments of a blinkered xenophobe jealously guarding the purity of his cultural tradition against contamination by the excluded "other." In fact, this cosmopolitan openness to other cultures has been the norm among Western intellectuals for most of the modern period. Thus it is hard to believe Nussbaum's adverb when she asserts that American college students in the past "rarely got...knowledge of non-Western cultures, of minorities within their own, of differences of gender and sexuality" (10). What they didn't get were melodramatic victimology and half-baked ideas like the social construction of gender or sexual preference.

Moreover, the issue of how to reconcile American ethnic differences with its core of liberal values—the burden of Nussbaum's argument—is an old one too, predating multiculturalism by decades. In the early part of this century, with the influx of immigrants from Slavic and southern Mediterranean countries, the debate was between "assimilationists"—those who believed cultural differences should be refined away in the WASP melting pot—and "cultural pluralists," whose position is very similar to Nussbaum's, as can be seen in this definition published in 1937: "[N]o one culture contains all favorable elements, but each group that makes up the total American population has unique values, and...the nation will be richer and finer in its cultural make-up if it, the country, conserves the best that each group has brought.... [T]heir natures, characters, and personalities are built out of a culture different from our own, and the method of effective cultural transmission requires that the fundamentals of their heritages be preserved for generations."[21] Apart from the assumption in "our own" that equates American culture with Anglo-Saxon Protestants, these sentiments are not that far off from the spirit of Nussbaum's argument when she says that "we need not give up our special affections and identifications, whether national or ethnic or religious; but we should work to make all human beings part of our community of dialogue and concern, showing respect for the human wherever it occurs" (4-5).

Nor is Nussbaum's concern with democratic education and cultural pluralism one that arose in the sixties with multiculturalism and ethnic studies. In the early forties a whole series of books addressed what was then called "intercultural education." Its intent was "to help our schools to deal constructively with the problem of intercultural and interracial tensions among our people" and to alleviate "the hurtful discrimination against some of the minority groups which compose our people." With the proper curriculum, the schools "can help to mitigate some of the present evils by teaching the young to see the unjust pain which certain of their present thoughtless practices and prejudices inflict on their fellows. They can in some cases help build respect for groups not otherwise sufficiently esteemed."[22] This concern with minority exclusion, moreover, is specifically linked, as in Nussbaum, to democracy: "The younger generation needs to know the facts about race, prejudice, and conflict of cultures, and to rethink the place of majority and minority racial groups in a society committed to making democracy a working reality."[23] As in Nussbaum's argument, this will be achieved by respect for different cultures along with commitment to the unifying liberal values: "Provided that individual and minority group patterns of thought and action do not run counter to the essentials of unity, the majority is required by the theory [of cultural democracy] not only to accept or 'tolerate' racial and cultural differences but to honor them as well."[24] Likewise Nussbaum: "This exposure to foreign and minority cultures is not only, and not primarily, a source of confirmation for the foreign or minority student's personal sense of dignity.... It is an education for all students, so that as judges, as legislators, as citizens in whatever role, they will learn to deal with one another with respect and understanding. And this understanding and respect entail recognizing not only difference but also, at the same time, commonality, not only a unique history but also common rights and aspirations and problems" (69). Clearly, the issues with which Nussbaum is concerned have been on educators' minds for many decades, which makes one wonder just who is that "traditionalist" conservative so terrified of the culture of the "other."

In fact, many contemporary presumed conservative critics of multiculturalism have been, like Arnold, proponents of exposing students to a great variety of cultures and traditions. Camille Paglia, a trenchant critic of identity-politics multiculturalism whom Nussbaum takes great pains to ignore, co-taught a course which originated in "the pressing need of American students for a broader international understanding." Paglia and her co-instructor had as an aim "to sketch out the possibilities, to find threads of connection. We imagined the course as a mutual exploration."[25] This sounds pretty much like what Nussbaum recommends. But more importantly, Nussbaum's definitions of liberal education and her call for Socratic education are not new and can be found in the work of her favorite "conservative" bogey, Allan Bloom.

Throughout Bloom's writings, one finds statements remarkably similar to Nussbaum's. Consider Nussbaum's definition of liberal education: it "liberates the mind from the bondage of habit and custom, producing people who can function with sensitivity and alertness as citizens of the whole world" (8). Again: "For the only kind of education that really deserves the name *liberalis*...is one that makes its pupils free, able to take charge of their own thought and to conduct a critical examination of their society's norms and traditions" (30); such students will be free "because they can call their minds their own.... They have looked into themselves and developed the ability to separate mere habit and convention from what they can defend by argument" (293). Compare now with the definitions of Bloom, Nussbaum's epitome of the exclusionary traditionalist: "By *liberal* education I mean education for freedom, particularly the freedom of the mind, which consists primarily in the awareness of the most important human alternatives."[26] Bloom too sees liberal education not as the force-feeding of "traditional values" but as helping students gain the power to seek the answers to the perennial questions of human value and identity, and to resist the dominant habits and customs of their society: "A liberal education means precisely helping students to pose this question [what is a human?] to themselves, to become aware that the answer is neither obvious nor simply unavailable, and that there is no serious life in which this question is not a

continuous concern.... Liberal education provides access to these alternatives [i.e., answers to the question], many of which go against the
grain of our nature or our times. The liberally educated person is one
who is able to resist the easy and preferred answers, not because he is
obstinate but because he knows others worthy of consideration."[27]
Finally, like Nussbaum, Bloom sees critical argument as the lifeblood
of liberal education: "The essence of philosophy is the abandonment
of all authority in favor of individual human reason.... The most
important function of the university in an age of reason is to protect
reason from itself, by being the model of true openness."[28] If Allan
Bloom's sentiments about liberal education are so similar to
Nussbaum's, who then is the reactionary traditionalist she repeatedly
constructs and knocks over in her book?

But doesn't Nussbaum differ from Bloom in advocating non-
Western works as well as Western, whereas Bloom wants to restrict
students to the so-called canon of Western "great books"? Nussbaum
attempts to show Bloom's ethnocentrism by distorting a point he
makes in *The Closing of the American Mind.* In the passage in question,
Bloom is arguing that required courses in non-Western cultures, as
well as taking up time not being spent on the Western tradition,
usually are little more than exercises in bashing the West for its ethnocentrism rather than a serious study of another culture. For a close,
honest look at non-Western cultures would show that *they* are ethnocentric, the West alone showing "some willingness to doubt the identification of the good with one's own way."[29] Hence the study of non-
Western courses done properly should lead to the conclusion that to
prefer one's own way is best—"exactly the opposite of what is intended
by requiring students to study these cultures." Bloom's point is that
the multiculturalist course, by ignoring non-Western ethnocentrism,
ironically validates the Western view of ethnocentrism: "What we are
really doing is applying a Western prejudice—which we covertly take
to indicate the superiority of our culture—and deforming the evi-

dence of those other cultures to attest to its validity."[30] Yet Nussbaum takes the quote about the West's uniqueness in rejecting ethnocentrism, rejects it as false without any evidence or examples to the contrary, and then distorts Bloom's conclusion to be that Bloom "judges the West to be superior and the non-West to be not worth studying" (132). Bloom, of course, says no such thing; rather he is talking about a certain *way* of teaching non-Western societies in order to further a political program, and he is pointing out the contradictions of a multiculturalism that criticizes the West on the basis of Western values. But Nussbaum needs her straw man to be a Eurocentric white-male elitist, all the easier for her to knock down.

But in actual fact Bloom, like Arnold before him, does not close off liberal education from non-Western cultures or restrict it to some canon of "great books." We have already seen in his comments about liberal education an emphasis on providing students with "alternative" answers to the perennial questions of human value and good rather than "implied answers...which exclude other possible alternatives."[31] Likewise in *Closing of the American Mind*: "Freedom of the mind requires not only, or not even specially, the absence of legal constraints but the presence of alternative thoughts. The most successful tyranny is not the one that uses force to assure uniformity but the one that removes the awareness of other possibilities, that makes it seem inconceivable that other ways are viable, that removes the sense that there is an outside."[32] And elsewhere Bloom makes it clear that these "possibilities" or "alternatives" can come from anywhere: "I appreciate and need further information. So do we all. The serious scholars in non-Western thought should bring us the powerful *texts* they know of to help us. The true canon aggregates around the most urgent questions we face. That is the only ground for the study of books. Idle cultural reports, Eastern or Western, cannot truly concern us, except as a hobby...." And as Bloom goes on to note, this has always been the case with Western intellectuals like Nietzsche and Machiavelli: "Male, female, black, white, Greek, barbarian: that was all indifferent, as it should be."[33] Again, these points are exceptional only to those who believe in the canard that the West has traditionally been resistant to other cultures, and that traditionalists worship some secret list of "great books" rather than, like Bloom, being concerned with critical consciousness and the tradition in which it is best embodied.

Not only is Nussbaum's view of liberal education similar to Bloom's, but her championing of Socratic critical examination (15–49) was also anticipated in Bloom's work; indeed, the whole point of *The Closing of the American Mind* is ultimately the need for Socratic education. Even before that book, Bloom had written that "it would be easy to demonstrate that the questions are the same today as they were for Socrates. It is these questions which are permanent and the consideration of which forms a serious man. It is the role of the university to keep these questions before its students."[34] In *Closing* he asserted that "the academy and the university are the institutions that incorporate the Socratic spirit more or less well"; this spirit should be the "soul" and "essence" of the university, which exists "to preserve and further what he [Socrates] represents." His conclusion was that the "contemplation of Socrates is our most urgent task."[35] Like Nussbaum, Bloom saw the essence of liberal education *not* as the injection of perennial "values" into students but rather the inculcation of the habit and techniques of critical questioning and contemplation of alternatives, particularly the questioning of the larger society's dominant values in order to protect the freedom of the individual mind. Bloom opposed multiculturalism because he viewed it, correctly in my view, as instead attempting to indoctrinate students with a tendentious ideological program that at its heart is incoherent and antiliberal and that limits students to the prison-house of race or ethnicity or gender. I find it hard to reconcile Bloom's Socratic emphasis on "questions" and "alternatives" with Nussbaum's caricature of the narrow traditionalist who wants to preach a uniform doctrine to all students. On the contrary, it is the multiculturalists who, in Finkielkraut's words, "demand the right of everybody to wear a uniform."[36]

If multiculturalism is at heart a species of identity politics inimical to Enlightenment liberalism, then Nussbaum's central claim—that Socratic education can be found today not in the classrooms of traditionalists like Bloom but in the courses of her like-minded friends—rests on an egregiously false analogy. Worse is Nussbaum's equation of her multiculturalists with Socrates, and the traditionalist critics with those who executed the philosopher because they were frightened of his questioning: "Socratic questioning is still on trial. Our debates over the curriculum reveal the same nostalgia for a more obedient, more regimented time, the same suspiciousness of new and independent thinking, that find expression in Aristophanes' brilliant portrait" (2; cf. 15–16, 22, 26). We have already seen that this traditionalist straw man is literally incredible; nothing in Bloom's work or that of any critic that I have read calls for "regimentation" or "obedience," or distrusts "new and independent thinking," or is afraid of anything that might "subvert traditional values" (37). How could they, when the essence of the tradition they champion is precisely the critical questioning of everything? On the contrary, the basis of most criticism of multiculturalism is that it demands obedience to a particular ideology that *stifles* "independent thinking" and opinion and questioning. On my campus it was a women's studies professor, not a traditionalist, who called the police to have a student removed because his "Socratic tendency to ask for reason and arguments" (22) annoyed the instructor. Speech codes and sensitivity training whose effect, if not their intent, is to curtail Socratic inquiry are proposed by campus multiculturalists, not by traditionalists. When unpopular speakers appear on campus, it is not the traditionalists who shout them down and organize protests to silence them as the radical democrats silenced Socrates. Finally, the protest against teaching non-Western or minority "cultures" derives not from any objection to non-Western or minority cultural products per se, but from the politically loaded and illiberal *way* these are taught, not to mention the fact that increasingly, multicultural courses *replace* rather than supplement courses in the Western tradition, which hardly is taught at all anymore.[37]

The greatest insult to the reader's intelligence, however, is Nussbaum's comparison of herself and other well-heeled academics to the impecunious Socrates: "We live, as did Socrates, in a violent society that sometimes turns its rage against intellectuals. We may be embarking on a new era of anti-intellectualism in American life, an era in which the anger of Aristophanes' father [Strepsiades] is all too real a force" (49). This is pure bathos. The only risks Professor Nussbaum runs by promoting multiculturalism are another notch on her CV and another rung up the academic *cursus honorum*, where she is even more unlikely to encounter the "other" over whom she frets. For the fact is, multiculturalism *is* the establishment these days, the reigning ideology from kindergarten to university, from television to advertising, from sit-coms to Disney cartoons, from the government bureaucracy to the corporate fief, where Diversity Trainers make big bucks schooling white folks on their insensitivity to the "other."[38] On college campuses "multiculturalism" and "diversity" are the favorite mantras of the ambitious school administrator and professor alike, for whom "diversity" functions as a secular religion, a sort of Apostles' Creed that certifies one's superior social conscience and sensitivity to the "oppressed other" who always seems to live on the other side of town.[39]

The reason for multiculturalism's triumph in the culture is obvious: it gratifies the new cosmopolitan "aristocracy of brains" in both its academic and corporate guises. As Christopher Lasch pointed out, multiculturalism suits both "to perfection, conjuring up the agreeable image of a global bazaar in which exotic cuisine, exotic styles of dress, exotic music, exotic tribal customs can be savored indiscriminately, with no questions asked and no commitments required. The new elites are at home only in transit, en route to a high-level conference, to the grand opening of a new franchise, to an international film festival, or to an undiscovered resort."[40] Multiculturalism provides the peripatetic careerist and rootless consumer, whether of cuisine or ideas, with a wide variety of lifestyle options and choices, "bits and pieces they can try on for a while, taste and enjoy, and throw away,"[41] all the while that their trivializing consumption is justified as "tolerance for the other" and "sensitivity to difference."

Contrary to Nussbaum, she and her friends *are* the ruling class in academe, the establishment it doesn't do to criticize unless one wants to be charged with the modern version of "corrupting the young"— being sexist and racist. If anybody can be compared to the crotchety Socrates, the late and oft-despised Allan Bloom fits the bill better than Nussbaum. Honest about his elitism, Bloom shared the philosopher's disdain for the masses, and he recognized the distrust with which a democracy views the elites who devote their lives to critical examination.[42] If we want Athenian models for Professor Nussbaum, we should look to the Sophists, those spin-doctors of the ancient world who "made the worse argument the better" and were well paid for their efforts. So it is with Nussbaum, whose sacrifice of sound argument and critical examination to the political prejudices of the academic elite has its own rewards. But the mantle of Socrates won't be one of them.

CHAPTER 2

JOHN HEATH

SOCRATES REDUX

Classics in the Multicultural University?

⌇

Like Bruce Thornton, I conclude in this review essay (which I wrote not knowing that he was working on the same topic) that Nussbaum's attempt to "spin" multicultural identity politics as Socratic examination and liberal education is a fraud, her argument redolent of the fifth-century Sophists who "made the worse argument the better." Unfortunately, Nussbaum is a public intellectual with widespread influence, one whose patina of liberal values masks rampant careerism and intellectual dishonesty, and therefore her career and book represent a phenomenon even more dangerous than that posed by the many obscure theorists cashing in postmodernism for eminence and lucre.

⌇

"THIS book began from many experiences stored up from twenty years of teaching at Harvard, Brown, and the University of Chicago and from travels to dozens of American campuses, both as a visiting lecturer and as a Phi Beta Kappa Visiting Professor" (ix).[1] It is hard to imagine a more ominous opening to a book on reform of higher education. Extrapolating from her "teaching" at three elite universities (one quickly infers that Professor Nussbaum has not waded through many half-baked blue books over the years), communiques with faculty she "knew and could trust," cursory visits to other campuses as well as the notes and tape recordings garnered by her four research assistants dispatched on similar missions, and an extremely narrow interpretation of classical antiquity, the Ernst Freund Professor of Law and Ethics sets out to restore our faith in the new developments in the liberal arts. The resulting *apologia* aspires to be the feel-good book the academic Left and university administrators have been waiting for. After taking so many hits in the culture wars, could it be that American higher education has finally landed a counterpunch?

Martha Nussbaum proposes to answer the following questions: "What are faculty and students really doing, and how do newly fashionable issues about human diversity affect what they do? What sort of citizens are our colleges trying to produce, and how well are they succeeding in that task?" (2). Her answer, to summarize boldly, is that special studies programs (she limits herself to African-American, Women's, and Gender) and the study of non-Western cultures have found important places alongside more traditional fare because they shape "world citizens" steeped in Socratic argument who can empathize with differences on an increasingly multicultural, pluralistic planet. She claims that these approaches need not—and she wants us to believe that in fact most do not—embrace the most controversial tenets of the New Humanities and Social Sciences, notably interest-group identity politics, radical epistemological skepticism, and moral relativism. As proof of the success of these innovations in liberal education, we are offered numerous anecdotes primarily in the form of sketches of classroom sessions and course syllabi. Indeed, by providing so many little vignettes, the book becomes a veritable ideological Kama Sutra for multiculturalists, depicting various positions and approaches attempted by a handful of pliant instructors across the nation to encourage their students to lead more tolerant and empathetic lives.

But a word of warning: don't try these contortions at home. They may look tempting, but upon even mildly close inspection their initial attraction gives way first to incredulity, then to surfeit, boredom, and finally to revulsion. Although Nussbaum poses as a sensible, classically based reformer, the book follows a pattern perfectly predictable by anyone familiar with its author's previous excursions into the culture wars. Partly because of a remarkable naivete about teaching and college curricula that can be possessed only by today's on-the-road, TA-dependent academic, partly because of her thinly veiled political agenda, but mostly just because of sloppy argumentation, the various strands of thought agglomerate over the 300 pages into a messy ball of contradictory and muddled assertions and, at best, timid and derivative recommendations. Professors and administrators of the academic Left waiting for a defense of their leadership of the academy must continue their anxious vigil. This Multiculturalism-Lite just won't do it.

The first chapter, an argument for "Socratic Self-Examination," quickly reveals the weighty problems that sink the book, and so it warrants a careful review. Nussbaum begins reasonably enough by defending Socratic argument against those who see it as a male, Western device constructed to empower the oppressors. She insists that its purpose rather is the activation of each student's independent mind and the production of a community that can genuinely reason together about a problem, not simply trade claims and counterclaims. But Nussbaum creates a false dichotomy in the history of education that she bases on a simplistic reading of the *Clouds*. One branch of thought, she argues, insists that the function of education is to promote acculturation to the time-honored traditions of a society; the other, modern approach emphasizes a "more Socratic education that insists on teaching students to think for themselves" (16). The old system, one apparently in place until just a few years ago, is bad: "We are now trying to build an academy that will overcome defects of vision and receptivity that marred the humanities departments of earlier eras..." (112). But Nussbaum misses the larger significance of Aristophanes' play, that of the dramatic dispute itself. The comedy offers a mock debate that pokes fun at both adversaries while simultaneously insisting that such disputation is essential to the discovery of how one is to be educated to live a good life.

One of the greatest oddities in this book of oddities is that it seems never to strike Nussbaum as noteworthy that among those "time-honored traditions of Western Civilization" is Socratic argument itself. Yes, there have been proponents of mindless obedience, but the important deliberation about liberal education (leaving technical training aside for the moment) has been whether those skills of argument, logic, and persuasion should be put to personal and professional advantage (Sophistic) or to the pursuit of some larger, universal truth (Socratic). Nussbaum herself has ably written on the confusion of the Sophists with Socrates. But in her praise of Socrates she rarely notes that he saw a purpose in his pursuit: truth. "Socrates himself made no appeal to truths that transcend human experience..." (40). What is missing throughout Nussbaum's discussion of Socratic dialogue is the ultimate purpose of this argumentation: to decide what is the better course of action and then to *pursue* that course while trying to persuade others to follow as well. Without this crucial link between intellectual deliberation and decisive action we are left in the realm of the Sophists, and there is nothing to counter the inevitable moral relativism—you think x, I think y, and so be it. This failure to address the Greek connection between word and deed taints her entire argument.

For example, Nussbaum does not include among the four reasons she gives for emphasizing a Socratic education the most important—that only through reasoned discourse can we sift through conflicting claims of truth. Instead, we are to follow Socrates (she includes the Stoics as the foundations for this self-examination) for the following four reasons:

(1) *Socratic education is for every human being.* Well, yes and no. Nussbaum has to make a tricky (one page, 26) distinction between Plato and Socrates. Plato was an intellectual elitist and an opponent of democracy, and even Socrates was done in by a hostile *demos*. But Nussbaum's approach means that parts of the *Republic,* for example, can be used to demonstrate her point (e.g., Socrates on women's education), but others must be left aside (e.g., the entire hierarchical structure of Socrates' utopia and in particular his educational scheme).

(2) *A Socratic education should be suited to the pupil's circumstances and context.* This too leads Nussbaum in directions she claims she does not want to go:

> It must be concerned with the actual situation of the pupil, with the current state of the pupil's knowledge and beliefs, with the obstacles between that pupil and the attainment of self-scrutiny and intellectual freedom. Socrates therefore questions people one by one. The Stoics, concerned with the broad extension of education to all, are not always able to do this. But they insist that individualized instruction is always, in principle, the goal. (32)

Bizarrely, she takes this to be a lethal challenge to a "great books" curriculum. Yet her main point is precisely that Socrates—now a walking, breathing great book thanks to his famous pupil—provides her universal model for education. Moreover, she must now side with identity politics far more than she admits, for if we are to adapt the curriculum to the student, we must address the "obstacles" to the student's intellectual freedom—what could she mean by this but issues of race, gender, sexuality, and so on? (That she does not examine issues of class is extremely revealing and typical of the elite liberal academic, who cannot imagine a poor white student more deprived than a wealthy minority. Supervising the senior philosophy theses of three upper-class minority students does not qualify one for combat pay. On her self-contradictions about identity politics, see below.)

But even more remarkably, Nussbaum does not see that Socrates is criticizing her entire *modus operandi* and that of the modern elite academic. The point is that the teacher must *work* with the student. Individualized instruction in the Socratic sense does not mean developing a curriculum to suit the context of the student, but teaching each student with as much personal attention as possible. This requires attention to the individual intellectual progress of the student, not lecturing to hundreds. It means small classes, not auditoriums. It means, in modern terms, grading every exam, reading every paper, meeting with every student, finding the right buttons to push for each learner. It is, in other words, a nearly impossible goal at many of the nation's universities, but it is a worthy goal nevertheless. Nussbaum has nothing to say about the un-Socratic structure of the modern research university in which she has spent her entire professional career. We should not be surprised. Socratic teaching could never mean spending an afternoon talking to a handful of philosophy majors at one more school on a ten-day junket, or sending out graduate students to do your teaching and research for you. Socrates didn't lecture to a crowd of a hundred at Sparta in the morning, then depart to Argos in the afternoon leaving Plato behind to answer questions. Socrates didn't abandon a position at Athens for one at Syracuse because it meant more money, more time to publish, and less conversation with the people. It was the Sophists, of course, who represented the modern academic so well, both in the way they lived and in their similar support for relative rather than absolute values.

(3) *Socratic education should be pluralistic, that is, concerned with a variety of different norms and traditions.* Nussbaum, against most of the evidence known to me (and she cites none to support her premise), seems convinced that the world is becoming increasingly diverse rather than increasingly homogeneous, indeed, increasingly Western. "Today's teachers are shaping future citizens in an age of cultural diversity and increasing internationalization. Our country is inescapably plural" (6). "The present-day world is inescapably multicultural and multinational" (8). But the entire thrust of "internationalization," for good or ill, is the breakdown of "cultural diversity." I will address this more directly later. But again, Nussbaum does not say what she means, for she doesn't really want students to deal with *all* difference, *all* different norms and traditions. Her entire insistence on a Socratic, rational model of argumentation as the basis for education, for example, reveals that she too believes that certain cultures have better ways of addressing human problems than others. And, like it or not, she has chosen a Western approach to her topic that has been decidedly insensitive to the traditional "dreamtime" norms of indigenous populations throughout the world.

(4) *Socratic education requires ensuring that books do not become authorities.* Again, this is a strange argument coming from someone who bases her book on the received wisdom found in a handful of books. Here, as often, Nussbaum assumes that philosophy alone can teach Socratic argument and avoid the "great book" syndrome. Literature, in fact *all* texts except those read by philosophers, "can indeed tone up the slack mind, giving it both the information it needs to think well and examples of excellent argument," but are "all too likely to become objects of veneration and deference," especially those produced by Western civilization (35). To learn Socratic logical argument, one must enroll in a philosophy course. "The disciplinary base of such courses should not stray too far from philosophy, or the rigor of analysis so

important for the Socratic virtues of mind will be diluted" (42). She concedes that philosophical "reflection may also be infused into a broader humanities course or set of courses, but in that case it is very important that philosophers participate in the design and teaching of these courses" (46). Clearly one of the reasons philosophy departments have been far more immune to the fraudulent epistemological claims of the New Humanities than departments of history and especially literature is their more rigorous skills of logical argumentation. But Nussbaum provides no evidence that in the courses she cites as examples of proper philosophical orientation students have developed any of the skills she seeks in her program of reform. So fuzzy is she in fact on just how Socratic self-examination is to be instilled that at one point (47) she insists that students at Brown, where there are no general education requirements of any kind, engage in Socratic activity merely by choosing their courses!

The function of literature is, as we learn in a later chapter entitled "The Narrative Imagination," to develop sympathy in order to understand (but not judge) difference. This can certainly be one of the most powerful aspects of art. But to focus on difference rather than similarities, and to limit art to the affective, would result in the most deformed kind of pedagogy. Nussbaum's brief essays into literature reveal the limitations of her approach. Her discussion of the *Philoctetes,* for example, concentrates on the role of the chorus, who "vividly and sympathetically imagine the life of a man whom they have never seen, picturing his loneliness, his pain, his struggle for survival. In the process they stand in for, and allude to, the imaginative work of the audience, who are invited by the play as a whole to imagine the sort of needy, homeless life to which prosperous people rarely direct their attention. The drama as a whole, then, cultivates the type of sympathetic vision of which its characters speak" (87). Are we to imagine an audience racing out to help in soup kitchens and tutor the poor after witnessing Philoctetes' prideful suffering? Is that really the impact of

Sophocles' tragedy? The nobility of Philoctetes is his *refusal* to seek mindless sympathy, his unswerving faith in the absolute justice of his case, and his insistence on bearing the consequences of his intransigence.

Nussbaum's strange and limited sense of compassion is now the hallmark of the apparently guilt-ridden academic Left. Compassion is primarily to be reserved for difference, for the Other, rather than for man's plight in general and the tragic nature of humanity. As becomes more clear in the following chapter, the focus in Nussbaum's "world citizen" is on difference rather than on commonality, on race, gender, and sexual orientation rather than on dilemmas that link us all. Her world citizen, despite her insistence on critical analysis, is primarily someone who develops a rational "strategy" to tolerate and sympathize with everything and everybody. She says that we are to retain judgment, but virtually nowhere in the book does she pursue the consequences that might follow from such critical reasoning—a *rejection* of some elements of difference as inferior, for example. Ignored or conveniently forgotten is Socrates' dictum that the greatest evil is *not* to exercise one's critical judgment by punishing wrongdoing.

Her conclusion to the opening chapter is thus necessarily skewed. "We live, as did Socrates, in a violent society that sometimes turns its rage against intellectuals. We may be embarking on a new era of anti-intellectualism in American life, an era in which the anger of Aristophanes' father is all too real a force" (49). Are professors now being attacked in supermarkets? Mugged on the streets? Forced to drink hemlock by concerned politicians and shopkeepers? Called "four-eyes" by mean-spirited teenage computer geeks? The "rage" here refers, one must assume, to the fact that the public, legislators, and administrators have begun asking faculty to be accountable to their constituents, the tuition-paying students, parents, and taxpayers. The "violence" is a position canceled, a tenure denied, a promotion delayed (an endowed professorship in an elite school of law and divinity rather than in its classics department?), a spate of books pointing out the very un-Socratic behavior of faculty and administrators, particularly at graduate institutions. Recent reports from the Carnegie Foundation for the Advancement of Teaching and in *Harvard Magazine* (is Nussbaum's alma mater turning on her?) simply document what we already know about the lack of commitment to undergraduate teaching at research universities. Nussbaum wants to demonstrate the validity of Socratic reasoning for a flourishing democracy—all well and good—and then gives a perfect argument in the remainder of the book of just why her "reformed liberal education" has come under such attack, not just by vocationalism, but by defenders of the liberal arts and democracy as well.

The goal of a liberal education, according to Nussbaum, is to produce "citizens of the world." In a chapter of that title, and another on the study of non-Western cultures, she fails to identify exactly what she means by Western, and so it remains unclear what skills and values—other than Socratic argumentation and an easy compassion— this new citizen should possess. Here is another irony in Nussbaum's project. She insists that the concept of "world citizen" is borrowed from the classical tradition but that this "form of cosmopolitanism is not peculiar to Western traditions" (53). Her only attempt in the book to prove this point is the citation of two writers supposedly outside the West who have discussed the idea of a world citizen. But upon closer inspection one turns out to be an Indian philosopher who "self-consciously melded them [older Bengali traditions] with Western cosmopolitanism" (53) and the other is a Ghanaian philosopher who we are later informed is the "son of an Englishwoman and a London-trained lawyer...educated at Bryanston and Cambridge, an expert in modal logic..." (149). If Nussbaum wants us to devote more time to non-Western cultures, then she must show us what they have to offer. This is a legitimate project, but one that is not attempted here.

Nussbaum never seems to catch the irony that this so-called cosmopolitanism of the classical world is in fact the utopian dream of a few intellectuals and cranks primarily in the West. Seneca and Marcus Aurelius never contemplated exchanging their culture for that of the barbarians on their borders. They never considered all cultures to be equal or that Romans should in fact abandon their values for a new world order. Neither Socrates nor any other classical Greek believed that non-Greek cultures were superior to that of the polis. Different, yes. Interesting, quite possibly. But to emphasize cultural diversity over chauvinism is simply un-Greek and decidedly un-Socratic. A few antisocial freaks like Diogenes—a favorite of Nussbaum's—were entirely Greek in their critical spirit, but not in their rejection of the concept of the polis.

On the other hand, these very questions about culture, sometimes posed in the form of literary utopias, are in fact primarily the product of the West. The West is uniquely self-critical, uniquely prone to compare and contrast its own way of doing things with that of others. And so the argument really should be that if we want to explore something outside of our own cultures, we should first understand how that very impulse derives from the Greeks. It is Western culture we should master first. Instead, Nussbaum suggests that her book is based on the classical civilizations merely as an accident of her training:

> It was through ancient Greek and Roman arguments that I came upon these ideas in my own history. The Greek and Roman versions of these ideas are immensely valuable to us as we pursue these debates today, and I shall focus on that contribution. But ideas of this sort have many sources in many traditions. Closely related notions can be found in India, in Africa, in Latin America, and in China. One of the errors that a diverse education can dispel is the false belief that one's own tradition is the only one that is capable of self-criticism or universal aspiration. (ii)

But she provides not a single example to support this statement, and one must assume that once again she does not really mean what she says. As concerned as she is with the study of women, race, sexuality, and religion in the rest of the book, can she really be suggesting that we can find such a rich critique of religion in China, sexuality in Saudi Arabia, women in Africa, or race in Japan?

Nussbaum herself is so deeply embedded in Western thought that she can find no other way to go about her study. When she writes, "Whether we are discussing the multinational corporation, global agricultural development, the protection of endangered species, religious toleration, the well-being of women, or simply how to run a firm efficiently, we increasingly find that we need comparative knowledge of many cultures to answer the questions we ask" (115), she is Western. Or when she observes, "When they [students] encounter violence against women, or assaults on democracy, or discrimination against members of a religious or ethnic minority, they are likely to say, 'Well, that is their culture, and who are we to speak?'" (137), she is asking questions that are addressed primarily in the West and whose answers have come almost solely from the West. When she glibly insists that "real cultures are plural, not single" and suggests that we "would easily see the defects in a monolithic portrayal of 'American values,'" (127) she reveals either her biases or a lack of serious thought on the matter. Freedom of religion and speech? Private property? Democracy? Free markets? A citizen army? A great majority of Americans would find these to be values and institutions that are embedded in our culture and are being adopted the world over. Instead of coming to grips with the dangerous dynamism—the exploration and destruction, the creativity and exploitation—of the West, Nussbaum says we should study non-Western cultures "partly because in so doing we come to understand intellectual and moral wrongs in which our predecessors have been implicated" (116). Once again the liberal academic guilt is found to be the pressing motive behind her discussion. She fails to see that the sins of the West are the sins of mankind and that it's primarily in the West that the spirit of self-criticism has led to an amelioration of these evils.

There are further ironies. A true exploration of "world citizenship" would focus on the similarities in human nature, on common denominators of experience and response that could unite us. But Nussbaum instead chooses to concentrate on the cultural differences. Permit me to quote a passage in full to give a fair flavor of the kind of anecdotal evidence and odd conclusions that pervade the book:

> Anna was a political science major at a large state university in the Midwest. Upon graduation she went into business, getting a promising job with a large firm. After twelve years she had risen to a middle-management position. One day, her firm assigned her to the newly opened Beijing office. What did she need to know, and how well did her education prepare her for success in her new role? In a middle-management position, Anna is working with both Chinese and American employees, both male and female. She needs to know how Chinese people think about work (and not to assume there is just one way); she needs to know how cooperative networks are formed, and what misunderstandings might arise in interactions between Chinese and American workers. Knowledge of recent Chinese history is important, since the disruptions of the Cultural Revolution still shape workers' attitudes. Anna also needs to consider her response to the recent policy of urging women to return to the home, and to associated practices of laying off women first. This means she should know something about Chinese gender relations, both in the Confucian tradition and more recently. She should probably know something about academic women's studies in the United States, which have influenced the women's studies movement in Chinese universities. She certainly needs a more general view about human rights, and about to what extent it is either legitimate or wise to criticize another nation's ways of life. In the future, Anna may find herself dealing with problems of anti-African racism, and with recent government attempts to exclude immigrants who test positive for the human immunodeficiency virus.

Doing this well will require her to know something about the history of Chinese attitudes about race and sexuality. It will also mean being able to keep her moral bearings even when she knows that the society around her will not accept her view. (50–51)

This may be one of the silliest passages yet in the culture wars. Anna could have majored in Chinese culture for four years at the best university in the country and not known all this. Moreover, as Nussbaum herself admits without seeing the contradictions, Anna "had a rough time getting settled in China, and the firm's dealings with its new context were not always very successful. A persistent and curious person, however, she stayed on and has made herself a good interpreter of cultural difference" (51). So on the practical level, Anna didn't need all those women's studies courses after all. What she needed was some intelligence, a desire to succeed, and the ability to think critically which she could have received in any solid course of study in the traditional liberal arts. It is also curious that a professor of Greek and Latin who has claimed to have the best current working knowledge of philosophical Greek, who has boasted of a competency equivalent to the ancient Greeks themselves,[2] should fail to mention that Anna would be best served by learning a little Chinese.

Who would disagree that we must be made aware of cultural variety in order to become a "sensitive and empathic interpreter" of others? But one might more reasonably argue that it is the rest of the world that has learned to act like the West, to understand how we do things. The world is becoming more Western, just as Nussbaum would have us dedicate more of our education to cultures who want to be or are simply forced to be like us. Why would we want to deprive our students of the very material that Nussbaum has found so stimulating and is the source of her own sensitivities?

Faculty and administrators who remain grounded in the quotidian realities of teaching undergraduates know that a curriculum can accomplish only so many things. Could we ever design a course of study that would have prepared Anna for every possible event life might throw in her way? Well, perhaps—the traditional liberal arts are exactly what students need in today's fast-changing world: to learn to think, to learn to learn, to learn to act in accordance with their reasoned thoughts. Yet Nussbaum seems to want to dilute the learning of the process and the study of the West in favor of sensitivity training.

Nussbaum's argument also runs aground on the moral sandbar of cultural relativity. She wants to reject moral relativism—"World citizenship does not, and should not, require that we suspend criticism toward other individuals and cultures" (65)—but she in fact never suggests what we are to do when cultural values clash in such a way as to require us to make a choice. And what criteria are we to use, if not Western, as the basis for this criticism? For example, the famous case of clitorectomies is frequently raised in her text. What are we to do? Talk. Sympathize—it's okay to disagree. Argument, in other words, not for truth or action, but apparently for therapy and mutual understanding. Another of her telling anecdotes again proves the exact opposite of what she is trying to demonstrate. In an attempt to show that a nonjudgmental approach to moral issues in other cultures based on Socratic argument is optimal and can be successful, Nussbaum cites the example of a class taught by a teacher with a "nonrelativist moral view." The paper receiving the highest grade is one with which the instructor, a Professor Stoddard, vigorously disagrees—a defense of a "hands-off" relativist position toward female circumcision:

> "Because it is impossible to judge a practice so foreign to our own conception of establishing social identity," writes Student Q (a male), "it is better to take a neutral position on the issue, and to accept...choices made by a culture with graciousness." Stoddard writes in the margin, "Where do you draw the line? If a country were slaughtering all male children, should we intervene?" As the argument unfolds, Stoddard commends parts of Q's strategy—his

insistence, for example, that internal critique and opposition are likely to be more knowledgable and precise than Western judgment at a distance; she commends his careful exegesis of material about two African cultures from books read in the course. (209)

Nussbaum's logic simply fails here. If she agrees that "internal critique and opposition" of a culture are likely to be more knowledgable (and therefore superior?) than another culture's views, her argument for applying Socratic argumentation to all courses of study falls apart. Any internal critique, whether based on tradition, divine revelation, the king's word, or holy text, must be considered more valuable for understanding another culture than Nussbaum's own Western dialectic. But Nussbaum doesn't believe this herself—her thesis is that we need Western, rational thought to overcome the flaws in our culture. So which is it?

Moreover, if the "best" essay hasn't taken into consideration the logical consequences of the moral stance—the professor asks a good and obvious question but apparently does not expect the student to have thought of it—what can this possibly say about the worse essays? Since the entire Socratic and reason-dominated approach Nussbaum advocates is Western, why is it commendable to subordinate that tradition to, or even equate it with, another? If argument is supposed to arrive at a defendable answer and not mere acceptance of difference, why would we want our students to accept practices that can't be defended logically? Apparently the universal standards we use to condemn all the dreaded -isms of our own culture are to be suspended when judging behavior in other cultures.

Though she also claims to reject identity politics (109-111), Nussbaum nonetheless defends its practitioners on the most peculiar of grounds. "Indeed, it seems a bit hard to blame literature professionals for the current prevalence of identity politics in the academy, when these scholars simply reflect a cultural view that has other, more powerful sources" (110). And what are these? Market economists, of course. She quotes Milton Friedman, "who said that about matters of value, 'men can ultimately only fight.' This statement is false and pernicious." But why? Wasn't our Civil War primarily fought over "matters of value"? Didn't millions die in Europe in this century over "matters of value"? Whether the values are good ones, or worth fighting over, should be subject to argument, but again, where but in the West is there such a long tradition of open and rational critique of the causes and necessities of war? There *are* different values, and they *do* conflict, and sometimes one must act on the basis of those values in order to defend them. All disagreement must not, and does not, lead to battle, but what would Nussbaum, who proudly discusses her adopted Judaism throughout the book, have had us do in the early 1940s? Were we to try to understand and sympathize with the "different" cultural approach taken to the value of human life by the Third Reich?

What is especially troublesome in this attack is Nussbaum's hypocrisy. How much longer will we have to listen to self-proclaimed liberal academics criticize the open market system while they negotiate higher salaries, lower teaching loads, and demand more perks for themselves, bouncing one offer against another as they travel the world lecturing for pay on the evils of capitalism?

Nussbaum's agenda is clear, but her solution to the perceived problems is not. After thirty pages of misunderstanding the uniqueness of the West as well as misrepresenting it (who, if not the Romans, stumbled upon a notion of religious toleration unlike any that was to be seen for the next 1,500 years?), what are Nussbaum's recommendations for an improved curriculum? They are three: a world religions course, foreign language proficiency, and the study of one non-Western culture. These are remarkably tame and sensible, and many universities already have them. Still, would this not-so-new curriculum accomplish Nussbaum's goals, would it have helped poor Anna clear the hurdles in China? Even if she had taken "Introduction to the Religions of Asia," a year of Chinese, and "Women in Contemporary China," my guess is that she would still have been lost in Beijing. And what if Anna had ended up in Moscow instead?

Two chapters on African-American Studies and Women's Studies follow parallel paths. A few anecdotes from contemporary classrooms are followed by the institutional histories of these programs at Harvard, from which conclusions about their necessity and usefulness are then drawn. Nussbaum desperately wants to appear to be arguing against identity politics and insists that the primary reason for these studies is to foster world citizenship. She tries to ignore the remarkable politicization and extremism of many of these departments and programs, but she avoids any serious examination of the frequent critiques made by critics of the university. She dismisses the arguments of such censors of academic feminism as Christina Hoff Sommers, and Daphne Patai and Noretta Kortge, as based on a "small number of anecdotes" and the comments of anonymous and "disgruntled individuals." She then supplies a small number of anecdotes and comments from a few nondisgruntled individuals to prove the success of these courses. As Nussbaum herself admits, one of the differences may be that Hoff Sommers looked at Women's Studies programs, whereas Nussbaum concentrates on courses on women in traditional departments, although even here she again must concede that "a number of courses I visited seemed to err in the direction of withholding criticism" (205) in rather un-Socratic fashion. Still, she defends even Catharine MacKinnon, whose conclusions about men's "perverse" control of women's preferences are notoriously extreme.

Nussbaum concludes: "Critics of feminism are wrong to think that it is dangerous for democracy to consider these ideas, and dangerous for college classrooms to debate them. Instead, it is dangerous not to consider them, as we strive to build a society that is both rational and just" (221). Few critics of academic feminism argue against any form of rational debate, and Nussbaum's attempts to sidestep the charges of indoctrination simply draw attention to the problem. The issue has almost always been the reverse, that advocates of special studies programs feel rational debate to be an attempt to undermine their authority, to impose male, Western, hegemonic discourse upon others. That is the reason they, and Nussbaum, talk so frequently about "exciting new methodologies" that inevitably call in the social constructionists and epistemological skeptics who hypocritically argue against the possibility of meaning and truth in jargon-laden academic prose we are supposed to accept as a true account of the subject at hand.

Nussbaum also fails to make any serious effort to prove that *academic* feminism is necessary for a "just" society. In fact, she completely ignores her basic question, which is whether Women's Studies is necessary at all. That people should study the role of women in history and culture and political policy, and so on, is denied by few. But her examples—for instance, Sarah Pomeroy's work from the mid-1970s—are hardly representative of modern academic feminist scholarship, at least in classics. Pomeroy used—and continues to use—very traditional methods to open up a new area of study. What Nussbaum needs to do is demonstrate why we need special interest programs now, when she herself admits that there is little to justify them methodologically or curricularly (194–195).

Her final chapter on special interest programs—the study of human sexuality—begins, as we would expect, by defending Foucault's claims that sexuality is a "social construct." She uses the work of Dover, Halperin, and Winkler in classics to demonstrate the importance and possibility of investigating "sexuality historically and scientifically, without losing one's sense of moral urgency about one's choices" (256). To accomplish this sleight-of-hand she must completely ignore the criticisms of Foucault, not to mention those of Halperin and Winkler, that have challenged the validity of this work. If Nussbaum were really interested in argument and Socratic disputation, she would have to discuss the criticisms of such scholars as Camille Paglia and Bruce Thornton, who demonstrate with all logic and clarity that most of the work in classics based on Foucault is flawed, not just because the great man himself was inconsistent and extreme, but also because he was gravely misunderstood by his acolytes. Indeed, if she cared at all about honest argumentation, she would have recused herself from any discussion of Colorado's Amendment Two, in the court case concerning which she has been accused of lying under oath.[3]

She closes her analysis by comparing the acceptance of special interest programs at two different religious universities, Notre Dame and Brigham Young. One final time Nussbaum gives us her argument and then betrays it.

> It seems plausible that a religious university can thrive only if it protects and fosters inquiry into all forms of human culture and self-expression, providing students with the mental tools they need to confront diversity in their own lives as citizens, workers, and friends. This does not entail a hands-off attitude to criticism of what one encounters; it does entail respect, and a sincere and prolonged effort at understanding. (259)

But eventually one must make a choice. Can homosexuality be part of the good Christian life? Do women belong in the upper echelons of religious institutions founded upon divinely inspired texts and dogmatic exegetical traditions that exclude them? Is abortion permissible? Nussbaum continues to treat education as a matter only of the mind, not of action. As long as we're talking, it's good. And especially as long as we're talking from the right perspective, it's good. But this academic approach is exactly what is wrong with the current curriculum. The good life isn't merely self-examination, but acting upon what one believes is right on the basis of that self-examination. Socrates drank the hemlock.

Nussbaum's argument—that Notre Dame is more open to discussion of sensitive social issues and therefore a better university—is a bit of a non sequitur but generally acceptable taken on its most basic level. Once again, though, her methodology is weak. Her voice for the Catholic institution is primarily that of Philip Quinn, who "is a leading liberal on faculty issues of gender and sexuality" (264). But the campus as a whole, as she admits, is divided on these issues, and even a reader like this one, who considers Brigham Young to be an unlikely place to find much provocative teaching or research in the liberal arts, has to feel a bit of sympathy for that institution after Nussbaum's muddled attack. For example, she suggests that at BYU "the doctrine of 'continuing revelation'—conspicuously invoked on June 9, 1978, to alter long-time church policy by admitting African-American males to the priesthood—makes it perpetually unclear whether the statements that seem most authoritative today will continue to bind tomorrow" (280). Yet just eleven pages earlier she had indirectly praised an identical flexibility of the Catholic Church, when she commented that in 1954, "conservative theologians in Rome tried to get [president] Father Hesburgh to withdraw a book published by the University of Notre Dame Press because of an article by liberal Jesuit John Courtney Murray on religious liberty in a pluralistic society—defending positions that are by now official positions of the church—Hesburgh fought vigorously..." (269). When Mormon officials change their mind, they make the university a difficult place in which to think. When the Catholic Church changes its mind, it has wisely adopted liberal Jesuit thinking promoted by the university. In general, the entire approach is offensive. Nussbaum passes judgment on these two institutions—and Notre Dame, in the minds of Nussbaum and Quinn, has far to go—on the basis of their openness to special studies programs. Nussbaum is finally ready to judge, but only with a litmus test of institutional sensitivity to her extremely politicized social agenda. Indeed, she could have examined the role religion can play in opening or shutting the mind by a much more interesting comparison of the way theology, for example, is taught at

Notre Dame and at a Vatican-chartered campus like the Catholic University.

Nussbaum concludes her study by misinterpreting what is really going on in the culture wars.

> By portraying today's humanities departments as faddish, insubstantial, and controlled by a radical elite, cultural conservatives—while calling for a return to a more traditional liberal arts curriculum—in practice feed the popular disdain for the humanities that has led to curtailment of departments and programs and to the rise of narrow preprofessional studies. When critics such as Allan Bloom, Roger Kimball, and George Will caricature the activities of today's humanities departments by focusing only on what can be made to look extreme or absurd, they probably do not promote their goal of increasing university support for traditional humanistic education. (298)

Again, as so often in this book, Nussbaum tells half the story. If "the state legislator or parent who reads such attacks" disdains the humanities, that is not the fault of critics like Harold Fromm or Dinesh D'Souza. They tell far more ugly (and equally true) anecdotes than Nussbaum tells pretty ones, if one must rely on tales, and they often use statistics, whereas Nussbaum uses none. And the cultural critics of the modern university also have the reams of jargon-ridden, epistemologically skeptical, morally relativistic research to quote. Nussbaum rarely cites recent academic research from the special studies programs she supports, and with good reason—it would prove her vision of the modern liberal arts wrong in nearly every case.

The one curricular experiment, the one reform of higher education that has not been tried on a vast scale in the last twenty years of an increasingly diverse student population, is that of an intensified Western culture sequence. Such a program would accomplish most of Nussbaum's goals—the inculcation of Socratic argumentation, an understanding of the importance of culture and cultural difference, the need to question, and the significance of the blending of reason and emotion in one's study and life—while avoiding the glaring weaknesses of her reformed curriculum: intellectual inquiry put to simplistic, political uses; the emphasis on cultural, racial, and sexual difference rather than the common bonds of human nature; the shutting down of judgment; the loss of truth as an object of intellectual pursuit; and the neglect of action as an essential element in morality. It would also do a great deal to explain how the world got to where it is today, and even suggest what we might do to get it where we would like it to go.

Ultimately the trouble with *Cultivating Humanity* may be that Nussbaum's brain knows better than to lead where her politics want to take her. And so she has written a classical defense of reform in liberal education, one that unintentionally but resoundingly calls for a reform of the reformers. She never sees the irony in one of her opening sentences, the connection between what has happened to liberal education and its failure to take root in the university or the public at large: "Never before have there been so many talented and committed young faculty so broadly dispersed in institutions of so many different kinds, thinking about difficult issues connecting education with citizenship. The shortage of jobs in the humanities and social science has led to hardships; many have left the professions they love" (2–3). Captain Nussbaum doesn't appear to wonder why the crew of her ship has thinned out as she orders it full speed ahead into the looming iceberg. And one suspects that the Ernst Freund Professor of Law and Ethics at the University of Chicago will not be going down with her ship.

PART II

VERY BAD THEORY

CHAPTER 3

✲

JOHN HEATH

MORE QUARRELING IN THE MUSES' BIRDCAGE

For the men of the *Iliad*, the heroic life was simply defined: to be a speaker of words and doer of deeds. The trick was to make your words become actions and not mere substitutes for them. Thus after warriors meeting one-on-one had engaged in their customary taunting, it was quickly time to turn speech into deed. Aeneas's words to Achilles are typical:

> "But come, let us no longer stand here talking of these things
> like children, here in the space between the advancing armies.
> For there are harsh things enough that could be spoken against
>   us
> both, a ship of a hundred locks could not carry the burden.
> The tongue of man is a twisty thing, there are plenty of words
>   there
> of every kind, the range of words is wide, and their variance.
> The sort of thing you say is the thing that will be said to you.
> But what have you and I to do with the need for squabbling
> and hurling insults at each other, as if we were two wives
> who when they have fallen upon a heart-perishing quarrel
> go out in the street and say abusive things to each other,
> much true, and much that is not, and it is their rage that drives
>   them.

You will not by talking turn me back from the strain of my
 warcraft,
not till you have fought to my face with the bronze. Come on then
and let us try each other's strength with the bronze of our spear-
 heads."
He spoke, and on the terrible grim shield drove the ponderous
spike, so that the great shield moaned as it took the spearhead.

          (20.244–60, trans. Lattimore)

  This link between what we say and do, so central to Greek
thinking, has of course been completely severed in the modern
university, where we are judged solely by what we write or say to a
handful of colleagues and not at all on how this matches what we
do or how we live. This disparity is found on both sides of the
ideological divide. The two books reviewed in this chapter represent some of the best that has been written by reasonable academics concerning the perversities of the current curriculum and
publishing "agendas" in the New Humanities. And they also persuade us—if we still needed persuasion—that the plight of classical studies is merely one small part of the much larger collapse of
the humanities in the university over the past few decades. Yet
one cannot help but be struck by what is missing from the discussion—nowhere here will you find an earnest examination of
teaching loads, course-release policies, classroom pedagogy, grading, tenure and promotion protocols, graduate school training,
much less a plan of any sort to attempt to eradicate the sophistic
crop that has taken root in the humanities.

  This is perhaps one of the most uncomfortable aspects of
academic populism—it requires us to act differently, to spend more
time with students and less in research centers, to teach more
classes, to write for a broad audience, and to trust in our material. If we limit our efforts to the admittedly important task of
documenting the degeneration of the quality of our discipline—
especially if we do so for fellow academics in the comfort of reduced teaching and skipped classes—we can hardly expect to bring
about change. At some point in the near future—and books like
the two under review here convincingly reveal just how much work
is to be done—we must, like Aeneas, stop our talking and hurl the

spear, even if we are doomed to fail. Aeneas loses his battle with Achilles and even his final, brutal triumph over Turnus is filled with ambiguity, but he ultimately changes the world.

‿ꝛ

"Can this be? Here is a strange thing that my eyes look on.
Now the great-hearted Trojans, even those I have killed already,
will stand and rise up again out of the gloom and the darkness..."
Iliad 21.55-57, trans. Lattimore

I. KILLING THE BOGEYMAN

*L*iterature Lost. The Killing of History. Can Classics Die? Who Killed History? The Death of Literature. Who Killed Homer? The stench of death seems to be wafting about the humanities these days. Despite the promises of youth evoked by "New" Historicism and the "New" Humanities, despite the hope of regeneration implied in the replicating manifestations of the prefix *post-*, one senses an aura of decay poorly concealed, like the powdered and perfumed cheek of an aging relative. We've smelled it before, of course, many times. But this is more serious, we are told, something different from the time-honored contest between the liberal arts and vocational studies, the yin and yang of Western education that have always kept scholars of the humanities honest, that made them come down from the ivory tower once in a while to joust with the knights of commercialism. The enemy is the worm within the apple this time, and it has grown fat on the ever-diminishing fruit. Inevitably, and sooner than we'd imagine—"But please, oh please, let it be after I retire," we mutter—we'll have only bloated worms presiding over an empty orchard, that is, cultural studies.

The two books reviewed here—*What's Happened to the Humanities?*, edited by Alvin Kernan, and *Literature Lost*, by John Ellis—examine the

practice of current scholarship and, to a lesser degree, the curriculum, in the humanities, particularly literary studies.[1] Although neither book specifically lays out the principles that link the various
schools of the New Humanities, it would be helpful to review quickly
the basic tenets that shape this scholarship. This task has been done
concisely by Keith Windschuttle in *The Killing of History* (in this respect, John Ellis's book might be fairly termed "Windschuttle Lite"),
who finds the following four common denominators:

> *Knowledge*: These theories are united in the view that inductive rea-
> soning and empirical research cannot provide a basis for knowl-
> edge. They challenge the concepts of objectivity and certainty in
> knowledge, arguing that different intellectual and political move-
> ments create their own forms of relative "knowledge."
>
> *Truth*: They believe that truth is also a relative rather than an
> absolute concept. The pursuit of unconditional truth is impossible,
> they argue. What is "true," they claim, depends on who is speaking
> to whom and in what context.
>
> *Science*: They claim that science cannot be value-free or objec-
> tive. They also agree that neither the human sciences nor natural
> science provides us with what could be called knowledge. We invent
> scientific theories rather than make scientific discoveries.
>
> *Disciplines*: Most believe that the traditional divisions of aca-
> demic disciplines, especially in the humanities and social sciences,
> are inappropriate. The established disciplines should all become
> far more multi- and cross-disciplinary. The adoption of the term
> "studies" reflects the new emphasis. Supporters of the movement
> advocate that, instead of being organized into disciplines such as
> history, law, and English, teaching and research be reorganized into
> new, cross-bred fields such as "cultural studies," "textual studies,"
> "women's studies," "peace studies" and "media studies."[2]

Most of the twelve contributors to *What's Happened to the Humanities?* (*WHTTH?*) are in essential agreement with John Ellis's thesis in
Literature Lost that the abuse of critical theory and the politicization of
literary and historical research in obeisance to the above principles

have had drastic consequences: reasoning and evidence that lead to conclusions receive minimal attention; intellectual curiosity and freedom, along with the complexity of literary and historical works, are reduced to a low level; opposing viewpoints are rejected on moral and *ad hominem* rather than intellectual grounds; the political arguments themselves are opportunistic and ephemeral. One also finds in these essays an underlying concern that the spread of the new is not merely diluting the old but replacing it. Like some irrepressible exotic moss, the New Humanities have deoxygenated the pond, killing off previously thriving and important species, leaving nothing in the water but, well, moss.[3]

These are damning charges, not infrequently heard, to be sure, although they are not usually found in publications from university presses.[4] And, to be honest, despite the intelligence, sincerity, and broad learning on display throughout these two books, even to a sympathetic reader it's all beginning to feel a bit stale. If there is a consensus among these sensible and serious scholars—one finds little of the passionate disgust of Bloom or the insightful wit of Paglia here—about what is wrong, then what can be done about it? How much more analysis can we stand without action? *Logos ergou skiê*: speech is the shadow of action, runs the Greek proverb. For although these books successfully undermine the intellectual foundations of much of the New Humanities, I am not convinced that they can account for the rapid metastasis throughout the academy, and they offer few prescriptions for a cure. The New Humanities have been dissected and irradiated hundreds of times over the past twenty years, but they keep coming back in new and more virulent forms. If success in the modern university truly depended upon the quality of ideas, the "posts" would have been buried and forgotten long ago. But as we all know from the sequels to slasher movies, you can't kill the bogeyman. The humanities, by any definition that seeks to avoid parody, are in fact fading away. The antihumanists have proudly, and to a large degree successfully, proclaimed the "death of God" and the "death of the individual subject," indeed, the "death of man." Apparently, these constructed entities gave their lives so a few academic careers could thrive at the end of the millennium. *Requiescamus in pace.*

II. Some Facts

Since much of the scenery on this road will be familiar to readers of this volume, perhaps I can be forgiven for taking a rather tortuous route through the arguments. First—philosophical wrangling aside for the moment—what exactly *is* the current status of the humanities in the classroom and the bookstore? It would require little effort to believe that philosophies based on the denial of objective truth could appeal to today's casually cynical youth, a generation whose lack of engagement is vividly symbolized by the dispassionately shrugged "Whatever" echoing across America's campuses.[5] Nor would it be difficult to see why minorities who historically have suffered from discrimination might devote themselves to a curriculum that speaks endlessly of a power structure that privileges hegemonic groups and insists that Western culture consists primarily of a conspiracy to keep a white, male cabal in control. We would not be surprised, I think, to learn that university students might prefer cultural studies that rein-force their limited experiences, prejudices, and identities of race, gender, and class to works that challenge their preconceptions and demand hard-earned skills of rational argumentation and analysis. And who would be shocked if adolescents flocked to faculty who turned scholarship into confessional accounts of personal traumas, who transformed the classroom into an arena of self-hype and wounded self-esteem?

But this is exactly what has *not* happened. The enrollment and graduation statistics presented in the appendices of *WHTTH?* reveal dramatically that over the past thirty years the New Humanities have failed to attract much interest beyond the scholars themselves and their critics. The decline of the appeal of the humanities, in fact, oddly coincides almost directly with the rise of "race-gender-class scholarship," as Ellis refers to it. "Meanwhile, falling enrollments in the humanities carry a message that is not getting through: students are voting with their feet against the direction that the humanities have taken recently" (86). Overall, the percentage of bachelor's degrees in the humanities has declined by over 40 percent since the late sixties, from 20.7 percent of total degrees in 1966 to 12.7 percent in 1993.[6] Doctoral degrees in the humanities declined from 13.8 percent to 9.1 in the same period, which is a good start. A recent article in *Harvard Magazine* summarized other aspects of the slide: humanities faculty representation in the university has decreased (in 1960, one of every six faculty members taught liberal arts; in 1988 one of thirteen); the verbal scores of the SAT and English literature scores on the GRE have plummeted; humanists receive on average the lowest faculty salaries by thousands or tens of thousands of dollars and rely on adjunct part-time, nontenured appointments more than those in other fields.[7]

Students, it turns out, are wiser than the revisionist gurus give them credit for—they recognize the difference between indoctrination and education, even if their professors don't. As one Berkeley student recently said when asked why he watched the crude TV animated series *South Park,* "It's so anti-PC, which I love, because we are so bombarded with PC stuff here."[8] And why would those students who are actually interested in absorbing the new dogma choose to enroll in half-baked humanities courses when the whole meal is waiting for them across the hall in sociology and communication departments? Minority students are not interested in the theory or social agenda either—they take fewer B.A.'s and fewer doctorates by percentage in the humanities than do whites (*WHTTH?,* 20). And university presses, finding it increasingly difficult to survive by publishing the cant-ridden prose of academic scholarship, much less the intentionally obscure and illiberal research of the new academic Left, are turning more and more to general interest books.[9]

Moreover, the past thirty years of affirmative action, segregated housing, cultural studies programs, and increased emphasis on a non-"oppressive" curriculum have created more racial resentment among college-educated whites and blacks than among those without a college education (Ellis, 112). There is no evidence that students of the humanities are now more civil, judicious, caring, and empathetic than earlier generations or than their coevals in the natural sciences, business, or engineering. The inevitable coalescence of most academic multiculturalism—enforced respect for rather than understanding of the Other—with identity politics (what Shelby Steele has called the politics of difference) could hardly lead to the social utopias imagined by the engineers of the new curriculum. Commitment among undergraduates to "helping to promote racial understanding" fell in 1996 to its lowest point in a decade.[10] Louis Menand aptly summarizes the situation in literary studies as it stands after thirty years of disintegration of disciplinary authority:

> Literary studies has existed since the 1960s in a heavily professionalized system in which the positions are subsidized, the research is subsidized, the journals and presses that publish the research are subsidized, the libraries that buy the journals and monographs are subsidized, and the audience is increasingly limited to peer specialists. There is no "reality check" on this work because the only reality is the rapidly shrinking profession itself, buoyed up by dollars that will now be disappearing. Almost no one outside the profession cares even to understand what goes on inside it; they will, given a choice, certainly not care to pay for it.
> (WHTTH?, 215–16)

Something has happened to the humanities in the past thirty years, something of a different order than ever before. As James Engell and Anthony Dangerfield summarize the "vital signs" of the field: "Past declines of the humanities were changes in degree. In 1998, with weakened faculties and less well-prepared students, we face an imminent, dangerous change in kind."[11]

III. THE NEW CURRICULUM

So, in one sense the "death" of the humanities hinted at by many of these writers accurately refers to the failure of recent scholars to attract student or public interest. One would think that the experiment would by now have run its course, the lab closed, the "retexting" experimenters deleted and the "unpackers" sent packing. But nowhere is the increasing isolation of higher education from the larger community, the remarkable unaccountability to the university and public more evident than in the curriculum of the humanities. The more students have rejected the courses, the more books sold by Bloom, Kimball, and D'Souza, the more legislators have threatened to shut it all down, the more tightly the revisionists have wrapped their tentacles around the throat of the curriculum. The New Humanities have spread with amazing swiftness through the American university system. Foreign exponents of cultural studies, for example, gasp in admiration at what has been accomplished here: "I am completely dumbfounded by it. I think of the struggles to get cultural studies into the institution in the British context, to squeeze three or four jobs for anybody under some heavy disguise, compared with the rapid institutionalisation which is going on in the US."[12]

Although the proselytizers for the New Humanities increasingly control conferences, journals, grants, promotional peer review, and professional organizations, more important by far for the future of the humanities is the place of these theorists in the curriculum and thus in the training and hiring of new faculty and program directorships. True, thanks to tenure, the transformation of the humanities faculty and curricula has been and will continue to be less furious than the feeding frenzy of publication. At present, most departments

represent some kind of mixture of old and new. Margery Sabin finds
a typical situation in the Amherst English department, where there is
a near "total separation between the traditional literary courses taught
by the 'old' Amherst faculty and the new courses taught by the young.
This conspicuous segregation spells trouble for both the present and
the future."[13] For now, the department is split, so the students are
exposed both to close readings and courses with explicit political agendas. But what will happen when the "old" faculty retire? Departments
will not merely continue to hire New Humanists who in time will
become the majority, but older faculty now often retire without any
replacement at all—the position goes to another school or program
(WHTTH?, 28).

Even if the various incipient countermovements pursuing traditional modes of scholarship were to have some influence on the curriculum, the posthumanists will shape the university. As Gertrude
Himmelfarb observes, countermovements, "like counter-revolutions,
never return to the status quo ante. Certainly the new subjects, which
now have so much institutional as well as ideological support—African American, ethnic, cultural, multicultural, feminist, and gender
studies—will not disappear."[14] Is there any reason to believe that methodologies will fare any differently?

If you have trouble picturing what such a humanities curriculum
will look like, let me suggest that you spend a few days out here on
the sunny West Coast. We in California—recent immigrants mostly,
where our traditions are dated in weeks—do not have the patience to
wait for the university of tomorrow. It is here, now, just an hour away
from where I sit.

Between 1960 and 1990 the number of institutions of higher education in the United States increased from 2,000 to 3,595, with the
number of public universities nearly doubling (WHTTH?, 4). These
schools, created amid much of the transformation of the humanities, often reflect a strange combination of traditional and novel cur-

ricula. California added three research universities, the most famously experimental being the now rather staid if slightly schizophrenic UC Santa Cruz, which spawned such influential practitioners of the New Humanities as Fredric Jameson, Hayden White, and Norman O. Brown, and provided shelter as well for such diverse figures as Angela Davis, Page Smith—and John Ellis.

But just last year a new state university was launched at Monterey Bay, and here we can see down which holes the posthumanists are leading us. The Cal State system (not to be confused with the better known system of nine research universities that includes UC Berkeley, UCLA, etc.) was established and has been developed over the past thirty years to prepare California students for practical success. The charge of these twenty-two schools is primarily vocational: nursing, counseling, teaching credentials, business and management, engineering, and more. Over a third of a million students are enrolled in this system that awards more than half of all the baccalaureate degrees in California.[15] Now, at the turn of the millennium, a new campus with a new curriculum is in the process of being established. How have we taken advantage of the opportunity to build an educational program from scratch? Where do the humanities fit into the new education?

We won't consider the uniquely Californian twist given to the CSU Monterey Bay "Vibrancy" requirement that seeks to create in the student "a holistic and creative sense of self including an ability to demonstrate knowledge of wellness theory." Nor is it completely certain that the combined "Equity and Culture" requirement fits under the rubric of the humanities, but given the expanding and disintegrating boundaries of literary and historical research we should consider it. The "Equity" requirement demands that students "produce an informed historical interpretation and analyses [sic] of contemporary issues of struggles for power as related to the oppression of various racial, cultural, social and economic groups of people in the U.S." This includes "an understanding of the differential and unequal treatment of people of color, females, gays and lesbians, the poor, and others from historically oppressed groups in the U.S....an understanding of strategies and policies such as affirmative action which are intended to address inequities in institutions such as schools, governmental agencies, and businesses," and an understanding of "how you, the student, have worked towards building a more inclusive and equitable society." (One presumes that an acceptable answer to the latter would not be "campaigned for the elimination of affirmative action.") For the "Culture" requirement, "students must grapple with cultural diversity within the U.S., or connections between cultural groups originating outside the U.S. and those within the U.S. We are particularly interested in students' ability to interact with and comprehend contemporary U.S. citizens—real people who are here, now—who differ culturally from themselves."[16]

Especially relevant is the "Literature/Popular Culture" learning requirement—the conflation speaks volumes—through which students are to acquire "the capability to understand, interpret, and appreciate literature and/or diverse forms of popular culture as artistic and cultural representation." This requirement can be met through one of twenty-nine courses or by various independent assessment mechanisms, one of which is a "20-page paper or three 5-8 page papers, which examine and interpret 3 issues related to race, ethnicity, gender, class, sexualiry [sic], disability, age, and/or nationality in at least 3 works of literature or visual representations and/or forms of popular culture." Not one of the twenty-nine courses, the titles of which I list here in a note, focuses on the European or American classics.[17] Shakespeare was not in the Cal State Monterey Bay curriculum last fall, and a visitor to the campus bookstore found no literature at all by British or European or American writers.[18] American literature is limited to American ethnic literatures and cultures, a syllabus defended by the instructor with the claim that "American people are from different cultures and should get rid of bad habits."[19]

This is the future as current trends would dictate: Shakespeare and Homer banished from the core, Latina Life Stories and Introduction to Teledramatic Arts and Technology representing the diversity of options for a literature requirement, and politically correct ideas about race, gender, and sexuality mandated for graduation.

The curriculum of the New Humanities—the curriculum of the future—has arrived in full force. So what—intellectually, that is—is wrong with that? That question, despite the neutrality implied by the title of Kernan's strangely organized volume, is what both these books set out to answer. Those familiar with the academic culture wars will find few surprises here, but the situation is laid out particularly well, if not in great detail, in Ellis's book (with a few important exceptions discussed below), and several of the essays in WHTTH? provide insightful analyses of the processes that have led us to the current situation.

IV. The Ideas

Ellis sets out to give the "new orthodoxy" the kind of careful scrutiny it has managed to avoid as it spread throughout the humanities. He wants to explain how in literature social activism—the question of oppression, particularly in the West, by virtue of race, gender, and class, with its superficial moral appeal and arcane language—has become the major purpose of literary criticism, and why this entire enterprise is replete with logical contradictions and false assumptions. Ellis is especially good on the contradictions involved in the West-bashing of such well-known literary scholars as Fredric Jameson: "Those in the grip of this impulse are critical of the Western tradition and define themselves by their opposition to it, yet the impulse itself is so much a part of the Western tradition that the attitudes it generates can be said to be quintessentially Western" (12). He traces how the West has idealized other civilizations in moments of self-doubt; the West alone fosters such fantasies. It will seem puzzling to classicists that, although he occasionally uses the word *sophist*, he traces the origins of multicultural theory—"or rather cultural relativism, according to which cultures can be judged only by their own standards" (21) to Johann Gottfried Herder, the major ideologist of the German *Sturm und Drang* movement.

Ellis rightly sees that the amelioration of racism and sexism has come and will continue to come not from the rejection of Western society but by an alliance with Western values. Western culture is uniquely self-scrutinizing. Since Homer, Thucydides, and Plato the tendency in Western literature, historiography, and philosophy has not been to support the regime, mouth platitudes, quote the emperor, or praise the status quo, but quite the contrary. Ellis makes the familiar—but no longer countenanced—argument for literature as a liberating and subversive force, rejecting such oafish remarks as Terry Eagleton's that "departments of literature in higher education are part of the ideological apparatus of the modern capitalist state" (quoted, 51). It is only in the West, and especially in Western universities, that students and scholars trained in the liberal arts are praised and promoted for their critical analyses of their own culture. The revisionists themselves are thriving and voluble witnesses against their own dogma.

J. Hillis Miller has condemned as "repressive" the practice of "forcing a Latino or Thai in Los Angeles, a Puerto Rican in New York, an inner city African-American in either city to read only *King Lear*, *Great Expectations*, and other works from the old canon." Denis Donoghue, who quotes Miller in his essay in *WHTTH?*, unravels this simplistic argument (note the words "forcing" and "only"), observing that Miller is cheating and "patronizing those students by claiming that they are not to be asked to read great literature or to be taught how best to read it" (135).

The cheating, however, goes well beyond the loss of mere exposure to great literature. By withholding the study of Western culture from minority students, teachers are depriving them of the single most effective way of learning about the culture into which they will have to fit to become a success. It is through this necessary acculturation that minorities and immigrants can best hope to become part of the mainstream society, to gain access to the skills, knowledge, and opportunities they have historically or geographically lacked and now desire. That's why they go to college. As David Bromwich points out in an excellent discussion of the problems of expansion and diversification of a communitarian curriculum based on cultural identity, the purpose of the New Humanities to immerse students in their own microculture is completely inverted (233). He criticizes Lynn Hunt's argument in the same volume that the demographic changes— more women and minorities are now enrolled in higher education than ever—must put feminism and multiculturalism "inevitably on the intellectual agenda" (19-20, 29): "The entry into universities of persons ever more various in their backgrounds might just as plausibly have prompted a stress on the value of scholastic rituals promoting unity and harmony" (230). They all would have been served better by a resurgence of the study of Western culture as a necessary aid for entering the larger, increasingly Westernized world.

The revisionists' fixation on oppression with regard to race, gender, and class misses the richness and complexity of literature; it searches instead for simple and monolithic answers to human suffering. What gets lost in this redundant pursuit, as Ellis argues, is the diversity of thought and experience of the "endless puzzles of human existence" (39). That is what makes Western literature "universal"—as important for the girl from the ghetto and the adult immigrant from Asia as for the burger-flipping white boy so despised by the radical academic. Anyone in doubt should read an account of how the Clementine Course in the Humanities—a rigorous exposure to traditional courses in literature, art, logic, American history (through documents), and political philosophy—changed the lives of a group of mostly minority poor from New York's Lower East Side. The creator of the program introduced the course to the first gathering of home-less, pregnant, drug-addicted, AIDS-infected, English-impaired, excon volunteers without compromise: "You've been cheated. Rich people learn the humanities; you didn't. The humanities are a foundation for getting along in the world, for thinking, for learning to reflect on the world instead of just reacting to whatever force is turned against you.... Rich people learn the humanities in private schools and ex-pensive universities. And that's one of the ways in which they learn the political life. I think that is the real difference between the haves and have-nots in this country."[20] The results of this program—based on (we have been told) canonical, hegemonic, phallocentric, and to-talizing texts originally composed (we now know) to oppress the underclass, texts taught in a variety of humanistic methodologies that fail (we have all learned) to grasp the authentic selfhood of man—proved him right:

> A year after graduation, ten of the first sixteen Clementine Course graduates were attending four-year colleges or going to nursing school; four of them had received full scholarships to Bard College. The other graduates were attending community college or working full-time. Except for one: she had been fired from her job in a fast-food restaurant for trying to start a union.[20]

Ellis takes the theorists at their word. He dissects their arguments to reveal their incoherence, contradictions, and illogic. He believes that their anti-Western rhetoric, which blames our ills always on soci-ety never on our nature, comes from a sincere if misguided wish for the fulfillment of utopian promises made by alienated intellectuals. That interpretation would be more credible if any of them ever vol-unteered to teach twice as many classes or to do their own grading in order to liberate the "proletariat" underclass of part-time teachers and graduate students; to turn down an offer from another institution without demanding that their own university match it; or to hit the streets to tend to the downtrodden races, genders, and classes about whom they are so concerned.

The intellectual foundations of the New Humanities are so easily skewered by Ellis because they were never really intended to stand up to scrutiny. A silly form of liberal guilt—"guilt spawns theory," as Julie Ellisons has argued[22]—added to a blatant desire for self-advancement equaled the jumble of the New Humanities. Margery Sabin comes closer to the truth in her summary of this process: "radical social protest in the late 1960s; deconstruction in the 1970s; ethnic, feminist, and Marxist cultural studies in the 1980s; postmodern sexuality in the 1990s; and rampant careerism from beginning to end. What else is there to say?" (*WHTTH?*, 86). Not much, really.

Ellis examines in three separate chapters the work of gender, race, and class critics. His basic premise is sobering: "The corrective to the view that literature has nothing to do with politics is that it has *something* to do with politics, not that it has everything to do with politics" (62). If his attitude seems old-fashioned, his analysis of feminist criticism is positively atavistic—and generally compelling:

> Two contradictory impulses are at work, therefore: the insistence that there are no good reasons for the past differentiation of roles pushes feminists in one direction, whereas the claim that there is a distinctive female contribution to knowledge pushes them in the other. The result is paralysis; a concern with new knowledge is often announced, but a recitation of grievances always follows, both because it is easier and because that is the nature of the underlying drive. (81)

This is decidedly unfair to a number of critics of the seventies and eighties who brought the study of the role of women in literature and society into the mainstream of research and the curriculum. But it accurately reflects the current state of much of feminist studies, at least in classics. We can see this, for example, in the recent spate of books on Penelope, who has become the focus of critical whining about the place of women in the ancient *and* modern worlds—and a project for reviewing decisions at midlife by disappointed classicists trying to come to terms with their failed relationships and stalled careers.[23] As Ellis concludes:

> It is easy enough to use the theory of a malevolent patriarchy as the basis for commentary on how Ophelia or Desdemona or Cordelia is mistreated, or how *The Taming of the Shrew* is full of misogynistic prejudice. But quite apart from the fact that this approach applies a historically unrealistic theory of relations between the sexes, it also applies indiscriminately a preconceived idea as to what will be important. We are back to the central critical sin discussed in the previous chapter—that of letting the critic's obsessions determine in advance what is going to be important for a particular work. (75)

It is no coincidence, for example, that it is a self-proclaimed feminist, Judith Hallett, who has led the APA-sponsored panels on the "personal voice," the classics version of the latest critical fad of subjectivism discussed briefly by Gertrude Himmelfarb. Himmelfarb describes this *égo-histoire*, or better, *nouveau* solipsism, as an approach to any subject that "is insistently personal, dwelling upon the feelings, emotions, beliefs, and personal experiences of the scholar" (*WHTTH?*, 155). Bromwich is again on the mark when he concludes that the "growth of confessional criticism shows [that] the talk of scholars about politics and their talk about 'complicity' has become, to a remarkable degree, uninhibited talk about themselves" (234).

Similarly, Ellis quickly outlines the logical inconsistencies of recent scholarship on the white European's mistreatment of other races. The now-familiar arguments from this school are examined, with special attention to those of Edward Said—"The novel, as a cultural artifact of bourgeois society, and imperialism are unthinkable without each other"—and Stephen Greenblatt—"Shakespeare became the presiding genius of a popular, urban art form with the capacity to foster psychic mobility in the service of Elizabethan power" (quoted, 90). What becomes clear here is not only the poverty of this recent literary criticism, but also the weakness of historical analysis in the hands of literary theorists. Ellis sums up the contradictions inherent in much of this scholarship:

> Here the position of race-gender-class scholars can be stated simply: they argue that objectivity and truth are naive illusions of traditional scholars and, more generally, of the Western tradition and that they have demystified these ideas. There are no value-free facts, they argue, because all knowledge is socially constructed. The odd thing about this position is that it is diametrically opposed to the reality of what both newer and older groups have actually done: first, as I have argued before, the race-gender-class scholar's commitment to his and her truths about the reality of sexism, racism, and oppression is as rigid as anything could be; and second, traditional scholars—both philosophers and critics—have often been skeptical about truth and objectivity. (191)

Ellis's chapter on class—and as he points out, many Marxist scholars are quickly reinventing themselves with the collapse of Marxism as a viable political system—is particularly depressing. Fredric Jameson insists even now that Mao's primary mistake in the Cultural Revolution was that he "stopped it too soon" (122). No less offensive is Jameson's defense of Stalinism: "Stalinism is disappearing not because it failed, but because it succeeded, and fulfilled its historical mission to force the rapid industrialization of an underdeveloped country (whence its adaptation as a model for many of the countries of the Third World)" (quoted, 122). Pol Pot and Paul de Man are similarly exculpated and extolled by this influential literary critic.

Ellis gauges the self-contradiction of the race-gender-class dogma, using Stanley Fish as an example in his exploration of Foucault's "PC logic." It is a logic of "adolescent sophistry" whereby all conflict is reduced to an issue of power.

The only puzzle here is why Fish does not then brand the whole
of race-gender-class a right-wing phenomenon, since it is surely
based upon a rigid set of social beliefs. He ignores the fact that if
race-gender-class scholars were forced to choose between their
hard-edged views of capitalism, sexism, and racism (on the one
hand) and their pretensions to epistemological sophistication (on
the other), there can be little doubt that they would abandon the
latter rather than the former. (179)[24]

Although Ellis concentrates on the intellectual vacuity of the
arguments, what he refers to as "ironies," "contradictions," "corruption," "mistakes," and "blindness" are surprising only if one assumes
that the scholars are personally as well as professionally serious.
Either Jameson, Fish, and their many acolytes are ignorant—and this
possibility cannot be excluded entirely, for their dismissal of historical fact is often embarrassing—or they are simply laughing all the way
to the bank. Can we really take seriously a scholar like Fish who
denounced "the increasing squalor that daily life in the U.S. owes to
big business and to its unenviable position as the purest form of
commodity and market capitalism functioning anywhere in the world
today" (quoted, 131) while he simultaneously held an endowed professorship at a university that owes its very existence to two of the most
brutally successful forms of commodity and market capitalism, the
tobacco and utility industries? Ellis's focus on ideas rather than on
behavior also logically requires him to treat *all* forms of the current
critical pathologies. It is impossible, however, to keep up with all the
"corruptions." Ellis does not include queer studies, porn studies, *c'est
moi* subjectivism, or whiteness studies in his account, all of which
have staked recent claims on the study of literature.[24] It takes more
than logic to kill the hydra.

Ellis is perhaps at his best in his examination of theory. The author of several excellent books on literary criticism, he points out
that what "is wrong here is not theory but *bad* theory" (181). He well
observes—and Bruce Thornton has also demonstrated (see chapter

five)—that "literary critics have always been prone to amateurish mis-use of borrowed concepts" (185). Over time, the word "theory" has become identified with ideological currents rather than with the ac-tivity of analysis. Ellis notes that Paul de Man claimed that opposi-tion to deconstructionism was a "resistance to theory":

> As theory became fashionable, there arose a theory cult in literary studies, and its leadership became a kind of theory jet set, a profes-sional elite with a carefully cultivated aura of au courant sophisti-cation. In this atmosphere, only recent theory counted; anything from earlier times was wooden and outmoded. The persistent igno-rance of prior theory was therefore no accident but an essential fea-ture of this new development. The new elite shared a set of assump-tions but not a penchant for analysis. (200)

What is intentionally abandoned by the new approaches is close reading. Sabin rightly fears that close reading at Amherst will be lost when "Studies in the Literature of Sexuality" and "Native American Expressive Traditions" take over the curriculum (88–91). After all, the point of these courses is to emphasize the political; the analytical, the logocentric, is the enemy. Donoghue, whose essay argues for close reading, worries that our students are losing the ability to read,

> or giving up that ability in favor of an easier one, the capacity of being spontaneously righteous, indignant, or otherwise exasper-ated.... I believe that the purpose of reading literature is to exercise or incite one's imagination, specifically one's ability to imagine be-ing different.... A good reading is in that sense disinterested, as we used to say. I know that disinterestedness is commonly denounced as just another interest, flagrantly masked, so I use the word only in a limited sense. But it is possible to distinguish a reading more or less disinterested from one demonstrably opportunistic. (123–24)

So, finally, how did we get to this sad state? These scholars, inter-ested as they are in the history of ideas, all have suggestions: the pres-sures of changing student demography; the weakness of the leadership of professional organizations like the Modern Language Association; a cultural desire for transparency deriving from a broader assumption that all knowledge is socially constructed; the collapse of disciplinarity and the rise of a narrow professionalism guided by the reaction against formalism and essentialism, with the familiar continental pedigree of posthumanism (Nietzsche, Heidegger, Derrida, Foucault) and the decline of liberal tolerance in the post-Vietnam War era. These suggestions all have plausibility, but I do not think they get to the heart of the problem, nor can they (and they are not meant to) get us out of the morass.

V. The Future

The antihumanists and self-contradictory literary critics and social theorists are winning the battle for space in the curriculum and slots in the faculty. Cal State Monterey Bay is not alone in its dedication to the social agenda. The impetus for these changes did not come from the West Coast (although Stanford's famous dilution of Western culture is one of the markers), and there is no reason that their fulfillment should stop at the Sierras. California is an odd state, to be sure, but it is not consistently liberal. We are, after all, the home of Richard Nixon, Ronald Reagan, property tax and immigration reform, and the elimination of affirmative action. Our U.S. senators may be liberals, but our previous governor was a conservative. There is no obvious reason the new curriculum should take hold in the present political climate.

Nor is the new charter merely a reflection of our notoriously diverse population. The freshmen at Cal State Monterey Bay tend to come from affluent areas, nearly half from the prosperous upper-middle-class towns of Santa Barbara, Irvine, and Huntington Beach.[25] And do not feel smugly comforted by the fact that California taxpayers are footing the bill for the incubation of this ungainly infant—we're not. Thanks to the hard work of then Monterey Peninsula congressman and House Budget Committee chairman, later White House chief of staff, Leon Panetta—coincidentally, he and his wife have made $1,400 a day as consultants to the president of the fledgling university—federal funds have paid for 90 percent of the cost (with three-quarters of the $200 million project left to be completed).[27] And the development of the university on the former grounds of Fort Ord is now being held up as a model of development of "downsized" government properties—Culture and Equity, not to mention Vibrancy, could be coming soon to an abandoned military base near you.

The curriculum is also a model for another proposed new CSU campus (Channel Islands), and the ideology has carried over to the new UC campus in Merced scheduled to open in 2005. This campus, to be a major center for research and graduate education like Berkeley, will eliminate the nasty rubric of the humanities altogether. Instead, because the "humanities are undergoing a search for new definitions to mark the boundaries and approaches of research programs," the campus will have a division of Arts and Cultures.[28] "These programs will provide explicit consideration of cultures of origin and the immigrant experience" and offer a "rich experience in cultural studies." In addition, "The study of Valley native cultures and immigrant, migrant and refugee experience will enrich understanding of the human conditions of place, movement, transition, adaptation and survival." In itself, the prospects are bad enough—the San Joaquin Valley alone, which the campus is to serve, is an area larger than ten *states* and has a larger population than twenty. The curriculum of a University of California campus is far more likely to influence other colleges and universities throughout the country than that of the Cal States.

Even so stately a critic as Frank Kermode answers his own question—"Does epistemic change come in different sizes or is it always catastrophic and total?"—with pessimism: "It is reasonable to believe that...the situation really has grown worse" (161, 175). Ellis too, who has traced the rise and fall of other approaches to literature in previous books, argues that the shifts are more serious this time, since departments within the humanities have tenured (and, for the near future, are likely to tenure) faculty who accept the principles of the New Humanities. Major Ph.D. programs—the system that trains future scholars and teachers—are the most likely places to find the leading members of the new wave. As Bromwich observes, choices have been made that affect the future in important ways. Even the history department at Yale—ranked number one in the nation at the time of Bromwich's essay—had no senior professor who made a practice of teaching the Founding Fathers, or the career of Lincoln, or the politics of the New Deal.[29] Abroad, things are a little better, if only because the institutions change at a slower pace. But as Windschuttle points out, new institutions in Australia and Great Britain have followed the same pattern as Cal State Monterey Bay, offering cultural studies, communications studies, and media studies while rejecting traditional historical or literary approaches and programs.[30]

The writers under review, most of them well-known scholars who have witnessed the transformation first-hand, offer little hope that current trends will change.[31] Obviously, if you have stock in the New Humanities, you should merely hold on tightly to your portfolio—you have already profited far more than anyone would have expected. And there is tremendous pressure on young academics to get in line. As Sabin observes, commenting on the plight of writing instructors, "professional success means investing in the same stocks of avant-garde radicalism—post-structuralism, social constructionism, and cultural materialism—that have brought such profitable returns to their prosperous colleagues elsewhere in the humanities" (99). But must we give up, merely hoping that the revisionists will devour themselves before they can finish off the rest of us?

Gertrude Himmelfarb—no stranger to these conflicts—concludes her essay by wondering if there is some middle ground: "In the meantime, traditionalists and postmodernists alike will have to tolerate and be civil to each other" (157). Sensible advice, no doubt—genuine civility is in short supply these days in the academy. But there is also an abundance of mock confrontation as well. Too often the leaders on both sides of the debate have seen this competition for the hearts and minds of our students as an intellectual game in which the participants duke it out at conferences by day and after which everyone chummily retires to cocktail hour like divorce lawyers after a busy day in court. Nothing is resolved, but careers are built on the papers, talks, and networking. Gerald Graff's concept of "teaching the conflicts" is an especially unhappy example of this tendency. As Menand notes, this "represents a kind of perverse consummation of professionalism, the last refinement on the isolation and self-referentiality of academic studies: it makes what professors do the subject of what professors do" (214-15). The great works and historical issues come ready-made with all the tensions, ambiguities, and complexities needed to raise the important questions.

VI. A Proposal

Let me offer what may seem a bizarre course of action, a plan for reform that combines the romanticism of the *Odyssey* with the tragic necessity of the *Iliad*. The cure I propose will seem almost worse than the cancer—I don't expect it to be taken seriously. Yet this dose of chemotherapy to the diseased humanities may do its job, obliterating the tumor just short of destroying the patient. Yes, it is just as likely to kill us all as well, but the facts suggest that, without some drastic intervention that everyone admits will never come from within, we're fading fast anyhow. Anything is better at this point than writing another analysis of the problem, than merely whimpering to our pals about the deconstructionist bullies down the hall. *Pantôn to thanein:* in the long run, no one gets out alive.

As several of the authors of *WHTTH?* point out, the tightening of the purse strings will play a greater role in most of academics, especially at state schools. Legislatures and elected officials are currently engaging in another round of "faculty-bashing." A recent article by William Honan in the *New York Times* entitled "The Ivory Tower Under Siege" summarizes the criticisms:

> The main complaints are that faculties have usurped control of educational institutions and run them chiefly for their own benefit, not the student's; that they are accountable to no one, and that colleges have failed to increase productivity and that they cost too much.
>
> The critics also contend that all too often, students are unable to graduate in four years because faculty members are off pursuing hobbies masquerading as scholarship or research, and not teaching enough sections of required courses. And, they say, as a final slap to the taxpayers who finance public institutions, professors have created an inflexible tenure system that guarantees them lifelong employment at a time when almost no one but Federal judges and Supreme Court Justices enjoy that privilege.[32]

James E. Perley, president of the American Association of University Professors, admits in the article that he is denounced almost everywhere he goes. "It's 360-degree bashing. All around us, people are throwing things. I've been a teacher for thirty-three years, and I can tell you it's never been this bad." In another recent article in *Business Week* on "The New University," we learn what we already knew: over the past fifteen years government support for higher education has been cut, tuition has soared, and—even assuming current spending cost trends do not get worse—there will be a $38 billion shortfall in 2015 in what schools require to meet expected student demand. Except for only the most richly endowed universities, something is going to have to change—is, in fact, already changing. "Universities are rethinking the big lecture halls, faculty tenure, discrete academic departments, and other features that have defined traditional institutions for a century. They are designing curriculums more relevant to employers, communities, and students. Schools are pursuing fiscal discipline, forcing accountability on organizations that for decades have expanded as they pleased."[33]

In other words, departments, programs, and disciplines are going to have to justify their existence. If the curriculum does come under careful scrutiny from outside, here's my advice: embrace the process, welcome the philistines (that is, the politicians, journalists, and parents, many of whom are a good deal brighter than the academics) into the camp, open your cupboards and bring out your oldest wine. Only by creating a venue for debate can anything change. Currently there is no place in the academy for genuine disputation, since the proponents of the New Humanities philosophically reject the possibility of using the "indeterminacy and contrariness of language" to arrive at a "better" answer, much less the "truth." That is, they know they'll lose.

Humanists are hoplites standing in an open field, vainly hoping their opponents will crawl out of the groves of academe to meet them head on. There simply is no real dialogue about these issues, only separate and impenetrable camps. Bromwich, in discussing the "exigent resistance" that led to the revision of the *National Standards* for teaching American history in grades 5–11, draws the following conclusion: "If the result suggests that a licensed curricular project may, in the current climate, eventually produce an appropriate curriculum for public schools, it also leaves in doubt to what extent such pragmatic effects are probable without intervention from an articulate public" (230). Perhaps a similar intervention can work for the humanities as a whole, at least regarding the curriculum. But before the traditionalists invite public scrutiny, their own camp must be put in order. This will involve two changes.

First, old-style humanists—wiser now for not taking for granted the "traditional" benefits of the study of literature, history, philosophy, and so on—must stop mumbling to themselves about loss of status, stop deferring in self-loathing, uncertainty, and timidity to the arrogance of the literary critics and social theorists. Donoghue puts his finger on the problem:

> As humanists—in the special and limited sense in which we are teach-
> ers of the humanities—we are unable or unwilling to say what we
> are doing, or why our activities should receive support in the form
> of salaries, grants, and fellowships. We are timid in describing the
> relation between training in the humanities and the exercise of the
> moral imagination. (123)

When legislators come knocking on the door, when the presidents and deans complete their transformation of higher education into just another $250 billion business, it is time for some of the old arguments to come back. As Sabin concludes, "Those in a position to influence academic currency now have the obligation to reconsider the distinctiveness of humanistic reading and writing that can no longer be taken for granted" (101). The focus must once again be placed on the value—and values—of an education in the traditional humanities.

Once it was thought that scholars of the humanities taught because they believed in the intellectual rigor of their enterprise, the sensibilities it cultivated, and the connection between thought and action—sometimes called morality. As Ellis proclaims (but does not emphasize enough):

> The standard defense of the humanities, on the other hand, was
> that humanistic education provided all kinds of rewards, but the
> least important was the enrichment of our leisure through great
> literature and the arts. The most weighty arguments were that the
> humanities enabled us to see ourselves in perspective, to become
> more enlightened citizens, and to think more deeply about impor-
> tant issues in our lives. A society of people educated not just for a
> vocation but for full and intelligent participation in a modern de-

mocracy would be a far better and happier society—so ran the argument—and this overriding social usefulness of humanistic education compensated for its not leading directly to means of earning
one's living. (3-4)

It also taught a discipline of mind that enabled students not only
to separate stronger arguments from weaker but also to learn a trade
and master a vocation better. And since the humanities were based
on great, profound works particularly from the West, they taught
above all self-criticism, a ceaseless questioning tempered by duty and
responsibility to something larger than the self. The single activity
that warranted the expense was teaching—humanists were to share
their skills, implant their enthusiasm, develop sensibilities, impart
information so that students might lead more productive lives. This,
in effect, is what most liberal arts colleges still claim to do. The classic
modern formulation of this realizable ideal is still that of John Henry
Newman, who more than a century ago defended liberal learning,
since the student

> who has learned to think and to reason and to compare and to
> discriminate and to analyze, who has refined his taste, and formed
> his judgment, and sharpened his mental vision, will not indeed at
> once be a lawyer...or an orator, or a statesman, or a physician, or a
> good landlord, or a man of business, or a soldier, or an engineer, or
> a chemist, or a geologist, or an antiquarian, but he will be placed in
> that state of intellect in which he can take up any one of the sci-
> ences or callings I have referred to...with an ease, a grace, a versatil-
> ity, and a success to which another is a stranger.[34]

Most of the undergraduate teachers of classics I know still believe this, although they would concede that the benefits of research
need to be blended into the mix. And so does much of the public,
which wants little to do with political correctness in their universities. A 1993 pilot study of public attitudes towards the liberal arts
revealed that corporate leaders, educators, parents, and students all

saw the great value of the humanities, but thought the current curriculum failed to deliver.[35] Ironically, the one truly radical curriculum that has *not* been tried on a large scale since the number and diversity of students in higher education increased dramatically is one based on a *strengthened* core of Western culture and traditional humanities. Once the student population started to shift, academic opportunists and administrative quislings retreated from the curriculum.

Old-style humanists who wish to take back the curriculum must demonstrate to the outside world why their vision of the humanities is superior to that of the new school and why it has any value at all to the physical and metaphysical well-being of the public. And this can only be accomplished by doing research and teaching courses that have some meaning to someone outside the academy. Admittedly, we still do need books such as these two under review, books that effectively dismantle the claims of the New Humanities. Mary Lefkowitz's patient efforts, for example, have done much to bring to an end Martin Bernal's fifteen minutes of fame. And of course we still need the traditional scholarly monograph.

But we need more books that display the value of our profession. One can appreciate Christopher Ricks's confession in his contribution to *WHTTH?*:

> When this collection of essays was being bruited, I found myself saying at an explorers' meeting that instead of everybody's talking, yet once more, about "the state of the humanities" and the changes and chances of late, those of us who resist the claims of certain recent developments—as not truly or not sufficiently developments at all—would do better to get on with such work as we believe in. (179)[36]

Indeed, Ellis's book would be more helpful if it also told us something about the German literature he has devoted his life to, about the issues and ideas that are raised in works little known to anyone outside the academy. Robert Alter's *The Pleasures of Reading in an Ideological Age* (1989) is a model worth following in this respect. Windschuttle's book also has the great advantage of demonstrating the superior explanatory power of traditional scholarship in comparing the results of various approaches to a series of historical issues. He *does* some history—readers can see what each side has to offer and make their own choices. Why must it so often be the talented amateur, a David Denby or Michael Wood, who brings ancient literature and history to the public? The three thousand copies of *WHTTH?* are mostly in the hands of people who have already taken sides in the academic culture wars. Michael Wood's book on Alexander sold fifteen thousand copies before the PBS series even aired.

The best way to uproot the new curriculum is to put the argument back into the familiar competition of liberal studies versus vocational studies, which is exactly where the public wants it.[37] The New Humanists cannot win a battle waged in this fashion, since they have joined the enemy. Ellis again puts things into perspective:

> We would have been amused by predictions of what was to happen, because it would have been impossible to imagine that professors of literature would throw away their advantages. Who could have foreseen so complete a reversal that philistines who had never seen any value in studying Milton and Keats would eventually derive their most convincing arguments and draw their strongest support from professors of literature themselves? Or that *they* would be the ones to tell the world that great literature, far from broadening the mind (as they used to say), actually narrows it by implanting constricting, socially harmful attitudes. (205)

Today's students—and their parents—are more concerned than ever that a college education lead to a good job. Nearly 75 percent of freshmen surveyed this past fall chose "being well off" as the most important goal of their education, while only 40.8 percent opted for "developing a philosophy of life." These numbers are reversed from

1968, when 40.8 percent wanted financial security and 82.5 percent were looking for something more meaningful.[38] The New Humanities have nothing to offer these parents and students—and nothing to counter their understandable pragmatism.[39] That is, the literary critics and social theorists explicitly reject the emphasis on traditional "linear" skills of analysis, "hegemonic" rationality, and "value-laden" approaches that have for so long been the tools for real social reform, including the challenge to the rampant materialism that the revisionists actually embrace so fervidly in their own careers.

Some of the modern academy will come out fighting, claiming what is good for society is their curriculum. But they have little ammunition and, like the Roman boys educated in the schools of rhetoric on obscure and fanciful tales of pirates and rapes, they won't be able to perform under public scrutiny. Their ideas do not stand up to rational review, as these books and others have revealed. Their curriculum has not improved society over the past thirty years. They don't even like their material, as Kermode concludes: "For we all have colleagues who hate or despise literature and the study of literature, and institutional change has given them power" (177).

To be politically realistic, like it or not, most of the cost-cutting elected officials do not share the liberal politics of the academic multiculturalist. When Californians voted overwhelmingly to abolish state-supported affirmative action, the faculty senate at Stanford bravely countered by voting unanimously in favor of affirmative action.[40] These freedom fighters, safely snuggled in their half-million-dollar houses in the faculty "ghetto" and the elm-lined streets of Palo Alto, opened their mouths and lifted their pens once again in support of the minorities whose bad schools and difficult lives will continue to keep them on the other side of the eight-lane freeway that divides them from their "virtual" mentors.

Even Ellis himself, who takes their ideas so seriously, ultimately must concede their true motives are not social reform or intellectual "paradigm shifting." He points out that unlike in the natural sciences, where a new discovery opens up new fields and career opportunities, often in the humanities it means that there is now one less thing to say. So, to make a career in academic publishing, one must reinvent what the humanities mean. Like Joseph Smith in the New York woods, one must dig up hitherto unknown texts and apply the magical lens of revelation to decipher the scribblings. Indeed, with everything now a text, there is no end of new material and new fads. How refreshing it is to read from Louis Menand what seems so obvious to those outside the academic world:

> It may be that what has happened to the profession is not the consequence of social or philosophical changes, but simply the consequence of a tank now empty.... Literary history is one thing that the academic structure is good for enabling. There was a job of periodizing, of establishing texts, of exhuming neglected or forgotten work, of producing critical biographies, and so on that could only be undertaken on a massive scale, and with due quality control, in a university setting. This work has now, possibly, largely been done. The only interesting new work being undertaken today is an extension of that old work: the business of exploring canonically "marginal" writing. The interest of this activity is largely historical, and it will eventually run out. There will always be scholarly problems to solve, of course, and there will always be room for critical revisionism. But the notion that work that seemed done a mere twenty or thirty years ago now needs to be entirely redone is a notion suggesting that the larder is pretty bare. Academic literary criticism is now largely in the business of consuming itself. (215)

Here is the Achilles' heel of most of the New Humanists: they are hypocrites to the core. No doubt some are politically sincere, convinced that the old humanities reinforce social realities which they find abhorrent. But they do not live the lives they profess. As even Ellis must conclude, the "self-dramatizing and self-absorption are real, the politics of social conscience is literary-critical" (211). They criticize capitalism because doing so pays financial dividends. They advocate multiculturalism because it promotes them out of the classroom and away from the lowly undergraduates, the people their curriculum is supposed to liberate. They have the sincerity of Orwell's dancing pigs, who devour the resources in order to "save the oppressed": "You do not imagine, I hope, that we pigs are doing this in a spirit of selfishness and privilege? Many of us actually dislike milk and apples.... It is for *your* sake that we drink that milk and eat those apples."

But (and here's shift number two) humanists can only exploit this hypocrisy—that is, the public will only be convinced—if they have the courage to reject the entire package of the modern academy. If academic politics replace reading, thinking, teaching, and writing, we are indeed lost. Professors must stop wanting or expecting anything from their profession other than the decent salaries they already earn. Not atypical is the following excerpt from an article on Cal State Monterey Bay:

> Two experienced academics familiar with the campus (but not affiliated with it), interviewed for this article, expressed unhappiness about the lack of European American or European authors in the reading lists. Neither was willing to be identified, observing that if they were named, jobs and relationships could be imperiled.[41]

What, some celebrity theorist-of-the-day might snub these "experienced academics" at the next annual meeting? Their colleagues would have confirmed what was always suspected, that these two academics had minds of their own? A grant application, think-tank invitation now at risk? When was it, exactly, that the academy became the repository for audacious charlatans, sycophantic wannabes, and tremulous *apragmones*?

It is time to return to the model of Socrates and to turn away from the Hellenistic version of the university. Indeed, Peter Green's analysis of the rulers and scholars at Alexandria seems uncannily appropriate for the denizens of the modern university as well: a foreign elite living among a people whose language and ways it wants nothing to do with in daily life, a world of raging ambition, lack of real political power, intellectual alienation, and urbanism. Despite claims of a radical divorce from the past, they instead reveal a "fantastic desire for stability," the prime aim, always, being to better one's position within the system as it stands. The Museum itself—where critics thought of themselves as superior to the artist—was attractive especially for the perks: free meals, good salaries, pleasant environment, good lodging, and plenty of servants (graduate students). There was even the equivalent of today's race-gender-class utopian agenda in the development of Hellenistic pastoral, likewise an idealized daydream of an urban elite, living on patronage, who would never be caught dead with a sheep. Green aptly refers to the lampoon of Timon of Phlius, which describes the Museum as a wicker coop where academics are maintained like high-priced birds: "In multicultural Egypt, many grow fat as subsidized bookosauruses, endlessly quarreling in the birdcage of the Muses."[42] We need more of Homer, less of Callimachus; more Sophocles and less Menander; a whole lot more of Plato and *very* little of Epicurus.

Faculty must stop expecting the public to subsidize publication. Research fellowships to individual faculty investigators should be eliminated. John D'Arms laments that the number of these grants, which he approvingly accepts to be "the lifeblood of scholarly research in the Humanities," declined from 250 to 150 between 1980 and 1994 (35-40). Not enough. The Fellowships for University Teachers go to scholars at major research universities already paid to do research. These scholars have the lightest teaching loads in the world. Nowhere have I ever seen it demonstrated that this research would not be undertaken if my tax dollars didn't remove them from their campus duties. Indeed, the cup of humanities research runneth over. And over. That such grants could be called the "lifeblood" of research indicates just how anemic the humanities have become, how desperately we need to be weaned from mother's milk and grow up. It is an insult to the huge majority of scholars who publish without having ever received a penny of outside money. The Fellowships for College Teachers and Independent Scholars, of which most of the winners come from elite liberal arts colleges and smaller research universities like Notre Dame, UC Santa Cruz, Dartmouth, and Georgetown, should mostly dry up as well. Why waste federal money on research that will get done anyway? If, as a nation, we desire to sponsor humanities research, then let's take a chance on faculty who teach eight large classes each year to students needing extra attention, professors who may need—and never otherwise receive—the rare opportunity to collect their thoughts and write something important.

In the over five hundred pages of analysis under review here, I found only one acknowledgement of perhaps the greatest transformation of all in college and university teaching over the past half-century, which is that, despite the huge increase in the number of both students and faculty, "over the course of the Cold War period, the amount of time professors at research universities spent in the classroom shrank from an average of nine hours a week to an average of four and a half hours a week"[43]—with a month less of class to boot! Humanities professors may spend more time in the classroom than faculty in other divisions, but at research institutions in particular this is hardly "quality time." As recently reported by a commission created by the Carnegie Foundation for the Advancement of Teaching, baccalaureate "students are the second-class citizens who are allowed to pay taxes but are barred from voting, the guests at the banquet who pay their share of the tab but are given leftovers."[44] With sabbaticals, grants, leaves, and released time, it has been estimated that as many as one-fifth of professors are not teaching at all during any given term.[45] A 1991 survey of over 35,000 faculty found that only 10 percent believed their institutions valued and rewarded good teaching.[46] As Sabin points out, even undergraduate courses in the humanities now are often little but narrow research foisted upon the unwary (91). The price of "being" an academic is high.

Tell the truth and be prepared to be despised, or worse (apparently), ignored. Achilles, Ajax, Cassandra, the Melians, Socrates—these should be our models, not Ismene who merely wants to be loved in comfort and safety, not the chorus, who merely want it all to go away. If it should suddenly become profitable to teach—that is, if jobs suddenly were dependent upon offering—more classes on familiar authors and historical subjects in traditional disciplines with humanistic methodologies, the New Humanities would quickly fade away. There would be so many conversions and reinventions in the academy it would feel like a revival meeting.

Could we ever be comfortable leaving curriculum decisions in the hands of politicians or alumni? Of course not. We have no reason to think that the presence of outside arbiters will lead to change in any positive direction: we may well soon have mandated courses on creation science, corporate tax-sheltering, and sports psychology. Moreover, the proponents of the New Humanities share with public officials and academic administrators a gift for schmoozing, an unctuous facility for ingratiation. They infiltrated the university by being political, not logical; private, not public. They work behind doors, networking late nights on the phone, born hustlers all. The nature of their success is transparent, as Joseph Epstein noted in his farewell column to *The American Scholar* after being booted out by the academic revisionists:

> Phi Beta Kappa's Senate, far from being representative of the organization at large, is almost wholly made up of academics, and in academic argument, I have noticed, the radicals almost always win, even though they rarely constitute a majority. Conservatives, dependably a minority, usually don't care enough to take a strong stand against them. Liberals, the poor darlings, though generally the majority, are terrified about seeming to be on the wrong side of things and so seek compromises that inevitably favor the radicals.

The model here is the Russian Duma, with the minority of Bolshe-viks cracking the moderation and ultimately the backs of the Mensheviks.[47]

So even if there were to be a public debate about the role of hu-manities in higher education, the leading posthumanists would send out their apparatchiks to take a painful but meaningless beating by the humanist thugs, while the politicos themselves made their deals offstage.

But in spite of the likelihood of failure—perhaps *because* of the very slim chance for success—academics concerned about the collapse of the humanities must take aim at something bigger than their own careers. Call it Millennial Fever. Homer, Shakespeare, the Founding Fathers—they deserve to go out with one final suicidal run, a Pickett's charge to victory or into oblivion. We little men and women owe them at least that much.

CHAPTER 4

✦

VICTOR DAVIS HANSON

"TOO MUCH EGO IN YOUR COSMOS"

—Rudyard Kipling

The use of the personal voice in scholarship and criticism has a long tradition. At the end of his monumental history, Edward Gibbon finished with the moving admission that "It was among the ruins of the Capitol that I first conceived the idea of a work which has amused and exercised near twenty years of my life, and which, however inadequate to my own wishes, I finally deliver to the curiosity and candor of the public." Indeed, what makes John Keegan the most widely read military historian of the present age is not just his mastery of language and knowledge of war across time and space, but also the occasional glimpses of himself in his formal narrative.

The personal voice, then, when used cautiously, economically, and without ideological bias, is a precious resource in the scholar's limited arsenal for making history and literary criticism come alive. But what is so bothersome about the efforts of Professors Judith P. Hallett and Thomas Van Nortwick in their edited collection, *Compromising Traditions: The Personal Voice in Classical Scholarship*, is not the use, but rather the abuse, of this hallowed tradition. For as I point out in the following review essay of their book, in their hands the personal voice—angry, whiny, passive-aggressive—intrudes on almost every page. It brings in images and stories—sex, breakdowns, tenure decisions—irrelevant to scholarship and better left out on grounds of good taste alone. Who wishes to hear about the various authors' clitorises or episodes of past sodomy?

The "I's" and "me's" convey neither experience nor insight, but rather are used mostly to complain about career disappointments and the general injustice of the university at large—predictably its purported unfairness to women and almost anyone other than the stereotyped oppressive white males.

Three other flaws of *Compromising Traditions* form the basis of my unease: the book is intellectually dishonest; it achieves the opposite effect of what is intended; and it has nothing to do with scholarship. First, the authors do everything but "compromise traditions": all are academics sharing a fashionable posture of radical feminism, postmodernism, and general hostility to what they variously call "old boys," "white males," and "WASPs." There is not a single dissenting opinion, not a conservative, not a traditionalist, not a poor soul in the book who might be anything other than an academic classicist who believes that white heterosexual males have made a mess of things. By choosing the title *Compromising Traditions* the authors compound their disingenuousness by suggesting that they are compromising something. They don't. While it is unusual to include the pronoun "I" thirty to forty times on a page, their professed politics are now the mainstream on campus and echo all the clichés about race, gender, and class that we've become accustomed to in the last twenty years. A far better title would have been *Timid Whiners Upholding Orthodoxy*.

Second, for all scholars who use the personal voice—veterans who remark of their own experience in war when writing military history, architects who confess to the puzzles of engineering when discussing the great cathedrals, artists who remark on brush strokes when critiquing the Impressionists—this book is treasonous. Any fair-minded reader will come away so assaulted by the overuse of "I" and "me," so put off by accusations of racism and sexism, and so bored with the tales of baby-boomer angst that they may well conclude that no one, at any time, should dare use the first person lest it degenerate into something like this book.

Lastly, the greatest untruth about the book was the inclusion of the word scholarship in its title. There is no extended literary criticism or historical analysis here, nothing about the ancient world that could benefit from the experience or insight of the authors, nothing at all really about the Greeks and the Romans. *Compromising Traditions* is not even an account about the use and method of the personal voice, but simply an embarrassing memoir of some very upset, upper-middle-class white academics who wish to talk about themselves, their graduate school horror stories, and their unhappy careers, rather than Sophocles, Plato, or Thucydides. Their time would have been better spent, and their anguish better ameliorated, by tutoring the underprivileged in Latin at local grammar schools. They are all far more concerned about themselves than about their field.

Yet, it came as a great surprise to see the authors suggest that they were somehow populists in their shared disdain for entrenched white male philologists. No better reminder of C. Vann Woodward's caution about the misuse of the word "populism" exists than *Compromising Traditions*. One surely can object to elitism on campus, the avoidance of teaching, and the ascendance of careerism without sharing a single thought of the Personal Voice "populist" authors.

Even more so than when I concluded the review with a quote from Homer's *Odyssey* ("may all perish who should ever do these things again"), I now feel that *Compromising Traditions* is a metaphor of what academia has become:

> If personal voice theory, at least as it appears here, is to be the golden mean between narrow philological pedantry and incomprehensible post-modernist theory, then we classicists really are, and should be, through. This is all so very, very sad.

After publication of the following review, others in classics expressed similar concern—I know of not a single subsequent favorable appraisal of this nonbook. But most astounding was the response of coeditor Hallett herself, who chose not to reply in print, but rather took an entirely different tack, quite unexpected for someone who is a professed woman of the Left. Apparently— and I say apparently, because no one has yet quite figured out her behavior—the present essay had the unintended effect of sending her scurrying to the FBI for assistance. (See the epilogue for Professor Heath's essay on the Unabomber incident.) In a notorious admission, Hallett confessed to calling the FBI to report the authors of *Who Killed Homer?* as possible terrorist suspects in the nationwide hunt for the Unabomber. But as Heath shows, at the time she asserts that she called the FBI hotline (October 1994), the Unabomber's views were *not* known to anyone, nor had Heath and I even begun collaboration on *Who Killed Homer?*, in which Hallett is scarcely mentioned.

What, then, prompted her fantastic announcement of going to the FBI on a global Internet list-serve group (for her admission, cf. http://omega.cohums.ohio-state.edu)? One can only speculate, but many of us suspect she never did call the FBI and was instead brooding about this present review rather than *Who Killed Homer?* Again, when she claims that she called the FBI, the Unabomber had *not* published his manifesto, and we had *not* written a word of *Who Killed Homer?*

Confirmation of that suspicion may be found in her further admission to the *Wall Street Journal*. When asked for an explanation of her actions by Mr. Jody Bottum, the literary editor at *The Weekly Standard*, Professor Hallett strangely replied that "Victor Davis Hanson should acknowledge that I voluntarily went to a law enforcement agency and likened his and his collaborator's view to that of a deranged killer when he is asked to assess my work and my life" (*Wall Street Journal*, May 28, 1999, W11). Again, Professor Hallett fails to acknowledge that at the time she claims that she contacted the FBI, John Heath and I had not even begun *Who Killed Homer?* nor had the Unabomber issued any of his public manifestos; but I had, just prior to her confession in spring 1999, published the following review—as she reminds us when she shifts from the plural to the singular, "when *he* [emphasis added] is asked to assess my work and my life."

Of course, neither the FBI nor the CIA—see below—contacted either Heath or me, and we doubt Professor Hallett ever called them at any time—and we hope not, since innocent lives depended on the FBI's ability to screen out crank calls like hers rapidly in order to glean real information that might lead to the killer. Rather,

Hallett's embarrassing confession was apparently designed to elicit some disclaimer from me in the future: from now on Hallett apparently wishes me to preface my reviews of her work with something like the following: "I cannot be fair since Professor Hallett called the FBI on me," or perhaps better yet, "I must confess that Professor Hallett once called the FBI on me, and that's why I unfairly criticized her otherwise excellently edited book." To paraphrase Edmund Burke, in her fanciful explanations: "fiction lags after truth, invention is unfruitful, and imagination cold and barren."

To this day, Professor Hallett has offered no clarification of her contradictory chronology and says she is reluctant "to provide more information on why I decided to help the FBI in this instance because I'm not sure how much I can share publicly about my other interactions with them, and the CIA" (*Wall Street Journal*, May 28, 1999, W11). Nor has the American Philological Association officially reprimanded her, though it is often prone to issue statements about bothersome practices in society at large that appear sexist or homophobic to scholars.

In the meantime we all await the much-promised volume two of *Compromising Traditions,* said to be due out shortly.

᪾

For myself, I shall simply set down its nature, and explain the symptoms by which perhaps it may be recognized by the student, if it should ever break out again. This I can the better do, as I had the disease myself, and watched its operation in the case of others.

History of the Peloponnesian War 2.48.3, Crawley trans.

I.

I N Book Two of Thucydides' history, the once-exiled author describes the horrific plague that struck Athens in the second year of the Peloponnesian War. In his discussion of the disease's origins and causes, Thucydides suddenly breaks into the first-person narrative to add poignant detail and empirical data drawn from his own illness. He returns to the use of the first person later in his fifth book, as he once more interrupts his rather solemn account to offer a more "personal voice" in his discussion concerning the length of the war.

> I certainly remember that all along from the beginning to the end of the war it was commonly declared that it would last thrice nine years. I lived through the whole of it, being of an age to comprehend events, and giving my attention to them in order to know the exact truth about them. It was also my fate to be an exile from my country for twenty years after my command at Amphipolis, and being present with both parties, and more especially with the Peloponnesians by reason of my exile, I had leisure to observe affairs more closely. (5.26.4–5)

The personal voice in nonfictional, nonautobiographical critical writing, whether that be history, science, oratory, or political theory, is as old as the Greeks—even the purportedly detached Thucydides is not immune from the temptation of its use. The ancients did not believe that the occasional employment of the first-person pronoun, the excursus into personal remembrance, or the citation of individual expertise and experience was in anyway antithetical to objectivity, accuracy, or gravity.

But notice carefully *why* and *how* Thucydides uses the personal voice. He believes that he has had unusual experience that is germane to particular discussions—most of them scientific—within his history: his recovery from the plague allows him first-hand knowledge about the symptoms of the disease and projects empathy with its victims. The horror of contagion is heightened by the knowledge that not even the historian escapes infection. Thucydides' exile after the setback at Amphipolis and his own relative youth, we now see, has given him an extraordinary opportunity to chronicle the entire struggle and to travel unmolested among the warring parties. Under the veneer of a detached and impersonal voice resides a man with enormous expertise about war and a wealth of tragic experiences.

That inclusion of personal information, then, explains a great deal in Thucydides' history. The reader no longer wonders why he seems to learn so much from non-Athenians and over such a long period of time. Notice the tone of Thucydides' remarks: matter-of-fact, grave, and restrained. Given the horrendous sequelae of the plague—described so vividly in the narrative—we should imagine that Thucydides himself must have suffered a variety of postinfectious maladies. None is recorded. No "I could not reach Melos because of my poor vision after the plague." From what we can piece together from other sources and incidental detail in his own narrative, his exile after Amphipolis was at best unfair. Surely there was a host of personal agendas and generally disreputable behavior behind the Athenians' decision to oust the historian from their society. Again, we are to hear none of it. No "My loss of office and exile were results of a personal vendetta engineered by Cleon."

When the first-person voice enters the narrative of the Peloponnesian War, the sentence structure, the level of emotion, and the use of imagery remain unchanged. Thucydides is neither more angry nor more frenzied when his own circumstances are discussed, suggesting that he, too, like the *dramatis personae* of his history, is subject to the same cruel irony and fate that all humans alike must face. And so when the author's voice leaves the narrative, we want to hear more, not less of Thucydides the individual—we are intrigued about what is left unsaid as much as about what is told. He is selective and guarded, not promiscuous, in his disclosures. His own person is, in short, tantalizing. We never know exactly when he will reappear to us as battle veteran, political infighter, traveler, or survivor of the plague. His personal voice is thus mysterious and subtle, and it possesses a certain dignity by the restraint in its use, the surprise of its entry and exit, and the critical and relevant expertise that it conveys. And while postmodernists and sophisticated theorists might laugh at the historian's "fiction" of both professed objectivity and restraint, Thucydides' purpose in using the explicitly personal voice is really more to assist the reader's understanding of his ideas than to elicit sympathy for his own suffering.

Consider, in addition, the nature of Thucydides' personal revelations: war, exile, plague—the traditional biblical host of abject catastrophes. Surely other problems arose in the historian's life—petty discrimination, perhaps maltreatment as a result of his Thracian pedigree, financial setback, loss of public repute, his marginalization by a more liberal Athenian democracy, and vindictive treatment by demagogues. Yet, again, none of these is ever explicitly mentioned. In the historian's eyes, such experiences are not relevant to the elucidation of his story. I would surmise that Thucydides felt such unfairness and maltreatment to his person to be inferior in magnitude to battle, disease, and forcible expulsion—to be, in other words, the relatively normal cargo of frustrations that we as humans all share in a frequently unpleasant, often tragic, and all-too-brief world, and hence of little value in adding either insight or information to his narrative.

II.

Far different from Thucydides' practice is a recent movement among classical scholars to embrace the "personal voice"—the "explicitly autobiographical intervention within the act of criticism." Judith P. Hallett and Thomas Van Nortwick have combined to edit a volume of nine essays, drawn from recent American Philological Association and British symposia and framed by their own introductions and conclusions, which seeks to change radically the way classicists interpret and present their scholarship.[1] The personal voice is to be an inclusive tent, where feminists, postmodernists, and assorted theorists can go far beyond "academic discourse" to swap storytelling and thereby reinvigorate classical scholarship in its eleventh hour (23).

We are reminded that personal voice theory is akin both to feminist scholarship, which emphasizes "the role played by gender, race and class in the production and reception of knowledge" and to poststructuralism, which questions "the validity...of the ideals of the detached scholar and impartial reader" (1).

As would-be revolutionaries manning the barricades and "compromising traditions," the authors expect opposition from traditional philologists. Professor Hallett is ready for it and throws down the gauntlet: "Such discursive concessions to the conventions of professional acculturation not only loom large during our days as novitiates, but long after we have taken our final vows. By employing the personal voice as part of our classical scholarship—with the goal of creating a more expansive and authoritative form of classical scholarship, one which acknowledges the distinctive differences among its practitioners as vital sources of strength—we are at last seeking concessions from *the other side*" (emphasis added, 14-15).

Hallett is surely right that by past standards of classical scholarship this collection is rather bizarre and does compromise at least the Thucydidean tradition of first-person usage that many scholars have on occasion employed. Classicists as diverse as Bernard Knox, N. G. L. Hammond, Michael Jameson, W. K. Pritchett, and Vasily Rudich, to name a few, have drawn on their own experiences—battle, field reconnaissance, military service, life in China, political repression under the Soviets—to lend expertise to particular discussions of the military, topographical, colonial, or political life of the ancient world. I am equally guilty of the practice in occasionally comparing my own blunders as a farmer with the realities of ancient Greek arboriculture and viticulture as practiced in a similar Mediterranean climate. But perhaps Hallett and Van Nortwick, and most others whose work is included in the collection, would see such traditional usage as limiting, anecdotal fact-gathering, unduly restrictive of the full potentialities of the employment of "I," "me," and "my," which should properly capture feelings as well as experience and thereby bring the irrational to the fore of scholarly discussion.

Whereas the Thucydidean tradition narrowly centers on the correlation between the special *technê* or experience of the author and the particular subject at hand in the narrative, the new version of "the personal voice" draws randomly on emotions and confessionals of all sorts, albeit overlaid with admitted orthodox "political agendas" (64; cf. 124, 173). And everything, we must understand, is now to be fair game for the classical scholar—drunken parents (19), midlife crises (16-17), tenure denials (121-22), gossip (94, 126), teenage sexuality and body appearance (41, 56), the clitoris (41), the penis/phallus (90, 107), sexual acts both heterosexual and homosexual (154-55), AIDS (177), mean boyfriends (26), mental breakdowns (91, 94), failed marriages (17), federal sex discrimination lawsuits (170), spousal abandonment (35), personal slights (122), insensitive former thesis advisors (39, 155), and far too many other topics to be summarized here, but which in their totality offer a literary and polished version of the more tawdry and rawer exposés presented daily for the less educated on the daytime television talk-show circuit.

There is to be no Thucydidean economy in this latest manifestation of personal intervention—it is not uncommon to find the first-person pronoun used forty to fifty times on a single page (cf. 17). So much for Susan Wiltshire's assurance that "we will want to avoid intruding ourselves carelessly into our writing.... The purpose always is to call attention to our subject, not to ourselves" (178). Nor is there any of the suspense or unpredictability of Thucydides' personal voice. The contributors are quite honest that this is to be a collection in which the author's life, thoughts, and angst will be missing from scarcely a paragraph. Borrowing a line from postmodern theory, they believe "all writing is personal" anyway (170, cf. 70), so why not just come out and be honest, abandoning the myth of "the detached scholar" and "impartial reader." Ostensibly these so un-Hellenic revelations will not merely elucidate the text, but allow readers to come to know the author not as a removed critic or unbiased observer, but as a real person like themselves. When we can emphathize with the travails of the modern classicist, we will at last empathize with the real Greeks. In the entire collection there is literally not more than a single page or two where "I" and its oblique cases are not found—the sincere, though naive, belief of the well-meaning authors is that their litany of disappointments and neuroses (what they call "confessing...shameful youth" [22]) will attract rather than repulse most readers. They are oblivious to Voltaire's warning that *"Le secret d'ennuyer est de tout dire."*

Sometimes the ego-disease can infect the embryonic sentence even before it can start out in life: "So it seems to me now, at this point in my thinking on this subject (which is not the same as twenty-two months ago, when I first started thinking about it, or as it will be twenty-two months hence)..." (49). Oddly, such halting personal prose in this case is offered to us as the author's clear corrective to the dull "depersonified academic voice" (39) of scholars of "superior detached status" (40), who have contributed to the "removal of my idiosyncrasies, the individual stylistic variants of my prose, any hint that 'I' existed as a real flesh and blood person with feelings" (39). Ironies, then, abound throughout the collection.

There is also no recognition of, or perhaps no concern with, the embarrassment that the collective experiences of most academics who matured in the last four decades are, to be honest, not especially interesting, much less unusual or heroic to most readers. All these voices lack Thucydidean *gravitas*. There are no wars, plagues, exiles here, and no apologies for their absences, either. Instead of the ancient notion of pathos, we feel real modern bathos. The stress, pressures, and accompanying fixations of contemporary Western suburban existence in general and the melodramas of academic life in particular are now to be as legitimate as were Thucydides' infection and expulsion. Instead of Thucydides' first-hand encounters with rotting corpses and sinking triremes we read of journal articles rejected (161), tenure denied (121), and rude department colleagues who were inattentive listeners (94).

Again, do not expect in this book a recent returnee from Bosnia or Rwanda to explicate the insanity of stases at Corcyra, someone with jail experience in a federal correctional institution to ponder Socrates' refusal to break out, a Vietnam veteran to talk of the "mile" run at Marathon, a journalism major to comment on Rumor, or even a former elected official to offer musings on the tumult of the ancient *ekklêsia*. Instead, the *Sturm und Drang* of a self-proclaimed, exclusively white, presently secure, self-conscious, mostly middle- or upper-middle-class, highly educated, well-traveled, urban professoriate—free from the horrors of war, revolution, grinding poverty, physical labor, mayhem, and hunger—are to elucidate, in a way classical philologists cannot, the lives, culture, and thoughts of a mostly agrarian and relatively poor ancient citizenry a harvest or siege away from ruin.

The authors, though, might retort that they think the use of the personal voice is critical for another reason as well—to identify the present political affiliations of a scholar (e.g., "the other side" [15]; "our own political agendas" [64]; "in honor of Bill Clinton's inauguration" [124]; "at a small campaign gathering for Albert Gore, Jr." [173]; "The Republican party, if it has its way..." [32]). Such honesty would end the sham of disinterested anonymity where "authors and referees are not supposed to be cognizant of or concerned with one another's identity" (135). Co-editor Hallett presents a disturbing scenario in her critique of the supposedly anonymous and "'objective' assessment" of scholarly articles (135):

> Here, for example, I have explained why I am a committed feminist who regards gender as a matter of major importance, and why I consider that my identity as a feminist scholar enriches and eluci-

dates my identity as a classicist. I appreciate similar efforts at honesty from colleagues, direct acknowledgments of where they are "coming from," because such efforts in turn help me assess those colleagues' criteria for assessing others. (134)

There is, of course, some danger in explicitly politicizing the personal voice through "direct acknowledgments." From the sad history of the twentieth century we all know where professed self-identification can descend. Ultimately the primacy of political correctness drowns out individuality, eccentricity, dissent, passion, and honesty—the only true stuff of art and literature. Long ago George Orwell—"if it paid better they would be fascists"—warned us that within such a politicized environment there would always be a rivalry to gain acceptance for ideas often of dubious worth by parading one's purer affiliations.

In the context of publishing scholarly work, perhaps we could affix detachable I.D. stickers to our submissions that say something like:

Dear Co-Editor Hallett,

As a strong feminist and long-time admirer of your own work, who feels the need for progressive scholars to counteract the "objective assessments" of white male privileged elites, I hope you will appreciate the enclosed effort at providing a strong feminist, though often silenced, personal voice.

Then sympathetic editors could turn to their Rolodexes replete with potential reviewers' "race, class, age, as well as gender" (cf. 128) to "help...assess those colleagues' criteria for assessing others" (134)—for example, no to this "white, wealthy, fortyish, heterosexual reactionary" reviewer; yes to that "Pacific Islander, lower-middle-class, postretirement, feminist woman" reader.

But Professor Hallett is worried not so much about the wisdom of requiring self-identification ("honesty" and "direct acknowledgments of where they are 'coming from'") as she is that others may not hear of it: "But are such efforts at honesty likely to become accepted professional practice? As the associate editor of a scholarly journal, I am frustrated by the reports of referees who find no fault with argumentation or the documentation of a submission, but dismiss its approach or choice of topic on the grounds that they are not 'important' or 'interesting'" (134). According to this logic—that everything is always political—because the present reviewer finds *Compromising Traditions* neither "important" nor "interesting," any criticism by him must be attributed to "where [he] is coming from," that is, membership in a gender, class, race, or power structure different from that of the contributors. Could it not be simply because I find the "argumentation," "documentation," "approach," and "choice of topic" (134) of this volume wanting?

Writers in Eastern Europe, Communist Russia, and Mao's China all knew "where they were coming from" and they were as eager to use those "criteria for assessing others"; but the result of seeking such progressive solidarity was not literature, art, or honest criticism, but mediocrity, repression, intolerance, and, of course, far, far worse. Given that academics are not known for their bravery, we would soon not be reading of personal voices, but rather hearing a shrill howling as the pack cynically bounded after each new scent that promised career rewards.

Indeed, we already see far too much of that calculated orthodoxy and monotony in this present volume. Otherwise, why is there so much mutual back-scratching? The authors in this collection, quite apart from the formal introduction and response, constantly quote one another by name and refer to one another's talks and work—not in the traditional and valuable manner of intravolume scholarly cross-references, but in a more grating sort of informal chit-chat and gratuitous back-patting ("If any Tom, Judith, or Susan can get published by confessing their shameful youth" [22]; "When Vanda was a student of mine"; "my Bristol colleague, Vanda Zajko, who was facing her PhD examination" [40, 38]; "A prestigious secondary school whose alumni include Professor Charles Rowan Beye" [120]; "Judith Hallett, whose paper at the conference and whose challenging questions during the discussions" [108]; "My excitement in discovering that my friend and colleague of many years Susanna Morton Braund" [107]).

But the authors, of course, warn those in "reactionary quarters" (129) ahead of time not to label as "unscholarly 'whining'" (129, 132), "white male bashing" (130), or "lack of tact" (178) their revelations of "my pain" (16), "deep feelings of inferiority" (123), and "emotional scars" (132). We are not to react "with distress, or embarrassment, or anger, or a combination of these" (94) when we read such often lurid revelations. To do so is to valorize the old "depersonalized academic voice...which manifestly bore attributes of gender, race, and age: male, white, and middle-aged" (40). It was a sinister enough voice that supported the "hierarchical, competitive model for doing business in our field." Its "anxiety about standards," we are warned with Foucauldian frequency, "can be a device for hoarding power" (22). These students of ancient logic have forgotten the fallacy that the constant anticipation of criticism is not synonymous with its rebuttal.

Sadly, despite their claims of bravery and radicalism in "compromising tradition," most contributors remain quite worried (15, 39–42, 59–63, 132–35, 178–80) about what those in the Old Guard might do when they get their hands on this book, hence the constant disclaimers and worries: "Most obviously, by revealing something about ourselves and why it is we ask the questions that we do, we contributors have compromised ourselves and our writing in one basic sense: that of exposing ourselves and making our writing liable to suspicion and disrepute" (2). None, however, goes as far as Charles Martindale, who gives us his heartfelt pledge not to engage in personal voice slumming again: "Nonetheless my own experiment with this approach is not one I would necessarily wish to repeat, or recommend to others" (94).

III.

Before examining some of the individual essays drawn from this self-confessed "middle-class suburban world" (31), let me enumerate a number of contradictions in the collection.

First, the purported aim of the book is to bring us the past via the experiences and feelings of the present. Specifically, classical literature can seem relevant in 1998 through an empathetic demonstration of how it can still explicate and change our own lives. But how many of these authors actually discuss classical antiquity? Do any explicitly and at length connect a problem in ancient literature with something that they themselves have experienced? In fact, only two of nine do so—Judith de Luce in her analysis of the topos of abandoned female helpers and Patricia Moyer in her reflections on Euripides. The rest of the contributions are not really essays on the past, but are mostly revelations about the angst of the present by authors who just happen to be classicists and thus scatter about a few references to Odysseus or Virgil. The only genuinely shared themes of these personal memoirs are criticism of classical philology and the simple fact of authorship by academics.

Fair enough—let us not criticize the book not written, but rather turn to what we have, an unhappiness with traditional classical scholarship spiced with intimate details about the contributors' lives. The central thesis of all of them is that traditional philology has left us with a grinding monotony in both approach and style. Who can argue with that? Anyone who has perused the program of APA talks, the table of contents of classical journals, or university press catalogues can agree. Too many classicists—sometimes both philologists and theorists alike—can be obscure, pedantic, distant, timid, and cold in their writing, and they are too often interested in problems that have little relevance for the typical college undergraduate, much less the average American. They teach too little and write too much for too few. But is the medicine offered here any better than the disease? Does this type of personal voice provide more engaging images, moving prose, and original themes and stories sure to make the ancient world come alive either in print or in the classroom? Thomas Van Nortwick asks, "What does knowing the metrics of Plautus contribute to the overall health of the Nation?" (186). Some might answer, About as much as being told that Mr. Van Nortwick (along with all too many millions of other Americans, including the present reviewer) is the son of an alcoholic. In other words, absolutely nothing in both cases.

The authors are confused about where such a true diversity of presentation might arise. To alleviate the boredom and repetition inherent in classical scholarship, aren't we in need of great stylists, creative writers and artists, eccentrics who may come into the field late and leave early, men and women of action who have lived lives beyond the dorm, library carrel, and faculty lounge, or even the sometimes reckless who smile at, not cower before, the official rebuke of their more entrenched peers? Don't we need idiosyncratic Schliemanns, Ventrises, and Parrys who seek to short-circuit academe and commune directly with ancient texts rather than with texts about ancient texts?

The writers of *Compromising Traditions* feel no such need. Diversity in this collection is apparently *uni*versity, involving relatively small differences of religion, gender, rank, and education—"We are six women and three men, ranging in age from early thirties to mid-sixties and in rank from Lecturer to Distinguished Professor" (6). That one has a Ph.D. from Michigan rather than Harvard or prefers Virgil to Homer is presented—embarrassingly—as difference: "We are Latinists and Hellenists, gays and straights, Jews and Christians. We hold advanced degrees from Stanford, Tulane and Big Ten state universities as well as from Ivy League strongholds in the U.S., and from Nottingham, Exeter and Bristol as well as from Oxford and Cambridge

in the UK" (6–7). In other words, we learn that a group of well-educated, white, upper-middle-class, liberal, and like-minded professors
were not educated at the same schools and have different research
sub-specialties within the tiny field of classics. And while being Jew-
ish or homosexual might constitute real variance in Des Moines, it
does not seem terribly disparate in the university.

Once our diverse and courageous rebels are identified, however,
we can then unite and move on to round up and condemn the usual
suspected enemies of storytelling. At the millennium we, of course,
all know who he is. The nomenclature of disdain shared by the contributors reflects an eerie type of group-speak, as if they were all working from some commissar's dog-eared script—though I was enchanted
to learn that this toxic species is allowed to have slightly diverse sub-
species. Sometimes he is the "WASP" (153) or "straight WASP male"
(12), or even "that most detested of creatures in contemporary American academia, a WASP male of the monied class with a Harvard PhD"
(153), more often the "white, middle-class male" (8) or "white, middle-
aged, middle-class male" (43), not to be confused with the "male, white
and middle-aged" (40) or "white, educated and heterosexual male"
(64) of "white middle-class, middle-American style" (162), or "old boy"
(133), "good old, straight old boy" (156), or just plain old-fashioned
"privileged white males" (129) or mundane "male classics professors"
(121). And he is responsible for all sorts of bad things, from "Newtonian
physics" (185) to the "Boston Brahmin" (154) and "America's ruling
class" (157), keeping us out of his "masculine preserve" (189), "traditionally male preserves" (23), "traditionally male...world" (172), "male-
defined world" (169), and contaminating us with "traditional notions
of masculinity" (14), "masculine reason" (189), "male-authored texts"
(9, 61), "the male's quest" (31), "male ideology" (9), the "male's voice"
(161), the "quintessential languages of masculine scholarship" (59),
"male writing" (162), and "dominant male culture" (35) of "male reviewers" (48), whether really "male or their female clones" (161), and

keeping us within "the purview of men" (169). He and his ancestors have made women feel "non-human" (34) and the equivalent of "the animal" (35), and he is an expert at "depersonalization" (39, 40, 41), this creator of "patriarchal culture" (33), "orthodox patriarchal assumptions" (23), "patriarchal lies" (61), and "modern misogyny" (189). All this stereotyping is somewhat surprising coming from a book whose professed aim is to inaugurate new idiosyncratic paradigms of expression outside accepted generalization.

But who are these horrendous pale monsters of America? Almost all the white middle-aged males I see out here in rural California are not elbow-patched, wire-rimmed, loafer-wearing, nasal-voiced, journal-article-rejecting, and tenure-denying chairmen and deans ready for pasture in the New England countryside, but of lower-middle-class status or already among the unfortunates of American life—filthy tractor caps, missing teeth, financially insolvent, and often dirty, disabled, and exhausted. Prior to being enlightened by this volume, I had considered such "white males" more the victims than the beneficiaries of the oppressive "post-industrial West" (190) these affluent, pampered, and tenured academics profess to despise. I wonder what the reaction would be should these self-proclaimed "courageous" contributors venture into the local auto parts store, cafe, or similar "traditionally male preserves" and inform the assembled "good old, straight old boy[s]" that there aren't going to be any more "orthodox patriarchal assumptions."

Can others play at this labeling game? If so, after reading this collection, I suggest we all agree on a new species of Anglo-American: the "white, upper-middle-class, well-paid, securely employed, summers-off, intercontinental-traveling, smug, frustrated, pouty, whiney—and mostly unhappy—desk-bound academic," whose published work few read and whose classes most undergraduates increasingly pass by. That stereotype is about as crude and unhelpful a label for the hundreds of hard-working classicists in little-known undergraduate programs as the constant "white male" calumny is for millions of Americans.

But the white male miscreant turns out to be less toxic (and more frequently identified and named) when he either agrees with the approach of feminists (the work of John Henderson is a particular favorite [42-43; 74-76]) or publicly recants the "cultural baggage we do not want to carry" in apologizing for "orthodox patriarchal assumptions" (23). Mr. Van Nortwick is particularly paranoid in worrying that classicists are sometimes unjustly accused by multiculturalists who claim that when "we in the Classics department teach Aristotle, we must endorse his views on women and slavery, and so proselytize innocent minds." Then he offers an inappropriate comparison to the Inquisition and the Nazis. "Do early modern historians endorse the Inquisition? Were Hitler's biographers all Nazis?" (188). But how many of us really worry that a zealot in Ethnic Studies thinks assigning Aristotle means advocacy of slavery or sexual discrimination? And I find, as most others would, Van Nortwick's further implication even sillier, if not reprehensible—that Aristotle's philosophical prejudices are in any way to be placed in the company of those of terrorists and sadists like Torquemada or the Führer.

True, among classicists it may be difficult to find real diversity as most Americans define it—diversity born of some life intimacy with the brutality, monotony, danger, and tragedy of the workplace. But given the book's showy promise of real variance, we might have at least expected to find here, if not the underbelly of America, then the voice of one right-wing nut, a Christian fundamentalist, or a millionaire capitalist—and there are actually a few such classicists—who could make the ancient cosmos of reactionary coups, extremist religion, or Athenian banking speak to contemporaries. But again the purpose of this volume is not to use personal experience or expertise to elucidate Greek literature, but apparently to complain about the "hoarding" of "power" by conservative elite classicists.

The authors make a terrible error in thinking that because academics' left-of-center views are at odds with most of America, somehow they are also unorthodox, even radical or courageous (2, 24). They are not. Any diversity that exists in this volume is the intramural squabbling and petty rivalry of the lobster bucket, where claws and pincers snap at others in oblivion. The easiest, not the most courageous, stance in the world of the 1990s (and beyond) humanities department is for a professor to attack the "middle-age, middle-class, white, heterosexual male." Alas, the voices here constitute a chorus of yes-men, not mavericks.

We miss, then, Danton's revolutionary *"De l'audace, et encore de l'audace, et toujours de l'audace!"* The fact is, *true* radicals damn the torpedoes and press on full speed ahead. If they entitle their book *Compromising Traditions,* then we should expect these would-be brawlers to give up their easy straw "white" men and forgo "the nameless and the dead" (133) and the constant unsupported chit-chat. Rather we should expect them to cite examples, name names, quote abhorrent policy statements, and thus make the case that living, breathing, and identifiable white, middle-aged males in the APA, Ivy League, Oxbridge, and the think tanks marginalize women and people of color through their enforcement of WASPish forms of argumentation, bloodless expression, and their "aristocratic aversion to public exposure" (189). Do they not remember Thucydides' "Men make the city not walls or ships without men in them"? As Frederick the Great said to his timid Guard, "Rascals, would you live forever?"

But I suspect many of us know why these tenured radical reformers parade the names of supporters (42–43, 74–76, 108), but leave mostly unnamed those culpable white men who have caused them such pain and anguish "and feelings of scholarly inadequacy" (127). Perhaps in a volume to come, we as a profession can ask who these dreadful white men are at Harvard and Oxbridge ("a pair of archaic institutions" [41]), and what those who "compromise traditions" are going to do to end their hurtfulness. If he is not named or quoted, can we believe the evil "white, educated and heterosexual male" really exists? Once authors such as these take up the language of invective (e.g., "outrageous misrepresentations and lies" [123]; "patriarchal lies" [63]; "most detested of creatures" [153]; "they have been a disaster" [167]; "philistine and ignorant" [166]; "lamentably incapable of even beginning to diversify the sorts of voices heard" [41]), then they have entered the arena and must play by the tough rules of the thrust and parry—and that requires names and quotations and citations if it is not to be cowardly or untrue.

So I am troubled over a revolutionary fervor that trashes the unfairness of footnotes and data collection—and then quite timidly gossips (121–22, 155); feints attack only to quickly hedge, prevaricate, and backstep (39–40, 62, 133); presents unsubstantiated rumor (126, 133) and unsigned e-mail (137); snipes at unnamed foes (94); ridicules now-retired dons (123); cites documents full of "outrageous misrepresentations and lies" but not their authors (123, 136); produces as evidence anonymous, unsigned questionnaires (142–48)—or promises not to do any of this again (94)! Professor Hallett's disclaimer— "unless I am citing their published work, or they have given me permission to use their names, most classicists who figure in this essay are either nameless or dead" (133)—only emphasizes, not excuses, her pusillanimity and is itself the truly *unprofessional* stance, especially when *she had argued for ending the practice of academic anonymity in peer review and for identifying scholars by their professed ideologies* (134–35). When we are told that so many "patriarchal" published texts abound, why is it then necessary to attack unnamed or unpublished correspondence, or to make generalized sneers without citations? Again, this volume is not supposed to be a novel or even a memoir where anonymity is standard, but an "act of criticism" and a new method of "classical scholarship."

There are plenty of living, breathing Ivy League males—powerful enough white heterosexual men in the field who sit on journal boards and graduate school admissions committees, referee fellowships, hold APA offices, and hire endowed professors, and who have written articles, policy statements, even whole books critical of feminists' views, whom Professor Hallett (again, the professed advocate of ending anonymity in scholarly peer review) could identify, quote, and footnote at length as examples of pernicious "privileged white males." Instead we get mostly ankle-biting on Professor Philip Ambrose of Vermont—a gifted, humane, and hard-working classicist at or near retirement, who has done as much as anyone in the country to encourage undergraduate education—for his liberal and elegant defense of internationalism and his justifiable worry over the bashing of foreigners (125–26, 140). In short, I find the targets of attack here misdirected and the studied exclusionary language of invective careerist, calculating, and, in the end, a very unpleasant sort of dissimulation. It is as if Demosthenes, in the secret hope of a spot on the royal Macedonian staff, were to rail endlessly to an in-house audience about all those anonymous hurtful "Northerners" without mentioning Philip or his accomplices in Athens by name.

And what are we to make of the constant smug dismissals of the anonymous white male when we read in Susan Wiltshire's essay near the end of this book that "one of the most compelling arguments for recognizing and appreciating the personal voice in classical scholarship is that it keeps us from attacking personally others who do their work differently. Ours is a spacious discipline, with ample room for many different approaches" (180). After all of the anger, we are reassured that "we American classicists inflict enough, needless, [sic] pain on one another" (131). As the arsonists' fires rage, can't we all just get along?

At first, Judith Hallett asks "Who the hell cares?" about the silly pedantry of "mean-spirited British classicists" who have been hurtful to her (121–24). But then, after her "first reaction" passes, she gives us pages and pages of generic bombast that prove she cares very much indeed. All this anger leads to the obvious question that lies at the heart of this entire collection—are these "radicals" angry over a culpable system that rewards dullness and irrelevancy, that harms the daily fight to interest American students in the Greeks and Romans, or are they merely depressed and hurt that at midlife their own careers have not met the expectations of a tiny elite? Is not the real worry of these middle-aged—but seemingly perennial—graduate students the state of their own careers rather than the sinking ship of classics? At least the Ivy League grandee, secure in his patriarchal values and privileged position, does not suffer the wages of hypocrisy as do these sunshine patriots who profess martyrdom but fear the bullet. So much mock heroism in this volume, so little real courage.

Another implicit claim of this volume is that the language of the personal voice is accessible and egalitarian (22–24, 94, 132–35, 177–80, 184–87). But why do the authors believe their often ungrammatical sentences (45–47) and I/me/my/mine revelations of the most intimate details of their lives are any easier to read than (say) the Pauly-Wissowa? Sometimes their exemplary personal voices are hilarious and turn the argument of this entire collection on its head—as, for example, when they compare John Henderson's prose with that of a traditional philologist. I shall let you be the judge of which voice is the clearer and more engaging by quoting the last two lines of the two respective texts offered to us for comparison by Charles Martindale (74):

> David West: "Because Horace does not put his hand on his heart and sigh, his love poetry is usually underestimated."

> John Henderson: "*Phew!* There, *that's* better. But...O scholarship, industry of avowal & deniability! Those *men*! They *would* say that, wouldn't they?" (emphases his)

I will wager any of the contributors that the undergraduates of

America will find West, not Henderson, the more comprehensible; the former seeks to pass on information and enlightenment, the latter, inside jokes and allusion among the tiny and chatty elite whose class the authors so vehemently denounce. And when an advocate of personal voice theory introduces the book with "discursive concessions to the conventions of professional acculturation" (14), we may legitimately ask against whose impersonal, dry, and lifeless language this movement should be railing.

Does the inclusion of dirty words at this late date really "contextualize" obscenity and offer a challenge to "those who wield power in our profession"? Susanna Braund compares J. N. Adams's work with that of Amy Richlin and blithely remarks, "What is refreshing here, and throughout Richlin's book, is that she does not shirk the relevant 'four-letter words.' She has broken with tradition in introducing words like asshole, cunt and fuck into her text" (48). What reactionary tradition is that in 1998? There is nothing compromising or untraditional, much less personal or "refreshing" about "four-letter words"—anyone can and, of course, does use them now in print. An author's preference for "fuck" adds nothing that a contemporary reader does not already see and hear every day on television and the radio, tells us nothing about the author except that she is pretty much a product, like the other two or three billion on the planet, of the modern age. The issue is rather one of decorum and taste—in 1998 using "fuck" in print rather than "intercourse" is about as courageous, refreshing, and unusual as talking publicly about an alcoholic parent.

A virulent anti-British and anti-Germanic theme runs through the entire collection. Hallett, in response to an imposed metrical correction of one of her Latin poems, exclaims, "Let those mean-spirited British classicists write some Ovidian verses about their leaders—elegiacs about the lunchtime amores of Tory MPs, or hexameters on Prince Charles' wished-for metamorphosis into a paper product for feminine hygienic use!" (124). Are we to laugh or weep? So much for

Ms. Hallett's earlier expressed anger over the unfairness of personal invective, the "disparaging remarks leveled at myself and others because of our gender" (11), which we all were supposed to deplore. Charles Beye then ups the ante: "When I once learned that the discovery of a 'controlled substance,' as it was called, in the pocket of a foreign national is grounds for instant deportation without a hearing, it took every ounce of Christian forbearance to prevent me from trying to improve the playing field for American classicists with this strategy" (167). A nativism that contemplates the commission of felonies, or an anti-Christian's (166) embrace of Christ, to rid us of the English presents more irony. Not only did a few of the anonymous, refereed submissions to this book turn out in fact to be British, but the one genuine example of an Oxford don's arrogance and cruelty—Kenneth Dover's gruesome admission of near-complicity in the death of a colleague—is not condemned (65-7) but instead offered as a more or less positive inspirational model (54-55; cf. 2) of personal voice usage!

Hallett and Beye argue that the Brits cannot teach (often true). They take jobs away from Americans at the top research universities (I suppose so). They are not sensitive to the American muse (of course). And they often fire us and make fun of us (not always wrongly). But why then have the most innovative and popular contemporary classicists—Peter Green, Peter Brown, Bernard Knox, and M. I. Finley—been either British-born, British-trained, or British-employed? Perhaps it is the greater British tolerance of eccentricity—a trait sorely lacking in these essays—that encourages the rare and gifted to break away from the crowd. It is hard to make the argument that all British classicists are aristocratic and dull as a group when the most successful popularizers of our profession—such as Michael Wood or Michael Grant—are English. My own minor brushes in graduate school with snobbery here and abroad were mostly from American wannabe Brits, not the real thing; the latter (who once numbered nearly half the senior faculty at Stanford) were usually quite unconcerned whether their American students went to "a prestigious secondary school" (120) or grew up in the farming backwater of central California. The English professors in Palo Alto and Athens as a rule cared only whether we knew Greek—the prep-schooled and East-Coast-trained Americans cared more about who we were and where we were from.

Ms. Hallett's and Mr. Beye's academic nativism is a little hard to swallow when it is passed off as a sort of broad-based populism. If we are going to suspect Europeans, then why not go whole-hog—less hand-wringing and whining about journal articles rejected, Latin pronunciation corrected, and tenure denied, and instead more honest nativism and xenophobia in the good old-fashioned, paranoid American style that Richard Hofstadter once so ably chronicled?

But if we are to trust only in our own national voice and not worship foreigners, why then such a heavy reliance on French thinking (163)? Scarcely a page can be turned without the intrusion of the old gang of Barthes (52, 82–84), de Man (78, 86–87, 185), Derrida (78, 86–87), Lacan (107), the "French feminists" (60), Foucault (65–66, 69), and their numerous American acolytes. Yet French-inspired postmodernism has done more to squelch individualism, emotion, and spontaneity than all the British philologists, empiricists, and positivists put together. Quite simply, according to Mr. Foucault, there is no such thing as a personal voice, much less a need for its expression. It is simply a concocted fiction of no value at all. Indeed, our poor contributors are on the sharp horns of a dilemma: how to quote their beloved Gallic ontological nihilists and yet maintain that their own individual voices are in any way valuable and unique—anything other than the epiphenomenon of an arbitrary fictive discourse fashioned by the invidious machinations of power networks. Constant apologies over that predicament and a few contorted escape plans characterize the entire volume (1–2, 23–24, 60–61, 78–79, 102, 107–8, 185, 188).

Personal voice theory is purportedly at odds with academic capitalism, the pernicious system of hierarchy that puts such a premium on status, salary, rank, and influence (19–22)—"the race for money, prestige, and comfort" (22). The clear intent here is to suggest that these contributors are not one in spirit with the Ivy League and Oxbridge grandees who lust after "power," "bigger salaries," and "prestige." Rather, the Compromising Traditionalists are normal folks in the trenches (128). They dance to a different tune than the Anglo-inspired elites and bravely write "not for any careerist reasons, nor for any admission into the patriarchy" (118). They have rejected "the race to bigger salaries and more prestige" (186) and sneer at "in-bred cliques, bent on reproducing themselves and so cranking out clones to feed the Dean's relentless bottom line" (186). We are told by one of them that "I am not interested in the power games played by so many academics.… One of my strongest principles is social justice: equal opportunities and self-realization" (52).

The lady doth protest too much, methinks, for these critics of the Anglo-American rat-race in general and the academic scrabble in particular seem obsessed with publicizing prep schools (120, 133), department chairwomanships (43, 52), journal associate editorships (134), directorships of honors programs (169), Ivy League educations (18, 153, 155, 169), Distinguished Professorships (6), Ph.D.'s (6, 38, 62, 154), grants (175), prizewinners (3), praise of one another (22, 183), postdoctoral sojourns abroad (122, 129), presidential addresses (3), and conferences (4–5, 91, 123, 125). All that bumper-sticker identification has little to do with explication of the Greeks, but it might tell us a great deal about elitist professors' own insecurities and real aspirations. Why do almost all the authors parade their own prior "pioneering" (3)—previously published work and conference papers (16, 21, 51, 125, 126, 138–39, 161, 173, 176)—and go on to explain the triumphs of their own "modest" careers (52)? For those who are so angry at British snobbery, why so many off-the-cuff and meaningless references, such as an association with George Bush's boyhood academy ("a prestigious secondary school" [120]), or personal contact with the current vice president ("I noticed that Gore seemed somewhat distracted" [173])?

Consequently, even the artificial and contrived efforts to display populism inevitably succumb to unintended but hilarious aristocratic pomposity. Judith Hallett confesses that she started Latin "late" at thirteen (127). Take another example, Susan Ford Wiltshire's pastoral, Wendell Berry-reading (174) image of herself thinking about her own book while propped up in an old rocker: "I finally gave up puzzling over the proper arrangement of the book and took some time off. As I sat in a rocking chair on a porch by a creek, thinking about something else altogether, I thought of the *pas de deux* in ballet" (174).

Leopards really cannot change their spots.

IV.

I shall end by summarizing four of the essays. By far the best effort is the penultimate response of Professor Beye (153–67): a crude, often funny and outrageous, but sometimes cruel rumination against Christians (166), heterosexuals (154–55), the British (166–67), and the tacky Americans in general (166). Beye, like Gore Vidal, combines the smug elitism of his upbringing (153–54) with a general, unapologetic, left-wing hatred of middle America (162, 166). He writes as well as any of his well-educated generation and lacks the stern joylessness of all the other aging and angry baby-boomers in the collection, whose lives and careers are not quite turning out as promised. As a modern-day Trimalchio who reviews his larger-than-life career at the table of his inferiors, this bon vivant relates his some thirty years of professional and sexual experience (e.g., 155) with the classical hierarchy. Of the Greeks' interest in the young male and his own difficulty with the dispassionate restrictions of scholarly discourse, he chimes in with: "Can one imagine how perverse it is to speak in utterly neutral tones with a distanced sensibility about the institution of erotic physical contact between two males when the speaker is himself a veteran of more such encounters than he could possibly count?" (156). Beye is indeed fortunate that he managed to speak in "utterly neutral tones." Had he revealed to his young students any personal-voice ruminations about his own "encounters"—much less acted on them—application of the many feminist-inspired speech and sexual-harassment codes on the present-day campus would have landed him in the academic pokey.

Nevertheless, this "veteran" has offered us a let-it-all-hang-out exposé that is honest, funny, and unusually perceptive—and which does not really have much to do with the art of using the personal voice. How can it, when a serious literary critic is asked to respond to talk-show chit-chat? Some of his casual comments surely must have bothered the stern political correctness of the first-person sisterhood: "I personally could argue that as a gay male I much admire Odysseus' capacity for lying" (158); "I sometimes found [one of his professors'] celebrated lunches...mildly titillating sexually, but most of the time an exercise in S & M that left me trembling" (155); "to the extent that the personal voice theory derives from the feminist movement and to the extent that women (in the USA at least) are acculturated to analyze other persons—what dismissive males call 'gossip'—such endless speculation can perhaps please the one sex and repulse the other" (160).

Beye is far too honest a critic not to notice the general vacuity of the volume, and he is the only one astute enough to see the hypocrisy of his *Compromising Traditions* peers concerning matters of their own privilege (157). His fellow contributors, who are eager to identify males by their "class" (e.g., 8, 43, cf. 2, 128) and decry exploitation inherent in their own society, should examine carefully their own exclusive positions and material comfort—where they live, where they travel and vacation, where their children go to school, with whom they socialize—inasmuch as they are among society's most highly educated and well-compensated elites. On a rare occasion the bounty and freedom of that hated Western culture provides a tad of embarrassment that must be quickly "efface[d]" away: "My own present position as an employed woman with financial independence and intellectual freedom would, in many contexts, make identification with the majority of women in the world seem distasteful. However, by choosing to efface certain differences and investing in a group identity, people the world over have become able to lobby for what they want" (63). Distasteful? Tap your slippers three times, Dorothy, whisper "Efface, efface, efface"—and presto, "contexts" disappear and "group identity" arises among the world's veiled and circumcised in their mud huts and these Anglo university professors who "compromise traditions."

It is just as cheap and easy to ridicule students' interests in grades and security (cf. e.g., 22), but rather sobering to think that their indebted parents are subsidizing work like this present volume. Whatever the contributors' complaints about their former thesis advisors, male professors, and "old boy" mentors, it is at least clear that they were offered a far better education at far less cost than the quite expensive but therapeutic and politicized "voices" given to today's financially strapped and poorly educated students. While Beye confronts honestly these embarrassments of class, his own decades-long and commendable wars with the pomposity of the philologist and the smug European have left their scars, and so pull his heart where his mind otherwise would not go. I suppose someone so talented can be forgiven for endorsing so mundane a collection, if we keep the Arabic adage in mind that "the enemy of my enemy is my friend."

Thomas Van Nortwick is the doyen of the school and at times he can write good prose. Thus the poverty of thinking evident in his two essays (16–24; 182–90) is especially sad, the more so as it is replete with all the standard clichés about power and marginalization from the guilt-ridden, white, middle-aged, middle-class male that will come back to haunt him and thousands of other trendies in the years to come. His contribution is not about a personal-voice explication of Odysseus' journey, but once more about the idea of using his personal voice: thus very little Odysseus, very much Van Nortwick ("I have written and published five autobiographical responses to works of classical literature in the last eight years" [16]).

The only real interest here is Van Nortwick's curious but doomed attempt to reconcile the irreconcilable notions of the therapeutic personal voice with postmodern nihilism, spiced now and again with flip slurs on the world of the old white guys. Thus we read (emphases added): "In the midst of *my* pain" (16); "*my* own journey from post-adolescence to middle age" (16); "painful changes in *my* own life"; "*I* was entering middle age and feeling..." (17); "theorists who made *me* feel inadequate" (17-18); "*I* was a fraud" (18); "*I* felt isolated" (19); "*I* was alienated from *myself*" (21); "When *I* was able to get help and begin to face *my* problems" (19); and on and on. This therapeutic soup is thick with postmodern crackers like "hierarchical, competitive model" (22); "constructing contingent selves to fit various communities of assent" (23); "ontological relativism of postmodernism" (23); "challenging patriarchal assumptions" (23); and "radical subjectivity that inevitably follows from postmodernists' paradigms undermines any search for 'real' antiquity" (185). Finally, the entire mélange is to be randomly peppered with "hierarchies" (184), "Newtonian physics" (185), the "privileged position," the "post-industrial West," and the "fragmenting of [the] Western social fabric" (190).

But the postmodernist rebel, nursed on authorless "texts" that are merely empty signifiers, the brave critic of the "hierarchical, competitive model for doing business in our field," is in a quandary—self-identification and person-less fictive texts really do not mix (pace Hallett [1]). But in the end, the author of "five autobiographical responses...in the last eight years" will at least believe in signing his name and expecting something in return for it: "Odysseus—remember you heard it here first—was the first postmodern hero!" (23).

Odysseus is not, and we did not hear it from you first, Mr. Van Nortwick.

So, at middle age, Van Nortwick is troubled about where his personal voice will lead, as the leaden weight of personal voice theory is forcing him ever closer to the choppy sea of not pleasing someone, with one foot precariously on the old philological dock and the other stretched too far atop the unsteady and drifting postmodernist boat. Will he jump to one side, swim on his own, or simply drown? Who will win? The id, or the old elite that run things and hand out "goodies," or the "courageous" postmodernist feminists? Unfortunately, all and none, sort of, and so he will slowly split apart—but only "for the moment":

> Then I must confront directly the implications of postmodernism for self-knowledge. I have struggled with these issues for some time, and here are my conclusions for the moment. I cannot get comfortable with the idea that I have no essential self to which I must be true. I harbor thoughts that would be considered unclean by a strict postmodernist: I think there is something called the meaning of my life, and I want to know as much of it as I can; I believe that the deepest essence of it is part of something that transcends my life and is larger than my comprehension; my struggle is to come to trust that what that larger truth gives me, though it is definitely not always what I want or think I need, is what I am supposed to have. (24)

Well, "for the moment" and "directly" we promise not to tell anyone about this shocking and "unclean" admission. Yes, Mr. Van Nortwick, there really is "something called the meaning of my life." It might even be something more concrete than "something that transcends my life"—a soul perhaps, God, or—who knows?—even Hell. And, yes, it may even be the meaning of Life rather than just your life. It is tragic that an academic renegade, professing the courage to abandon the professional norms of an acknowledged tiny sinking profession ("the Dodo bird" [23]), must be afraid—notice the Clintonesque use of "for the moment," "I think," "that would be considered," "cannot get comfortable with"—that a few Gallic provocateurs will now find him quaint. And, of course, they surely will. Thirteen personal pronouns in a single sentence may unfortunately answer Van Nortwick's query whether his writing was "not theoretical enough" (24).

And you, parents, who might object that you advanced all that borrowed money to Oberlin for an education that should have included Homer, not Mr. Van Nortwick's own personal voice confessions, beware! Your children, according to Mr. ("remember you heard it here first") Van Nortwick, are really grade-grubbers who merely want "sorting devices in the business of handing out the world's goodies" (22). You and they foolishly went into debt for the *Odyssey,* instead of properly instructive personal revelations from Mr. Van Nortwick about how corrupt we all are: "If we conduct our classes in a way that exposes for students the dominant assumptions behind our educational system—that what counts is acquiring accurately measurable skills by which they can compete in the race for money, prestige, and comfort—is that necessarily a bad thing?... If we want them to take the *Odyssey* seriously as a reflection of something important in human life, then we cannot insist that, having acquired some perspective on the competitive, hierarchical assumptions that govern the poem, they must automatically respond in a way that affirms those assumptions" (22). What spooky times we are in! Since it is impossible now simply to appreciate the beauty and learn from the tragedy of Western literature, we might as well explicitly indoctrinate our students about poetry's "hierarchical" and "dominant" "assumptions."

Judith de Luce (25-37) offers "Reading and Re-Reading the Helpful Princess," the only example in the entire book of real personal voice theory and classical criticism. She is upset about the ubiquity of classical themes of heroic abandonment, especially those involving deceitful men like Jason, Theseus, and Aeneas. She wrestles with the dilemma of why there are so many of those rather "ruthless" white heterosexual privileged males, ancient and modern, who use young princesses to advance their careers—only to abandon them when they are out of danger. (Question: can someone guess where Professor de Luce's personal voice is leading?)

Yes, the answer comes but a few lines later: "Like many women, I have found myself performing the role of the helpful princess too often" (26). Other stories follow—for example (and perhaps some of us have heard this particular one before), the anonymous hard-working woman friend of Professor de Luce who was abandoned after putting her yuppie, careerist doctor husband through medical school. But thanks to feminist thought, Professor de Luce was at last able to correlate the ancient motif with her own personal experiences. "It was while I was in graduate school that I first became involved in the growing women's movement, however, and began to question that assumption of female sacrifice" (28). Thanks again to critical texts and a reexamination of these heroines—Ariadne, Medea, and Dido— de Luce at last discovered the truth of Julia Wood's empirical study proving that "caring grows out of culturally constructed subordinate status rather than sex-role socialization" (33). Professor de Luce was thus saved by feminists from yet another "ruthless" white male—once she learned that a "culturally constructed" society, not her own hormones, made her do it.

There are two fatal shortcomings in de Luce's essay, which even an amateur literary critic attuned to the difference between mythical motifs and literary portrayal could spot. First, of course, is the matter of characterization of the male hero. Since de Luce did not see these white men on vases, or hear folk stories about them, or read about them in public inscriptions, she must know that she finds these cads so distasteful precisely because authors like Euripides and Virgil have made them so morally bankrupt. Yes, authors do exist and they can more or less craft even traditional characters as they please. De Luce sees the male trait of spousal abandonment as reprehensible because ancient white male authors may well have wanted Theseus, Jason, and Aeneas to appear just that way. Incidentally, de Luce also fails to notice the irony that the shame culture of ancient Greece, even as it appears in sophisticated literary portrayals, puts the onus of public reproach squarely on the white male heterosexual scoundrel who did not honor his word. In our own narcissistic and guilt-ridden society, the "ruthless" male need only seek help for career angst and midlife stress, cite childhood trauma or repressed memory, blame his parents and teachers, or confess guilt over his race and gender—and society will understand if not approve of his misdeeds.

I leave the other obvious criticism of her discussion to the keen wit of Professor Beye. In his response, he reminds us that such encounters can become tragic if the quid pro quo is not honored—sexual favors and moral support for the male careerist in exchange for a chance for commitment and a share in future spoils (159). I agree and often have seen such abandoned princesses as shamefully maltreated as Professor de Luce and her friends once were. But I am also always curious why at least a few of the victims, even when they often have had an array of loyal, faithful, and dependable suitors, chose to forgo the more ordinary and staid men in order to share, if only for the moment, the excitement offered by the reckless, egotistic, and ambitious thug—who incidentally in both myth and actuality can be handsome, adventurous, royal, and wealthy. This is high-stakes courtship that involves the unpredictable and raw human spirit and, as Beye reminds us, has "been tragic since the beginning of time" (159). But melodrama (not tragedy), the evil of one sex (not the ignorance and manipulation of both), and female victimhood (not the tragic lot of man), are now the only stuff of feminist theory as it appears here.

I shall close with Professor Hallett, who is so very angry (1–15, 120–52). Since she has written by far the most in this collection—roughly a fourth of the book is hers—her wrath, along with Van

Nortwick's self-revelation, tends to define the tone and spirit of the movement in general. Her formal contribution, "Writing as an American," has nothing to do with the ancient world directly. It is one of the most confused and unorganized essays I have ever read, but nevertheless it is also a strangely intriguing, weird, passive-aggressive confessional that alternates between real hurt and wild fury. The first four pages recount her graduate school tribulations, followed by an animated discussion of her dismissal from Boston University. The next eight are further personal recollections of past conferences, laced with references to her own published and committee work, the theme of which is her own unpleasant run-ins with British academics. Then we get an "Afterword" of over three pages where she suddenly posts afterthoughts about her revelations and replies to past criticism of herself that she has had a selective memory and has been unfair in both her presentation and analysis of the past twelve pages of recollections. I'll skip yet more of the irony found here. Finally, an eighteen-page "Appendix" concludes, in stream-of-consciousness fashion, stitching together a series of quotations from published works, her unfavorable tenure report, signed and anonymous e-mails, the text of an Irving Berlin song she performed, a reader's critique rejecting one of her Latin compositions, more quotations from her own published articles, anonymous responses from questionnaires, and, lastly, quotations from other critics of European classicists.

The apparent themes throughout revolve around the ubiquity of British academics, the power of male elites, the insistence on needless academic formality, the cruelty of white males in power, and the cumulative effect of all this to rob her of a professorship at Boston some eighteen years ago: "In retrospect I suppose I am thankful for those initial, and rationally groundless, expressions of little-to-no confidence in my professional 'promise.' They toughened me to survive various criticisms and dismissals of my pedagogy and scholarship in years to come" (121). If the reader thinks I exaggerate the centrality of her last-

ing hurt in this essay, then consider her appendix where her unfavorable tenure decision of nearly two decades past is quoted, or at least
sort of quoted—it is heavily edited and does not identify its author.
There is, as is true of the entire book, unintended irony here as well.
Her inclusion of the tenure report is designed to offer contrast (in
her favor): the white male philologist's prejudices have unfairly deni-
grated the real quality of her work as we can now quite clearly see in
the present article.

Let us take up the challenge and work from her edited transcript.
I shall call the unnamed villain Chairman X.

• Professor Hallett, as she tells us, *in costume* recently invited the audience at an academic conference in Bristol to sing the opening lyrics
("in their best Bill Clinton accent") of *Annie Get Your Gun* (123, 137, cf.
163).

*Eighteen years prior Chairman X wrote that Hallett was "shallow" and
added that some students "deplore[d] the quantity of 'trivia' she interjects in
classroom lectures" and added that "she does not hesitate to sacrifice substantive comment for mere entertainment" (136).*

• Professor Hallett writes frequently "of my feminist identity" (122),
"race, class and age as well as gender categories of analysis" (128), "privileged white males" (129), her "identity as a feminist scholar" (134), the
"white, middle-class male" (8), "theoretical (partly deconstructive and
postmodern) perspective" (9), "misremembering" (132), "normalizing
depersonalization" (8), and so on.

*Eighteen years prior Chairman X wrote of "her insistence on terminology
inappropriate for ancient Rome...and her use of fashionable jargon."*

• Professor Hallett, in her review of her own career, somehow has
managed in a single article to mention Philips Academy in Andover
(120), Bill Clinton's inauguration (124), Wellesley College (120), George

Bush (120), a postdoctoral year in England (122), APA conferences (130), an English and another unnamed conference (125), as well as her own past articles and reviews (138–41).

Eighteen years prior Chairman X wrote of "her constant attendance on professional committees (any committee), her developing of professional contacts.... She seems at every opportunity to try to cloud the intellectual poverty of her work with quantity, or just with names."

• Professor Hallett writes passionately of "expressions of little-to-no confidence in me" (nearly verbatim three times in two paragraphs, 121–22), of an unnamed person who "devalued me as an individual owing to my gender," of "deep-rooted and painful feelings of inadequacy which such insensitive and cruel treatment has instilled in me" (132), of the "outrageous misrepresentations and lies" of this report (123), and of a British prejudice against her education: "I am often regarded as comically inadequate" (124).

Eighteen years prior Chairman X wrote, "I noted that she conducted herself more like a teacher of early elementary school children than a college professor."

Professor Hallett is obviously a hard-working scholar, but she shares a troubling naivete characteristic of this entire book. Since the contributors continuously offer personal-voice-inspired compositions juxtaposed next to old-fashioned "detached" and "impersonal" reasoning and presentation, they should at least be sure that their stilted comparisons do not achieve the very opposite of the intended effect. Readers like myself, who do not know either Professor Hallett or her teaching, on the basis of the quoted evidence she has provided us (albeit heavily edited and incomplete), may well come to the opposite conclusion of the one she had intended. Out of politeness, I shall forgo that judgment, but I do add in closing that, whoever Chairman X was, it is clear that he was perhaps needlessly insensitive to Professor Hallett and even at times pedantic. But he was also intellectually honest, unafraid, forthright, and unapologetic—traits sadly lacking in most humanities programs in the last two decades.

V.

The authors of *Compromising Traditions* are rightly worried about the death of classics. But this volume, despite its extravagant claims for personal voice theory ("an embarrassment of scholarly riches" [4]), is yet more proof of why we are dying. All of the book's initially promising claims fall by the wayside page by page: personal voice theory as it is presented here is not anticareerist, but career-obsessed. Its language is not clear, but jargon-laden and often incomprehensible. It is not a diverse and spontaneous voice, but tired, intolerant, and predictable. It is not a radical and courageous stance, but conservative and timid. It is not about being a lone wolf, but about joining the pack. It is not about enlightening the reader, but about parading the self. And it does not improve on the dullness of the impersonal and scholarly voice, but explains, as no philological zealot could, precisely why such a depersonalized and abstract voice arose in the first place and why, within general parameters of usage, it is so vital and so will surely continue. Whoever the icy seigniors in the Ivy League and Oxbridge are, they must be chuckling with glee over this volume. In contrast, reformers in classics must be wondering, with friends like these, who needs enemies? *Errare malo cum Platone quam cum istis vera sentire.*[2]

The authors here also fail to make the critical distinction between philology and a particular type of distasteful philologist: philology itself is noble; many of its practitioners are not. The use of the Greek and Latin languages to uncover and explicate the culture and literature of antiquity is the touchstone of classics, the common currency without which we cease to be a profession. The zeal here, then, should not be directed against philology per se, but should prompt a careful analysis of the practice of philology itself. The reference to philology should be one of deference, not condemnation, and so we miss especially here a nuanced argument over exactly how some philologists in their professional lives and published work have fallen short of their calling to embrace and advance a worthy profession—and that critique must consist of more than philologists' being rude or hurtful to some contributors of this volume.

Retired Oxford don Hugh Lloyd-Jones is one of the rare few quoted by Hallett as a negative example of narrow philology and British bias against American classicists. But unfortunately, as is the case throughout this book, once more irony abounds: this volume offers confirmation, not refutation, of Lloyd-Jones's clairvoyant warning about American faddists: "The enemies of exact scholarship can easily find an audience there, and gifted rhetoricians find it possible to set themselves up as local gurus, teaching a method which rapidly produces fashionable results" (137). And what are we to make of a collection that, in claiming to bring morality and humanity (179-80, 189-90) to the fore of scholarly writing, condemns Lloyd-Jones's defense of tradition (122-23, 136-37) only to side step or excuse Dover's ghoulishness (54-55, 65-67)? Somebody's feelings are really not the same as someone's life.

A real diversity, of course, is needed to save classics from both narrow word-gatherers and the French-inspired postmodernists, those smug theorists who cannot write anything readable and whose comfortable lives are at odds with the nihilism they profess. We desperately need classicists who are, or who have been, athletes, dancers, singers, poets, workmen, doctors, carpenters, soldiers—almost anything other than the traditional academic—to bring that diverse real expertise into their scholarship and present it in new and interesting ways to the general public. These true compromisers of tradition should welcome, not whine about, the ridicule of an entrenched elite who have watched classics die. They must feel it a badge of honor, not feel "inadequate" that a pedantic magnifico finds their real diversity irritating. It is a testament to how far we have fallen from the spirit of the Greeks to even imagine that this present volume is in any way populist or that its authors are renaissance figures at odds with the status quo. If the personal voice is to help us, then we need it in the style of Thucydides, not Athenaeus.

In the present culture of the academy, it would be cruel, but not unfair, to ask academics who insist in their scholarship on giving us the most intimate details of their personal lives that they at least should have had lives outside of the university. Whatever the general public or the undergraduates of America expect from their public intellectuals and professors, we can be sure at the millennium it is not more confessionals and psycho-melodramas from the desk-bound class. If our readers and students really do desire more public revelations of sex, mental instability, baby-boomer angst, and narcissism, they can get it with far more originality and panache from Jerry Springer and company than from what is found in these dull pages. After reading this collection, I think what is really needed is a thorough study of why (upper-middle-class guilt? self-loathing? sheer boredom? excessive affluence? too much leisure? suburban blues? voluntary segregation from the muscular and poorer classes? the angst of middle age?) so many well-compensated, white, suburban academic elites—with lighter work loads than ever before, with more travel opportunities than at any time in history, enjoying far more equality than any prior generation—are so unhappy and angry at the very material culture that they obviously take for granted, if not enjoy. Routledge would do far better to publish that book, rather than this embarrassing confessional.

In the end, the intimate details of these lives, heirs to the Hellenistic but not the Hellenic legacy, turn out to be nothing but boring, and they cannot sustain an extended analysis of ancient literature at all. By the conclusion of the book the repetitious litany of breakdowns, alcoholism, genitalia, professional slights, conference gossip, unkind British dons, corrected accents, bad boyfriends, hurtful white middle-class heterosexual males, broken marriages, and sexual trysts with other professors is monotonous and trite—less interesting than a philological excursus into the many uses of δέ. If personal voice theory, at least as it appears here, is to be the golden mean between narrow philological pedantry and incomprehensible postmodernist theory, then we classicists really are, and should be, through. This is all so very, very sad.

ὡς ἀπόλοιτο χαὶ ἄλλος ὅστις τοιαῦτά γε ῥέζοι.[3]

CHAPTER 5

BRUCE S. THORNTON

THE ENEMY IS US

The "Betrayal of the Postmodern Clerks"

I first became aware of the problems of using theory to understand and interpret literary works and other cultural artifacts in
graduate school. From 1979 to 1983 I was a student in comparative literature, the hotbed of theoretical ferment. At that time,
Derrida and deconstruction were out of fashion for the
cognoscenti, who deemed both fit only for the second-rate
wannabes in the English department. The comp-lit hep-cats knew
that most deconstructive criticism in practice ended up as mere
self-indulgent formalism, the old New-Critical close reading
tarted up with Continental rhetoric. The *soi-disant* "leftist" comp-
lit graduate students and faculty needed a theoretical perspective
that spoke to their liberationist pretensions, and that allowed
them to pretend that their privileged, elitist academic existence
was *really* all about freeing the oppressed by unmasking the devi-
ous machinations of power, the hidden mechanisms that ac-
counted for literature, culture, language, consciousness, gender
roles.... Remember, those were the bad-ol'-days of "Reaganism"
and the national repudiation of received wisdom from the sixties. The only "cause" activists could find to champion were the
thuggish Sandinistas. Thus Michel Foucault and his "analytic of
power" were all the rage.

Having perforce to acquaint myself with these fashions, I immediately began to notice some peculiarities. The complex epistemological, ontological, historiographical, and linguistic issues with which poststructuralism concerned itself were radically reduced and simplified by Derrida et al., and even more so by apprentice literary critics who showed no evidence of having mastered the intellectual traditions that had long ago identified the numerous Gordian knots. Ideas contested for millennia were simplified into buzz-words and jargon smugly bandied about with a blithe disregard for their incoherence and self-canceling implications. It was like watching someone trying to buy groceries with Monopoly money. But I also noticed that the value of these ideas and their attendant patter lay in their power to confer status. It didn't matter if the ideas themselves were useless or incoherent: terms like *différance* or "archaeology of knowledge" or "death of the subject" were talismans warding off critical scrutiny from banal conclusions and bad criticism and establishing their possessor as someone hip, in-the-know, *au courant*—in short, better than everybody else. As Camille Paglia would suggest later, for the lit-crit academic on the make, Derrida, Foucault, and Lacan served the same purpose that BMW, Cuisinart, and Rolex did for Wall Street wolves.

Years later, when I examined the books reviewed in this chapter, I found the same problems I had noticed then among both the theorists and my fellow comp-lit grad students: (1) a reductive, clumsy handling of complex ideas coupled with an utter lack of awareness of just how contested those ideas are, overlaid with a laughable ignorance about just how dull was the presumed "cutting edge"; and (2) a barely concealed careerist agenda, an aggressive touting of novelty in order to vault a few rungs up the academic ladder. Perhaps most annoying were the intimations that liberationist boons were supposed to follow from the obscure, muddled thinking of elite academics and their epigones talking to each other in the subsidized academic Lilliput. I had spent too much time around poor people of all races in rural Fresno County to have much patience with *haut bourgeois* white folks preaching revolution from comfortable groves into which the oppressed never wandered, except as janitors.

A further dishonesty I discovered results from the essentially empirical methodology that the writers continually fell back on even as they referred to poststructuralist ideas that proclaimed empiricism impossible. Finally, in all these books one finds a ham-handed approach to literature and poetry that completely misses the aesthetic qualities and complex engagement of the human condition that have kept classical literature alive for 2,500 years. And this, finally, is the greatest crime of all—that "things of beauty" have been defaced with intellectual graffiti.

๛

THESE are perilous times for classics in America. The dwindling of higher education's economic resources, the steady drain of money which accelerated in the early nineties and which at the present has only temporarily slowed, is leaving the study of ancient Greek and Latin ever higher and drier, and hence ever more vulnerable to sharp-eyed administrators, trustees, and state legislators scrambling to squeeze the most out of every pedagogical buck. This assault, moreover, comes from both ends of the political spectrum. After all, the utilitarian Right, anxious about keeping up with our economic rivals, sees nothing useful in classics beyond offering a compendium of whatever "values" are convenient to the new global economic order. And the therapeutic multiculturalist Left, obsessing over the self-esteem of the victim *du jour*, has even less use for what Bernard Knox has wryly called the "deadest white European males," those bad boys who invented patriarchy, oppression, sexism, colonialism, and God knows what other crimes.

Despite this imminent threat, however, the profession itself is mired in a "Phony War," a debate between "traditional" philology and the "new" theorists. Yet as John Heath argues in chapter 6, this battle "is not...a Manichean duel for survival, but rather a skirmish of elitists for the advantages of elitism.... The pampered doctors are argu-

ing over the complexion of a patient dying from their own malpractice."[1] Heath goes on to argue that the true crisis in the profession
results from the vertical division between a teaching *dêmos* and a non-
teaching *eupatridai* that monopolizes resources growing ever scanter
so that they can teach less and write more that is read by fewer.[2] This
elite, composed of both traditional philologists and new theorists,
preoccupied as it is with its game of careerist musical chairs, for the
most part has done nothing to show parents, trustees, and legislators—that is, the citizens who foot the bill—why anyone should care
whether classics survives in the university and in American society.[3]

This is the context for evaluating the claims of the new theorists
that the "new ancient world," as one publisher's series is called, is
more politically inclusive and attractive and hence, as Heath articu-
lates their implicit claim, can "invigorate the discipline."[4] As we begin
the new millennium, it is instructive to look over a few examples of
this decade's classical scholarship in the theoretical key and ask
ourselves these questions: (1) Do the theoretical assumptions guiding
this scholarship offer the profession anything genuinely new and
useful? and (2) What do these works do to justify the study of classics
in an economically straitened academic world?

I.

John Peradotto has been in the forefront of those who argue for the
use of *la nouvelle critique* in studying the classical world. Through his
own work and through his editorship of the journal *Arethusa,* he has
for years successfully advanced the cause of structuralism and poststructuralism. Like Peradotto's election to the presidency of the American Philological Association, his collection of essays, *Man in the Middle
Voice: Name and Narration in the Odyssey,*[5] a volume in the Martin Classical
Lectures series and one made possible by the usual prestigious institutional largess duly noted in the Preface, testifies to that success.

Given that theoretical interest, Peradotto's collection of essays presents itself as a study of Homer's *Odyssey* that "shows unabashed signs of contemporary theoretical and semiotic perspectives" (4). Indeed, all the "signs" are there: the building and knocking over of the flimsy straw man of "traditional" perspectives, the tone of critical daring, the portentous jargon, and the dropping of Continental names. Peradotto heaps up a mountain of theorese from which ultimately crawls a modest mouse of an idea that traditional philology could have midwived with a fraction of the labor this book demands of the reader.

Peradotto indulges in poststructuralist affectation in the Preface: "If this book were perfectly consistent...with its own misgivings about 'the ideology of the person' and the proprietary claims attending it, its author would have had to remain anonymous" (xiii–xiv). Right from the start Peradotto reveals one of the key weaknesses of the "theoretically correct": the unexamined acceptance of shaky poststructuralist ideas that have for years been subject to intense criticism. What Peradotto calls "the conventional view of the stable subject" (xi) has in no way been definitively exploded, nor even seriously challenged outside the rarefied chapels of the professorial elect.[6] Stanley Corngold argues persuasively that "[t]he deconstruction of the subject is a project that...lies always ahead of us. It has not been done, and on the evidence of those who are attempting to do it, it cannot be done, neither factually nor by right."[7] The pedants keep telling us the "bourgeois subject" has dissolved into a field of conflicting social and linguistic forces, yet everybody—including, even *especially,* these same professors—go on living their lives like "stable subjects," integrated egos that write and plan and choose and get upset when people misunderstand or criticize their work. It puts me in mind of de Maistre's parody of Rousseau's "man is born free" dictum: sheep are born carnivores and everywhere eat grass. The subject is dead, and everywhere subjects are telling us the subject is dead.

The "death of the author" that followed the "death of the sub-ject" may have been mildly daring twenty years ago when Roland Barthes proclaimed it, but its emptiness as an idea became obvious when a very lively Jacques Derrida claimed John Searle had misunder-stood his work,[8] and hence *a fortiori* Derrida repudiated his disbelief in the possibility of stable linguistic meaning; or when Derrida and other poststructuralist grandees came to the defense of Paul de Man, who suddenly ceased being a linguistic effect.[9] Worse than this obvi-ous hypocrisy, the attack on the subject is part of the larger antihu-manism at the heart of poststructuralism, and as such has some un-savory political bedfellows.[10] The revelations of Paul de Man's war-time collaborationist writings and his lifelong "deconstruction" of his odious past confirmed the sinister uses such an idea of a fluid self could have.[11] On a more mundane note, I presume Professor Peradotto has paychecks made out to him, not to the "locus of responsibility." Some readers may still find this sort of affectation sophisticated, but by this late date, I think it is merely jejune.

Worse than jejune, though, is Peradotto's dismissal of his neanderthal colleagues in classics who refuse to swing with Barthes and Foucault: "This study may strike literary analysts outside the field of classical studies as less sophisticated than it could be, given the state of theoretical discussion. That is in part because it is designed largely for my colleagues in a profession long suspicious of theory..." (xiii). Engaging in a "conspiracy of silence" (6), these colleagues have "relentlessly and...successfully resisted the inroads of current meth-odological inquiry arising from ongoing philosophical reflection and interdisciplinary dialogue," and they have found semiotics "a special object of revulsion" (5). Peradotto attributes this resistance to theory to "the general character of the discipline" (8) whose members appear (Peradotto's hedge-word) to form "the most conservative [*terribile dictu!*] group" (9); hedging again, Peradotto wonders if classicists are afraid of semiotics because it "inevitably makes ideology explicit" (10), which implies that classicists have invested in an ideology so unsavory they want to keep it hidden. Thus traditional philologists "[turn] their back on a dialogue so fearfully oriented" (12). In short, classicists who reject theory are a collection of thick-headed, conservative, establishment flat-earthers fearful of having their reactionary ideological assumptions laid bare—unless Peradotto practices exegesis in simplified terms they can understand.

Apart from describing an insulting straw man—Peradotto never names any of these "colleagues"—this picture is dishonest. Peradotto's professional eminence gives the lie to his characterization of the profession.[12] Other classicists, as Peradotto well knows, have also read ancient literature through the structuralist and poststructuralist lens. Charles Segal's *Dionysiac Poetics and Euripides' Bacchae* (1982) engaged Barthes and Derrida almost a decade before Peradotto's collection, and Segal certainly has not been denied the profession's esteem. Enough poststructuralist classics had been done by 1990 to undermine Peradotto's claim that the "general character of the discipline" was as reactionary as he describes it. More serious, however, is Peradotto's implication that the theoretical ferment of the last twenty-five years constitutes some sort of Kuhnian "paradigm shift," a new model for looking at language and literature that has rendered obsolete all previous ones, just as the heliocentric cosmology superseded the geocentric, and so philologists who ignore it are like the church-man who refused to look in Galileo's telescope.

But these theories, as numerous commentators have demonstrated,[13] are for the most part highly speculative and filled with arguable assumptions, wanton speculation, vapid jargon, and dizzying leaps of logic, all overlaid with what J. G. Merquior has called the "glamour of a manichean grand-guignol."[14] Critics have identified some very good reasons for ignoring poststructuralism, not the least being that what Peradotto flippantly calls "discredited humanistic values" (12) are only "discredited" in the minds of some Western intellectuals who continue to enjoy those values (and, I might add, in the minds of totalitarian thugs eager to destroy them). To allude to these theories without recognizing such challenges is an act of scholarly bad faith.

Peradotto's first chapter delves more deeply into the issue of traditional philology's lamentable intellectual conservatism. He sees its resistance to theory as arising from the discipline's unfortunate investment in a "humanism [that] appeared [prophylactic hedging again] to be undermined by the dissolution of the subject inherent in structuralism" (10). Those familiar with poststructuralist ideology know that it views "humanism" with all the suspicion of a right-wing Christian fundamentalist: at best it is a quaint, unsavory relic of an earlier age, like whale bone corsets; at worst an insidious rationalization for elite, white male dominance. Moreover, Peradotto goes on, among classicists this commitment to humanism is buttressed by certain "entrenched positions" (13) of the discipline, positions poststructuralist thought presumably had swept away: "language as mere instrument, constituted wholly by an autonomous subject"; an "epistemologically naive realism, coupled with a view of language as a representation of things"; a "deep suspicion of 'unconscious meaning'"; a "further suspicion of the presumed impoverishment of meaning resulting from structural and semiotic approaches"; a "belief in an 'objective' interpretation of the past"; and the "myth of 'disinterested scholarship'" (14–15).

Needless to say, none of these "positions" has been definitively disproved, and Peradotto's characterization of what he calls "naive realism" (17) displays elitism—notice his lofty dismissal of the "folk knowledge" of the "Standard Average European" (15) and the "realist man-in-the-street" (16); it reveals as well an ignorance of the complexity of the issue and the force of the arguments against poststructuralist epistemic nihilism.[15] Moreover, indulging the trendy epistemic angst that characterizes poststructuralism leads one into fatal contradictions, as David Hirsch has pointed out:

[T]here is no absolute truth, except the absolute truth that there is no absolute truth; consciousness (the subject) is historically determined, but, at the same time, there is no subject; the subject (read individual self) does not exist, but the deconstructionists must speak and act as if they were individual subjects; the poststructuralists-deconstructionists are opposed to all forms of authority (the authority of the text), except that they claim authority for their own writings.... Language, they insist, speaks itself, but they sign their essays and books "Jacques Derrida," "Roland Barthes," etc., not "Monsieur Language." Are they plagiarists, then, or do they believe that language speaks itself, but speaks itself differently through different, and hence unique, individuals?[16]

If Peradotto really believed in the force of *his* positions, he would not even bother to write. The fact that he *does* write, that he believes he is offering through language a worthwhile and accurate interpretation of what is going on in Homer's epic—itself a piece of reality Peradotto presumably believes his words accurately describe—renders his talk of "epistemologically naive realism" so much self-canceling rodomontade.

Having described the pitiable intellectual backwardness of his colleagues, Peradotto then goes on to explain how such a state of "intellectual reclusiveness" (17) could have come about. To do so he calls on Michel Foucault's *The Order of Things*, which purported itself to be an "archaeology" of the shift in "epistemes" that began in the seventeenth century. Foucault identifies three epistemes: a Renaissance, based on resemblance and analogy; the classical, based on representation and analysis; and the modern, based on function and history. To Peradotto, classical philology never made it out of the classical episteme, and indeed the discipline has been shaped "fairly consistently by opposition to the great changes in epistemic suppositions that have occurred since the classical age, and that hardly seem reversible" (24). Thus Peradotto sees classics "as operating with the episteme of his [Foucault's] classical age, with a view of language as transparent representation, with a rationalism that would see itself threatened by Nietzsche's invitation...to a radical reflection on language..." (24-25). A few lines later, though, Peradotto speculates that classics is stuck not in the classical episteme, but in the *shift* between the classical and modern, between "an endeavor to fit new concepts to the lingering system of representation" and "the abandonment of representation altogether" (25). Wherever classics is languishing, its problem is that, to put it simply, it does not display enough suspicious self-conscious-ness about the duplicity of language and its inability to refer to any-thing other than itself.

The reader should not bother with looking for any historical evi-dence that such a process did indeed occur, for any examples of clas-sical philologists so unfortunately mired in passé "epistemes," for any analysis of the shortcomings of their readings created by their episte-mological backwardness. The representational truth of Peradotto's argument is ultimately beside the point. If not, he would have had to confront the serious problems with Foucault's model. Despite Peradotto's implications that Foucault has discovered a historical truth, in fact the model is riddled with unargued assumptions and depends on highly selective supporting evidence.[17] But a more imme-diate question is why, in a book about Homer's *Odyssey*, do we need this unconvincing excursus into the history of classical philology? Is Peradotto just showing off, or is he bringing in Foucault to intimi-date the reader into accepting his own idea? Or, what I suspect to be the case, is Peradotto involved in academic *marketing*, giving his ideas a sheen of theoretical newness to make them more attractive to the academic consumer?

Finally at page 26 we get to learn what Peradotto wants to do with Homer—"narrative analysis" (26)—though he remains cagey about pin-ning down what he is up to. At any rate, whatever it is will involve three "fundamental operations": "description," which Peradotto uses Todorov to define as the attempt "'to obtain, on the basis of certain theoretical premises, a rationalized representation of the object of study'"; "theory development," which questions the theoretical premises; and "reading," which Peradotto leaves undefined (27).

At this point the reader's jaw must drop if he remembers those poststructuralist "positions" Peradotto endorsed earlier. What possibly can be the force of the concepts of "rationalized" representation and "object of study" given those positions? Will not Peradotto's "description" involve a use of language that will accurately "represent" that "object"? And would not any traditional philologist, *mutatis mutandis,* be doing pretty much the same thing as Todorov recommends for narratological analysis? If narratology is all Peradotto wants to do, he does not need to indulge in all the fancy theoretical footwork that consumes so much of the book. In fact, he has danced himself into a difficult corner, for like many critics trying to wed theoretical perspectives to a basically empirical procedure such as narratology, he ignores or plays down the conflicts among various strains of poststructuralism and fails to respect the full force of the latter's nihilism.[18]

Here Peradotto ignores the adversarial development of poststructuralism out of structuralism, the way the former became "the severest critic of its [structuralism's] new methodism," as Howard Felperin put it.[19] Todorov has pointed out that structuralism was not incompatible with the search for meaning that characterized other critical approaches like New Criticism: "Structural analysis, like its predecessors, aspired to furnish a better answer to the same question [what a text means], calling attention in this case to the internal construction of literary works."[20] The break with this sort of structuralism came in 1966 with Derrida's "Structure, Sign and Play in the Discourses of the Human Sciences" and its deconstruction of Levi-Strauss's structuralist anthropology.[21] The consequences of Derrida's move are described by Terry Eagleton: "The advent of the concept of *writing,* then, is a challenge to the very idea of structure: for a structure always presumes a centre, a fixed principle, a hierarchy of meanings and a solid foundation, and it is just these notions which the endless differing and deferring of writing throws into question."[22] Peradotto, for all his poststructuralist posturing, is really in his reading of Homer engaged in what Merquior calls "kaleidoscopic" structuralism, the search for "a ground of identity, a matrix composed of just a few, recurring elements"[23]—what narratology, with its "narremes" and "kernels" and "functional units," is up to.

Finally, Peradotto's footnote (27 n. 10), brushing aside this theoretical jumble—a "lack of methodological unity" is nothing to worry about "as long as no logical incompatibility or inconsistency results"— gives the whole game away, for Peradotto's endorsement of those poststructuralist positions enumerated earlier means that "logical incompatibility" or "inconsistency" is meaningless, a chimera spawned by the anxious desire to fix the free play of signifiers over the abyss. One can only conclude that Peradotto ultimately is engaged in an empirically based interpretation whose only difference from traditional philology is the poststructuralist rhetorical packaging.

Thus Peradotto's thesis, when we encounter it in chapter 2, does not need for its force all the numerous theoretical references and discussion with which he tricks it out, and the omission of which would facilitate the reader's comprehension. Peradotto sees the *Odyssey* as informed by two types of narrative, one of which he calls myth and the other *Märchen,* or folktale: the former is the "narrative of desire frustrated," the latter the "narrative of desire accomplished" (49). Thus the numerous tales Odysseus tells or others tell of him reduce "to the two basic possibilities of our model: one, the tale of the master trickster (*polymêtis*) and technician (*polymêchanos*) who achieves his purposes in a hostile environment; and the other the tale of one who has little choice other than to endure the full load of the world's resistance (*polytlas*)" (52). Myth and *Märchen* are further identified with the Russian critic Mikhail Bakhtin's centripetal and centrifugal forces, the former "unifying, centralizing, homogenizing and hierarchizing...closely associated with dominant political power"; the latter a force exerting a "disunifying, decentralizing, stratifying, denormatizing influence; these forces tend to be associated with the disempowered..." (53).[24] Homer's text, then, oscillates between these two voices, each not allowing the other to dominate or to pin down the force of Odysseus's name and character or to achieve closure in its own terms, although Peradotto ultimately believes the voice of *Märchen* has the last word. Homer is politically correct, in other words, aligning himself, like our author, with the "disempowered" and the "open" and the opposers of norms and official language. After all, is that not what Peradotto fancies himself to be doing, bringing a centrifugal, poststructuralist voice to the staid authoritative drone of traditional philology?

Actually, I am sympathetic to Peradotto's distinction of myth and *Märchen* in the *Odyssey*, particularly as these are seen as part of the broader concern with the collision of culture and nature, since these two forces create the field of possible Greek human identity. Thus I agree that identity is fluid in the *Odyssey*, and that Odysseus during his wanderings is relearning and reconstructing what it means to be human in his world's terms by experiencing alternatives, whether these are idealized, like the Phaiacians', or horrific, like Polyphemus's. However, Peradotto's need to elevate his own ideas by associating them with what he presumably feels are more authoritative theorists subjects the reader to unnecessary divagations and complications. For example, for Peradotto to articulate his model, we do not really need the twenty-page excursuses into Levi-Strauss, Propp, Genette, and Bremond, with the attendant pseudo-scientific terminology and pretentious symbols and charts, that precede it.[25] One gets the feeling Peradotto is more anxious to display his theoretical prowess than to communicate an idea to the reader. And dragging in Bakhtin's ideas, especially since Peradotto oversimplifies them, sows nothing but confusion. We know what Bakhtin meant when he talked about voices sanctioned by political power—they were probably bugging his phone. But what "political power" does Peradotto have in mind when speaking of Homer? What authority? We do not know enough about ancient Greece or even the date of the *Odyssey's* composition to speak in these terms. I suspect Peradotto is concerned more with giving his reading a politically correct subtext than with elucidating Homer.

The rest of Peradotto's book proceeds in the same fashion: he puts his model through its paces, considering in chapter 3 the text's refusal to endorse a definitive end that validates either myth or *Märchen*; elaborating in the final three chapters on the fluid quality of Odysseus's name and identity as they are constructed by the play of those two voices; and overlaying these potentially useful interpretations with clots of theoretical explication unnecessary to the points he wants to make. Moreover, sometimes Peradotto's obsession with the arcana of narratology skews his readings of specific passages. For example, in chapter 2 he includes an unnecessary discussion of the "distinction between the function and motivation of a narrative event": "its function is the purpose it serves in advancing the narrative towards its conclusion, its motivation is that which it finds necessary in dissimulating its function"(45). He then discusses the scene in Book 9 where Odysseus first encounters Polyphemus and does not name himself. To Peradotto, the internal motivation for Odysseus's not naming himself is weak, for "the suppression of one's own name is unusual" according to "the point of view of a verisimilitude inferable from the *Iliad*" (46). Later Odysseus gives himself the name Outis, "noman," likewise a weakly motivated action: "In retrospect, we see that his anonymity and the choice of that precise name, Outis, is functionally necessary to the pun that saves Odysseus' life, but its motivation in the progress of performance is extremely arbitrary" (46).

Peradotto here shows the danger of reading in terms of an abstract theoretical model rather than imagining the concrete situation the poet describes—a drawback resulting from the unexamined assumption that writing is about writing rather than about life. When Odysseus enters Polyphemus's cave, he confronts not another human warrior who shares Odysseus's heroic conventions, but a monstrous one-eyed creature that immediately establishes its disregard for the humanizing codes that define Odysseus's world. This inhumanity is made obvious with Polyphemus's first words to the Greeks: "Strangers, who are you?" (9.252), a rude question inverting the normal ritual of hospitality, in which this question is asked only after the guest is greeted and fed. The response of Odysseus and his men testifies to their recognition that they have left any recognizable human world: "Our spirit was broken" (9.256).

In this savage world, the "verisimilitude inferable from the *Iliad*" doesn't mean a thing. Odysseus knows immediately that heroic force or persuasion is useless and that only an unheroic craftiness will save him and his men. So he needs to maintain the element of surprise, and he needs Polyphemus to undervalue him. If he stupidly identified himself, as Peradotto wants him to do, Polyphemus would be more on guard. Indeed, given that Polyphemus knows in advance that it is Odysseus specifically who will harm him (9.512), in all likelihood he would simply destroy Odysseus on the spot—as he nearly does later when Odysseus rashly reveals his true identity. Typically throughout the epic Odysseus's *métis* displays itself in his caution, his ability to exploit the element of surprise, to work through disguises in order to learn the lay of the land. In the inhuman world of Polyphemus's cave, radically different from the relatively homogeneous heroic world of the *Iliad,* suppressing one's name is not at all unusual or "weakly motivated." It's a damn good idea. Likewise with the false name Outis. Of course Odysseus does not foresee the precise chain of events that will make the pun work. That is not the sort of abstract intellection which *métis* represents. Odysseus's craftiness, like a good chess player's, works not by foreseeing a precise sequence of cause and effect, but by

creating favorable *contexts* in which Odysseus will find an advanta-
geous option. It is plotting on "spec," so to speak. When forced to
give a name, Odysseus reserves the element of surprise *and* creates a
potential advantage by giving the name Outis.

Throughout Peradotto's book the tug of theory distorts his readings, blinding him to the obvious—and more interesting—interpretation. For example, Peradotto uses a speech of Calypso in Book 5 to
exemplify the Bakhtinian conflict between the centripetal voice of
myth and the centrifugal one of *Märchen*. When Hermes tells Calypso
that Odysseus must return home, she attributes the necessity of
Odysseus's homecoming to the jealousy of male gods who do not
like goddesses sleeping with mortal men (5.118–20). Peradotto hears
in Calypso's protest the centrifugal voice of *Märchen* "representing
revolt against a system whose order is made to depend on the suppression of female sexual desire in a way not expected of males" (55).
Besides distorting Bakhtin's ideas, this interpretation is so far off the
mark I can only think Peradotto here is throwing a proleptic sop to
any feminist Cerberuses anxiously monitoring his gender-sensitivity
quotient. Calypso is not being forced to release Odysseus because of
male-god jealousy—that is *her* piqued interpretation. Odysseus has to
go because it is *fated* (1.16–19), and fate is a limit even the gods must
respect. Calypso must release Odysseus for the same reason the patri-
arch Zeus must watch his son Sarpedon die and Apollo must abandon Hector—that is the way it must be. Nor is the issue the question
of the "suppression of female sexual desire," for Calypso has been
indulging hers at Odysseus's expense for seven years. And what could
Peradotto possibly mean by the word "system"? What system? One
that can be reconstructed from Homer's work, filled with powerful
female characters? One current in Archaic Greece? If the latter, what
literary or epigraphical or archaeological evidence could Peradotto
present that would define such a "system" for us? Sappho's fragments,
notorious for their reticence about female sexuality? Peradotto has

two lenses he reads through: one of theory and the other of modern academic political pieties.

Man in the Middle Voice presents us with an object lesson in just how damaging to a scholar is the impulse to be theoretically *au courant*. A good and potentially useful idea is here buried beneath a mountain of digressions, jargon, and explications that do nothing to advance the thesis or to persuade the unconvinced. When the text itself is engaged, readings are skewed by the need to display mastery of dubious Continental theories and to grind a politically correct axe. If Peradotto's intent was to display the efficacy of theory for the interpretation of ancient texts, the result, for anyone even casually conversant with the terms of theoretical debate of the last twenty-five years, proves precisely the opposite. No one slogging his way through the clotted prose of these essays will be moved or excited in new ways by Homer's *Odyssey*, nor will he discover anything that would help him to move or excite others.

II.

Like Peradotto's collection, *Innovations of Antiquity*[26] is intended to advance the cause of theory in classics. As its title brags, this collection of sixteen essays aspires to present the profession with the latest in theoretical sophistication, a "showcase for more advanced investigations of Greek and Roman literature" by "a new generation of classicists" (xii) who have made "some of the most significant advancements in our understanding of classical literature" (xvii) and who in this volume are making further "interpretive advances" (xii)—thus the whole volume has, according to its editors, a "progressive thrust" (xv).

However, despite this insistent rhetoric of novelty, redolent of the stentorian hectoring of television commercials, the essays themselves, when they even bother to "do theory"—a point to which I will return—mainly reflect the formalist theoretical fashions, especially a defanged deconstructionism, that culminated in the mid-eighties: Derrida's is the name to drop in this collection, not Foucault's. Editors Ralph Hexter and Daniel Selden inadvertently reveal the dated quality of their enterprise when, obeying the current faux confessional strictures to "situate" oneself, they reprint the letter they sent in 1987 to their prospective contributors. In it they quote from then-president of the Modern Language Association J. Hillis Miller's 1986 Presidential Address, in which Miller touted the "almost universal triumph of theory" (xi). The irony here is that Miller's address was significant not for his debatable claim about the triumph of theory, but for his attack on the new kids on the block, the New Historicists, who were challenging the deconstructionist ascendancy and echoing earlier criticisms of deconstruction for its self-indulgent ahistoricism, its eagerness "to demonstrate the history-transcending qualities of the text," and its tendency "to be an activity of textual privatization."[27] Indeed, Miller was fighting a rearguard action, for the battle was soon to be lost, at least outside of classics. The numerous criticisms of deconstruction mentioned above, especially those from the Left which recognized that American deconstruction had degenerated into ahistoricist "New Critical readings in Continental dress";[28] the scandalous apologetic contortions Derrida and his American acolytes went through to excuse Paul de Man's wartime collaboration with the Nazis; the revelation that Martin Heidegger, the intellectual godfather of deconstruction,[29] was a supporter of Hitler and remained unapologetic about it until his death; all of these led to deconstruction and Derrida losing their "former questionable prestige."[30] It is only the bureaucratic inertia of tenure that accounts for the continued presence of deconstructionists on campus, just as one can still find the stray New Critic. Thus, like the essentially formalist interpretations of most of the essays, this introduction is curiously ahistoricist, failing to take into account the institutional power-struggles that determine which theory triumphs at any given time—and that is the fashion in criticism these days: showing how all cultural productions are epiphenomena of some oppressive power structure jealously guarding its prerogatives, something few of these essays do in any but a very general sense. Hexter and Selden's silence concerning the shifting institutional fortunes of critical enterprises reveals their claims of "innovation" and "advancements" to be yet another instance of academic marketing.

But this collection has a much more serious problem than the somewhat dated quality of its theoretical pretensions. Given the current promiscuous eclecticism and vague attacks on "power"—the Foucauldian phlogiston of the theoreticist humanities—some changes in vocabulary and phrasing could probably make most of these essays pass, particularly since many of them are in a general sense concerned with "gender" issues, the current hot topic for those desiring to unmask the machinations of power. The real problem, however, is that *all* of the essays except one are not really theoretical at all, in the sense of consistently endorsing or displaying the epistemic nihilism or skepticism about the "subject" and meaning in language that characterizes genuine poststructuralist and deconstructionist criticism. Instead, like Peradotto's, these essays engage in an empirical procedure not that different from "traditional" philology's: their authors make what they believe to be truthful generalizations about the ancient world based on interpretations of texts buttressed by close readings and by extensive footnotes locating the interpretations in the tradition of scholarship about their subject. To put it in utterly unpoststructuralist terms, these authors are rational subjects making truth-claims about the meanings of ancient literary artifacts which have an objective independent existence apart from the authors' interpretations. Moreover, the essays' authors believe that these claims recover more of the innate meaning in the texts than had been previously noticed.

The editors imply as much when they state that their title, if the genitive is subjective, locates the "moment of innovation...not in our own time, but with the ancients.... [W]hat the essays also make clear is that these works [of ancient literature] are theoretically in advance of the point at which we find ourselves today..." (xxii). That is, these essays have a higher *truth value* than previous interpretations and are recovering more of the truth about the ancient world because the essays' theoretical assumptions more accurately match up with some meaning in the ancient texts. This implicit assumption—that the essays can say something truthful about the ancient world in rationally coherent arguments supported by textual evidence—means that anything "theoretical" about the essays functions on the cosmetic level and consists of superficial references or rhetorical flourishes or pretentious jargon that do not affect the essays' essentially traditional and *conservative* methodology.

Astonishingly enough, the editors themselves admit that despite their request that the contributors "make explicit the *methodological* principles on which [their] reading was based" (xiv; emphasis in original), they found "that many of the essays...were not, in fact, particularly theoretical" and so most of them "failed in [their] assignment" (xvi), a failure due, the editors sniff, "to the current state of literary criticism in classics, which in this respect is only just beginning to find its bearings" (xvi) and to the fact that "the move from theoretical to pragmatic considerations...is inherently more problematic" (xvii). The first reason recalls Peradotto's false claim about the intransigent intellectual conservatism of classics. Here it is equally dishonest, given the *age* of some of the current essays—Winkler's was first published in 1980, Halperin's was begun in 1982, and Margaret Ferguson's was begun in 1975. I think the discipline has had plenty of time to "find its bearings." The second reason is no reason at all, simply a reliance on the academic weasel-word "problematic." I submit that the *real* reason that these essays "failed in their assignment," as the editors put it with schoolmarmish petulance, is simply that all

scholars do pretty much the same thing, and only the subject matter—which does not depend on any particular set of theoretical assumptions—and the self-conscious packaging make any difference.

The editors' admission, then, and the traditional methodology
of most of the essays not only vaporize the raison d'être of the collection, but cancel out the references in the Introduction to throwing
the "spotlight on questions of critical procedure" (xiv), to engaging
"issues that are theoretically more demanding" (xix), or to their gran-
diose hope that the collection "will contribute...toward the eventual
restructuring of the profession" (xxi). What is demanding, however,
is the opaque style and dull poststructuralist clichês that appear occasionally in some of the essays and the editors' introductions. The
editors themselves suspect that some readers might object to these
obfuscations, and so they try proleptically to defuse such criticisms
with a cheeky apologia that must be quoted at length for the reader
to savor fully its arrogant duplicity:

> All of [the essays] make conceptual and stylistic demands which
> exceed the norms of classical scholarship today and, to the extent
> that they are methodologically challenging, they require a genuine
> liberality on the reader's part. The ideal of a transparent, tempered
> and accommodated prose, which still predominates in academic
> circles, goes back to a moment in neoclassical aesthetics when the
> middle or conversational style of the canonical *genera dicendi* be-
> comes the approved mode of expression for the society and values
> of the newly empowered middle class.... This ideal of an urbane and
> purified language of criticism, in which anything "foreign," "bar-
> barous," "archaic," or "technical" is systematically eschewed, betrays
> not only the nostalgia for a natural idiom, but the project to re-
> make the language of the modern nation-state in its image. De-
> spite this pretense to an unartificial diction, however, the refine-
> ment of a style that elutriates all sense of labor inevitably turns
> critical prose into a commodity, whose distribution of ideas for
> ready consumption shares the economy of the marketplace it so
> desperately desires to elude.... To the extent that [the essays] defy

the "prose of the center," their language constitutes a break, and hence something of a scandal, whose efficacy can be measured by the degree to which it resists facile assimilation. Style here begins to acquire the rigor of a method, and it would be naive for any reader, even the most seasoned, to expect that criticism of this sort could be entirely absorbed, much less exhausted at a single sitting. (xx, xxi)

This "solipsistic cant," as Heath puts it,[31] is one of the most shameful rationalizations for bad writing I have ever encountered outside a freshman composition course, and I want to point out its numerous affronts. First there is the implication that classics today, at least as practiced by "traditional philologists," is undemanding, that is, simplistic. Does anyone think that the work of, say, Moses Finley or Bernard Knox is "undemanding" just because it is clearly written? This is an example of what Cedric Watts, way back in 1983, called the poststructuralist "jargonish fallacy," which occurs "when a critic claims or implies that to use a very difficult or obscure mode of expression is to demonstrate one's integrity (for one thereby opposes the conventional and therefore the ideologically conservative), whereas to express oneself clearly and intelligibly is to compromise with the conventional and therefore to support the bourgeoisie."[32] This "preposterously silly idea," as Peter Medawar called it[33]—that complex ideas necessitate convoluted syntax, incoherent organization, and pretentious jargon—is one we would expect from a clever undergraduate defending an empty term paper. Moreover, Selden here is blatantly contradicting the blurb he contributed to the back of Winkler's *Constraints of Desire,* in which he praised Winkler's "precision and liveliness" and touted the book as "consistently clear, logical, and persuasive."[34] Has Selden changed his mind since then, or was the earlier praise of phallogocentric clarity and logic merely a sales pitch?

Next we get a vaguely Marxist potted history of just how "transparent, tempered and accommodated prose" came into being: as a phallogocentric, patriarchal, capitalist tool of hegemony that benefits the bourgeois "nation-state" and its economic system of "commodity" and "consumption." Must we, at this late date, once again be subjected to *haut bourgeois* academics—themselves involved in the utterly middle-class pursuit of academic prestige, power, and pelf—indulging antibourgeois banalities? And if anything is a "commodity," it is this collection, which exists to circulate—and in some cases *recirculate*, since some of the essays have already seen print—its "products" throughout the academic marketplace and create "profits" (promotion, tenure, release time, grants, think tank sinecures, more prestigious positions, endowed professorships) for its editors and contributors. Finally, and most shamefully, is the implication that if the reader does not understand the essays it is because he is just not smart enough and so had better go back and read them again. Indeed, any lack of understanding or any rejection will automatically function as a sign of the collection's intellectual profundity—not, as is more usually the case, a sign of a bad argument or bad writing. This shabby ad hominem trick is akin to the old Marxist reliance on "false consciousness" or the Freudian on "repression" whenever these ideologies encountered criticism.

The truth is, unclear writing is usually the sign of unclear thinking. Muddled prose is an instrument "for concealing or preventing thought," as George Orwell put it in "Politics and the English Language," an essay Hexter and Selden should be compelled to read.[35] Maybe then they could avoid such sentences as the following: "Augustine not only *fleshes* out the existential *stakes* inherent in rhetorical structure, but ultimately reverses the classical *poles,* exiling exile, as it were, and *marking the land* of metaphor as the proper home for language" (67, emphases added). From painting to gambling to electricity to surveying, the metaphors mingle promiscuously, reminding me of Orwell's observation, in the same essay, that bad writing "consists less and less of *words* chosen for the sake of their meaning, and more and more of *phrases* tacked together like the sections of a prefabricated henhouse."[36]

This introduction, then, is an exercise in packaging and marketing and does not address forthrightly the issue of contemporary theory and classics. A much more honest, but still troubled, discussion of these issues can be found in Charles Segal's "Epilogue on Method: Relativism, Eclecticism, and Interpretation," which follows his essay on the *Hippolytus* (444–50). As we have already noted, Segal has long been a practitioner of classics interpretation in the French key, and his use of structuralism to analyze Greek literature has led to some valuable criticism, for the simple reason that, as he put it in *Tragedy and Civilization: An Interpretation of Sophocles,* the Greeks themselves structured thought in terms of polarities and antitheses, and so structuralism *can* be, in the right hands, a "powerful conceptual tool"[37] for uncovering the meaning of Greek literature. But it is important to repeat here the point made earlier regarding Peradotto's narratology: structuralism *per se* does not necessitate any doubts about the critic's ability objectively to recover the "deep structure" creating meaning in the texts, or any doubts that the meaning exists apart from the critic and relates to the larger structures of meaning operating throughout the culture as a whole in which the text is produced—thus Segal's image of structuralism as a "tool" that the rational mind wields on an object to discover its truth. This is a far cry from the tenets of poststructuralism and its epistemic nihilism.

The drive to pluralism endorsed by Peradotto and Segal and other "theoretically minded" classicists necessitates repeating again the incompatibilities between structuralism and poststructuralism, as described here by Thomas Docherty: "The impetus towards totalization which was inscribed in structuralism was exploded by the unsettling maneuvers of some poststructuralist thinkers, and was most obviously displaced by deconstruction. Structuralism's desire to rest critical analysis on the same foundation of a scientific linguistics was frustrated by deconstruction's constant displacing of that ground, and the concomitant drive towards sceptical undecidability."[38] Segal notes this conflict between the two (447), but I think he too facilely glosses it over. If one takes seriously poststructuralism's disbelief in any recoverable meaning in a text, its belief that "there is something in writing itself which finally evades all systems and logics," that the "concept of writing...is a challenge to the very idea of structure,"[39] then it is utterly incompatible with the sort of structuralism Segal practices—and, I might add, the kind of clear, coherent prose that he usually writes. If poststructuralism in general, and deconstruction in particular, are differently defined—as Segal observes when he predicates "epistemological indeterminacy" of "*some* forms of deconstruction" (456, n. 87, emphasis added; cf. also 447)—then it is not deconstruction or poststructuralism, but rather an emasculation of those theories similar to Peradotto's, a taming of their excesses for smoother consumption by the American criticism industry.

This domestication of deconstructionism and poststructuralism, which usually characterizes both when they appear in classics, needs to be remarked on further. Most classicists of a deconstructionist bent practice what Felperin calls "soft-core" deconstruction.[40] The latter, created by the popularizing activity of critics like Jonathan Culler,[41] allows the aspiring deconstructionist to practice an unrestrained formalist criticism without falling into "the dizzying aporia of the Derridean perspective," as Felperin puts it.[42] J. G. Merquior has called this form of deconstruction "a technique for unreading texts" that avoids Derrida's "epochal ontological stakes."[43] Hence its attractiveness to classicists—they can continue to interpret texts empirically, as they have been trained to do, and to propose new meanings they believe have truth value, all the while dressing up the whole procedure in poststructuralist high fashion. This is what the "pluralist" position of Peradotto or Segal amounts to, but as many critics have pointed out, pluralism can work only by draining deconstruction of its self-cancel-

ing nihilism—and hence its true significance. Thus Segal's statement
that his own essay draws on "contemporary semiotic, structuralist,
and post-structuralist" approaches (421) and on "deconstruction" (445)
again glosses over the contradictions between structuralism and
poststructuralism. This confusion runs throughout his "Epilogue,"
as in the following:

> The major interpretative division that affects (and afflicts)
> classicists...is that between a historicist and a linguistic-semiotic
> model. In the former the text contains a message (however complex)
> about a world outside itself that the critic can recover. In the latter
> the text is a construct of conventions and operations which relate to
> other families of texts (other such constructs) rather than to a final
> historical truth. Meaning, in the semiotic model, is not something
> immanent in the text itself; it is a construct dependent on the
> context(s) into which the interpreter decodes the text's networks of
> relations (psychological, political, sociological, etc.). (444-45)

As well as adopting the rhetoric of the "Phony War" I mentioned
at the start, Segal here creates a false antithesis for a number of reasons. More broadly (leaving aside for the moment the true division in
the profession, the vertical conflict between academic grandees and
helots), I would say that the conflict these days (and back in 1992 as
well) is not as he describes it. Rather it is between those scholars who
believe it is possible to make defensible generalizations about ancient
literature and society based on an objective analysis of evidence and
containing some truth value, and those who *claim*—their actual practice is another matter—that given the undecidability built into language and the insidious control of "power networks," any interpretation can be only a misinterpretation serving some ideological purpose, since "truth" and "objectivity" are bourgeois chimeras. Next,
there is no real conflict between "message" and "construct"—any literary message is a construct, if only of language or genre. Who would
argue with that? And where, if not in the historicist's "world outside"

the text, would Segal's "conventions" and "operations" and "other families of texts" and "networks of relations" and "social and historical background" (445) and "social and historical determinants" (446) reside? Are not those "conventions" and "families of texts" historically true? Segal does not make them up. And *something* exists in the texts—codes, for example—that contribute to their meaning and thus is "immanent," at least the way my dictionary defines the word. What else could Segal mean when he says that the critic who focuses on one interpretive method "runs the risk of neglecting the full range of possible meanings *in the work*" (446, emphasis added)? Segal must believe, moreover, that those meanings are "true," else why would he write? Segal has hedged with the adjective "final": I know of no scholar with any intellectual integrity who would claim that he or she has discovered the *final* truth about anything, though we all may sometimes talk as if we had. But we all try to recover more of what is in the texts we study, to give "fuller adequacy to what the text of the work seems to be saying" (446), even as we all realize we will never exhaust their potential meaning, particularly in classics, where the evidence is fragmentary and so our conclusions provisional. Thus, we have "to accept at least a certain measure of [interpretation's] indeterminacy" (445). Given the loophole of "at least a certain measure," who in our profession would disagree?

Segal, I think, has built a traditionalist straw man and then knocked it over. Worse, the theoretical spin he gives to his work is unnecessary. What he does in terms of *practice* is ultimately no different from what, say, Bernard Knox does. Only the emphasis or focus changes, as it necessarily does from critic to critic. And if all interpretations are not equal—as Segal clearly implies when he says, "One interpretation...can take a *fuller* account than another of the text's context and content. It can describe and illuminate *more* of its details" (449, emphases added)—then that is because those interpretations are more *true*, which in turn means that no matter how diffi-

cult, *some* objectivity is possible—the position of traditional philology. As Segal says, "We can try to correct for our inevitable biases by
alertness to the otherness, the difference of the text and its own concerns and ways of organizing meaning" (450), which implies a *true*
meaning our biases can keep us from seeing—an idea anathema to
the genuine poststructuralist. Thus, contrary to what Segal asserts,
interpretation *does* involve something not situated "in our own time
and place and informed by our own concerns" (449)—the text's "concerns" and meanings which are recoverable because, rather than being forever deferred by the free-play of signifiers, they exist objectively
apart from our interpretations.

Segal, then, cannot resolve the contradiction flawing the
poststructuralist "project": quite simply, if you really believe in
deconstruction or Foucauldian constructionism, then, as the novel-
ist David Lodge put it, you're sawing off the epistemic or ontological
or linguistic branch you're sitting on. But Segal and most of the scholars in this collection proceed as we all do, and so by implication *do*
believe that we can uncover truths about the ancient world that transcend our biases and ideologies. Which raises the question: why all
the huffing and puffing about the necessity of engaging theory? All
most critics gain from theory is perhaps some methodological self-
consciousness, which can be salutary if it leads to humility, and a
wider range of subject matter, but both of these can be acquired without revelations from Paris. But the essence of these critics' procedure
is the same as the most hidebound reactionary's: survey the evidence,
come up with a generalization you believe to be true, support it with
specific textual evidence, and locate your interpretation in the tradition of scholarship concerning the subject as documented in footnotes. And do all this in language that is clear and coherent so that
your idea can be communicated to your community of scholars. This
is the ideal: we all fail at times, but when we do, we can be sure that a
sharp-eyed colleague will pounce on our mistakes and correct them.

Ulrich Wilamowitz's interpretation of Sappho fragment 31 as a heterosexual epithalamium was not just an alternative interpretation, one of many like "the different 'interpretations' of a piano or violin concerto by different soloists or orchestras," to use Segal's own analogy describing the "pluralist" position (444). Wilamowitz's reading was simply wrong, or as Denys Page put it, a "mere delusion."[44]

This collection of "innovations," then, consists for the most part of essays following a traditional practice that reflects the authors' philological training, and anything theoretical, as I said before, consists of superficial verbal gestures or fashionable name-dropping or truisms ponderously restated. The best essays, however, do not even bother with those cosmetic retouches. J. J. Winkler's "Lollianos and the Desperadoes" (5–50), for example, does not in the least depend on any theoretical viewpoint for its clearly written narratological analysis of fragment B of the *Phoinikika*, since narratology, like structuralism, is perfectly consistent with old-fashioned notions of critics rationally analyzing elements of literature they believe to be in the text. Thus when Winkler says that his essay "traces the pattern of narrative, the basic plots and formulae of popular entertainment" (6) and that the fragment is "closer to ancient melodrama, mime, and thrilling travel tales than to the little we know of mystery cults" (6–7), he is doing nothing that would offend the most traditional of philologists. He is simply taking sides in a critical debate, elaborating a reading that supports a tradition of interpretation dating back to K. Bürger's work in 1902 (38 n. 5). So much for "innovation." Nothing poststructuralist here, and certainly nothing "New Historicist," which is the *real* latest fad. In fact, the interpretation Winkler argues *against*—that the fragment reveals information about historical mystery cults—could more easily be reconciled to a New Historicist interpretation than Winkler's essentially formalist analysis of generic narrative conventions.

Some of the essays, unfortunately, do not follow Winkler's example. Like Peradotto, their authors feel compelled to gussy up their conventional practice with fashionable references and allusions that either are irrelevant or confuse their ideas. Sometimes we are subjected to self-important restatements of the obvious, a bad habit of Hexter and Selden's in their brief introductions to the eight pairs of essays. For example, when they introduce Winkler's essay they inform us that literature is not mimesis but rather "a system and specific signifying practice" (3). To whom is that a revelation? And why can't a "signifying practice" be mimetic as well? Or consider this: "Any reference to the codes of religion or history in the *Phoinikika* is not documentary, but strictly subordinate to the structure and requirements of its plot" (4). Of what piece of fiction is this not true? What writer worthy of the calling does not want to tell a good story rather than remain faithful to his documentary detail? And some writers—Joyce, for example, or more recently Charles Bukowski—manage sometimes to do both; thus the antithesis here is false. Either Hexter and Selden are critical tyros, or they assume their readers are. Why else repeat such truisms?

This habit of restating the obvious is even more annoying when the banality is given the imprimatur of some preferably poststructuralist authority. In his own essay "Ceveat Lector: Catullus and the Rhetoric of Performance" (461–512), Selden tells us that "Jacques Derrida speaks of 'the irreducible excess of the syntactic over the semantic'" (466), a trite restatement of Keats's advice to Shelley that he "load every rift with ore." Of course literary language promises more meaning than any act of interpretation can describe. That is why we still read Homer and Shakespeare. Tacking on a French label does not make a truism any less a truism. Or listen to Margaret W. Ferguson writing about exile in Augustine (69–94): she sees exile as the middle term of a dialectic "which J. Hillis Miller calls 'a basic paradigm of occidental metaphysics—the picture of an original unity, but in our present sad dispersal, to be regained at some point in the millennial future'" (69). First, this is the sort of vapid generalization one expects to find in suspect popularizers harping on a fixed idea; second, what makes J. Hillis Miller, a literary critic, an expert on "occidental metaphysics"? This practice is nothing but intellectual name-dropping, an attempt to revive tired ideas with a spurious authority.

Worse than these irrelevancies, however, are the references to (once) trendy deconstructionist ideas that add nothing to the writers' arguments and indeed saddle them with unresolved difficulties. The problem is the same one we noted in Peradotto's essays: speculative poststructuralist interpretations of conundrums are presented as demonstrated truths everyone else must now acknowledge.[45] Margaret Ferguson, for example, writing about exile and figurative language in Augustine, says the "exile is defined negatively with reference to what he is not; his essence is determined by a *difference* portrayed as a lack" (70, emphasis in original). Ferguson wants to link this idea of the exile to metaphor as a "home away from home, a detour in the road whose goal is union—or reunion—with truth" (70). But Ferguson cannot be content just to present these ideas and develop them. First they have to be sanctioned by appeal to what was, in 1975 when she first published the essay, the ultimate Gallic Big Daddy, Jacques Derrida:[46]

> A metaphysical concept of truth as "presence," according to Derrida, underlies both the Judeo-Christian metaphor of human life as an exile from God and many traditional formulations of the theory that language imitates or represents something essentially *unlike* language, something that is often conceived spatially as behind or beyond the medium that imitates it. (70)

Ferguson is referring here, of course, to Derrida's conception of "logocentrism," which John Ellis fairly defines as "the illusion that the meaning of a word has its *origin* in the structure of reality itself and hence makes the *truth* about that structure seem directly *present* to the mind."[47] As Ellis points out, Derrida is simply flogging the dead horse of essentialism, the idea that our conceptual organization of reality has an existence in reality independent of language, an idea considered untenable by philosophers and linguists long before Derrida.[48] That Ferguson seems not to realize how unoriginal—and, stripped of their camouflage of neologism and jargon, commonplace—are Derrida's ideas illustrates the parochialism that, ironically, afflicts so many theoretically "innovative" scholars. Is not this allusion to debatable ideas or to theories without mentioning, at least in a note, the major criticisms of them, contrary to the usual practice in our profession? Is the silence on Ferguson's part the result of carelessness, ignorance, or fear? Finally, and most importantly, what is this reference to Derrida doing here in the first place? I invite any reader to omit from this section of Ferguson's essay (70-71) every reference to Derrida and his questionable theories and see if Ferguson's thesis suffers. He or she will find that it does not.

Another example of this same insecure appeal to Gallic authority occurs in David Halperin's thrice recycled essay on Plato's *Symposium*, "Plato and the Erotics of Narrativity" (95-126), which sees narrative as "an expression of desire: the successive narrators and enduring narrative of the *Symposium* enact the very process of loss and renewal, of emptying and filling, with which Plato's dialog as a whole is concerned.... [I]ts complex narrative structure is itself designed to manifest and to dramatize the working of *erôs*" (102). But as Halperin elaborates on this idea and relates it to other issues such as orality, writing, and interpretation, he cannot resist the urge to show off Derrida with all the eagerness of the campus nerd who has just made friends with the captain of the football team:

> [Halperin reads] Plato in opposition to Derrida not as a metaphysical dogmatist but as a kind of deconstructionist *avant la lettre,* a cunning writer fully alive to the doubleness of his rhetoric who embraces *différance* and who actively courts in his writing an effect of undecidability. The *Symposium* exhibits a series of alternating doctrinal and counterdoctrinal pressures, and interpreters of the Dialogue need to remain sensitive to each set of pressures. It would

be wrong to conclude from [Halperin's] reading of the work that it contains no positive doctrine, that it lacks any genuinely Platonic philosophical content, or that it merely spoofs the notion of an erotics of narrativity, being wholly ironical in purpose and designed simply to demonstrate the futility of philosophical inquiry or to satirize the quest for a true doctrine. (114)

Do not be fooled by Halperin's disagreement with Derrida. What is more significant is that he accepts as a discovered truth Derrida's questionable theory of *différance,* which apparently to Halperin is a descriptive truth about language akin to gravity, waiting millenia for that Newton of philosophers Derrida to discover and define it.

But of course *différance* is no such thing: it is rather a highly speculative—and ultimately poorly constructed—*theory* about language deriving from a misreading of Saussure's insight that the *concepts* that words signify arbitrarily organize reality and are themselves part of a system that creates meaning by differences and contrast between the system's terms. Out of this misreading, as Ellis demonstrates, Derrida creates his neologism:

> Derrida's first move is to introduce the word *play* and substitute it for a word such as *contrast,* so that now we have the play of differences as the source of meaning. *Play* is no longer a matter of specific contrasts—it is..."limitless," "infinite," and "indefinite"; and thus meaning has become limitless, infinite, and indefinite. This thrust is developed with both spatial and temporal ideas. Since play is ceaseless, it is temporally extended; by playing on the two meanings of the French verb *différer*—to differ and to defer—Derrida argues that the play of differences means that meaning is not present to us but is *deferred,* i.e., postponed into a future rather than a present. And the spatial sense of "present" comes into his notion that the absence of an independent concept ("transcendental signified," as he calls it) means that meaning is never present to us.[49]

Ellis goes on to point out that as well as shifting Saussure's meaning without logically justifying such a shift, Derrida, in his obsession with

"absence," confuses here "signification and the analysis of signification"; as Ellis observes, "All words are, in a sense, present for possible
choice, and then all but one rendered absent by actual choice; that is
how language works. The absence is not something that necessitates
a search or a diagnosis of absent meaning; absence is meaning when a
systematic choice is made."[50] In short, Derrida's idea is incoherent
and useless as a statement of the way language actually works.[51]

Halperin's problem, however, is not just that he ignores, like
Ferguson, the serious criticisms of Derrida's ideas. What is worse is
that he uses Derrida's *différance* in a wholly un-Derridean sense, and
so is practicing a "soft-core" deconstruction that is a contradiction
in terms.[52] To say that a text has a "double rhetoric," which I suppose
means it can send more than one message or have more than one
meaning, or to say that a text displays an "effect of undecidability" is
obviously *not* what Derrida means by *différance*. All literature often
presents us with a self-conscious undecidable conflict among several
meanings. That is why there is so much interpretation. Derrida's point
is that *any* meaning, not just those that are undecidable or conflicting, is irrecoverable, constantly deferred, an absence bearing the traces
of the play of differences. Thus it is astonishing to hear Halperin speak
of "positive doctrine" or "philosophical content" in Plato's dialogue,
terms necessarily meaningless if we accept seriously Derrida's notions,
which tell us that *no* text, *no* writing contains anything that can legitimately be called "positive doctrine."

Halperin, then, like Ferguson, complicates his argument needlessly by bringing into it theories long subjected to serious criticism,
theories which apparently he either does not fully grasp or consciously
etiolates and whose elimination from his essay would not hurt its
argument a bit. Moreover, his fixation on the (once) trendy Derrida
blinds him to other scholars who would have been much more useful
for his purposes. His concern with the "doubleness of rhetoric" could
have found much stronger support in the work of Mikhail Bakhtin,[53]

and his interest in the connection of narrative and desire could have been more fruitfully linked to the work of René Girard or, more recently, Patricia Meyer Spacks.[54] Instead we get garbled, irrelevant references to long-exploded theories. But Halperin and Ferguson derive several advantages from Derrida's presence: he functions as a sort of talisman to deflect the reader's critical scrutiny, and he adds some Continental panache to their ideas, increasing the ideas' academic marketability in much the same way that ordinary jeans increase in value once a French designer label is attached to them.

In Halperin and Ferguson the *morbus Gallicus* of theory manifests itself only occasionally; in Ann Bergren's "Architecture Gender Philosophy" (253–305) the disease rages out of control. In Bergren's favor it must be said that she alone has taken the editors' charge, as well as the implications of deconstruction, seriously, and has alone produced something utterly unlike what one would expect from traditional philology. Hers is an essay whose undecidability of meaning and rejection of suspect repressive strictures like logic, coherence, and clarity exemplify perfectly Derrida's vision of language as a riotous dance of signifiers over the abyss. If, as the editors claim, the success of the essay is dependent on how stubbornly it resists "facile assimilation" (xxi), then Bergren's essay is a *succès fou,* for it resists *any* assimilation, facile or otherwise.

As its title suggests, the essay wants to uncover—or "demystify," I suppose I should say—how architecture and philosophy collude to reinforce and "ground" one another by ignoring the way they arbitrarily construct gender, a construction essentially appropriative and repressive: "The mutual edification of philosophy and architecture in the *Timaeus* entails the construction of gender between them. Their 'ground-as-support' requires their complicity in the stabilization of *chôra.* In deconstructing this cooperative 'choral work' resides the potential for the dislocation of Platonic ontology as formulated in the *Timaeus* and of Platonically informed architecture" (253–54).

This statement needs to be scrutinized, for the whole essay depends on the linkage established here among *chôra*, architecture, and gender. Bergren's first move is to define *chôra* as "space" instead of "receptacle" or the "stuff without property"[55] out of which the demiurge creates the cosmos by the imposition of form. This notoriously difficult idea in the *Timaeus*—Plato has Timaeus call it "difficult of explanation and dimly seen" (Jowett translation)—requires from Plato a whole host of images: "receptacle" (*dechomenê, dexamenê,* 50b, 52d, 53a; *dechomenon,* 50d; *dexesthai,* 50a), "recipient" (*hupodochê,* 49a), "womb" (*mêtra,* 50d, 51a), "nurse" (*tithênê,* 52d, 49a), "place" (*topos,* 52a), "seat" (*hedra,* 52b), "matrix" (*ekmageion,* 50c), and "space" (*chôra,* 52a, 53a), as well as analogies that compare the demiurge's activity to molding gold (50a) and blending perfume (50e). Obviously, *chôra* is just one of many images Plato uses to describe a difficult abstraction, and it is not even the most frequent. There are those who have argued for "space," in the sense of empty space or extension, as what Plato intended to describe,[56] but there are serious difficulties with this interpretation, not the least being that it is hard to see how empty space so defined can "[sway] unevenly hither and thither" or be compared to winnowed grain (52d).

The important point, however, is that Bergren makes absolutely no reference to this disagreement of interpretation, gives us no argument why we should accept "space" as the meaning of the "receptacle," makes no effort to distinguish between the ordinary sense of "space" and what Plato intends with *chôra*, and cites no previous scholars who have worked on this problem. Thus her use of *chôra* throughout the essay is misleading and inaccurate. This silence leads one to conclude that Bergren is critically analyzing not Plato's philosophy and the tradition of interpretation of its difficulties, but rather his imagery, teasing out the implications of it to suit her desire to talk about Derrida's essay "*Chôra*" and his joint architectural project "Choral Works." Thus what is important to her is not an accurate assessment of the interpretations of Plato's difficult thought in the *Timaeus*, but rather the assertion of a link between philosophy and modern architecture and gender, one based on a superficial understanding of Plato's ideas and on a formalist overemphasis of his expressive imagery—a procedure which certainly will *not* result in the hubristic goal of a "dislocation of Platonic ontology."

The next term of Bergren's triad, "architecture," is equally troublesome. The naive reader probably would assume that Bergren means here to deconstruct "architectural theory," not real-life buildings, which everyone knows are deconstructed with dynamite. But, alas, buildings and parks in the real world are intended here, since the essay's topics include a design by Derrida and Peter Eisenman for a section of the Parc La Villette in Paris, the so-called "Choral Works." The reader mystified by the idea of "deconstructing" something as concrete and useful as a building should listen to Mr. Eisenman: "My tendencies are all towards the anthropocentrism, aestheticism, and functionality which I am trying to critique.... I must constantly work against this sensibility in order to do the architecture I am interested in" (274). In other words, he wants to design ugly buildings no human being can use—something one would expect from a graduate of Swift's Academy of Projectors at Lagado, whose architects attempt to build houses from the roof down.[57]

But even granting the existence of deconstructive architecture, the more serious problem for Bergren's argument is the sleight-of-hand by which she gets the idea of "architect" into the *Timaeus*. Just as she chooses one of many images Plato uses to describe the "receptacle," so she interprets Plato's word *dêmiourgos* in terms of one *possible* meaning—one, by the way, not listed by Liddell, Scott, and Jones—and then substitutes *that* meaning—"architect"—throughout the essay, giving the impression that "architect" is the commonly accepted translation of Plato's *dêmiourgos*.[58] As with her use of *chôra*, the substitution of "architect" in her essay for Plato's *dêmiourgos* is unfounded and deceptive (e.g., "The treatment of the *dêmiourgos* in Plato repeats the rhetoric of the female and the architect in pre-philosophical texts" [263]). If Plato intended "architect," why did he not simply use the word Bergren herself makes reference to, *architektôn*, a word that Herodotus uses (3.60) and so we know was available to Plato?

Analysis of Bergren's third term, "gender," necessarily takes us into the murky depths of a common academic superstition, "constructionism." That is, gender has little to do with biology or nature but is an arbitrary social construct: "Psychoanalysis and anthropology [*ipsi dixerunt*!] have analyzed gender as the constellation of characteristics and values, the powers and powerlessness, attached by a given social group to sexual difference" (255). The issue being glibly oversimplified here is the complex and intricate interrelations between culture and nature, or heredity and environment, a problem as old as the Sophists and currently being worked on in fields such as ethology, genetics, biology, and sociobiology as well as in pseudosciences like psychology, sociology, and anthropology.[59] Thus Bergren reveals the parochialism of the humanities scholar when she speaks as though the final word has been definitively spoken by "anthropology and psychoanalysis" when in fact just the opposite is true.[60] But nature, as Horace said, is not so easily disposed of, and Bergren herself throughout her essay vacillates between her ostensible interpretation of "female" as a term in an arbitrary system of differences that has nothing to do with biology and her repeated references to what can only be real-life women who suffer exploitation and subordination because of their biological differences with men. Compare the following passages:

> Architectural theory does not appear conscious of this issue as essential to its self-understanding and thus germane to male or female, practitioner or theorist as well. This relative absence of theoretical reflection finds a practical counterpart in the male dominance, both ethical and statistical, among the stars of the profession. (255)

The moral and social status of the *dêmiourgos* is of the same marked, ambiguous structure as that of the female: despised for their manual and material labor, while magnified for their intellectual ingenuity. (262)

What does "female" refer to in these passages, a semiotic marker or real-life subordinated women? Obviously the latter—you don't despise a "construct." Then how do these women relate to the marker "female"? The connection is muddled, never spelled out or clarified. When it suits Bergren, "female" is an arbitrary signifying term; when she wants the justifying moral force that comes from contemplating the suffering of women in the flesh, then that is what "female" means. This confusion, as with most constructionism or cultural determinism, results from the oversimplification of a complex problem the solution to which still evades us.

The problems arising from Bergren's sloppy handling of her three terms vitiate her whole argument. Nor are matters helped by her opaque presentation, her nearly free-associative frenetic bouncing from one idea to another, her technique of argument by superficial connection (e.g., *mêtis* is associated with the female, *mêtis* is associated with the architect, ergo the architect is associated with the female [257–62]). And there are other problems. We find occasional distortions of fact: "Outside of the poetry of Sappho, virtually no speech or writing by Greek women has been handed down" (257)—so much for Corinna, who bested Pindar in song, so much for Praxilla, of whom Lysippus made a bronze statue, so much for Telesilla and Erinna. And Bergren should make clear that accidents of transmission, rather than patriarchal plots, account for the absence of the work of some other women poets such as Myrtis, Charixena, Cleobulina, and Morê, just as we lack the work of numerous male writers attested to in ancient sources. Then there are the clumsy symbolic readings, such as her interpretation of decapitation as "feminization by castration" (262), an egregious non sequitur; or her labeling a thunderbolt "a flashing phallic power of the sky" (292, n. 47)—on the logic, I suppose, that anything longer than it is wide is "phallic." And of course we are treated to the dreary deconstructionist patois of ugly neologisms ("genderization" [255], "architecturalization" [265]), meaningless compounds ("Phallo-political" [260]), obscure words used in some private sense ("[d]iathectic" [260]), cute tricks pulled with parentheses ("gen(d)eric" [257], "(il)legitimacy" [268], "(re)production" [269], "(w)hole" [283]), and orthographic Frankenstein monsters like "hom(m)o/auto-erotic" (264, 266).[61]

Ultimately, however, what damns this essay the most—and gives the lie to the editors' rhetoric of scholarly "advances"—is its stale ahistoricism, its complete lack of any awareness of the historical contexts of cultural artifacts separated by nearly 2,500 years. No indication is given of the significant differences between an ancient and modern architect, between ancient and modern women. Bergren's three terms float timelessly, abstract counters in some academic game or, as Frank Lentricchia puts it in his criticism of deconstruction's solipsistic formalism, "an ultimate mode of interior decoration whose chief value lies in its power to trigger our pleasures"[62]—except that in this case, the pleasure can belong only to the author and to those who take seriously poststructuralism's vision of language as a carnival of indeterminacy. And this, finally, has to be allowed to Bergren—she at least has integrity. She writes as though she believed in the poststructuralist vision, rather than occasionally slumming in its gaudy rhetoric all the while knowing there is a prim empirical procedure waiting back home.

Fortunately—from my traditionalist perspective—most of the essays in this collection are closer to the standards of Winkler than of Bergren; again, that is because their authors follow the usual procedure for scholarship in our profession, the accepted practices to which we all adhere. Why, then, this assertion of novelty on the part of the editors? The answer should be obvious by now—academic careerism.

Without the rhetoric of novelty and advancement, there would be no reason for this collection to exist. Its essays could appear in scholarly journals and still make their contributions to the profession. But just as laundry detergent manufacturers add useless colored crystals to their soap and then tout it as "new and improved," so Hexter and Selden package their collection as the latest in theoretical sophistication—the irony, of course, being not just that, as the editors themselves admit, the essays are not particularly theoretical, but also that when they are, they are dated by their ahistoricist formalism. But *curricula vitae* must grow, conferences must have themes, books must be published, money must be cadged from the NEH and robber-baron trust funds, all so that the careers of ambitious academics can flourish. Why else would Halperin's essay be seeing its fourth incarnation, this one financed by a sabbatical and a Mellon fellowship? How many times does the profession have to pay for one idea? And that, finally, is where this collection is "situated": not in the desire to say something worthwhile about the ancient world that might communicate its importance for us today and justify the study of classics, but in the good-old philistine pursuit of money, status, and power.

III.

The latest example of what has by now become a permanent mini-industry of classical criticism, *History, Tragedy, Theory: Dialogues on Athenian Drama*,[63] records the fruits of a similarly named conference that was held at the University of Texas in 1992 and that was partly financed by money from the Robert M. Armstrong Centennial Fellowship in Classics. Like the previous two collections, then, this one is made possible by the institutional largess that testifies to the secure market share theoretically minded classicists have carved out of the profession.

This security may account for Barbara Goff's toning down of the usual claims of marginalization and theoretical derring-do against stubborn, entrenched traditionalists that we encountered in Peradotto and in Hexter and Selden. But the claim still turns up like some Homeric formula: "The reaction of classics to self-consciously theoretical work has often been hostile and defensive, but it has never been exclusively so, and the increasing institutional importance of 'theory' has required the discipline to reflect on its assumptions and procedures in a way that should be welcomed by all those who value intellectual commitment" (1; also 14). The recognition of the theorists' success in the profession is a welcome abandonment of the fiction of an embattled avant-garde, yet the characterization of those who oppose theory is still reductive, finding the answer to resistance in two-bit psychologizing ("hostile and defensive") rather than in any acknowledgment that the ideas promoted by theory are seriously flawed.

That Goff, like Peradotto and the rest, believes that these ideas are irreversible, definitive truths about the nature of language and literature and culture becomes clear when she starts talking about deconstruction. She immediately tips her hand by saying that the activity of deconstruction's "detractors" (n.b., not "critics"), besides generating "heat," has been characterized by a "corresponding lack of light" (2) and is an "extreme reaction" (4). Does Goff ever name some of these critics or refer to the refutations of their murky criticism? Of course not. Would you bother to refer to attacks on the heliocentric cosmos? Further confirmation that Goff believes Derrida has discovered some permanent truth can be found in her claim that "[d]econstruction has thoroughly disrupted the traditional humanistic inquiry into literature" (4). Where was that question-begging adverb earned? Or consider this hubristic absurdity: "Deconstruction has instead made problematic any comfortable or comforting relationship that could be maintained with literary texts, because of its rigorous exposure of the effort required to sustain the humanist categories of analysis, such as truth, intention, and referentiality, against the destabilizing potential of language" (4). The parochialism of this assertion is breathtaking. Millennia-old, fiercely contested philosophical issues (remember the Sophists?) have all been settled by the "rigorous" Derrida, according to Goff, and all those millions of people with their "comfortable" relationship with literature, all those myriad analyses and discoveries of truths from courtrooms to laboratories, all those daily successful uses of language to refer to reality—all mere chimeras, the fantasies of ovine chumps with their logocentric false consciousnesses.[64] Goff's arrogance makes one wonder how high a premium she herself places on what she claims traditional classics ignores: the "self-conscious examination of its assumptions" (16).

What soon becomes clear in the Introduction, though, is that Goff is not so much trying to make new converts as sorting out the various conflicting theoretical approaches. We are in theory's post-Nicene phase, with the poststructuralist *filioque* firmly in place and a few christological and trinitarian disputes left to tidy up. Thus Goff surveys the various strengths and weaknesses of the new historicism, "[a] mode of inquiry which at its most productive moments seeks to take account of the history within texts as well as the textuality within history" (5), which she faults for its tendency to forget the "deconstructive claim that the object of historical inquiry is itself textual, and that its meaning has never been self-evident" (8). She gives an obligatory passing nod to Foucault and his presumed achievement of "a radical rethinking of the self and of agency" (10)—a highly debatable claim, as we have already had occasion to note. Various conceptions of ideology get their innings, as does feminist criticism, the latter congratulated for its "relatively respectable position within classics" (15). But the point is that *never* are the assumptions of any of these theoretical positions challenged. Goff's worry about New Historicism, for example, concerns the danger that it might "presuppose a stable point from which to view a complex situation"; she wants to make sure that we "recognize the usefulness of the deconstructive claim that the object of historical inquiry is itself textual" (8), that is, we must beware of slipping back into the discredited yearning for a stable historical past available through a transparent language. But a more serious—and threatening—problem is raised by Felperin in his discussion of what he calls "new contextualism":

> Yet the problem of the language of literature as something distinct from the language of history, which has been neatly sidestepped, makes its embarrassing return the moment we ask how the study of literature can be founded on or explained by history, when what constituted history may be nothing other than literature, since both are "inscriptions" of "ideology." How can fiction be "explained" by reference to what is only another fiction, or the explicator's explanations extricate themselves from the ideological torsions and coercions that produced the fictions he sets out to explain? The concept of ideology, begging as it does the question of its linguistic status as history or fiction (since it seems to be capable of being defined as either or both), introduces a radical circularity into the project of "explanation," a circularity no less self-enclosing than that of the moral formalism and formal moralism that characterized practical criticism.... The moment "history" is recognized as "discourse-specific," as having no location outside language, i.e., as neither past nor present nor even the presence of a past, but as a *myth* of a presence, a *mediation*, it ceases to be a reliable *ground* for literary criticism, let alone for political action, since a mediation can never be a ground but only a problem, an occasion for more discourse.[65]

The problem is more complex, and the stakes of deconstruction's vision of language are higher, than Goff admits. The issue cannot be dismissed with the breezy and banal half-truth that the "object of historical inquiry itself is textual."[66]

But Felperin's level of sophisticated critical analysis is never reached in Goff's self-congratulatory presentation of the various theoretical positions. They are all presented as received truths whose minor quarrels with one another—at the conference, Goff is pleased to report, "fundamental differences were productively aired" (24), and there was a lot of "productive variety and disagreement" (31; note the soothing tone of the therapeutic bureaucracy)—do not challenge either their self-definition against that of the profession's unnamed traditionalists mired in humanistic delusions, or their confident assumption of self-evident validity. Both of these flaws can be found in Peradotto's and Hexter and Selden's collections, and seem to have become a trope in this genre of classical scholarship.

We noted earlier another annoying byproduct of what Frederick Crews calls "theoreticism,"[67] the striking of vaguely leftist political attitudes in an attempt to get a moral leg up on the traditionalists. The motif of the "conservative" classicist in Peradotto, as we saw, suggests certain unpleasant political ideologies the reactionary is too afraid to confront. When Hexter and Selden speak of their collection's "progressive thrust," we know they are talking of more than just theory. Goff, unfortunately, follows this convention as well. At the end of her Introduction, in an attempt to demonstrate that esoteric cogitations over "history" and "tragedy" and "theory" have relevance beyond the comforts of the conference room, she remarks on some newspaper reports of a 1992 production of *Medea, Trojan Women,* and *Electra* in Bucharest:

> Are these reviews a simple celebration of what in Greek tragedy really is human and timeless and can therefore unite disparate cultures? Or is the East's production of Greek tragedy useful to the West as a most compelling proof that the "others" wish to Westernize? These reviews tell us that the post-Communist countries can help us to discover once more the marvels of our Greek heritage. So in this narrative what post-Communist societies teach the West is the superiority of Western products. (33)

We all know the first question hides a sneer about anybody who believes that Greek tragedy can be "timeless" and universal. The second question is simply incoherent. How did Romanians, who live in a Christian country once a Roman province and who speak a Romance language and who were shackled for half a century by a Western political philosophy, suddenly become Eastern and "other"? Eastern European is still European. Those Greek tragedies and their obvious excellence are the Romanians' heritage as much as ours, as meaningful to them as to us. And the answer to the question is yes, they want very badly to "Westernize," if that means acquiring the political freedom, property rights, equal protection under the laws, and material comfort that bourgeois professors take for granted. As they did for the ancient Greeks, the issues of oppression and freedom in those tragedies have a meaning for theatergoers in Bucharest that spoiled and self-loathing Westerners can only imagine.

Needless to say, the combination of unexamined theoretical assumptions and anti-Western political postures will not do much to recommend the study of classical antiquity to either students or the tuition-paying parents and taxpayers. The complex of attitudes Goff advocates serves only the interests of a professional elite consolidating its institutional power. Goff inadvertently lets slip this bias when she recommends that classicists "theorize their practices as fully as possible, not the least if they want to continue to make sense to students who are increasingly habituated to quite demanding relationships with texts" (31). Who possibly could these students be? The few-score aspiring classics Ph.D.'s, who will leave school with their "theorized practice" and, if they are lucky enough to find jobs, discover that they have to learn some way to teach Latin and Plato and tragedy in translation to working-class and minority students? If you pull that patronizing "other" stuff or pretentious jargon on them, they walk— and the administrators start sharpening the knives.

The ultimate problem with this collection, as with the previous two, is not that the essays have nothing valuable to say. The problem is that the self-conscious display of theory never displaces an essentially traditional procedure in which rationally coherent arguments are presented in order to develop an idea the author believes to be true. Michelle Gellrich's "Interpreting Greek Tragedy: History, Theory and the New Philology" is, compared with the previous essays, a nuanced and complex argument that "our habits of critical thinking about tragedy operate in accordance with a binary logic that falsifies the complexities of interpretive choice" (51). She calls for a Derridean analysis that demonstrates "an unravelling of the logic of opposi-tional thinking; the center of the system cannot hold because neither term obeys the principles of identity, exclusion, and complementarity that the order of binary thought assumes" (52). She then uses the Dionysus in the *Bacchae* as an illustration: "He does not so much destroy or confuse distinctions as configure the nondifferentiation out of which such distinctions eventually arise" (53).

I'll buy that—but do we need Derrida's ideas (once more presented without any recognition of the numerous challenges to them or of the stakes much higher than the mere dissolution of binary opposi-tions) to understand this point? Of course not—Euripides' play al-ready has shown us how much of reality beyond (and within) the human eludes the rational mind's categorizing structures. There's always more disorderly nature than culture, and it's an act of hubris to think, like Pentheus, that the latter can control the former—mainly because nature can never be completely excluded from culture, nor passion from the rational soul. And finally, Gellrich herself does not really believe in Derridean epistemic nihilism—her writing is clear and coherent, presenting a fixed meaning by means of a rational argu-ment light years from the wanton signifying and undecidability that Derrida claims characterizes *all* writing and that he demonstrates in his own. Gellrich, quite simply, is a traditionalist in this regard. Thus how seriously can we take Gellrich when she touts deconstruction as providing "a critique of Aristotelian biases that continue to drive our ways of making sense" (55), when her own writing "makes sense" in terms of those same so-called "biases"?

This same by-now-familiar combination of traditional procedure tarted up with occasional references to unexamined poststructuralist writers also characterizes Peter W. Rose's "Historicizing Sophocles's *Ajax*." Rose gives a fairly useful reading of the play on various levels—mythic, rhetorical, and historical. But he does so by ordinary textual explication and historical references to "fifth-century Athenian realities" and their "social and political relations" (69), all presented in a logically coherent argument supported by references to primary and secondary literature. But, of course, this empirical procedure must be "theorized" and given a patina of shiny innovation: "For not only are 'events' texts, but, as Foucault reminds us, 'to say something is itself an event' (1991: 126) and 'the cultural product is also part of the historical fabric' (1991: 129)" (60-61). What revelations! What else can a "cultural product" be if not part of the "historical fabric"? The most hidebound formalist would admit that much. And how can saying something *not* be an "event"? Unless Rose and Foucault are talking in some private code, these are painfully obvious banalities. Or consider the following: "If one is willing to grant that this sort of language is intended to evoke for the Athenian audience a very strong identification with Ajax and his followers, to interpellate them, in Althusser's term, as ideological partisans of Ajax..." (70). We don't need the main clause to see that the phrase with the fancy word "interpellate" and the dropped French name add *nothing* to the sense of the sentence. They are there not to communicate but to strike an attitude. Rose apparently fancies Althusser's "interpellate" because he uses it again, equally without need, on the next page.

Rose's use of deconstructionist interpretation likewise reflects the same dilution—or even misunderstanding—we have encountered in the other collections. Commenting on the third monologue, Rose asserts that "Ajax himself deconstructs through his self-reflective ironies all the overlapping binary oppositions that constructed his former identity: birth versus obscurity, hard versus soft," etc. Rose obviously thinks deconstruction means merely the undermining of binary oppositions rather than the undermining of *all* possible linguistic meaning and logic, including his own. That is why Rose, a mere one sentence later, can say, "In the very process of standing outside his own previously unquestioning adherence to the aristocratic code, Ajax offers a withering critique of its alternative, summed up sarcastically in the virtue of 'safe-think'" (76). Rose is absolutely right—*unless* he really believes in Derridean deconstruction, which tells us that the infinite play of signifiers scored with the traces of lost presence makes "Ajax" and his "critique" an inauthentic simulacrum conjured up out of Rose's nostalgia for a stable presence that can stand apart from and cast the cold eye of analysis on the codes of culture. What "cries out for a deconstructive reading" (76) is Rose's own "logocentric" writing.

Finally, Rose gives us an example of self-righteous political posturing when he attempts like Goff to salvage some political relevance out of his elitist privilege, and thus establish his politically correct credentials and distance his work from that of those reactionary traditionalists:

> But I think we too in our culture need to come to grips with our deep emotional investments in our own John Waynes, Charles Bronsons, Chuck Norrises, and Clint Eastwoods—with figures whose essential brutality, moral obtuseness, and gender-based emotional blockage we are constantly invited to forgive for the little behavioral crumbs evincing their stunted potential for human feeling. And why? Perhaps because we are dimly aware that, as a society, our privileges derive from the genocide of Native Americans, from the crushing of Japan, the devastation of Korea and Vietnam, and—not least—from the systematic brutal repression of the criminal element at home effected for us by our military and detective heroes. (79)

This is sheer sophomoric cant. Let's leave aside for the moment the fact that poststructuralism does not allow any of these statements to mean anything. (Indeed, no self-respecting postmodern critic would betray such a prissy lack of ironic distance from the products of popular culture.) What we have instead are the tired clichés of the academic leftist who has missed the bus of history: the reductive and snobbish psychologizing about the unwashed masses and their heroes, the pompous tone of unearned moral superiority, and an irredeemable stupidity concerning history.

IV.

If we return to the question raised at the start—does theory add anything new and useful to the study of classics?—I would argue that based on these three collections the answer is no. Time after time we have seen critical procedures, indistinguishable from traditional philological practice, repackaged with name-dropping and half-baked references to highly contested philosophical ideas, without any indication that those ideas are the sites of a fierce and complex debate. This duplicitous practice contributes to what Merquior calls "theorrhea": "ambitious 'theory' as a pretext for sloppy thinking and little analysis, fraught with anathemas against modern civilization."[68] Moreover, given the epistemic nihilism at the heart of poststructuralism, this wrapping of empirical procedure in the robes of radical linguistic indecidability can only be characterized as either incoherent or fraudulent—these poststructuralist tight-rope walkers always work with the net of empiricism stretched over their "abyss."

Nor is the spurious political relevance claimed by some theorists likely to convince anyone outside the cells of the elect. For one thing, the various causes these "activists" endorse—gay rights, women's rights, anticolonialism, and so on—laudable as they may be, nonetheless are all untenable by anyone genuinely endorsing poststructuralist social constructionism and linguistic indeterminacy. Those theories necessarily reject some minimum of shared human nature which forms the necessary ground for universal human rights that transcend the particularities of time or place. This contradiction became obvious in the later Foucault, as Ferry and Renault note:

> Under these conditions [of radical historicizing] antihumanism can only take on a particularly radical form, that of hatred for the universal, such as Foucault expresses right up through his last writings: "The search for a moral form acceptable to everyone, in the sense that everyone must submit to it, seems catastrophic to me" [*Les Nouvelles littéraires,* June 28, 1984]. Obviously, we have to wonder how, from this point of view, the significance of a theme such as the rights of man can be saved, a theme Foucault took up militantly in the last years of his life. Similarly, what happens to the values of the "republic" in its etymological sense, as the *res publica,* when, along with the disappearance of communication behind pure relations of force, the very possibility of intersubjectivity and thus of a real "public space" seems to be called into question?[69]

The fact is, to the honest poststructuralist, a phrase like "gay rights" or "human rights" has no meaning. Rather, is it not a mere freezing of the play of signifiers, the inauthentic conjuring of the subject's spurious essence, one wrought by the machinations of a relentless economic and social power-network consolidating and extending its control over a contested field of human identity, a field arbitrarily marked and traversed by the discourses those same networks manipulate?

Second, this political posturing is rank with a hypocrisy that most students can see through in five seconds. These professors are not street activists fighting the establishment. They do not proselytize in the ghetto or on the assembly line. They are all elitists enjoying the financial and institutional privileges that accrue to their profession. As Crews notes, "they are members in good standing of the academic establishment from which they claim to be freeing us.... [T]he benefits they seek are conferred, not upon the huddled masses, but upon themselves, at the expense of others."[70] This contradiction between endorsing a liberationist agenda while aggressively pursuing careerist

ambition has been noted for years—"Blessed are the academic revolutionaries," Russell Kirk wrote in 1978, "for they shall know tenure."[71]
Recently Harold Fromm has been our best analyst of the unholy alliance of poststructuralist politics and careerism:

> [W]hen I look at today's deconstructors of unconscious agency, I
> see consumers, trendies, exploiter-beneficiaries of "capitalism"—in
> sum I see ordinary people no better or worse than you or I, except
> for their pretensions. I certainly do not see St. Francis monks in
> hair shirts renouncing the evils of the "capitalism" on which they
> in fact thrive as they race about to conferences in jet planes, enjoy
> the benefits of computer technology, barter their articles and books
> for upward mobility in the academy, but I do see much to lament in
> the use of stylized moral jeremiads as coin to obtain yet a bigger
> share of the very spoils that are being denounced. I lament this as a
> postmodern betrayal of the clerks, who (to recall Johnson's *Rasselas*)
> talk like angels but live like men.[72]

Given that both the theory and the leftist manifestos are at the service of self-advancement, the politics can be only a mere "symbolic
politics," as Russell Jacoby recently put it, "a replacement for, and
diversion from, the gritty politics of the community and street."[73]
Unlike sloganeering, concrete political activity takes time away from
padding one's *res gestae* and risks alienating the establishment of which
one is a member.

We return, then, to Heath's point that the crisis in the profession
arises not from the challenges of a politically informed theory to a
traditional philology, but from the self-aggrandizing activity of a professional elite, whether traditionalist or theoreticist, conservative or
liberal, of the Right or of the Left. This problem, moreover, must be
understood in the larger context of the long decline of higher education in America. As Robert Nisbet argued twenty-five years ago, the
vast infusions of federal money into the universities and colleges,
coupled with explosive growths in enrollment, set the stage for the
corruption of the university's mission by a bureaucratized careerism

smoothly assimilable to the utilitarian demands of government and industry. The result was what Nisbet calls the "academic capitalist, the professorial entrepreneur" whose intellectual activity—"conspicuous research"—was subordinated to and driven by career advancement.[74] This is the historical context (if I may historicize the historicizers) that explains the theory explosion of the last thirty years. The glut of research—driven by the demands of tenure, promotion, grant acquisition, think tank and institute membership, and professional upward mobility—created an anxiety that little remained to be said about literature: "That question...haunts a critical industry whose reckless growth in the quarter century after World War II has now been succeeded by a painful stagnation; the sense that 'everything has been done' turns to panic as opportunities for appointment and promotion disappear."[75] Crews wrote those words in 1982, just before the oft-decried "Reagan-era greed" ended the stagnation and underwrote the growth of the Theory Industry. For just as it appears the market for humanities Ph.D.'s will dry up, leaving the grandees with fewer graduate students and hence the horrifying prospect of teaching undergraduates, some theory comes along as a new mill in which to grind the old texts, and the whole industry can keep humming along with more books, more articles, more conferences, and more money—at least for a few more years, until the cycle of boom and bust ends in the profession's crash.

If the theoreticized classics represented by these three collections, then, is dominated by this careerist ethos, we already know the sad answer to the second question this essay raised: what do they do to justify the study of classics in a world of fewer academic dollars? The answer is obvious. Nothing. For the antihumanism, the trite antirationalism, the sloppy thinking, the turgid jargonish prose, the political hypocrisy, the relentless self-advancement are all evils of intellect and character a genuine classical education is supposed to free one from. William Arrowsmith years ago made this point about the inconsistency between the classical character and its professional caretakers:

> Our professors and graduate students now compete only for pro-
> fessional plums, ever fatter professorships and fellowships. When it
> comes to their lives, they live as unclassically, as untouched by the
> humanities, as any barbarian. They are, almost all of them, the worst
> possible witnesses to the value of what they profess.[76]

Albert Jay Nock, making the case over sixty years ago for the central role of classics in the curriculum, described the benefits of a classical education as simply "a disciplined [and] an experienced mind" and "the views of life and the demands on life that are appropriate to maturity."[77] These are the very qualities that can liberate us from the mindless consumerism, intellectual vacuity, and mass-produced trivia polluting our public life. Given that disciplined and mature minds are rarer and rarer in this image-besotted, materialistic society, the loss of classics appears even more grievous, its abandonment by its guardians even more reprehensible.

But once the Greeks and Romans are deconstructed by these same guardians into sexist imperialists who oppress various "others" to con-solidate their own power; once their "monuments of unageing intel-lect" are demystified as the epiphenomena of insidious power net-works, no better than the eye-candy on MTV; once the students and parents witness the hypocrisy of elitists preaching a shop worn left-ism from the comfort of the subsidized seminar chapel and confer-ence hotel—once all this is wrought by scholars who themselves em-body not the humane critical consciousness classics can teach, but the worst of this society's philistine values as enshrined in the corpo-rate boardroom and in government bureaucratic fiefdoms, why should anyone spend another dime of public money on classics?

Quite simply, they won't. The classical bureaucracy is heading the way of all complex institutions that make self-perpetuation and advancement their only reason for being. The ever-decreasing number of classicists will continue to dwindle, like Mycenaen palace scribes manipulating an esoteric philological and theoretical syllabary, ignored by the peasants outside the walls until the lupine administrators and trustees, like some economic Sea Peoples, sweep us all away, leaving our works to molder in the libraries, as sterile as ashes and pottery shards. And we will deserve it, for our worst enemy will have been ourselves.

PART III

ELITISTS, CAREERISTS, AND ASSORTED OPPORTUNISTS

CHAPTER 6

ひ

JOHN HEATH

SELF-PROMOTION AND THE "CRISIS" IN CLASSICS

A few years ago I thought I knew why the field of classics was in trouble and so wrote a paper spelling out what I believed was wrong and what could be done to try to fix it. Entitled "Genitives and Genitals: Self-Promotion and the 'Crisis' in Classics," it argued that careerists from both extremes of the ideological spectrum (that is, pedantic philologists and "cutting-edge" theorists) were running a once-noble discipline into the ground. The article that emerged after two years of "insider" therapy and a steady diet of editorial tofu—and with a new and apparently less "hurtful" title—is reprinted here. But the story behind this essay proves its thesis about academic corruption far more incisively than I managed to do in the publication itself.

In January of 1993 I submitted the first version of the paper to *Classical World*, one of the standard journals in classics, published by the Classical Association of the Atlantic States and aimed especially at teachers of Greek and Latin and the problems they face in the classroom. A few weeks after submission, I received a phone call from associate editor Judith Hallett, who was both pleased with and overwhelmed by the piece. While noting that the article contained much of merit, she asked that I remove all "unsubstantiated hearsay" and then resubmit it for consideration. She had a point. In an effort to demonstrate the genuine disdain for teaching that is ubiquitous in graduate programs, I had included accounts of numerous conversations that I had personally witnessed over the years. The associate editor suggested that my argument was weakened by these unverifiable details and that the individuals involved might sue the journal. I understood her discomfort with publishing material that was not verifiable—*CW* would not want the expense of proving that what I said was accurate—and so I quickly agreed to remove these passages or to replace them with published material. I rewrote the article and resubmitted it in March, just a month after our conversation.

Seven months later—things in the academy do not move at a feverish pace—I received a phone call and then a written response from the new editor of *Classical World*, Matthew Santirocco, dean of humanities at New York University. The two self-avowed feminist referees, I was informed, had not liked my few comments (about one page in a twenty-three-page manuscript) on the unreliable link between feminism and populism. One of the readers did in fact recommend publication with substantial rewriting of that one page. For the other referee, however, the situation was intolerable. She complained that the "conservative bias of the paper shows even in the title, which clearly targets female classicists (or feminists) and, perhaps, a few gay men with the word 'genitals.'" It was never made clear exactly how a reference to "genitals" could be a specific criticism of female classicists, or feminists, or gay men, unless the referee believed that only feminists, female scholars, and a few gay men possess or are interested in genitalia. This same reader insisted that "to talk about the 'sirens of deconstruction,'" as I had dared to do, "is overtly sexist." By this reasoning—strange by any definition but especially odd for a teacher of Greek and Latin—all classical allusions are suspicious: a reference to the Lotus Eaters marginalizes vegetarians; the use of the word "cynical" should arouse animal rights activists; no doubt to speak of Aeolian wind is an attempt to humiliate those with intestinal disorders. One can only imagine the fury (oops) that must envelop this referee at every mention of Europe, a continent that is named, *horribile dictu*, after one of Zeus's many mythological rape victims. The reviewer at least made no efforts to disguise her bias: to cite a conservative scholar or journal is evidence enough to dismiss an argument as a "kind of anti-p.c. hysteria that is so frequently found in NAS (National Association of Scholars) publications": "Many of the persons cited by name and the publications (*The American Spectator*) are known to represent conservative ways of thinking about such issues."

To the editors' credit, they did not listen to everything their referees had to say. The associate editor agreed with many of the referees' criticisms—"genitals" had to go, for example, and my comments about academic feminism eradicated—but she was still interested and asked me to "re-write and re-submit the article yet again with the readers' criticisms in mind." Editor Santirocco was even more enthusiastic, writing that he had delayed in responding to me because he "...still wanted to publish [my] article and, in fact, to build an entire issue around the sort of professional questions it raises." My article, then, was seen as valuable in its critique of the existing classics hierarchy and, if purged of its embarrassing across-the-board criticism of careerism, more useful than not to feminists and gender-studies theorists on the barricades in the culture wars. Perhaps my general critique of Left and Right, philologists and theorists, might be valuable if it could be tilted and finessed more against the Right, less against the Left.

Still believing that change could come from within the system (such youthful optimism!), I rewrote the article once more "with the readers' criticisms in mind"—they had not changed my mind about the lack of a necessary connection between feminism and populism, however—and I resubmitted it in November. In January of 1994—*one year after I had first submitted the article*—the associate editor sent me seven single-spaced pages of comments, mostly on my latest one page of comments, and I wrote back to her a few weeks later withdrawing my article from consideration, noting that it would never conform to the editors' ideology. I was beginning to suspect—okay, I'm unusually slow—that *Classical World* was now more interested in protecting certain political agendas than in promulgating diverse ideas. Professor Hallett then called me, however, and insisted that the article was important, that the journal wanted it, and that I should rewrite the article one last time.

I can only say that she was doing her best to like the article and I was still trying to work from within. I rewrote and resubmitted the article yet again a fourth time in March, and in July I was informed by Editor Santirocco that the article had been accepted contingent upon (1) yes, one more rewrite based on two more referees' reports (the same individuals as before) and his own comments; (2) *Classical World* would publish eight responses to the final draft of my argument. By now even I realized I was being set up, but I didn't mind, as long as I got a chance to rebut the respondents without editorial interference. And so in August I resubmitted the article a fifth and final time. I would not have recognized its early incarnation, but I naively believed it might yet make a difference if it engendered discussion about how to address the plight of classical studies.

In May of 1995 I received the eight responses to my article, and a month later I submitted my rebuttal. On the fourth of July the associate editor called, accepting the rebuttal with only one mandatory alteration (one sentence) and four suggested rephrasings. Time was short—the printing deadline was approaching fast—and so she asked me to fax the changes. One of these suggested changes—*nota bene*—involved the wording of one of seven points I made in rebuttal to the reply of Professor Barbara Gold, a fellow feminist and friend of associate editor Hallett. Trained to be sensitive to the political nuances of address, she had nevertheless composed her entire response to me in the second person, complete with an introductory "Dear John" (the first such letter I have received from a professional journal), and asked such questions as, "Who and where are these 'feminists' that you target?"

I had concluded my long discussion of her reply with a short paragraph about this puzzling tone of familiarity in a rather inimical reply, beginning with the following observation: "Finally, and as an aside, I still do not know what to make of Professor

Gold's personal salutation and use of the second person. If I referred to her as 'Barbara' throughout this rebuttal, I am certain she and the language watchdogs of the WCC [Women's Classical Caucus] would cite me for my 'patronizing' tone."

The editors, again for reasons that were never articulated, objected to one word in this entire paragraph—"watchdogs"—and so I changed the phrase from "the language watchdogs" to "other vigilant members" and faxed off the change—along with the other four "suggested" alterations—on July 7. A few days later Editor Santirocco sent me a letter acknowledging acceptance of the rebuttal: "Thank you very much for your fax of 7 July. The 5 changes you have made to your reply will be incorporated. I think the volume will be very interesting and that you have provoked, and will continue to provoke, lively discussion of important issues in our profession. Thank you for working with *CW* on this project."

By all the standards of academic publication, beyond a bit of copy-editing the task was completed. My article had been accepted, eight responses had been solicited, and I had replied. Every word had been read and approved by the editors, referees, and staff as conforming to the standards of the journal and the profession. The next step would simply be correcting the page-proofs, at which point only minor grammatical or typographical changes are acceptable and affordable. Everything had been scrutinized and rewritten, so there would be no surprises. In the first week of September the nine contributors to the volume received all ten articles—my original article, the eight replies, and my rebuttal, for copy-editing. I did not bother to reread the eight replies, but my two articles seemed to be in good shape and I sent the galleys back to the editor, thinking that it was at last finished.

By agreement the eight respondents had not had an opportunity to read my rebuttal to the final drafts of their responses before (or so I thought), and when they did the phones at *CW* started ringing. As Editor Santirocco insisted in a hurried phone call (followed up with a hasty letter), I was accused by several of them of engaging "in flip or mordant humor that many *CW* readers will see as silly or hurtful." One Ivy League respondent objected, apparently to the point of threatening a lawsuit, to my summarizing his reply—quite charitably, I think—as "A Day in the Life of a Harvard Professor." It wasn't the first—and by no means the last—time that I was reminded that academics cannot laugh at themselves.

My reply, which had met with the approval of the editors to the point of requiring the alteration of only a single sentence, suddenly did not "conform to the 'professional' standards of our journal" as Editor Santirocco now insisted. Both he and the associate editor called me, urgently demanding drastic revisions—pressing legal issues had come up. It was obvious, of course, that this had nothing to do with professional or legal standards but everything to do with a lack of scholarly integrity, academic freedom, editorial courage—and plain telling the truth.

And it doesn't speak well for my courage either. In my twenty years in higher education, the only action I truly regret is that I actually listened to them one more time. I don't know to this day why I caved in. True, I was sick of it all, and true, I still hoped that my ideas might start a discussion that could result in change; certainly I had put enough time into it to hate to see it all wasted. By then I was already planning and working on a book that would do what I feared the article would not, especially in its weakened condition, so I did not care as much as I otherwise might have if my argument was once again diluted. But these are poor excuses. Cave in I did, and quickly. As Editor Santirocco later commented in a letter to me, "I enjoyed our telephone conversation today and appreciate your willingness to accommodate your final reply to the sort of discourse customary in a professional journal like *CW*." He sent me another copy of the page-proofs, this time with entire paragraphs crossed out, and asked me to cut out these "offending passages" and fax him the new version in "a day or two." After all, it was supposed to be at the printers! But wait, it gets stranger still.

In reading through the required cuts to the rebuttal, I noticed that one paragraph in the accepted version was no longer even printed in the text. Sometime between July and September the entire paragraph in which the once-offending phrase "language watchdogs" had appeared had been Trotskyized: discarded without comment or notification. So when I sent in what I thought would be the "final" version of the now-gutted rebuttal with all the dozens of requested changes made (save one), I restored the comments on Professor Gold's second-person address. As I wrote to Editor Santirocco, "I restored the last section on Barbara Gold's response which had been edited out without my approval. This paragraph—on Gold's use of the second person—now becomes even more important than before, since this entire re-write is based on 'professional norms.'"

This last wimpily defiant touch was cut off at the pass, of course. The editor called a few days later to thank me for accepting the changes, and he informed me that the paragraph could not be reinserted. When I asked him why, he said it was no longer relevant, since Professor Gold's reply had been altered, rewritten *after* my rebuttal had been accepted. And sure enough, when I looked back at the page proofs of the entire journal, Gold's article now had no "Dear John," no second-person address anywhere! The text had been thoroughly changed—even an original direct imperative to me ("Return now to my first paragraph") was altered with the hokey last-minute addition of a novelistically inspired vocative "Dear reader, return now to my first paragraph." In other words, the rules of the forum were now suddenly changed: the eight classicists who responded to my article (which could not be altered in lieu of their comments) had changed their responses in light of my rebuttal. Wrestling with the elusive logic of radical feminism is tricky enough without the editors' allowing the respondent to rewrite her argument and then requiring that you rewrite your own.

The editors were clearly embarrassed when caught at this duplicity and did not want to talk about it. But associate editor Hallett, angered for other reasons, has recently summoned up the courage to overcome her unusual reticence. Over the past few years she has repeatedly and publicly suggested that the first versions of "Genitives and Genitals," as well as my eventual rebuttal, were libelous and—I kid you not—that I "refused" to change anything!

For example, in defending her recent bizarre behavior (see the Epilogue), she wrote on the Internet that "Heath refused when asked, to remove personal attacks on individuals from these texts, and was backed by his collaborator Hanson. Editors other than myself, in consultation with legal counsel, found a number of these statements actionable, and insisted that they be changed" (e-mail). Perhaps she is just confused—I had no "collaborator" on the project at all. And could I (alas) have been any more compliant, in fact rewriting the article four times after the initial submission, always after lengthy and what I would term friendly (if occasionally heated) discussions with the associate editor herself? I also accepted the minor changes and then completely rewrote the rebuttal on short notice long after it had been accepted.

So, after all that, here is the "controversial" article, along with my rebuttal to the eight replies solicited by the editors. After its Orwellian metamorphosis, it is now tame and housebroken, but it still tells the truth (if not all of it). I like it because its two-year gestation reminds me of my younger, more innocent self (even if I cringe at how often I bent over backwards for the editors).

It is tribute to the system, a system in which editors with political agendas send articles to be refereed to their ideological allies (See Hanson's "Too Much Ego in Your Cosmos," chapter 4 in this volume), allow friends to rewrite their shoddy arguments in advance of criticism that is then preemptively edited, cave in to their hired thugs when the intended victim draws a little blood, and then brazenly lie about the entire process in an attempt to claim some bizarre sort of victim status. The saddest thing is that I think somewhere in the editors' hearts they really did at one point want to make a difference, that they knew classics was in trouble and thought they could contribute to the debate over the future of the field by making my article the focal point of the discussion. But ultimately they felt that protecting their own ideological alliances was more important than performing their professional duties of maintaining and encouraging a free marketplace of ideas. It is perhaps foolish in this era of the pursuit of "whatever-it-takes" success to look for strength of character in higher academics. Should classicists really be expected to struggle harder against human frailty just because we spend our lives studying Achilles, Antigone,

Socrates, and Jesus? Well, in a word—yes. Do we expect any less of our students?

༄

"Beleaguered Classicists Debate Strategies for Survival: Proponents of new theoretical approaches challenge traditional philological model."

—title and subtitle of article by Peter Monaghan,
Chronicle of Higher Education, January 6, 1993

IN 1989 a pointed question of some relevance to most classicists was posed in the now familiar volume edited by Phyllis Culham and Lowell Edmunds, *Classics: A Discipline and Profession in Crisis?*[1] The essays for the most part were in general agreement that the profession was at a crucial juncture which in fact might fairly be called a crisis.[2] The contributions fall into three broad groups (although the book is divided into four somewhat misleading sections): (1) historical background and state of various subdisciplines and organizations which, combined with a little study of demographics, present the "facts" of the "crisis"; (2) suggestions that the problems are primarily structural, the result of an increasingly sharply divided "two-tier" system of institutions, elite researchers at graduate institutions versus the rest;[3] (3) arguments that the profession is weighed down by an old, philology-laden hierarchy which has been too slow and self-protective to incorporate new, theory-driven (feminist, literary, anthropological, etc.) approaches which might invigorate the discipline. Some essayists concentrate on one of these arguments; some bring in two or even all three. Many of the articles also offer concrete suggestions for improvement, brief outlines for "survival."

What has happened in the five years since the publication of this collection is revealing and disheartening. One inevitable response has been the insistence that the term "crisis" is inappropriate, since the difficulties confronting the profession should instead be seen as "challenges we are facing [which] are exciting, rewarding, and can be met."[4] As comforting as this view may be, the public discussion and concern about the future of classics could not be so easily swept aside, and the debate has now taken an interesting turn. The concerns of the progressive, nontraditional third group listed above, and the responses of its philological targets, have come to dominate the public forum (as evidenced in the story in the *Chronicle* cited above).[5] The voices of the second group, which draw attention to issues of elitism, teaching versus scholarship, and careerism versus professional responsibility, have been largely ignored or forgotten. And the reason for this is not hard to discern. The ideological dispute is being advanced by elites on *both* sides, Left and Right, for the opportunity to continue the very class system challenged by the second group.

My argument is that the discussion of the two-tier system needs to be exhumed and the issues examined from a slightly different perspective. The debate on the future of classics must be focused more sharply on what it is to be a "successful" classicist. The present theory/philology wrangling among the elites must cease to dominate the discussion. As long as what I would call working classicists—the vast majority in the profession—allow a small minority of *optimates* to direct this debate, we are doomed. Finally, I append a few suggestions—some practical, some attitudinal—for ameliorating the present "crisis."[6]

I. Left-Right, Top-Bottom

The battle for the "survival" of our profession has been framed with increasing stridency in such a way as to highlight an ideological rift among classicists. We are led by some of our colleagues to believe that the salvation of the discipline depends completely upon which one of these two supposedly diametrically opposed visions comes out victorious. The participants in this struggle give themselves, and are given, various names (the most colorful of which I shall not include), but the antithesis is *always* set in a horizontal plane with the Left standing for "new" and the Right standing for "old." Other familiar terms for this schism are theoretical approaches versus the philological model, progressives versus reactionaries, deconstructionists versus positivists, liberals versus conservatives, multiculturalists versus preservers of Western culture, feminists versus male traditionalists. The sheer noise and authority of extremists on both sides of this apparent polarity continue to mask the *real* division in classics, that between top and bottom, a vertical rather than horizontal divide. True, the Left-Right dichotomy is important. It *does* and will and should affect all of us. It is not, however, a Manichean duel for survival, but rather a skirmish of elitists for the advantages of elitism. It has far less to do with Aristophanes' *Clouds* than with Plato's Thrasymachus. The pampered doctors are arguing over the complexion of a patient dying from their own malpractice. Let the debate continue among the few. For the present it has added complications to an already serious problem, but in the long run it will *not* determine the success or future of *most* classics programs. The significant *vertical* gap between classicists has always been present in academia, but it is growing at an alarming pace, and classics—especially classics—can no longer afford it.

Jeffrey Henderson's pointed essay in *Crisis* covers most of the important issues concerning the division in the profession, but there is a conflation of polarities in his account: "An ideal of careerism based on publication and hostile to academic citizenship now tends to divide the most prominent classicists (mostly graduate faculty) from the rest of the profession and to turn teaching and scholarship into separate worlds: publishing stars on the one side and on the other special interest groups who feel neglected, unfairly deprived of professional rewards, or excluded altogether."[7] I would argue that Henderson actually presents two very different divisions, which should not be confused. The first, careerism versus teaching, clearly is a vertical gap. Nearly all the resources associated with "prestige" (see below under "teaching") are absorbed by the few at the "top." The second division, publishing stars versus special interest groups, may traditionally have been a vertical division, but it is now primarily an ideological issue in which the two sides have far more in common than they would want to admit. Over the past few years some of the special interest groups have pushed their program with such vociferousness that they have succeeded in creating their own exclusionary hierarchy. This new "revisionist" elite can now boast of its control of journals, conferences, APA panels, hiring preferences, even publicly funded summer seminars for college teachers. So, the division as it now dominates the headlines is Left versus Right, but the real dichotomy in the profession is between on the one hand the elites, *both* Left and Right, whose primary concern is with self-promotion (grounded in ideological posturing and research "agendas"), and on the other the vast majority of classicists whose careers depend upon quality teaching, successful program development, institutional service, and research. Most classicists are dedicated, overworked teachers at small nonelite private colleges and large state universities who spend their time teaching, grading papers and exams, designing new courses, digging up students, giving honest advice to potential majors, chairing committees, and attempting to find a bit of time to think, write, and (*dis volentibus*) get to a reasonable library to do their research.

It is no coincidence, therefore, that the Left-Right debate is being directed and dominated by the grandees—it is a luxury most classicists cannot afford. What is needed is a reevaluation, a reordering of priorities. What is it that links most classicists together? What is it that most classicists do to make classics work in their own programs? How can we help one another to improve, to survive, to grow? It is the values, practices, and energy of *these* classicists, "the rest of the profession," upon which the future of classics depends. I am encouraging *these* classicists—the foundation of the classics pyramid—to take over and redirect the debate and not to leave it to a few elites, who are far removed from and indeed mostly unfamiliar with the real challenges which face our discipline, to determine the survival of the discipline. No matter what approach we take in individual classes on the ancient world, one professional ethos alone will save classics: good teaching, intelligent curriculum development, broad scholarship, and solid campus citizenship. That age-old creed, dismissed by the academic aristocracy at both extremes, is the only agenda that will bring students into the classes, that will bring students into programs and enable them to grow, that will satisfy administrators and preserve departments—and that ultimately will provide a future for both classics and classicists.

II. Teaching

Graduate programs may claim to teach students to teach, and some programs seem honestly to care about it, but in fact graduate students are more often presented with a model which tells them that teaching is at best a necessary evil and more likely a waste of valuable time. The message is presented in a thousand subtle and not-so-subtle ways, but nowhere else is it more clear than in the graduate departments' own promotional material, usually distributed in the shape of "The Newsletter of the Department of Classics." An introductory note, "A Message from the Chair," discusses the tremendous success the department had the past year in recruiting faculty, graduate students, and undergraduate majors despite university-wide budget cuts. Occasionally we are even informed that undergraduate enrollments are "holding steady" in these challenging times. The true values of the department, however, can be readily traced in the following paragraphs on "Faculty Activities." Here we read only of papers presented, articles published, speaking invitations accepted, grants pursued, conferences attended, trips taken abroad. Someone less familiar with the conventions would be surprised to learn that the faculty had taught any undergraduate (or even graduate) courses at all. They probably did teach a few classes, and some may even have done a good job, but there are no laurels awaiting such a revelation.

What is it that we tell our future faculty makes a successful classicist, and how well prepared are these students for the realities most will face when they do *not* "succeed" in making it "up" to a Ph.D.-granting institution?[8] Henderson summarizes the behavior of graduate faculty and the marks of success: "high salary, frequent leaves, grants, lectureships, conferences, travel, mobility, celebrity, the power to make or break careers. Anything else is ignored except when it might interfere with publication: then it must be evaded."[9] The common prize, then, is release time from students, particularly undergraduate students, as well as from the duties of responsible academic citizenship. This is particularly startling when one compares the regular teaching loads at elite and at nonelite institutions. The few are "burdened" by three or four courses a year, occasionally five, sometimes only two, while the many teach three, four, or five courses each semester![10] And small programs have no room for release time, no funds for replacements, no graduate students to do the "dirty work."

Most teaching by graduate professors is of two kinds: small graduate seminars on their narrow fields of expertise, and large lecture courses. In the first case, this is primarily an extension of research, necessary for the training of future classicists but, by definition, not much of a stretch for the teacher. At its worst, it degenerates into research on the instructor's next book performed gratis by the graduate students. And the second type of teaching involves walking into lecture halls, presenting a lecture, and leaving it up to graduate students in smaller discussion sections to do the explaining, the guiding, the challenging, the caring, and all of the grading. Done correctly, with great attention paid to the training of teaching assistants, running a large lecture course can be hard and important work, but this, unfortunately, is not the usual experience. What is the professor's attitude toward his or her assignment? Does he or she love to teach this class, and are the graduate students required to develop their own abilities and enthusiasm? If not, will this hurt the student's chances of getting a good recommendation? Henderson notes that members of "research" faculties who willingly make time for teaching are deemed untenurable or deadwood.[11] How many of the senior faculty at graduate institutions teach any of, much less the entire, beginning language sequence? And so are we to expect our young faculty trained in this miasmatic atmosphere to be excited by the opportunity to build up enrollments in their own Latin and Greek courses? Are we to be surprised at their dismay about the heavy load of courses in translation awaiting them in their first job? Graduate students quickly learn from watching their "models" that teaching courses with enrollments of twenty to fifty, leading discussions, grading papers, setting exams, holding extended office hours—that is, actually taking charge and caring about a student's progress—are activities which are of little value and bring no repute. These are plebeian concerns from which they should hope to graduate. Yet most classicists will spend their entire careers in exactly this fashion.

The battle for the soul of our profession is waged at the APA panels and elections, in special interest newsletters, and for positions at elitist institutions, but the only place that ultimately counts is the classroom. Both extremes, Left and Right, would prefer not to muddy their shoes in that infertile field. Quality undergraduate instruction instead is highly suspect, probably a sign of the inability to do something more important. A teaching award is a professional liability, the academic equivalent of the blind date's "great personality."[12]

Again, the difference here is not Left versus Right, but up versus down. The "lower classes" of the field—that is, most classicists—are almost by definition those who are concerned with the quality of teaching. And it is simply *not* true, as often seems to be implied, that the philological extremists are the only ones to think teaching undergraduate courses in translation and elementary languages beneath them; some on the elitist Left are equally disdainful. It is just that the philologists are more ready to acknowledge openly their impatience with undergraduate teaching. Note, for example, the implications of William M. Calder's approving remarks ("he was one of three Harvard teachers who made me a scholar") on A. D. Nock's teaching: "Although his lectures were hilarious, teaching seemed a pause from the more important. He lectured on Tuesday and Thursday and canceled all Saturday classes. His office hours were from 12 to 12:05 on Saturdays in the Widener Stacks, which undergraduates were forbidden to enter. He stated in his first lecture: 'My telephone is for the use of my superiors, my colleagues, and my few friends.'" To this day, we are assured, Professor Calder is "startled" by calls from students.[13]

How far have we come from a great American (though foreign born and educated) teacher-scholar in our field, Gilbert Highet, about whom the editor of his papers says,

> To students and his colleagues he gave constant personal attention, whatever the time and whatever their needs. He asked his "pupils" to visit his office, where they could talk "eyeball to eyeball," and went out of his way to help those who worked hard and with integrity. After every final examination he sent his students a typed, mimeographed letter in which he analyzed the results and provided valuable suggestions. He urged his graduate students to call him at any time, at school or at home, and set for them the same rigorous pace that he set for himself.[14]

The answer to the challenges ahead lies in hard work, not in methodology. Feminist scholars, for example, often claim to represent a more egalitarian and communitarian ethos which embraces undergraduate teaching.[15] This is a refreshing and welcome self-

representation, openly acknowledging the importance of the classroom in its agenda. To be sure, feminist scholarship over the past
twenty years has made important contributions by bringing previously neglected material into the spotlight. Many (most?) classics
programs offer courses on women in antiquity; more important,
more and more literature, history, and culture courses have come to
consider the study of all "outsiders"—women, slaves, barbarians,
blacks, children, and so on—as essential to understanding the "new"
ancient world. In this sense, feminist scholars can certainly demonstrate that their *scholarship* has embraced a wider and more diverse
approach to the ancient world. On the other hand, it is not obvious
that the *professional* or *personal* ethos of feminist scholars is necessarily more egalitarian or inclusive or dedicated to undergraduate teaching. That women are dramatically underrepresented in Ph.D. programs and therefore often "relegated" to undergraduate teaching
cannot be denied. This imbalance needs to be redressed, but it does
not have the bearing on the issue at hand that is sometimes claimed.
Of course women should be equally represented at Ph.D.-granting
institutions, but this has little to do either with critical approaches
to the ancient world or with a redirection of the discipline. Feminism
is no more monolithic than any other "ism," incorporating such
(often conflicting) variations as liberal, Marxist, radical, socialist,
and ecofeminism, to name a few.[16] Indeed, some strands of feminism
are distinctly separatist rather than inclusive. What evidence is there
that feminists are more dedicated to teaching than others? What
evidence is there that feminists or feminist scholars—the distinction
may be important[17]—are more communitarian than other groups?
Feminism certainly welcomes some individuals who feel alienated
from the philological Right or excluded from the traditional sources
of influence, but does it reach out to those who do not share its
particular political ideology (whichever one of the feminisms is under discussion)? Without such a demonstration, there is every reason

to believe that this ideology may provide yet another vehicle for self-promotion and careerism.

No methodology, no ideology can claim to embrace a middle-class work ethic *except* a middle-class work ethic. Indeed, several Ph.D. programs are already heavily influenced by the Left, either de jure or de facto, with no reduced hostility toward the classroom. My thesis is not that the wrong *kind* of exclusionist agenda is leading us astray but that the inculcation of elitism in general is killing the field. A more egalitarian ethos based equally on scholarship, teaching, and service—that is, based on professional deportment rather than on critical methodology—must be developed, encouraged, and rewarded.[18]

The fact is that an African-American woman teaching four classes a term at a state college may have more in common with a white male similarly teaching four classes a term at a liberal arts college than she has with *any* woman or male African-American at an elitist university. The gap is huge—"teachers" and "researchers" are divided during their first years of graduate school—and few ladders are available.[19] Karl Galinsky, in a 1991 article on the state of classics, cites as an example of the "mobility" within the profession the fact that "Princeton recently hired an ancient historian who previously taught at Montana State."[20] This is certainly the story of a bright young classicist's climb up the professional ladder, but it says little about the health of the profession. More significant would be the answers to such questions as the following: How strong were the Greek and Latin language and ancient history courses at Montana State? How many new majors were attracted? How many new positions were created? How many courses were taught, how often, to how many students? For these are the real, the only signs of "success"—survival—for most classics programs. These are the questions deans ask. Galinsky tips his hand here. After arguing that the "two-tier" system and "elitism" are not issues which need to be addressed, he finishes his discussion of "mobility" by claiming that "there is plenty of room at the top these days." The "top" according to whom, by what standards? In short, what does he mean by "top"? We all know the answer, of course, because the elitism is an accepted fact of academics.[21] Teaching simply does not count. Galinsky argues that we need not be worried about competition with multiculturalism, because "in the curricular free-market...classics can do very well indeed."[22] Of course it can, but only if we have well-trained, excited, and exciting teachers who have a set of values and priorities very different from that of their graduate faculty mentors. It is perhaps revealing that Galinsky nowhere mentions quality teaching as an area of concern or improvement. He no doubt assumes this will exist (he recognizes its importance in an earlier essay),[23] but classics can no longer make this assumption and hope to survive. The truth is that it will make little difference what we emphasize in our classes if there are no students in the classroom because the next generation of classicists either resents teaching or cannot teach. Both extremes are deadly. Morphology without ideas, theory without texts—these are useless in the classroom. The narrow focus by a few elitists is leading us away from more pressing concerns; and it simply ignores the substantive daily struggles by most classicists to make the profession move ahead.

III. RESEARCH

Even those who agree with some of what I have suggested in the previous paragraphs surely will have been shouting for some time now that this system serves a purpose—it rewards those who have new, "big" ideas with the time and resources to research and write. Of course research is the essential element in any field's progress, and who would not agree that every classicist must engage in original contemplation and writing? But it is the increasing *separation* of the two activities, the increased concentration of resources (available time and money) in specialized research on both traditional and revisionist extremes, and the effect this is having on many classics faculty (burnout) and graduate students (skewed expectations and values) that are so damaging.

This traditional view that our resources and authority should be placed almost entirely in the hands of those who do the most specialized research is loaded with serious problems in these days of budget cuts. First of all, this view is at least partially based on the general academic paradigm of grant writing. In other fields, particularly but not only the natural sciences, many grants of many hundreds of thousands of dollars are obtained in order to help fund entire programs (and in some cases divisions). This type of grant is extremely unusual in the humanities. Our grants, instead, are often trophies for the individual so he or she can *take time off from teaching* to do more research. It is a never-stopping carousel for those few who are invited to hop on. The results are quite destructive. If the same people continually absorb the available resources, using each award as a prerequisite for the next, how will the field ever get fresh ideas? The same people—elitists on both sides—obtain grant after grant and invite themselves and their friends to conferences and lectures. Camille Paglia and David Lodge have had their fun with this familiar scheme, but such public ridicule has done little to arrest this behavior, and so the situation grows worse.

One of the recent books, for example, from a leading member of the "progressives" has six chapters, five of which were published before. A closer reading of the footnotes reveals that there is nothing really new in this "book." The first chapter was in fact published three times prior—this is its fourth appearance in print, recycled under three different titles. It was given as a lecture thirteen times and requires expressions of gratitude to twenty-three people. Of the remaining five chapters, only one is unavailable in any other form, while the other four have been published previously in a total of *eight different places*. Incredibly, one of the three places in which the third essay had previously appeared was *Crisis* itself![24] This is a little like asking Julius Caesar to analyze the "crisis" of the Republic. Thirty-seven more individuals are thanked for comments on ten different lectures/panels. Two Mellon Fellowships were needed for the writing of the papers/panels/lectures/book.

On the other side, a book by a Harvard professor presents us with seven chapters, only two of which are new. What were the resources that went into these articles-turned-book? In addition to the acknowledgement of an NEH (National Endowment for the Humanities), a Guggenheim, and a Fulbright grant, thanks are expressed to the American Academy in Rome, the American School of Classical Studies in Athens, the Seeger Foundation, and the Hellenic Studies Committee of Princeton University.[25] How much capital and time are needed for these publications? And does the investment of our profession, in these difficult times, justify the return to us all?

The greatest irony of all is found in this trickle-down theory of academic progress. The theory sounds distressingly familiar: if you give those at the top enough, some good will come to those below. Now, trickle-down does not work, because, as Thucydides knew, human beings are, after all, human beings (and here my own ideology is showing). If you give those at the "top" most of the resources, they do not share them but simply use them to go back to the trough for more. The middle class is slowly squeezed until there is only a small group at the top and a lot of people working very hard for less and less down below. It does not take a genius to see through, or take advantage of, the disparities of this system. If you feed the birds in the tree enough, they are certainly going to fatten up nicely, and something is bound to trickle down, but how many of us really want to walk under that tree? This is largely a phenomenon of the 1980s and early 1990s, so the pungent irony here is that many academics—particularly those on the Left—deplored Reaganomics for the past twelve years just as they were increasingly adopting Reagademics as a handbook for their own careers: everything now is to be deconstructed except resumés.[26]

In an endless cycle those who have the most time to publish are those with the smallest teaching loads, and who in turn teach their own books in small seminars. In other words, fellowships, grants, and the concomitant course release time are generally awarded to those very people who least need them! Again the questions arise: release time from what? and for what? Our present system might self-destruct, but it would at least be justified if all this resulted in exciting advances which could trickle down to the rest of the profession and convince the general reading public of the power of our ideas. But the extremes on both sides—Left and Right, progressive and traditional—seem to produce more and more *abstruse* research, obscure in topic, method, and language, which is not only esoteric and thus primarily useless to most other scholarly investigation but nearly always valueless for the classroom.

Here I am not passing judgment on either body of scholarship, but merely repeating the stereotyped charges each side directs at the other. The reality is that both traditional philology and contemporary theory do have a place in the spectrum of classics, but to suggest that either should be *the* direction in classics is absurd. Neither approach, in fact, will "save" classics. Either extreme, left to its own, will simply continue to erase the discipline and so destroy us. The acolytes of each school usually teach at elite institutions where the students are brighter than most and are, in effect, self-taught. In contrast, most other classicists have to uncover ways of making the ancient world breathe in some meaningful fashion for students of only average ability. They cannot risk burying it in either linguistic or theoretical cant and then trust that the students will be bright enough to mimic the performance. And here, I think, interestingly enough, is what most closely binds the two camps, progressive and traditional alike, in their elitism. Both extremes appear to disdain the average student—and the entire middle class, for that matter. Yet those students, who were so ignored by Reaganomics and Reagademics the last decade, constitute the vast majority of students in our colleges and universities.

Finally, there is no more deadly label for a piece of scholarship than "popularization." This was not always true in our profession, but to write something now that might appeal to an audience larger than one's friends and colleagues is anathema. Here I do not mean coffee table books, but real work with original theses on broad topics which are accessible and of interest to the "average" intelligent human being. This effort should be viewed as the pinnacle of scholarly accomplishment, to take a new view on the ancient world and make it seem important not just to a few hundred (dozen?) classicists but to the reading public in general. Many other fields have been "popularized" by leading scholars. Faculty in history, for example, often measure their success not just by professional reviews but by the number of books sold, by book club selections, or even by the number of weeks on a best-seller list.[27] Are we really conceding that classics has nothing to offer the average reader? If so, then the field *should* be abandoned and not rescued.

This prejudice against big ideas and jargon-free writing may seem most obvious when applied to the philological side of the debate, and indeed here must be placed much of the blame for the initial collapse of classics on the college level in the middle of this century. The current theorists, however, are also self-contentedly obscure. What are we to make of the following celebration of "methodologically challenging" (a circumlocution of some schools on the Left for "bad") writing in a section of a book proudly entitled "*lectio difficilior*"?

> The ideal of a transparent, tempered and accommodated prose, which still predominates in academic circles, goes back to a moment in neoclassical aesthetics when the middle or conversational style of the canonical *genera dicendi* becomes the approved mode of

expression for the society and values of the newly empowered middle class: there might be differences of background or profession within the bourgeoisie, but there would be a common language, a vernacular of culture and intellectual pursuits. This ideal of an urbane and purified language of criticism, in which anything "foreign," "barbarous," "archaic," or "technical" is systematically eschewed, betrays not only the nostalgia for a natural idiom, but the project to remake the language of the modern nation-state in its image.[28]

Here, in marvelously solipsistic cant, one finds clear, precise, and comprehensible prose jettisoned into that all-too-fathomable deep of the imperialistic "bourgeoisie."[29] Teachers and scholars who attempt to communicate their ideas and share their excitement about the classical world are no longer the backbone of our profession—they have become the "methodologically challenged." Again, how far we have come from a Gilbert Highet, whose nearly twenty books and hundreds of articles include textual emendations (for the philologists), the translation of Otto Kiefer's *Sexual Life in Ancient Rome* (for those in gender studies), a textbook in beginning Latin and two books on teaching (for all classicists and academics), and readable scholarly books for both classicists and the general public. Classics desperately needs to find ways to reach a larger, more diverse (that is, less elite) audience. Soon.

IV. Suggestions

The current ideological debate will continue to grab the few headlines set aside for classics for the immediate future, and it will help to shape the curriculum.[30] Common sense will prevail here as in the past, I trust. Relevant approaches will become a natural part of the field, less productive ideologies will disappear. I have already noted the contributions of feminist scholarship in this light, and much of the anthropologically influenced work on ancient religion can be profitably transferred to the classroom. Structuralist interpretations of classical literature, on the other hand, seem to have outlived their usefulness, and the sirens of deconstruction are finding it increasingly difficult to convince the world that the corpses on their rocks are merely cultural constructs.[31] Philology will always remain at the heart of the profession—many progressives acknowledge this, while insisting that different questions be asked of the texts.[32] But despite sanguine protestations to the contrary by insulated magnificos, classics programs *are* under attack by number-crunching deans, Western culture-bashing provosts, and fund-seeking presidents. Programs at "top" liberal arts schools are fighting increasingly difficult battles to replace retiring faculty. Less established programs are simply losing positions. Entire award-winning state university programs have been threatened with extinction. How many institutions still fully fund all levels of both Greek and Latin? Perhaps many major Ph.D.-granting institutions have not yet felt the pinch (although my own alma mater has lost at least two positions in the past decade and may be about to lose more), but if classics is to survive, classicists cannot wait for the damage to work its way up. It is only common sense to spend more time on the strained foundations than on the wood rot in the attic.

The general thrust of the following suggestions is that those activities which promote the study of the ancient world should be encouraged and those individuals who encourage the study of the ancient world should be promoted. Good teaching; broad, original, and approachable research; aggressive curriculum development; and more equitably shared resources are the goals. The APA should reflect its constituency, which means that members of undergraduate classics programs and nonelitist graduate programs should be the dominant force. Change must take place from within and below.[33] The new "top" should be the familiar but overwhelmed teacher-scholar, and resources should be directed to support this ideal. Narrow researchers on both sides of the ideological debate should be encouraged to retire to the library, where they can do everyone the most good. *I do not pretend that these recommendations will be implemented or that, even if they were to be, the "crisis" would be eliminated or the "challenges" met.* My hope is to redirect the discussion, perhaps to *begin* a slight shift in approach and attitude. As Stephanie Quinn Katz observed about a slightly different polarity, "In practice the resolution will be long, difficult and uneven. Intellectually, the resolution requires nothing more than a shift in our habit of mind and discourse, a shift from rigid duality to flexible dialectic."[34]

1. Graduate Education

Several graduate programs already have some of these policies in place (how much do graduate programs share their ideas about curriculum?).[35] Graduate students must have it impressed upon them that throughout their careers they will probably spend more time preparing for class, teaching in the classroom, and grading than doing *any* other activity. In other words, the importance of quality undergraduate teaching must be stressed, both directly and indirectly. Graduate faculty should teach more beginning language courses and teach them the entire year. They should be actively engaged in discussions concerning the undergraduate curriculum. In many graduate departments there is something like an "Undergraduate Committee" comprising untenured (and thus inexperienced) faculty who are charged with the unpleasant duty of dealing with this aspect of the program. Graduate students should be closely supervised in their teaching and given constant feedback, and this should be an expected and evaluated part of the graduate faculty's responsibilities. Some dissertation scholarships, usually reserved for students attempting to follow in the footsteps of powerful members of the research faculty, should be set aside for top teaching students. This way students can see that quality teaching and research are not only not antithetical (as viewed from the "top") but in fact inseparable (as viewed by the "rest").[36] Since graduate institutions do have oppressive publication requirements, and also have a supply of cheap labor in need of teaching practice, course release ought to be targeted (awarded) to graduate faculty who devote time and energy to teaching and curriculum development. Now it often seems that the self-promoting publishers get most of the release time.

Graduate schools need to hire the best scholars available, of course, but there is a point of diminishing returns. If the scholar cannot teach, or will not teach, or is rarely available to teach, his or her value to the institution is primarily cosmetic. The department looks good on paper, but what kind of education are the students really receiving? (And as regards graduate students who have come to that particular institution because of the "scholars in residence," the support of such evanescent faculty borders on fraudulent advertising.) A better balance would be struck if graduate programs considered hiring an occasional teacher-scholar, that is, someone (of *either* gender) with a good publication record (in *any* classical field) and an excellent record of teaching instead of someone with a very good publication record and "potential" for more. Graduate students would then have another, in all probability more appropriate model for their own careers. Along these lines, Lewis Sussman's idea about an exchange program between graduate faculty and teacher-scholars at nongraduate institutions is a good one.[37] Sussman points out the benefits to faculty from both sorts of institutions and the possibility of closing some of the gap between the two tiers, but graduate students might also benefit greatly from this exchange. Imagine their surprise when they discover that a published undergraduate teacher can conduct a graduate seminar.[38]

2. Professional Deportment

The following suggestions run directly counter to the codes of the elitist cartel, but our profession can only do so much for so few.

Individual faculty members should be *discouraged* (*horribile dictu*) from taking repeated research grants and fellowships. Resumés with repeated course release should weigh *against* applicants. Faculty leave disrupts both the undergraduate and the graduate curriculum. (One local Ph.D.-granting institution has had at least five members of its department—nearly half—on leave in one year. Graduate students were teaching graduate courses as well as the usual undergraduate language classes.) Graduate students quickly learn that a faculty leave is a positive factor in career advancement, no matter how detrimental it may be to the program. Release time should be the exception, not the rule, a break from the heavy daily responsibilities of teaching *and* research. Similarly, faculty should be held accountable for their courses and not be allowed excessive leave to attend conferences, lectures, and so on. In fact, many undergraduate institutions have strict rules and limited funds which control such absences. Apply this across the board to all classics programs.

True, this is a problem endemic to academics, but classicists, now in the most danger, must take the lead as reformers of the entire university. Graduate students should be given the impression that teaching and research are the important determinants of a career, not "networking." Graduate students should at least for a few years of their academic lives be allowed to live with the belief that the classroom and the library are the crucial *fora* for a classicist, not a conference. Graduate students, terrified of not getting a job, are forced with increasing urgency to take sides. They are inculcated in the elitist model, but there is another, far more significant division in their field which they will have to face. Conferences—the sharing of ideas—should serve to break down the vertical division in the profession, not as retreats for members of one ideological extreme or the other. At their best, conferences can provide crucial opportunities, especially for geographically isolated classicists, to keep in touch with their fields and their colleagues, but they should not be viewed as substitutes for teaching and refereed publication.

Finally, editors should try to publish original material and limit the retreads by well-known classicists (which are included, no doubt, in the hopes of increasing the prestige of the editors' publications). Young untenured Ph.D.'s must publish bits of their (soon to be a book) dissertation, unfortunately, in order to become established and eventually be granted tenure, but there is no such excuse for established scholars. In a field where everyone can agree that more good research is needed, valuable space and trees are being devoted to too many reprints of old material.

3. Curriculum Development

Of course "good teaching" alone will not make classics thrive.[39] The best teachers in the world cannot justify a classics program to a dean if their offerings attract only three students because of the remoteness, obscurity, or narrowness of the topic. This is where one would have hoped that the "progressives" would be of some help. In fact, as I have suggested above, the recent ideological battle has not been on behalf of the community, but for the individual proselytizer. This self-promotion requires only a soapbox at the edge of the park from which one can shout out a coded message to a personal coterie invited to cheer the performance. As W. R. Connor has pointed out, there are several inherent reasons why this adversarial model has not produced a successful new alternative: it feeds on hyperbole at the expense of accuracy, it fails to provide an adequate rationale and sense of purpose for those who profess the classics, and it attracts those who are trying primarily to advance political or social causes. "If some classicists trivialize or devalue their material, no wonder the public is confused and easily misled."[40] How are we to hope for public support of *any* educational mission when the few headlines concerning classics tell the world only of two extreme responses to

the undeniable richness of the ancient world? Classics, already vulnerable, cannot survive the kind of public contempt hurled at the
MLA each year for its absurdly extremist convention.[41] Throughout
the country teacher-scholars are successfully teaching the classics in
a wide variety of ways, some with more traditional goals and methodologies, some with a mixture of old and new. These *pragmatic*
approaches to building classics must be uncovered, shared, high-
lighted, and celebrated. *This* is where attention should be focused,
not on the battle for "power" and control as it is currently constituted. While the extremists of the Left and the Right argue at length
about what is wrong with one another's definition of classics, most
classicists continue to have a steady but not uncritical confidence in
what they teach. After all, with the dwindling resources limited to
the padded resumés of the elites, it is a belief in the importance of
what they are doing which provides the *only* reason "the rest" remain
in the field. The discipline should listen to what *they* have to say and
what *they* are doing about the curriculum.

4. Professional Organizations

The APA should make it a high priority to facilitate this self-examination and renegotiation of what it means to be a successful classicist.
It is not surprising that recent scuffles for offices and panels have been
located on this Left-Right axis, because the APA is naturally the locus
of whatever power exists in the profession. The officers and interests
of the APA should more accurately reflect its constituency. I mean the
APA should represent the concerns of the majority of classicists, not
primarily the interests of a small minority of elites. Undergraduate
scholar-teachers should vote for those members who want to work on
their concerns—this is the purpose of the candidates' statements.
They should consider running for office even if they have not written
as many books as their colleagues at graduate institutions. (The irony

here, once again, is that it is only those with graduate-level teaching loads who have the time for such things.) Regional classical organizations do a better job at sharing both curricular strategies *and* meaningful scholarship, but the national organization should not be immune to the professional lives of the majority of its members.[42] This proposal will not meet with much enthusiasm, especially among those who think that the field is already populated and run by "hundreds of bookless, grantless zeroes."[43] But the issue here is how to keep classics, not a few comfortably ensconced classicists, alive. In voting for the Goodwin Award, the APA should also consider a book's breadth and potential to transcend the small professional circle. Teaching loads, as well as scholarship, should be taken into consideration for research grants (perhaps a tie-breaking factor on proposals of equal merit) at this extra-university level as well.

V. Two Final Notes of Caution

(1) This paper quite intentionally has not entered into the more popular media debate over why classics (that is, Western culture) should be taught or studied at all. In some ways, of course, this question is the one posed by those debating along the Left-Right axis. Unfortunately, the extremists are much better at describing the weaknesses of one another's approach than at constructing an argument for their own discipline. As I have tried to demonstrate here, this is primarily because those at each pole have been more interested in the polemics of career advancement than in the "mundane" and "middle-class" worlds of broad scholarship and classroom teaching, which demand a more encompassing perspective. I argued quite impressionistically that "most classicists continue to have a steady but not uncritical confidence in what they teach." But is this really true? And if so, why? This is not the place to address these questions, but I would suggest that classics cannot survive if the leading voices

do not *celebrate* the ancient world in some way. To study the ancient civilizations primarily to claim that they were *wrong* about some modern political preoccupation (Left or Right) is just as destructive as to warp—or limit—the ancient evidence to support a similarly personal agenda. We must believe that in some sense the classical civilizations, as we know them, were *right,* either in the questions they asked (a common and moderate position) or even in some of the answers they offered. It is this delight with our field that seems absent from the debate, but it is this delight which has always provided the fire in the best teachers and scholars, and it is this delight which convinces fellow academics and students alike that there is something here which *must* be pursued.

(2) The final irony: a murmur is beginning to be heard in the inner circles of academia about "the importance of undergraduate teaching." The public expression of this concern does not come from graduate faculty, of course, for most of whom "God's in his endowed chair—all's right with the world," nor even from undergraduate faculty (who, paradoxically, are usually not included in such discussions). The audible proponents of quality teaching have been nonfaculty scholars (usually securely protected from the classroom by the cyclopean walls of conservative think tanks) and, more significantly, university presidents who (rightly) see it as good business. The careerists are always the first to sense a change in the breeze (particularly when it blows from on high), and thus it does not take Apolline powers to predict that soon some elites in our profession will quickly reinvent themselves as advocates of teaching. The worry here is that these insincere calls for attention to this long-neglected aspect of Ph.D.-granting institutions will become merely the latest ephemeral source for self-promotion. Genuine, revolutionary reform is required. It cannot be expected to come, in the wake of pressure from administrators, from the very individuals who for so many years have proudly voted against the hiring and tenuring of out-

standing teacher-scholars in their departments in favor of the philological or theoretical obscurantist. The survival of classics requires good teachers, and the obvious truth (until now denied by no one) is that the existence of an effective, dedicated, and enthusiastic teacher at a major university is an accident, if not a "mistake." If the discussion heats up, we should be careful to distinguish the genuine voice of the "accident"—a voice which can and must lead from within both the university and the discipline—from the affected bellowing of the latest incarnation of the self-promoter.[44]

✌

Omnis Effusus Labor: On Futile Efforts and Inevitable Results

A REPLY FROM JOHN HEATH

"I am shocked, *shocked* to find that gambling is going on here."
—Captain Louis Renault in *Casablanca*

M Y first reading of these replies to my article, I must admit, left me feeling a bit like a plump, immobile piñata. Here came the graduate professors, clubbing my insulting caricatures, insisting after each whack "We do *too* teach!" Next up were the feminists, swinging their distaffs wildly with cries of "We're the solution, not the problem!" Even the undergraduate teachers were taking a few tentative pokes, like the Greeks jabbing at Hector's corpse, with depositions about their commitment to cutting-edge scholarship. Particularly disconcerting was the fact that at the end of each attempted thrashing everyone shouted in unison, "No more divisiveness!"

I was depressed, but like Captain Renault in *Casablanca,* not really surprised. My thesis, that there is a false horizontal split and a genuine vertical schism in our field that works to the advantage of a few but is destructive to the discipline, was dismissed as a red herring, the envious ravings of an enervated corporal down in the trenches. But the solutions offered by the respondents have already been tried. The 1970s and 1980s were devoted completely to their agenda. Ask yourself: Did the number of conferences, special interest groups, books that should have been articles and articles that should have stayed at home increase during that period? Did the teaching loads at major research universities go up or down during that period? And now ask yourself: Is classics better positioned in the university now? When Greek teachers now retire, are they routinely replaced? Are more classics departments being created or threatened with extinction? Is classics more respected in the community now? Are our future classicists better trained in Greek and Latin, more eager and better prepared to teach, ready to make the classical worlds relevant to nonclassicists? Not every reader will draw a connection between these two sets of questions as I do in my paper, but it makes *no* sense to argue that we need to continue what we have been doing when it is clear that it is not working.

Equally revealing was the more gentle condescension of those respondents who basically agreed with me but suggested that my thesis was exaggerated, that the field of classics is in fact directed by nothing but decent, hard-workin' folk. The argument that we should not worry about the few self-promoters in our field because classicists are "pikers compared to sociologists, political scientists, critical theorists, and even historians"—true though that statement may be—is no argument at all. On the purely pragmatic side, this is comparing apples and oranges. The cups in these other departments runneth over—classics can afford no such luxuries. More to the point: why are we so afraid to take a lesson from the Greeks and tell it like it is? Such behavior is selfish, wrong, detrimental, and should be stopped.

I cannot rebut formally or in detail all of the arguments and accusations presented in these eight papers. I stand by my original premise (classics is in trouble) and original argument (we and our skewed priorities are the primary culprits). To be sure, technology, blind allegiance to progress, and the glorification of material culture have put a great strain on abstract learning in general and classical education in particular during the past few decades. But the influential members of our field too often joined the looters, turning classics into a comfortable place of reduced teaching loads, extended leaves, think tanks, conferences, endowed chairs, grants, and petty power politics. What we have now in our discipline is not a healthy contest of ideas but a mock-epic struggle of nocturnal creatures croaking and scratching at each other for their tiny portion of an evaporating pond, one final *Battle of Frogs and Mice*.

The individual classicist may judge from his own experience whose analysis makes the most sense: Is the field being excised from the university (it is almost gone from the high schools and has already been removed from American life), or are things really not that bad and actually getting better all the time? Does the two-tier system contribute to increasingly trivial and redundant publication, poor preparation of future faculty, squandered resources, and complete elimination of the ancient world from public discourse, or is it merely the institutionalization of some wondrous kind of natural selection, a Platonic utopia whose guardians selflessly guide the profession and guarantee the healthy survival of our discipline? As Harvard goes, so goes Cal State Bakersfield?

My hope all along has been that my paper would stimulate a bit of reflection on the state of the field, and perhaps it will accomplish this in some small way. I support nearly all the suggestions made by the contributors for improving the field (especially those of Ron Mellor and David Porter), and even agree with some of the criticisms of my rather sweeping condemnation of the "elites." And I am pleased that most of us can agree that we need more good teaching, curriculum development, research, and leadership. But what I would like to address here are several specific interpretations of my argument which seem particularly off the mark.

I. Research

Several readers reach the puzzling conclusion that my frustration with the priorities of our field means that I am "railing against the desire to do research." Not only would I never mean that, I never said it. *Of course* we cannot advance the field, as it *must* be advanced, if we do not do research. *Of course* we cannot be effective teachers if we do not do research. *Of course* we are, quite simply, frauds if we do not do research. My purpose is not, and I never suggest that it is, to replace research with a pep rally for long-suffering unpublished undergraduate teachers. *Of course* most of us admire the quantity of the research of such scholars as Charles Segal. *Of course* there is a hierarchy, and should be. The Greeks were right: we are *not* equal. In Greek literature there are always those at the top, who are sometimes noble and talented, more often selfish, both bright and stupid; there are always those at the bottom, both deservedly so and often exploited and oppressed. The question simply becomes, what is to be the top?

My concern is about priorities, about the *nature* of the *optimal* hierarchy: What kinds of activity and behavior should be encouraged and emulated? What kinds of excellence should guide our profession? I argue that we have answered these questions much too narrowly for the good of the discipline. By holding up only one model, by concentrating authority and resources in the hands of only one group (which is falsely split into two in most analyses) with a very limited job description, we are hastening our own demise. This analysis is not about feelings of failure, but about what's good for classics. It is not about envy, but about what can keep a sputtering and extremely important field alive. It is not about an individual's drying up but about a discipline's withering away. It is not, believe it or not, about me (I have the ideal job, from my perspective, where teaching and research are given equal weight in tenure decisions, teaching loads are demanding but reasonable, fairly well-prepared students attend relatively small classes, and two excellent research libraries are right around the corner). Perhaps the most revealing responses to my argument are those which assume that all professional activity, even such futile gestures as writing or responding to this paper, must lead to some personal benefit for the writer; they must, in other words, be self-promoting.

And yes, I also argue that some kinds of research on the theoretical and philological extremes (and Thomas is right to note that this can be in the eye of the beholder) receive too much emphasis and too many rewards. We should just keep in mind the relative value of this work in the big picture. Is the promotion and self-promotion of this work going to convince ignorant administrators and legislatures (the easy targets and favorite whipping boys of several of the respondents), much less the "outside" world, that the study of Greece and Rome is important? I found nothing in these replies which even attempts to convince me that it will. I find everything in the trends of the last two decades to suggest that it will not. This faith in the status quo and Professor Konstan's own unimaginative caricature of broad scholarship as little more than "moral platitudes" are even more poorly supported than my own cynical vision. The barbarians are at the gate *because* we sent them an invitation engraved in deconstructionist gibberish and philological minutiae. This conclusion is not "philistinism" or "contempt for learning"—one's political opponents are always dolts—but a criticism of the priorities of the discipline. Those at the top may take some comfort in the fact that they will be the last to hear the midnight knock on the door: *après nous le déluge*. Still, their days are numbered, too, and their earnest protests—"But I'm a textualist! And I work nights!"—will fall on insensitive ears as the sniggering philistines toss them into the truck with the rest of us.

We can either de-emphasize the marginal Muse and demonstrate to those outside our profession who have the power to make or break us—and this especially includes our students—that classics is crucially relevant to the modern world, or we can smugly continue with the present system and simply wait for the end. And if we choose the latter and decide to go down without a fight against our real enemies— our own myopic selfishness on the one hand and inculcated timidity on the other—let's at least do it with some dignity. Let's not whine that "small-minded deans and college presidents and legislators (with the collaboration of a certain number of faculty members) at more and more colleges and universities are trying to increase teaching loads and take away time from the research...." Let's not snivel about "short-sighted materialism" while simultaneously slithering up the academic food chain and demanding more money for teaching less. (This hy-pocrisy of the *soi-disant* leftist academic is particularly annoying.) When the Roman senators awaited the invasion of the Gauls, they did so in proud silence, with no whimpering about their superior culture, no blubbering about their now useless cutting-edge battle tactics, no blaming the thick-headed victors. They had blown it, and they knew it. And remember, too, that they were butchered on the spot.

II. Missing the Point

There are several other peculiar but less serious misreadings of my paper. Professor Thomas, for example, reviews the article he would have written (on the university/secondary school hierarchy) instead of the one I wrote. Professor Konstan makes the surprising claim that I am advancing the cause of "chumminess," whereas I am in fact pleading with him, and every other classicist, to plant themselves in the classroom and the library and to *stay there*. Trade the chumminess of the conference, the fellowship of the think tank, and the brother-hood (or sisterhood) of the Internet for undergraduate teaching, office hours, campus committee work, and meaningful research.

These and other such misrepresentations are minor matters, but I cannot let Professor Barbara Gold's analysis of my brief argument go without some clarification. Let me correct a few of her more substantial misunderstandings.

1) She claims that my category of "special interest groups...turns out to be feminists." In fact, I use feminist scholars only as one "example."

2) She claims that my "anger is leveled" against feminists, when in fact I applaud them for opening up new avenues of scholarship and call their claim to represent a more egalitarian and communitarian ethos embracing undergraduate teaching a "refeshing and welcome self-representation."

3) She claims that I "stigmatize" feminists "as a homogeneous group," that I am ignorant of the fact that "there is not one feminism but many kinds of feminisms." What I say is in fact the exact opposite, fully agreeing with Professor Gold that "Feminism is no more monolithic than any other '-ism,' incorporating such (often conflicting) variations as liberal, Marxist, radical, socialist, and eco-feminism, to name a few."

4) She claims that I "say that the feminists in classics do not care about teaching or students." Instead, I ask, "What evidence is there that feminists are more dedicated to teaching than others?" I am delighted that some feminists put undergraduate teaching high on their list of priorities, but there are many types of feminists and not *all* are committed to the classroom. I ask for supporting evidence for the claim that feminists are in fact *more* committed to undergraduate teaching in some way which distinguishes them from the rest. Professor Gold does not supply such substantiation.

5) She claims that my argument that special interest groups (her "feminists") "have become a new elite who form a counter hierarchy to the old guard white-male classical elite...is sloppy logic and unfair hyperbole. To further claim that this 'group' has taken control of the

journals, conferences, APA panels, hiring, and NEH seminars stretches the bounds of reason." Let me share a brief summary of my experience with this very article, which was rewritten four times at the editors' request. (This process accounts, at least in part, for the embarrassingly tame and toothless tone of the final draft.) The associate editor in charge of the manuscript, Judith Hallett, is a feminist. The first refereed version of the article had about the same amount of material (although substantively different) on the role of feminists in the "crisis" as in the present version. The two referees chosen to comment on the paper were both self-avowed feminists. Like Professor Gold, they objected almost solely to this one page of my twenty-two-page paper (one of them enough to reject the article entirely), arguing that I was attacking "strawmen." In the subsequent rewrite I quoted from a paper sent to me by Professor Hallett herself, and was then told that I was jumping to incorrect conclusions because there was a whole history of the issue of which I was "not aware." The next version substituted a quotation from an editorial by the then-editor of the *WCC Newsletter,* but I was told that this was unfair because her opinions did not represent the majority of the WCC. (I mention this also to counter Professor Barbara McManus's objection that I did not bring the Women's Classical Caucus into the discussion; I tried but not in a fashion acceptable to *CW.*) If that is not "control" of a journal, then I stand corrected.

And so I cannot share Professor McManus's confidence that group activism will decrease the kind of elitism with which I am concerned and "save" classics. It may get certain members of the group installed in the hierarchy, but if that means ideologically driven misreadings such as Professor Gold's will increasingly dominate the profession, the battle is lost. Still, the basic thrust of McManus's argument is sobering and convincing: a middle-class work ethic is probably not "potent enough to counter our disciplinary socialization." After all, such a philosophy would lead to the classroom rather than the conference, the university curriculum committee rather than the APA, the library rather than the airport. And what kind of leadership would that provide?

III. Teaching

Although I can sympathize with the urge to demonize "dollar-minded administrators" and "small-minded" legislators—we are all victims in this therapeutic age—it turns out, of course, that the issue is not quite so simple. Some administrators and legislators *are* small-minded bean-counters, ignorant of and blind to the importance of classics and the liberal arts in general. One might ask—as I have—whether we classicists have made much of an effort to open their minds and eyes to exactly *why* we ought to study the Greek and Roman worlds. But don't blame them for wanting some of us to teach a third or fourth (or even a fifth or sixth) class, maybe even do a bit of grading, discuss and ask and challenge rather than merely lecture, see students in our offices (even—*horribile auditu*—talk to them on the office phone occasionally), stay on campus the entire term rather than disappear for conferences and guest lectures.

There is enough discussion now about low teaching loads, insulated faculty, and exploitation of part-timers and graduate students that we watch our tongues, careful even in our denunciations of exciting and "excited" teachers as speed-pushing showmen to insist that we are not being disdainful of good teaching, but it's just that others don't know what good teaching is. We talk the talk more often now in classics, but we have no intention of walking the walk. Perhaps by changing verbal behavior we can change attitudes, but I think Aristotelians would insist that *actions* shape attitudes, and I do not see classics *behaving* any differently in its graduate training, hiring, tenuring, or promoting than it did twenty years ago. In fact, the situation grows worse as the jobs dry up.

Professor Mellor could have been insulted by many things in my article, I suppose, but it should not be by my statement "that good teaching is just 'an accident, if not a mistake' at major universities." What I actually said was that "the existence of an effective, dedicated, and enthusiastic *teacher* [my new emphasis] at a major university is an accident, if not a 'mistake.'" My point here is that I do not know a single major university where the quality of teaching is given anything near the same weight as scholarship in tenure decisions. Many of these institutions list teaching as one area of evaluation, but in fact it is the quality—more likely, in fact, the quantity—of research which forms almost the entire basis for the decision. Now, a heavily published scholar may, *coincidentally,* also be an outstanding teacher, but he or she was not tenured because of pedagogical excellence. Good teaching is an adventitious byproduct at a research university. That is what I meant by "an accident." The "mistake" part comes in when, as Jeffrey Henderson pointed out in his original *Crisis* article, the scholar decides at some point to slow down on the publication in order to spend more time and energy in the classroom. Henderson observes that such individuals are termed "deadwood," and I frequently hear such expressions about them as "he's lost it" or "she doesn't do much anymore, does she?" I am certain that there are excellent teachers at graduate institutions, but my point is that the "coincidental" nature of their existence is a self-destructive way to run a profession. And, by extension, it is the "coincidental" nature of good teachers *anywhere* (since everyone, even the sanguine Professor Green, concedes that one does not learn to teach in graduate school) that is ultimately most ruinous.

IV. Conclusions

Well, this has gone on longer than any of us had hoped or desired. Far from inventing caricatures, my article listed specific behavior—even named a few names—and outlined solutions, citing others who have voiced similar concerns. There remains much to be said, especially an explanation and defense of what exactly is relevant and valuable about classics and thus why its demise is particularly tragic. Apparently there is also a need to explain and defend the pursuit of big ideas which, one would have thought, keep us all studying the ancient world. Scientists may study rat femurs in order to construct a general theory of evolution, but some of our leading classicists are "suspicious" of anything beyond their own particular rodent bones. This is our greatest crime, because we are running out of time to explain to the public just what classical antiquity has to offer the modern world, why *everyone,* not just classicists, now snugly buckled in for their "virtual" ride into the twenty-first century, should care that an alien and long-dead world is fading fast in the rearview mirror.

Over fifty years ago, Gilbert Highet (*The Classical Tradition*) raised several of these same issues. Bad teaching and narrow research, he argued, were hurting the field: "It is, then, the fundamental fault of modern classical scholarship that it has cultivated research more than interpretation, that it has been more interested in the acquisition than in the dissemination of knowledge, that it has denied or disdained the relevance of its work in the contemporary world, and that it has encouraged the public neglect of which it now complains" (499–500). And that was before the even more debilitating careerism and classical civilization bashing of self-promoting classicists during the past two decades. These warnings of Professor Highet, Anthon Professor of Latin at Columbia University, went unheeded by his peers, of course, as did the debate on similar issues sponsored by the APA nearly a quarter of a century ago and reported by this same journal (*CW* 65.8–9 [1972] 245–261). I certainly did not and do not expect today's barricaded residents of the Capitoline to heed my cackles of admonition. But merely to ignore the crisis, or to play the victim, will surely cast us into oblivion all the more swiftly.

CHAPTER 7

ॐ

VICTOR DAVIS HANSON & JOHN HEATH

WHO KILLED HOMER?:
THE PREQUEL

A few weeks before the book *Who Killed Homer?* appeared, the journal *Arion* published the following excerpt. This condensation and the subsequent appearance of the book set off a firestorm in the tiny world of classics that endured for more than two years. Most classicists were as outraged over our thesis—that the profession had abandoned advocacy for the study of classical antiquity at precisely the time advocacy was most needed—as the public was receptive.

We have, of course, been delighted by the response that *WKH?* received in the popular media from nonclassicists. Our intention in writing the book was that the Greeks—and how we classicists write and teach (and do not teach) about them—might become the subject of some discussion outside the soundproofed walls of the academy. The reviews the book received, almost all of them so far positive, in important review publications (e.g., *Kirkus*, *Publishers Weekly*), major newspapers (e.g., *Washington Post* and *Times*, *Los Angeles Times*, *Wall Street Journal*, *Cleveland Plain Dealer*), and mainstream journals of various political persuasions (e.g., *American Spectator*, *Dissent*, *Weekly Standard*) were also a pleasant surprise. Even more unanticipated was the interest a cranky book on the Greeks aroused among the producers of national and regional television and radio—the irony of our representing classics and classicists on *Talk of the Nation* and *NewsHour with Jim Lehrer*, as well as in numerous other radio and newspaper interviews, was not lost on us (or on the rest of our profession). Apparently, what we had to say has resonated with a number of people outside the classics frog pond who are genuinely interested in the Greeks and Romans.

That being said, it is not surprising that classicists have for the most part tried to avoid at all costs a public wrestling match with our tar baby. Yet the hundreds of personal e-mails, letters, and invitations to speak (!) from classicists and humanities programs throughout the country suggest that there are many teachers of the Greeks and Romans who have found something to like in the book, but do not have the time, energy, or stomach to get dragged into and smeared by the controversy.

Who can blame them? We too are glad that the immediate disputation died down, since we have spent a great deal of time writing personal letters of response, being adopted as philhellenes by a number of Greeks, and politely accepting and declining offers of all sorts of trips and interviews from (sometimes bizarre) groups and individuals. The "official" published response of the profession itself reveals the "highly idiosyncratic agenda" (as one angry reviewer put it, adding "perverse" in another paragraph) of the book: praised by Bernard Knox; trashed (on four occasions!) by a furious and seething Peter Green; praised and trashed simultaneously by Charles Beye; lauded by such diverse figures as Camille Paglia, David Kovacs, James Morris, Richard Rodriguez, Roger Kimball, John Silber, and Steven Willetts; dismissed as very unfunny by Mary Lefkowitz; and even deemed life-threatening to Charles Martindale.

WKH? is built upon three arguments which any critic, classicist, or pubic intellectual must address: (1) The demise of classical learning is both real and quantifiable; (2) The self-appointed leaders of our present generation of classicists have helped to erode classical education through an increasingly careerist approach to their vocation that runs directly counter to the spirit of Greek wisdom itself; (3) Greek wisdom is not Mediterranean but anti-Mediterranean; Hellenic culture is not just different from, but entirely antithetical to, any civilization of its own time or space. Connected to this proposition is our contention that the central institutions that derive from an underlying Hellenic core of values have shaped the modern West. We must therefore examine them if we are to understand, manage, and correct our own lives.

Most find this blanket assertion astonishing for at least two reasons. First, nursed on the mother's milk of academic specialization, most campus critics immediately object to our equation of Hellenism and Western culture: no, it was the Jews, the Christians, the Romans, the Renaissance, the Enlightenment, the Germans, the *et alia*....that created Western civilization. These critics forget that the core of Western culture, enlarged and enhanced by all of the above, first coalesced in Greece and nowhere but Greece.

Second, nearly everything that academics in the humanities value—appointments, fellowships, peer-reviewed publications, release time—is predicated upon a fashionable disdain for almost everything Western. Proclaiming that there was very little equality and quite a lot of racism, chauvinism, and elitism in ancient Greece is now the career creed of academic classicists; and when the other cultures of the ancient Mediterranean are invoked—Egypt, Persia, the Near East—it is nearly always to suggest that the Greeks borrowed or stole from them what was good and invented on their own what was bad. Very few classics professors seem to realize, much less argue, that Persepolis was not a *polis*, that the independent voices of Homer, Hesiod, and the lyric poets are not of the religious tradition of the Old Testament prophets, and that the monumental tombs of the elite in Egypt have affinity to Mycenaean and Hellenistic, but rarely to classical, Greece.

Because we see great value in studying and coming to grips with Greek wisdom—and because fewer and fewer Americans are aware of this wisdom—we also called for drastic changes in the way classics is structured. We hoped, at best, to raise the issue for debate, and that we may have accomplished to some small degree. The oddest reaction to our sample curriculum outline, in fact, was that many classicists objected to our proposal that classics be at the center of the way undergraduates are taught.

Our call for more and better undergraduate teaching, broad publication with less conference hopping, and so on, is not going to sit well with careerists in any department in the modern university: it "really chills the blood" of one phlegmatic reviewer. Still, it is fun to cull the comments on our proposal even from the most glowing reviews: "Their rigorous pedagogic program for returning classics to a pride of place in the humanities, however, involves too many Draconian measures—scrapping the doctoral dissertation, ending post-doc fellowships, junking peer conference junkets—to be practical"; "...too many forces in the universities that would prevent any such change"; "unlikely"; "likely too much to expect"; "Was ever a wish list so nobly at odds with its context?"; "utopian...or possibly harmful" (this quite favorable reviewer did not like our proposal to jettison the dissertation and replace it with a series of papers presented to the entire graduate faculty, despite the fact that of the over 1,400 theses started in the past ten years, less than half were finished by the end of 1997!); "their solution is a kind of academic boot camp"; "It is like a good B-movie plot; we know that it is too late." Yes, we do.

So, if our proposals for genuine change will be dismissed, what do the official candidates for American Philological Association (APA) offices suggest should be done instead? After all, their recent 1999 statements are filled with ideas for addressing contemporary "opportunities" and "challenges": they insist "we must increase our efforts to reach out to a literate audience beyond our classrooms" and call for "responsible" popularization and attention to undergraduate teaching. There is even a new ad-hoc Committee on Outreach—staffed for the most part, we cannot help but observe, by the same APA figures who have advocated the recent deleterious developments in the field. Others promise a new magazine for the general public that highlights the exciting research APA members are doing—the more they formally deny there is a serious problem, the more they look for ways to find salvation.

But the methods for achieving these noble goals which we outlined in the book—all part of the central argument of *WKH?*—are decidedly different from our own suggestions and are uncannily familiar: more links with other professional organizations, more cross-fertilization with other disciplines and alliances with other departments, more prizes, panels, websites (the Internet will save us all!), organizations, journals, conferences, sessions, colloquia on topics like the APA-sponsored three-year panel on "Ethnicities: Ancient and Modern," and papers on "The Relationship Between Gender and Ethnicity in Ancient Mediterranean Societies" and "Women's Culture, its Formulation and Transmission." In other words, more of the same kind of inbred behavior that got us in this mess to begin with, or at least has done nothing to get us out of it.

The *vitae* submitted by the candidates for professional offices in the APA give away the game: fellowships, grants, leaves, monographs, and administrative appointments pepper the landscape of their personal statements without a single mention anywhere of the variety or number of courses taught, articles or books penned for the popular press, or even the expressed intention of committing themselves to such endeavors in the future. How sad that we are to vote for those who give us the least amount of evidence that they have taught the ordinary student in any personal fashion or written anything anyone has read.

As for the suggestion that the Greeks can be saved with more colloquia on the state of classics, we can think of no greater waste of time or money. We already know what must be done, how it should be done, when it should be done—but the medicine is worse than the disease. For example, in June 1998, three months after the publication of *WKH?*, there was a conference at Stanford University (our alma mater), sponsored by the Department of Classics and Stanford Humanities Center. The working title of that conference—eventually retitled "Institutionalizing Classics"—was "We Killed Homer" (the website address ended in *wkh.html*), an unusual bit of candor peering through what was probably intended to be a joke. The colloquium featured seventeen speakers, including four scholars named in our "roll call of dishonor," on "current issues and controversies in the teaching, reading, scholarship, and public invocations of the classics." But, of course, there was no real interest in a diversity of opinions—no one critical of current trends in scholarship, curriculum, or graduate indoctrination was invited to participate. Indeed, it appears that no audience outside of the Stanford campus was invited to attend—to this day we have not heard of a single classics department in the Bay Area (where we live and work), much less the country, that received notice of the conference. The speakers, several on year-long leaves, reaffirmed that all was well with the field, and most of the speakers did in fact seem to be flourishing in the California sun. Much of the conference, we have learned from second-hand reports, was apparently devoted to suggesting that we were rightists (a euphemism) on questions of race, gender, and class. A similarly skewed and monolithic conference on the future of Ancient Studies was held in February 2000 at New York University. The reviewers of the conference for the *Chronicle of Higher Education* and *The New York Times* wondered aloud why genuine diversity of opinion had to be tracked down on the other side of the country. And the American Philological Association did devote a panel at their 1998 convention to discussions of *Who Killed Homer?*, but the range of topics proffered did not suggest that any classicist actually wished to discuss the arguments presented in the book: the dearth of jobs for classics professors, the ideological fads that promise expansion of popular interest in Greece and Rome but have actually eroded both readership and enrollment, and the value system of a profession that rewards undergraduate teaching hardly at all.

The simple fact is that classicists in charge of classics are *not* open to criticism of their field, and they are understandably but sadly so defensive about their failures that they are unable to deal directly with our blunt critique. We are still waiting for one of them—any one of them—to tell the world why our children should study, and why our neighbors should care enough to read about, those long-dead Greeks. And so here is a final great irony. The aforementioned candidates for APA office, who have demonstrably not been interested in real discussion, now, in typical academic passive-aggressive fashion, indirectly accuse us of trying to "silence" certain voices: "We fail the commitment to intellectual endeavor that is our primary legacy from the classical past, if we eliminate certain roads of inquiry in favor of others"; "What is most to be feared is the successful appropriation of the classics by a single, and single-minded, body intent upon imposing its will, forestalling dissent and thereby forestalling progress in scholarship and education." If there has been any attempt to silence anyone, it has come entirely from our critics, whose efforts have ranged from calling the FBI, to lobbying the University of California Press to forgo their paperback edition of *Who Killed Homer?*, to efforts by the editorial staff of UC Press to censor our updated edition.[1]

The claim of classicists to want to keep open dialogue and discussion is simply another posture, and so, sadly, *Who Killed Homer?* continues to remain about the only alternative voice in classics' eleventh hour.

⨍

I N a recent article about the state of classical studies, Garry Wills makes a series of remarkable assertions, but perhaps none is more surprising than the title of the article itself: "There's Nothing Conservative about the Classics Revival."[2] A political agenda is clear—more on that later—but what could Mr. Wills possibly mean by a classics *revival?* The only evidence he provides for "people beating their way...to clamber on board" the sinking ship of classical studies (38) is the connection of some recent scholarship to a few other disciplines and special interest groups in the academy—black studies, gay studies, women's studies, and comparative anthropology. To Wills, that a handful of academics can now find their own ideologies reflected in the scholarship of their colleagues down the hall in the classics department means that ancient Greece and Rome are alive and well in America at the millennium: "The ancient texts have become eerily modern in what they have to say about power relationships between men and women, gay men and war, superiors and subordinates" (42).

Wills himself, however, is aware of the tenuousness of his thesis. "Multiculturalism, far from being a challenge to the classics, is precisely what is reviving them. *If* [our emphasis] there is a resurgence of interest in the classics, it is because we are making them *our* classics..." (42). The conditional mood gives away the game: unfortunately there is no "resurgence of interest in the classics," and so Wills cannot adduce proof of growing university enrollments in classics, more B.A.'s awarded in classics, an upsurge in hiring of recent classics Ph.D.'s, new undergraduate programs, expanding readership for university press books on the ancient world, steady growth of Latin in the high schools, a renaissance in interest in the Greeks by the public at large—or any other hard data. In fact, Mr. Wills has nothing at all to support his assertions other than his ideological affinity for the fashionable causes of contemporary classical scholarship: if we mean well, then we are crafting a classical renaissance.

In fact, classics is *dying,* if not already dead, mostly *because* of the very approaches Wills cites as evidence for his imaginary revival. Multiculturalism has not "supplied blood for the ghosts," but drained the last drops from a fading patient. Like the narrow philology it replaced, the latest multicultural fad is hardly populist and inclusive, but usually in language and scope predictably elitist, narrow, and self-serving. Classicists now share an uncomfortable fate with Aesop's dying eagle. The Greek fabulist tells of an eagle, shot down by an arrow, which only at the moment of his death recognizes his own feathers on the shaft. What classicists have said and written over the past few decades—how we said it and especially why—has done its own part to kill off any lingering interest in the ancient worlds for all but a tiny cadre of professional scholars. For the first time in the centuries-long struggle to preserve Greek wisdom, the Greeks' traditional defenders have turned traitor to the cause and, consciously or not, abandoned the wisdom of the Greeks in favor of a hypocritical careerism.

I. Some Facts

If Wills means by a "classics revival" that professional scholars are publishing more than ever before on the ancient worlds, he has a point. In the single year 1992, for example, classicists published and reviewed 16,168 articles, monographs, and books about the Greeks and Romans.[3] The work of over 10,000 individual scholars appeared in nearly 1,000 different journals. We are a busy profession in our eleventh hour. Researchers on Homer's *Iliad* and *Odyssey* alone produced more than 200 publications in nine modern languages, not including the scores of studies of the historical, archaeological, and linguistic background to the Homeric texts. These articles and books represent officially published material; perhaps as much was written in relatively obscure journals or local academic newsletters and bulletins.

A comparison of the professional output of 1992 with that of 1962 reveals the remarkable growth in the industry of classical scholarship in just the past three decades: twice as many scholars now publish 50 percent more material in twice as many journals. A reference aid listing abbreviations of journals, series, and standard works "that classicists most frequently find in the scholarship of their discipline" lists more than 4,400 separate titles.[4] No classicist alive knows even the serial numbers of his trade anymore, so enormous has the machinery of academic production become. No one has calculated how much capital and how many ditched classes and ignored students were invested in this new experiment in mass publication.

Scholars cannot even keep up with the publications themselves in their own subspecialty within classics. The author of a recent 470-page book on the *Iliad*, for example, comments at the beginning of his bibliography (itself comprising twenty-five pages containing over 700 items): "A few sources mentioned in passing in the notes I have omitted, in the interest of economy [!], as peripheral; even in work central to the Homeric Question, there can be no question of completeness."[5] Even academics, who write for a few dozen or so, now confess that after reading 700 secondary works in their field, they cannot master their own bibliographies. Is this abundance of classical scholarship a sign of a healthy, flourishing, important, "reviving" discipline? Or is it, in fact, symptomatic—and explicatory—of its very demise?

Different statistics might tell a very different story. At the same time scholarly publication was soaring, the number of nonprofessionals in America actually reading about or studying the classical world took a nose-dive. There were 700,000 high school students enrolled in Latin in 1962; by 1976 enrollments had plunged 80 percent to 150,000. In but fifteen years over a half-million fewer Americans enrolled in this fundamental building block of classical studies. In this Golden Age of classics publication, the number of college Latin students plummeted from 40,000 in 1965 to 25,000 just nine years later, and enrollments have not recovered. The full data on the nineties are not yet in, but statistics for the first half of the decade reveal that the decline continues, if not at an accelerated rate.[6] In short, there are both more students in the university and fewer in classics than ever before.

Between 1971 and 1991 the number of classics majors dropped by 30 percent, as did Greek enrollments in one decade between 1977 and 1986. Of the over one million B.A.'s awarded in 1994, *only six hundred* were granted in classics, meaning that there are now five or six classics professors in the country for every senior classics major *and over thirty articles and books each year for every graduating student.*

One of the authors of a recent survey of the study of Greek in North America observed that enrollments in a new sequence of Greek courses at her university declined over four semesters, from twenty-five to ten to five to two. The sequence was canceled, she concludes, despite—and who says politicians have a monopoly on "spin"?—"the unquestionable success of the experiment."[7] Two students completing a Greek sequence at a major university is now labeled "success."

Falling student numbers are, of course, not the only symptom of our moribundity. The death of classics can be measured not just in the number of students, but also in the *kind* of students and the quality of their education. Classics majors in the 1970s had the highest GRE scores in the humanities, fifty points higher than majors in English. By the mid-1990s the gap had nearly disappeared, but the movement was in all one direction: the scores of English majors remained virtually unchanged, while the average for classics majors *dropped* forty-four points. By any objective criterion classics faculty faired just as poorly: there are now fewer doctoral programs in classics than in any other discipline surveyed; even with cut-backs at graduate programs, classics still has one of the poorest rates of employment in the humanities for recent Ph.D.'s and the second lowest salary on average in the humanities.[8]

We cite the above statistics simply to document the obvious: the Greeks, unfamiliar to the general public at large, are also now dying in the university itself. The claim of a "revival" is but yet another hoax from a school of thought that denies the existence of facts, that believes the Greeks exist "only when we rethink them as a way of rethinking ourselves" (Wills, 42). Today classics embraces a body of knowledge and a way of looking at the world virtually unrecognized, an almost extinct species even in its own protected habitat, the academic department. We classicists are the dodo birds of academia; when we retire or die, our positions are often either eliminated outright or replaced with temporary and part-time help.

So the real question becomes, why are the Greeks unknown *now*? America is at its wealthiest, its universities are larger than ever, the number of senior classics professors, endowed chairs, think tanks, humanities centers, graduate programs, journals, publications, and professional conferences is at an all-time high. Why such dismal in-

terest *now*, despite the availability of Greek wisdom through an unprecedented number of high-quality and affordable translations? At
the very moment in our history when Homer might be helping to
remind us of who we are, why we got here, and where we should go,
only a handful of Americans knows the Greeks—or cares that classics
is dying. If we are writing so much, why are others reading so little of
it? In our identity-obsessed age, why haven't we Westerners been led
by our very busy professors and scholars back to the beauty and the
wisdom—and the power—of our own culture?

II. THE PRESENT CRISIS

As the statistics reveal, the beginning of the end of the formal study
of the Greeks arrived in the 1960s. Classics—lonely *amo, amas, amat* in
the carrel, Demosthenes' hokey sermons on courage and sacrifice,
Livy's advice to fight the good war—became worse than irrelevant. The
entire package was viewed as part of the reactionary "establishment."
It had to be jettisoned. Curricular "reform," introduced by a new crop
of professional "educators," meant the abandonment of core courses.
The post-Sputnik panic also created an increased educational emphasis on math, science, and modern language. And the number of
students—and faculty—grew at unprecedented rates in the late sixties
and early seventies, greatly increasing the challenge of teaching
difficult subjects to the more poorly prepared undergraduates (a task
which was increasingly handed over to the burgeoning ranks of
graduate students). For these and other reasons, students of this new
age, no longer either compelled to memorize irregular comparative
adjectives or eager to soak up the bothersome wisdom of Sophoclean
tragedy, now needed to be *enticed* back into the traditional classroom.
Scholars were forced to win back their students and to convert the
now preoccupied public to their own particular enclaves.

Yet many old-school philologists, faced with these challenges, sadly became even more reactionary. If classics was to be extinguished by the uncouth, better to commit suicide with a tiny, loyal band in the bunker. They would not stoop to fight the barbarians hand-to-hand, to dilute the purity of their discipline with courses accessible to the "illiterate" (i.e., those with little Latin and less Greek). Teaching, of course, was rarely on the High Classicists' agenda (they had tenure; others to come did not). At the height of the crisis, Professor George Goold of Harvard University said as much at the national meeting of the APA in 1971:

> I think we are liars or fools or both, if we claim that the usefulness or relevance of classical studies constitutes the real reason why we cultivate them.... [W]e did not take up classics in order to teach it, and once we are honest enough to face that fact, we shall—when we actually do teach classics—be superior teachers for that very fact.... The real reason we study classics is its value: and that value is quite simply the pleasure it gives us. It is a pure, non-material pleasure, akin to the pleasure we derive from looking at pictures and listening to music; it is, for the most part, a passive, intellectual pleasure....[9]

The American public, then, was supposed to pay materially for a few professors to privately enjoy a "non-material" pleasure. These self-styled elite classicists—most not as candid or as intellectually honest as Professor Goold—shunned the task of winning new recruits to their "passive, intellectual pleasure." University and government money would always subsidize a tiny cohort of true classicists, who could read Greek in tiny enclaves.

After all, what was the alternative? Only "classroom showmanship," "middle-class dutifulness," "being excited in class," and "pushing academic uppers," as one Ivy League classicist scoffed recently—adding that the profession does not need "the pose of middle-class populism" or "good citizenship and chumminess, to the point of opening our homes to calls at all hours from students."[10] An ethos like that should win Professor Konstan the presidency of the APA. Yet our problem in classics has never been "calls at all hours from students" but, in fact, *no calls from anyone outside academia at any hour.* Most of our unemployed young Ph.D.'s in classics milling around the hiring board at the annual job convention would prefer the risk of middle-class populism to the certain doom of aristocratic elitism; many, we think, would prefer "calls at all hours from students" to no jobs at all.

In a sense, the self-proclaimed Old Guard of classics fiddled while Rome and Greece burned in their classrooms. Enrollments steadily declined even further, until a wise few saw the peril. Finally, in the 1970s, courses in Greek and Roman religion, mythology, and litera-ture in translation—many introduced and taught by new, more ener-getic faculty—came to play a more important part in the classics cur-riculum. Rousing new editions of Homer, the lyric poets, the tragedi-ans, the historians, Aristophanes, and the Augustans by gifted trans-lators such as Richmond Lattimore, Robert Fitzgerald, Peter Green, Michael Grant, William Arrowsmith, and David Grene became fix-tures in the syllabus. The field would have died completely had it not been for the popular efforts of such scholars and teachers. Their skill and imagination ensured that the themes of drama and epic, hard and tough lessons, now struck harmonious chords with students unversed in the niceties of iambic trimeter and epirrhematic syzygy.

Anemic and bandaged, but still breathing, Homer limped into the 1980s, leaning heavily on the goodwill of dedicated teachers, trans-lators, and "popularizers" who were struggling to save their programs (High Classicists at a critical time provided little leadership to cap-ture new students, other than staffing the offices of the APA). But much damage had been done—the vital organs had been reached, and worse still, too many classicists themselves were now confused and divided over whether saving classics meant killing it. Homer, then, required more new blood, more work to build on the successful undergraduate translation classes of the 1970s.

Instead, the 1980s and 1990s have seen another curricular shift in the academy and a much different challenge to Homer in the form of "theory" and "multiculturalism," the very movements Wills cites as responsible for our "revival." Multiculturalists generally belong to one of two camps. Some believe that all cultures are equal—the West no better or worse than any other. But others more dour are convinced that all cultures are equal *except* the West, which is uniquely imperialistic, hegemonic, nationalistic, sexist, and patriarchal and therefore to be studied only as an exemplar of what is *wrong* with the present world. Either way, the Greeks lose: if they are the same as the Thracians or Carthaginians, why study Greek instead of Greek/Phoenician/Hittite/ Egyptian? If they are worse, why study them at all?

Astonishingly, too many complacent classicists seemed to have learned nothing from the catastrophe of the 1960s and therefore have done little to fight back against this new, more virulent variant on the tired modernist accusation against Greek and Latin of "inappropriateness" and "decadence." Instead—and here are the eagle's feathers—they have enlisted in this crusade against the West. Like Ephialtes, classicists used their inside knowledge to lead the enemy around the pass at Thermopylae, and so to destroy the embattled and outnumbered Greeks and their entire tiny phalanx from the rear.

A new crop of "social constructionists" either trashed the classical world for not being multicultural (which is dishonest: no civilization has been or ever will be truly multicultural) or tried to reinvent the Greeks and Romans as multicultural (which is a lie). Greek wisdom is not only forgotten—it is now to be actively rejected. The last generation of classicists wishes to survive and be loved—by fellow academics—by guaranteeing to their anti-Hellenic colleagues that there will be few other classicists to follow.

Eager to fan the last ember of the dimming classics campfire by co-opting this latest fad, some programs in classics for a few years now have been adopting such misguided schemes of reinvention as the following:

> Our field is ripe not only for theoretical but also practical restructuring. Why Greek *and* Latin, to the exclusion of others? A department of Greek, Hebrew, and Syriac could be one very exciting place....[11]

So would a polyglot "Department of Greek, Hebrew, Syriac, Phoenician, Assyrian, Babylonian, Hittite, Egyptian," and so on—but to what end other than attempting to appease others at the university by killing the field? "Why Greek and Latin to the exclusion of others?" Why? Perhaps because there is a literature of Greek and Latin that *alone* in the Mediterranean is quite separate from religion, one that *alone* inaugurates the Western experience of self-criticism and abstraction. Perhaps because in these languages there are words for "citizen," "constitution," and "freedom" and a vocabulary of social dissent. Many now find that it earns dividends to deny that the Greeks were unique in the ancient Mediterranean, or that Western culture, ancient or modern, has any peculiar dynamism or imagination. Such a traditional view, we are told, is now hopelessly naive and outdated:

> I argue that the current sense of "crisis" has been misrepresented as a conflict between theoretical and traditional archaeology, or even between young and old. In fact it is just one part of the general collapse of intellectuals' attempts to define what 'the West' is and should be. Archaeologists of Greece had neutralized their material to protect the set of beliefs which gave prestige to classical studies; now that these beliefs are crumbling, they are left defending nothing.[12]

Are we to believe that this archaeologist and his many peers in their own lives really find the definition of the West—free speech, an independent judiciary, material bounty, private property, a market economy, separation between church and state, and constitutional government—to be mere "crumbling beliefs" amounting to "nothing"? Still, there is nothing particularly objectionable to "universal inclusivity" as a general warm and fuzzy principle—provided that faculty and students understand the real differences between these cultures. Like the Greeks themselves, classicists must never pretend *that all cultures are equal*. They know better than to speak the untruth that there is a *Phaedo* in Egypt, an *Oresteia* in Persia, or an *Iliad* in Assyria, much less democracy among the contemporary Germans or universities in fourth-century B.C. Gaul. The Pharaohs really did not have designs for airplanes, and Socrates, as Professor Mary Lefkowitz has demonstrated time and time again, was neither black nor a product of a stolen African philosophical system. The Romans learned much from Mago the Carthaginian's treatise on agriculture; but there existed nothing in Punic culture like the Theophrastean tradition of Western agronomy.

It is neither ethnocentric nor chauvinistic to admit that the court of Tiglath-pileser III was not a Socratic circle, that the citizens of Sidon did not craft law by majority vote, that everywhere outside of Greece there mostly were two, not three, classes, that hydraulic dynasties did not foster yeomen, that planned palatial economies did not create an empowered citizenry, that literature or philosophy apart from religion is rare beyond the Aegean. Yet the current multiculturalism on campus makes such truths unmentionable if not dangerous.

As one classicist recently insisted, "The patriarchal denial of the possibility of early matriculture found in traditional classics is elitist, (hetero)sexist, and insidiously racist and anti-Semitic, since it dismisses academic discussion—i.e., the production and dissemination of knowledge—of a matricentric and egalitarian early culture and discounts African influence on the cultural development of the West."[13] To argue—as the evidence overwhelmingly suggests—that Greek wisdom of the *polis* ultimately owes little of its core to other Mediterranean cultures now earns scholars the nastiest of labels. Who in fact now has "dismissed academic discussion"?

Even more strangely, some scholars have built careers in the past decade by insisting—again, by citing authors and arguments that have been thoroughly refuted—that the *polis* Greeks derived many aspects of their core culture from Africa and the Levant. Professor Wills merely repeats these discredited notions when he insists that "Eurocentrism, when it was embedded in the study of the classics, created a false picture of the classics themselves. Multiculturalism is now breaking open that deception. We learn that 'the West' is an admittedly brilliant derivative of the East" (42). Can Mr. Wills please demonstrate from what part of the East did the West brilliantly derive democracy, free inquiry, the idea of a middle class, political freedom, literature apart from religion, citizen militias, words like "parody," "cynicism," and "skepticism," and a language of abstraction and rationalism? And can Professor Passman explain *where* there was an "egalitarian early culture" outside of the classical world—Egypt? Carthage? Persia?

Martin Bernal is a historian of China who compares himself to Schliemann and Ventris—philhellenes both—because of his contributions to the study of classical culture despite his "amateur" standing in classics. He has urged us "not only to rethink the fundamental bases of 'Western Civilization' but also to recognize the penetration of racism and 'continental chauvinism' into all our historiography."[14] Not only are all cultures alike in this postmodernist world, but Greek wisdom turns out not to be Greek at all! Racism in "all" of our historiography has created Greeks who were not really Greeks. The paradox is unmistakable: Western culture is racist, sexist, patriarchal, but we nevertheless now are to claim that it all started in black Africa and Asia. These new critics cannot have it both ways: either Greece and the West are terrible and properly the baggage of an oppressive European culture that plagues us still, or they are not. The Greeks cannot both be deplorable and yet proof positive of a glorious lost African or Semitic legacy.

It is time to put aside the personal quibbling and concede that this latest attempt at "rethinking" the Greeks has failed—except at offering a false picture of the origins of the West and serving the professional aspirations of a handful of academics who publish too much and teach too little, who advocate one life and live another, who ridicule everyone's affluence but their own. Wills takes a particularly odd tack when he dismisses the comprehensive refutation of Bernal's thesis by "Mary Lefkowitz and a group of scholars...for what they take to be errors and overlooked information" (40). Bernal's thesis has been demolished by professional scholars from a wide variety of disciplines. They do not merely "take" his arguments "to be errors," but demonstrate them to be errors and half-truths and unsubstantiated inferences. What exactly does "what they take to be errors" mean? Errors or no errors in Bernal's "history"?

Diverse and impressive cultures populated the ancient Mediterranean, constantly interacting, borrowing, sharing, adopting, and rejecting from one another as they saw fit, all worthy of professional exploration. The Egyptians and Persians influenced the early Greek world, and the Greeks themselves were variously impressed with the Scythians, Celts, and Carthaginians. But all cultures have never been, and are not, the same. If names now must be changed to fit the times, it would be far more honest to call the true classics program of the next millennium the "Anti-Mediterranean Studies" Department. If truth were still a goal in American universities, then we should explore why and how such a tiny, poor country in the southern Balkans differed so radically from the general culture shared by its wealthier neighbors across the sea, its tenets still so radically more influential even as we speak.

When the Pharaohs were coercing labor on a mass scale to erect their own elaborate tombs, when the Great King of Persia was building palaces for himself and temples for the gods into which no commoner could step, the Greeks were constructing gymnasia, theaters, law courts, public dockyards, markets, and assembly places for their own lowly citizens. That *is* a different reality and *can* be evaluated on *absolute* criteria. In the classical age of Greece, there was no Pyramid of Pericles, no Great Palace of Epameinondas, no mummified Aristides. Giza and Persepolis are still beautiful and they are monuments to the ingenious marshaling of human and material capital, but they are also testaments of how and why that labor and treasure were used—and for whom. Again, whose values are "crumbling"?

While Cleisthenes and his successors were reorganizing Athens into a consensual democracy built upon assemblies, councils, and officials elected by citizens and lot, hereditary princes and priests were running the show for the Celts, Persians (whose "Great" king could "do as he willed"), Scythians, Jews, and Egyptians. There was no God-On-This-Earth Themistocles, no Lord Solon. As Greek farmers perfected a system of mass fighting in hoplite ranks to save their lands and their consensual *polis,* the Carthaginians still preferred mercenaries, and a professional military class had long since dominated in Persia and Egypt. Miltiades, elected by the Athenian people to command them at Marathon because of his proven record of leadership, defeated a forcibly conscripted Persian army led by the sons, sons-in-law, and nephews of Darius—mostly incompetent and frightened insiders appointed by the Great King to positions of command, the ancestors of Saddam's yes men and Iran's theocratic guard alike. Leonidas died with his men in the front ranks at Thermopylae watched over by King Xerxes enthroned on the mountains above. At Salamis, as Themistocles took to the water, Xerxes once again took to the hills—and then again to the safety of his harem. Yes, they "are just different customs," but all soldiers across time and space appreciate a general who looks, battles, and thinks like they do—who fights in front, rather than sits enthroned to the rear of, his men. Persians prostrated themselves at the feet of the King; Aristophanes made Athenian political leaders such as Cleon look like self-serving dolts, religious seers like mere oracle-mongers hawking phony wares. Whereas

Aeschylus could celebrate the emergence of a democratic form of trial by jury of one's peers in Athens, justice in Egypt was defined as "what Pharaoh loves."

Yes, the Greeks relearned to write by adapting an eastern alphabet to their needs. Yet the *polis* Greeks quickly turned their new, and now vastly improved, tool of writing into powerful lyric, drama, and history in the hands of the individual—not the state, not God, not the military—who asked and explained and challenged. The Achaemenids and Pharaohs, with their tiny cadre of scribes and priests, used their millennia of literacy to produce *ex-cathedra* pronouncements and royal records of what the big men did. Herodotus and Thucydides wrote history as free inquiry, something Near Eastern and Old Testament literates never really did. Government chronology, religious chronicles, campaign facts, priesthoods, religious adages, and dynasties are still not history. Eastern powers put their artists to work on small prestige objects and relief sculpture of their ruler's conquests or palatial tombs; the Greeks produced cheap utilitarian vases of unsurpassed beauty and public murals glorifying community bravery.

The *polis* may have entertained Asiatic-inspired cults or borrowed architectural orders from Egypt, but no Greek believed that there was a better political state outside of Greece. They all knew there was no *polis* out there. Thus when we in America speak of that paradox "multiculturalism," we classicists must be honest, even if brutally so, and say that we are enriched by different foods, music, fashion, art, literature, and language—as satellite experiences around our dynamic Western center. Even the most rigid defenders of the West have always acknowledged that other cultures offer aesthetically impressive, moving expressions of the human condition. A Chinese poem, an African play, a novel from the Punjab, or American Indian chants *can* evoke human emotion and reveal the tragedy of man on earth every bit as passionately and accurately as Sophocles or Virgil.

But not one of the multiculturalist classicists (despite the fashionable rhetoric) really wishes to adulterate our core values from the Greeks, to live under indigenous pre-Columbian ideas of government, Arabic protocols for female behavior, Chinese canons of medical ethics, Islamic traditions of church and state, African approaches to science, Japanese ideals of race, Indian social castes, or Native American notions of private property. What we say now as classicists and how we live have become two very different things—and for students of Socrates that has become a dangerous thing indeed.

Again, many classicists now seem to be unaware of or unimpressed with the uniqueness of the Greeks. They argue that the West is merely a construct of a privileged few whose beliefs are now "crumbling" and that its shortcomings are unique among other cultures, ancient and modern. Yet they suffer the wages of hypocrisy: all make their arguments in the comfort of Western institutions that guarantee their rights—rights that descend directly from the Greek vision of the world, rights that now incidentally include guaranteed employment for life and unquestioned academic freedom of speech, rights that are never acknowledged as unique or appreciated as life-sustaining. Intellectually naive at best, this form of academic multiculturalism is hypocritical to the core and, worse, entirely alien to Greek wisdom.

Most "theoretical" classicists who empathize with the oppressed from the safe distance of the university lounge identify themselves and their research as adamantly anti-Western and try to exhibit as many credentials, claim as many affinities, and list as many identities as possible to ensure they are *not* associated in any shape or form with traditional admiration for the Greeks and their legacy:

> I find it difficult rhetorically to lay out the ways in which Foucault's work has mattered to me without acknowledging the fragmented, disparate, split nature of my sense of self, a self produced in late capitalism, with gender, class, all those markers that locate one tenuously and ambiguously in the world. All of these affect the encounter with the great man. I am a psychoanalytic female subject, an

academic, a Marxist historicist feminist classicist, split, gender-troubled, in the midst of a book about Sappho. And I realize as I write that I could not have written this book without Michel Foucault. So how can that be? I have to take these various elements of whom [sic] I think myself to be, and look at them in relation to the work of Foucault.[15]

Note the repetition of "self," "me," "my," "myself," and "I"—twelve times in but six sentences. Perhaps we need a little less of Professor Page Dubois and a little more of why we should learn about the Greeks in the first place. Professor Dubois may be fragmented, disparate, feminist, split, psychoanalytic, gender-troubled, and adrift without Michel Foucault, but we wonder whether this "self produced in late capitalism" really does teach six to eight classes a year to the underclass, creates positions for the unemployed and exploited in her own field (and there are many), writes prose for those students unacquainted with the Greeks and the West, or as a self-proclaimed Marxist tutors the poor and uneducated. If she were to do all the latter, and spare us the therapeutic self-obsession, then we might witness a revival of classics, though one far distant from the pages of the *New York Times Magazine*.

In short, not until the late fourth century B.C. did the *polis* produce anything like what we would now reasonably and without calumny define as a present-day American academic: *a well-fed, elite, institutionalized thinker of the late twentieth century, who crafts ideas for his peers with the assurance that the consequences of those ideas should not and will not necessarily apply to himself.*

Thus, the crime of these "soft" multiculturalists is one of ignorance and omission, a serious enough charge against those stationed to protect a weakened discipline from enemies at every side. Other classicists, however, the "hard" multiculturalists, have made a direct attack on the Greeks. They do talk and write about the Greeks and the West, but concentrate only on the ugliness of that tradition, the oppression and brutality. "Why study the culture of classical antiquity," they ask, "if it was only the mechanism to extend slavery, sexism, racism, imperialism, patriarchy, and colonialism, the assault on the Other, the non-citizen, which continues unabated today?" These latter classicists are popular and in demand in the university—what better way to refute the West than have its own defenders lead the attack? What better way to destroy a discipline than offering rewards to the last generation who promises that love for the Greeks will end with them?

These classicists indict the classical world and the West on two grounds. First, they deplore the West's successful and brutal history of cultural imperialism (the fact of which is often quite true). Second, they often contend that the values embedded in the West are not merely dynamic, they are toxic. That is, academic multiculturalism of the "hard" sort often means that all cultures are equal *except* that of the West. Multiculturalist diversity turns out not to be a diversity of ideas at all, but rather a uniform chorus of head-nodders, who attack what started with the Greeks, who see history not as tragedy but as melodrama, where the task of the present-day smug academic is to round up all the usual nasty suspects—heterosexually inclined, free, European male citizens. But under examination, all of these charges of the hard multiculturalists turn out to be simplistic or hypocritical, or both. Let us examine some of the most common.

III. The Horrific Beast

The Beast—the sexism, chauvinism, slavery, and exploitation inherent in Western culture—was born, as we all know, in ancient Greece. And today's academic ideologues are content merely to flop him over and poke at his purportedly foul and scaly underbelly. Each critical thrust is accompanied by a sanctimonious cry of disgust and blame: "Down, Beastie, bad Beastie," as if censuring the Greeks for lacking modern sensibilities offered a meaningful vision of the classical world and its significance to our own, as if we can assuage our own middle-class guilt by blaming the dead. And so at a recent conference on "Feminism and the Classics" at Princeton University, feminist scholars—who could agree on little else—universally conceded that the *Antigone* is a hurtful and patriarchal text that primarily reinforces the subordination of women.

Yet this Beast is a much more complex and subtle creature than these would-be dragon slayers care to acknowledge. But before we examine this apparently loathsome brute in detail, remember three things about the Greeks. First, by and large, the sins of the Greeks—slavery, sexism, economic exploitation, ethnic chauvinism—are largely the sins of man common to *all* cultures at *all* times. The "others" in the Greek world—foreigners, slaves, women—were also "others" in *all* other societies of the time (and continue to be "marginalized" in most non-Western cultures today). If classicists can find a present-day matriarchal nonracist, classless utopia, and can trace that legacy back to an ancient culture where women and the Other were far better off than in Greece and Rome, let them step forward with "proof" rather than discourse. Millions in America no doubt would love to emigrate there.

A bloodthirsty Cortés did not have to teach the Aztecs about colonization, sexism, racism, religious intolerance, or slavery—much less the intricacies of human sacrifice. For the real brutality of killing children, civilian massacre, and gruesome disfigurement, examine primitive, prestate cultures outside the Western experience. Africa knew enough of human bondage and female subjection—and a bit more about human sacrifice, cannibalism, and torture—before Europeans taught them Western pathologies. The discussion of—and often redress of—those innately human failings, however, is most likely found in the West, and so often the tortuous path toward *solution* started with the Greeks. It is natural for the Western critic to lasso his own Beast, but there are really much greater ogres in the world's herd mysteriously left untouched.

Secondly, the march of centuries does give us latecomers advantages over our predecessors through the grasp of the mistakes of the past. Two-and-a-half millennia of review should result in some moral progress. The social contract does not suddenly spring mature from the head of Zeus, but is hammered out through centuries of hit and miss, through the laboratory of millions of personal tragedies. The better question, then, is not "why did not the Greeks move, as we have, to eliminate sexism and slavery?" but rather "why after 2,500 years has our own moral sense in comparison progressed so little?"

Thirdly, and most important, classical literature is its own most astute critic. Classical writers are far harsher on their own culture than is any contemporary multiculturalist, providing others the ammunition for their own execution. The Greeks present a picture of their culture and say: this is the way it is—this is what we value, this is what makes us who we are, this is who is included, who excluded—and then blast the entire conglomeration to pieces. What is most often misunderstood about classical literature is that almost *all* of it was composed as a critique of society and the very values that allowed it to flourish. The most important legacy of the Greeks and Romans is this uniquely Western urge to pick apart everything—every institution, tradition, and individual. Only in this manner do ideas change at all—and only in this way does the author find any credibility with the reading or listening audience.

The macho world created by Homer, the smug *polis* of Aeschylus, Herodotus's wild Aegean, even Virgil's holy Rome—all are held up for review and none emerges unscarred; the foundations begin to dissolve even as the superstructure is crowned. Even Xenophon, Spartaphile par excellence, cannot write a paean to Spartan culture without attacking the institutions he is supposed to be praising.

We are not saying that every Hellenic community was a republic or a truly autonomous *polis,* or that institutions like slavery and the political subservience of women were anything but reprehensible. What we mean by Greek wisdom is that at the very beginning of Western culture the Greeks inspired and sustained the ambition for an ordered and humane society, one whose spirit and core values could evolve, sustain, and drive political reform and social change ages hence: a Beast that could with time, after painful self-criticism and experimentation, know when and how to shed his more odious skins.

The Greeks become the cultural template that two millennia of critics of society know to be best. It is this manual we use when we stab Caesar, organize the legions, start a revolution, write a treatise, build a cannon, question male supremacy, or probe a cadaver. We are not claiming in the West an uninterrupted utopian *polis* of some 2,500 years—who could, given the Inquisition, the Holocaust, the World Wars, apartheid, and the brutality of colonialism?—but only a foundation for, at its best, an ordered and humane society. At its worst, the Western tradition is merely a dynamic and frightening scientific enterprise, one that gave Hitler the power to build Tiger tanks, invent V-2 rockets, and organize the panzers. But that same legacy also ensured that a coalition of liberal states would—and could—sacrifice their citizenry and national treasure to obliterate a vile enterprise, an aberration that we nevertheless knew had arisen at least in part from our own shared culture.

Classicists need not worry about offering sophistic alternatives to the West to today's undergraduates, since most students in state universities—poorly prepared, in debt, and at work at low-paying jobs—scarcely know anything about the origins of their own culture to begin with. And if classicists are really troubled over what Greece spawned, they should concentrate on the frightening dynamism—not weakness—of the West, whose marriage of market capitalism and democratic freedom seems to be sweeping the planet precisely by offering the worst of our material culture.

IV. THE BEAST IS US?

Classical literature, and most European literature that followed, is in some sense a comment upon and evaluation of contemporary custom. Cynicism, skepticism, parody, invective, and satire are all Greek and Latin words—a rich vocabulary of public and private dissent unequaled in non-Western languages. Apart from a few hackneyed court panegyrists, no important classical author, not even the subsidized Horace, ever becomes a mindless spokesman for the regime. Sophocles, Athenian patriot and veteran par excellence, wonders in the *Ajax* how courageous individuals keep falling through the cracks. Euripides, breathing hatred and venom at arch-rival Sparta, nevertheless dramatizes the brutalities of war and creates characters who question the way women and slaves are treated. Aristotle, no fan of the tyrant, has no belly either for turning the whole thing over to the mob. Both radical democracies and autocracies become his models of "deviant" constitutions. Socrates was not the last to tell us that the unexamined life was *not* worth living.

Beneath the veneer of Petronius's hilarious banquets and drunken orgies in his *Satyricon* is a devastating condemnation of Roman imperial culture, from the emperor to the lowliest slave. Later Rome became a more closed society, but the stuff of its imperial literature from Virgil and Horace to Seneca, Tacitus, Juvenal, and Suetonius was parody, satire, and invective against society at large and often the emperor in particular. Conflict, dissent, self-criticism, revolutionary critique—these are the burdens of our inheritance from the Greeks and Romans. The current scholarly criticism of the Greeks and the West, then, is as much a part of our Western tradition as slavery and the subjugation of women—a legacy far different from anything that emerged from the theocratic states, palatial economies, or nomadic tribes outside Greece. The irony is usually missed by the critics. But we must keep that self-critical tradition in mind when considering the following standard attacks on the Greeks by those classicists eager to repudiate the very literature they study.

Greek society subjected women to second-class social and political status and demeaned them in a variety of overt and subtle ways.

Sadly, yes. Greek women could not vote or hold office and lacked equal protection under the law, so the active political leadership of the *polis* voluntarily sacrificed half its brain power and any claim to true egalitarianism. Recent scholarship often seems content merely to demarcate the exact nature of the sexism of the Greeks and the West: "In the case of a society dominated by men who sequester their wives and daughters, denigrate the female role in reproduction, erect monuments to male genitalia, have sex with the sons of their peers, sponsor public whorehouses, create a mythology of rape, and engage in rampant saber-rattling, it is not inappropriate to refer to a reign of the phallus. Classical Athens was such a society. The story of phallic rule at the root of Western civilization has been suppressed...."[16]

Yet these same Greek men insisted on incorporating strong female characters into every aspect of their art and literature. The sensuous, proud Venus de Milo is no *Penthouse* titillatrix. Still too much a Barbie doll, you maintain? Try the armored Athena Promachos with her grim visage of martial probity. Greek tragedy is dominated by heroines, from Iphigeneia to Alcestis to Clytemnestra to Antigone, women who all direct lesser men in their midsts. We may wonder now if God is a woman, but Spartans, Argives, Eleusinians, and Athenians were convinced that Artemis, Hera, Demeter, and Athena were their patron deities.

Antigone sacrifices her life for the sake of a male relative, the Princeton conference feminists remind us. She condemns herself to death by burying her brother—but she is the most noble and forceful character in the entire play. Creon's arguably justifiable defense of his city becomes tyrannical and monomaniacal, earning the wrath of the gods. He is finally reduced to a wretched caricature of arrogance and incompetence when he brags that he will not fall victim to a weak woman. Sophocles surely had seen such men and knew that the male gospel of unquestioned intellectual and spiritual superiority was not supportable, an untruth that indicted any—man, ruler, the state itself—who would mindlessly embrace it. Women and the treatment of women were very much on Greek minds, and a few of the best saw the sexual contradiction at the very heart of the *polis*.

Whom do we remember, Clytemnestra or Agamemnon? The latter kills his defenseless daughter, who offers her throat to the blade heroically and bravely. His wife Clytemnestra finishes off the king, who perishes ignominiously in a bathtub. Both husband and wife are wrong, perhaps, and in Aeschylus's version it is clear that the male is to be preferred to the female (Athena, the female goddess with no mother, says as much). Yet the issue is raised before the assembled citizenry, the battle joined.

Penelope, a perfect match for Odysseus, surpasses in wit and wisdom her whiny adolescent son Telemachus. She is the sole person of action among a sorry group of gullible and indolent wannabe suitors. But that is not what we learn from the critics:

> Almost imperceptibly, the seeds of later misogyny are sown. Penelope yields to Odysseus her loyalty and her creativity. The traces of sexual subjugation and political exclusion, the violence that lies behind this act, are scarcely visible and might seem merely figments of our imagination, had we not already experienced them fully in the first half of the poem.[17]

The strange argument here is that Penelope may *appear* to be an equal match with Odysseus—but that is before the astute reader projects the fates of other females in the first half of the epic onto Penelope's marriage. Odysseus's "sexual dominance" of Circe, for example—we are not reminded by the scholar that Circe was just as eager for sex as Odysseus and would have transformed him into a pig had he not acted first—reveals the inherent (but "scarcely visible") violence in the "true nature" of male/female struggle for power. Penelope is a rape victim whether she—or the reader—knows it or not. This kind of misreading is typical of most postmodernist research, in which the themes of texts and the tensions in cultures can be dumbed down to an issue of power. Some feminists cannot decide whether Penelope was a clever, powerful subverter of male assumptions or a dupe who stayed home while her no-good husband philandered. Mostly, though, they just rail that she gets less air time than Odysseus.

> The narrative of the *Odyssey* incorporates as a significant element of its ideological strategy a commentary on the construction and differentiation of gender. The text self-consciously employs control over narrative production itself and the ability of a subject to guide this narrative as a means of differentiation. The story works towards the fulfillment of the goals of the masculine hero, which are represented as socio-culturally constructive. Females within the narrative are almost unanimously represented as constructing plots or narratives hostile or threatening to the hero's goal. The consistent denial of the completion of female plots, which is also a denial of female desire, subordinates female subjectivity.[18]

In fact, with Penelope—at the very beginning of Greek literature—the entire Homeric world of male adventure and dominance is undercut by the most unlikely of people, a woman behind the loom with more nerve and brains than all the men of the entire poem. Throw in Nausicaa, Calypso, Circe, Arete, and Athena, and it's no match. Men should feel slandered—"gender outrage"—that Polyphemus, Antinoös, and Melanthios are so petty, childish, and brutal precisely because of their exaggerated maleness. No wonder a few Victorians thought the author of the *Odyssey* must have been a woman. The roles in myth for women are limited, of course—wife, mother, daughter, inhuman witch or warrior, denizen of some shattered household, or beached nymph on a mysterious island. But the traditional tales are consistently manipulated to bring scrutiny on just these traditional expectations. The Greeks, it seemed, wanted to know why it had to be so.

Don't forget the hyacinths, moon, and stars of Sappho, the cucumbers of "silly" Praxilla—an entire alternative female universe to the shields and breastplates of Greek poetry. The Greeks often mused that the best lyric poetry was at times written by women. Corinna, poetess of backward Tanagra, they said, beat the old master Pindar himself five times in poetry competitions. So angry was he, the myth went, that he was reduced in rage to calling her a "sow." The point of that frivolous yarn was *not* to make Pindar venerated and majestic.

It would be difficult to argue that any of these authors was trying to revolutionize the *political* structure. Yet they raised the important issues, played on the tension created by this obvious and sometimes embarrassing gender gap again and again. The playwrights expected their dramatic enactments of competing ideas to be of great interest to the Athenian civic body at large—and to win them a prize. The examination of gender issues in tragedy was not, then, as some contemporary feminists argue, a mere sham. The discussion was not a phony sounding board designed to release safely male tension and assuage masculine anxiety about men's self-serving suppression of the opposite sex. At the very beginning of the long road to full egalitarianism, people in the West became aware of the contradiction between their ideals and their traditions, of the facts that talent and character knew no sex and that a free society which was half unfree was not free.

There was not a true Greek emancipation of women, perhaps because of the Greeks' quite different approach to politics and the law. They would not necessarily define equality of power solely by twentieth-century notions of statute and legalistic prerogative. No more than 30,000 to 40,000 free adult male citizens exercised full political rights at Athens out of a total resident population of perhaps 350,000-

500,000. In that sense even the most radical of Greek democracies was illiberal by modern standards. At the same time it is absurd to equate the absence of the vote with modern notions of exploitation and inferiority. The *oikos*, or household—man, wife, children—was the building block of the *polis*.

Religion, ritual, and cult—where women just as often were in control—could be as important as citizenship to the life and health of all in the *polis*. Priestess (*hiereia*) is a common Greek word, but one still rare in our own vocabulary. Greek religion does not insist—at least not to the degree found in much of modern Christianity, Judaism, or Islam—that women are secondary in formal ritual and religious expression, or prescribe that the gods may be reached only through the benevolence of male intermediaries. Antigone—long before the male priest Tiresias appears on the scene—alone understands the unwritten laws of the gods, serving as a remedial tutor to all of Thebes in the lost arts of piety and the true nature of treason. To the Pythagoreans, women were central to religion. Their active role in cult was essential to belief and honored as such by husbands who were to profess formally both their admiration and their fidelity. The Stoics assumed that women were equal to men, while Plato and Aristotle at times argued for equal opportunity of education.

The Greeks did not solve, but most certainly began, the discussion of the place of women in society, a dialogue that finally turned into equality in the West—and *only* in the West. Women—especially those who lose crucial steps on the cutthroat *cursus honorum* due to the demands of child-raising—may still bump up against glass ceilings in corporate America. But how many would trade their business suit for a veil, their contraceptives for infibulation, their inheritance for suttee, their Bruno Magli pumps for foot-binding, their 1.8 children for fourteen, their Lady Remingtons for clitoridectomies? If full equality is not yet here, it is not because the classical cultures did not allow women to vote. It is more likely because for centuries we ignored what the brilliant Sappho, Aspasia, Lysistrata, and Antigone had been saying all along, ignored that women held property and personal rights in Sparta and Rome far more liberally than in most societies for the next two millennia.

The study of women in antiquity, then, can tell us much about the values of the West, but *not* in the sense offered by much of today's feminist criticism:

> Feminist theory—Native American, African American, lesbian, psychoanalytic, French feminist, gynocentric, historical, anthropological, archaeological, literary—can open up the traditionally hermetic discipline of classics to the outside world. Once it is so transformed, it will be apparent to scholars in other disciplines that there is more to the discipline than the collections of "great myths" and clichés about the traditional values of "Western culture" currently portrayed in the popular press. In the end, then, theory can turn classics from a rarefied study for the leisure class (by means of which others are kept at bay) to a vital arena for multicultural dialogue in the next century.[19]

The "outside world" that will suddenly discover the importance of the Greeks as a "vital arena for multicultural dialogue" turns out to be "scholars in other disciplines," not really those outside the university gates who are relegated to the condescending "popular press." This smug rejection of Western culture—the primary aspect of the ancient world that could actually be of interest to anyone outside of academia—in favor of lancing another boil on the Beast, has kept the Greeks safely out of the "popular press" for several decades. And we suspect that the "leisure class" includes most new theorists who are better paid, have more time off, and travel far more widely and frequently than America's indebted students and their strapped working-class parents who are paying an increasingly stiff tab for the rather affluent and increasingly rarefied practices of American university faculties.

The Greeks and Romans developed an economy based almost entirely on chattel slavery.

No charge is more frequently cited by current multiculturalists than the charge that the Greeks, like racist southerners of old, were slaveholders. True, few Greeks had any universal notion of the inherent dignity of mankind that might prevent a fellow human from becoming the mere property of another. And the Athenian renaissance would have been absolutely *impossible* without the arms, backs, and brains of thousands who are now completely forgotten in the story of Western civilization, poor nobodies with names like Sosias, Thratta, Xanthias, Karion, and Manes, all vanished without a trace left in the historical record, but who we can be sure died in the silver mines, on triremes, and in dank shops. Aristotle and Plato at times—to their lasting discredit—argue that there is such a thing as a natural slave (their concern is not to discredit the institution *per se,* but to ensure that the properly dull and limited, not the gifted, are the ones enslaved). Aristotle calls the unfree a "tool," little more than a breathing wrench, a saw or hoe with a working brain. Nicias, the rich Athenian whom Thucydides praises as sensible and pious, made much of his fortune on the backs of hundreds of anonymous slaves, human shovels chained and forced to dig Attic silver, men who crawled into black tunnels with death their only escape—all to give Athens her silver owls and to keep Nicias in good repute.

But on closer examination the distinctions between slave and free, even in the most hideous and ubiquitous manifestations of the classical mind, are not so clear-cut as we are now led to believe. Even Aristotle assumed that slaves might be better treated than the poor, that their relegation to political nothingness did not, as in later times and other cultures, preclude all cultural, political, and social prerogative. His *Politics* seems to assume a large body of contemporary hostile critics ("*others affirm* that the rule of masters over slaves is contrary to nature"), who force him to defend his own (perhaps often unpopular?) views of natural human inferiority. Plato in his *Laws* writes that the proper way to treat slaves is to be more just to them than to those who are our equals. Bankers, accountants—professors too—were Greek slaves. Slaves could be chained and die in the mines, but the material conditions of the free poor, at least in modern terms, often could be little better. The true evil of slavery in the ancient world was more often the reality of a virtual nonexistence in the political life of the community, a forfeiture more bitter to any Greek or Roman adult male than is conceivable to us.

Rightists like the Old Oligarch (an anonymous fifth-century B.C. pamphleteer) and Plato worried about the absence of clear visual distinctions between free and slave under democracy. The Old Oligarch went so far as to claim one could scarcely tell master from slave at Athens and that slaves were on occasion as wealthy as free men and said whatever they wanted without fear of reproach. Even if an exaggeration, such a claim would have been inconceivable in any other slaveholding society. Poor stammering Claudius was accused of turning his empire of millions over to Narcissus and Pallas, intriguing ex-slaves who knew a little more about how to run Rome than did the inbred and dissolute Caesars. Ex-slaves in Petronius's *Satyricon* assume that slavery is often but a temporary state, a bad and unlucky start that can be circumvented by the more cunning who are able to outwit their witless masters and end up with cash, status—and slaves of their own. His potbellied freedman Trimalchio is an ancient Horatio Alger, a caricature of the wily slave who ends up quite free and more a Roman success than the tired and bankrupt class of old aristocrats. Horace claimed his father's kin were of slavish origins. No wonder that under such a mobile and changing social cosmology, Roman law in theory recognized some marriages between free and slave.

Examples abound in Greek history of the mass liberation of slaves. We hear frequently of slaves given freedom for fighting alongside their masters, made citizens in times of population decline, armed by cagey insurrectionists, manumitted upon the death of the master. One wonders if Isocrates was altogether exaggerating when he claimed, "No Athenian inflicts such cruelty on his slaves as the Persians do to their own free men." Slavery in the classical world was clearly a mutable and debated enterprise, with the distinctions between servile and free often blurred in a way unknown, for example, in the American South. Few if any ex-slaves tutored the children of Jefferson Davis, improved the accounting system of the Confederacy, or built their own plantations.

Modern multiculturalists often ignore these significant differences between slavery in antiquity and nineteenth-century America, forcing errant interpretations onto the past in their efforts to reveal the racism inherent in the West. So Shelley Haley, a self-labeled "Black feminist classicist"—such glitzy, bumper-sticker self-identification is now the trademark of the new academic who has such concern for others—argues from *no* evidence at all that the Macedonian Cleopatra was black, at least symbolically:

> Gradually, by reading my history and Black feminist thought, I perceived that Cleopatra was a signifier on two levels. She gives voice to our "anxiety about cultural disinheritance" (Sadoff 1990: 205), and she represents the contemporary Black woman's double history of oppression and survival. In the Black oral tradition, Cleopatra becomes a symbolic construction voicing our Black African heritage so long suppressed by racism and the ideology of miscegenation.[20]

Cleopatra may have been a "voice," "signifier," and "symbolic construction," but there is no evidence that she was an African black. The sheer familiarity of Greek masters and some slaves—Aristophanes, Demosthenes, and the Old Oligarch suggest that they often looked, talked, and acted alike—helps to explain the very persistence of the institution, which might have fallen into greater ill-repute had all chattels without exception been chained and sent into mine shafts below the earth. Spartacus, whom classical elite historians often describe as a better man than the Roman plutocrats and blue-bloods who conquered him, could not mass millions to overthrow Rome because, under the insidious system of slavery in Italy, not all slaves were starved and beaten by cruel overlords with whips and fetters. Nor were all masters bloated grandees who customarily drew blood from their servants.

A few authors like Epictetus and Plutarch, even at times Euripides and Aristophanes, chafe at the contradictions of slavery. In the ancient world slavery was not systematically predicated on color or purported racial inferiority, but quite often on the accident of fate—a siege, a pirate attack, an unlucky birth. Heraclitus says simply that war "makes some slaves, others free." A horrible institution, yes, but at least not always parcel of some larger nightmare of race, color, or pseudo-genetics. When Diogenes was purportedly taken captive and enslaved, he pointed to a Corinthian buyer and said, "Sell me to him, he needs a master." Despite what Aristotle claimed, natural inferiority was not felt by all Greeks to be the ideological underpinning of slavery, which explains why—contrary to the American experience—the existence of educated, brilliant slaves was apparently *not* fatal to the idea of the vile institution itself. An ingenious, brave black slave called into question the entire servile architecture of the South; an ingenious, brave Greek slave could be dismissed with, "Sorry, you or your parents were in the wrong place at the wrong time." A Greek was not terribly bothered that his slave was a better man than he—such are the vagaries of fate; a plantation owner presented with the same saw his entire pseudo-scientific creed crumble before his eyes. What bothered Aristotle and Plato was that all Greeks—women and children especially—were in theory only a captured city or losing battle away from enslavement.

The Roman philosopher Seneca advised: "Remember this, that the man you call your slave comes from the same species, enjoys the same sky, and breathes, lives and dies exactly as you do. You can imagine him to be a free man, he can imagine you a slave." Five centuries earlier the obscure rhetorician Alcidamas scoffed, "God made no man a slave." It may not have struck him that one should therefore dismantle the institution, any more than it did Thomas Jefferson or John C. Calhoun, but the topic of slaves—if not slavery itself—was at least open for discussion. How else could we ever have eliminated slavery at all?

The Greeks are slaves of reason, without the natural spontaneity and levity of other cultures. They are responsible for burdening their Western successors with the heavy cargo of rationalism, which has led only to the bottom line and taken the mystic joy of the inexplicable out of life. We who study the Greeks wrongly believe that truth and values are absolute and unchanging, and not mere constructions of those who hold power.

Multiculturalists argue—often in a patronizing vein—that we in the West do not appreciate other indigenous systems of discourse and reason, so burdened are we by Hellenic notions of "linear" thinking, positivism, and empiricism, so constrained are we by the silly notion that a text means what it says, that writing honestly can more or less describe a reality.

> Nor may the meaning be referred to referents external to the text, for the analysis also argues that the claimed referentiality of a text is irreducibly metaphorical, based on a distinction between inside and outside that is also shown to be a logical fiction. All texts, both the figurative and the ostensibly descriptive, are reduced to the level of rhetorical acts that strive to deny their rhetorical status in the pursuit of an elusive referentiality or "truth." In the philosophical context, this technique of reading, in its emphasis on the text's irreducible rhetoricity or "textuality," destabilizes the central enabling assumptions of conventional Western metaphysics such as "being," "presence," and "identity."[21]

If Professor Goff's book is also a mere "rhetorical act," and thus has nothing to do with any truth about ancient tragedy, why read it? Since its language provides no entertainment and "destabilizes" nothing, and itself uses the entire structure of "Western metaphysics" in its argumentation, the collection of essays is at best a bad joke, at worse hypocritical to the core.

Yes, the Greeks first taught us how to analyze the world systematically with logic in pursuit of the truth, but they also told us that we must acknowledge and then, sometimes reluctantly, sometimes joyfully, give in to the power of the irrational, of wonderful things we cannot always see, hear, or prove. Creating at once an enlightenment and romantic reaction is no easy task. Apollo, the god of rationality and measure, turns his temple over to Dionysus three months each winter. Dionysus, the god of irrationality, ecstasy, and liberation, must be given his due as the unfathomable power that somehow makes the juice flow in the veins of plants and animals alike. Pentheus, the legendary king of Thebes, tries to deny the divinity, the power, even the very existence of this "new" god. He is overwhelmed and succumbs to his own repressed irrational desires, and is finally torn to shreds by his delirious mother.

The irrational is always dangerous, but it is thoroughly embedded in our natures; even Plato makes it a part of our souls. Phaedra's illicit passion for her stepson Hippolytus must result in the destruction of the entire family, but we should not forget that it is Hippolytus's calculated and complete rejection of Aphrodite, passion herself, that begins the disastrous chain of events. Aphrodite only wants a little recognition, or so she claims—but how is Hippolytus (with his "big thick books") to dedicate himself both to the sexual purity of Artemis (an odd desire for a male in the classical world) and acknowledge the importance of sex at the same time? Is smug prudery as evil as indulgence in the call of nature? Egos, ids, and super-egos are scattered throughout the pages of classical literature, demanding that we examine the contradictory and conflicting aspects of human nature. It is no coincidence that Freud and Marx—both critics of much of Western society—were armchair classicists who used that very training to press their attacks.

Our tradition of self-criticism, of analyzing who we are, how we live, what we believe, and what we value, is the source of Western progress. To the Greeks and Romans we owe our constant questioning: Why do we do this? Why do we do it this way? Is there a better way to do it? Is our society really moral? We inherit these queries from Prometheus, our prying intelligence which saved us from our bestial existence by bringing us "fire": science, manual skills, communities, technology. And often when we reach the limits of our reason, we turn to faith, religion, and mysticism.

Those who decry this "Western paradigm" of progress, restlessness, dynamism (the fruit of rationalism), of needless tearing down and building anew, who argue that our ceaseless itch to move ahead has not brought happiness, has not always improved our lives, should be warned: the Greeks were there long before them. For every Aeschylean myth of Prometheus and the advance of civilization, there is a Hesiodic Myth of Ages, an ironic Sophoclean ode about progress, a primitivistic vision of human life which sees degeneration, not amelioration, over time. The Golden Age has passed, as have the Silver and Bronze—the era of heroes and demigods has slipped by. We live now in the Iron Age, a time of moral decline: "Would that I were not among the fifth generation of men," Hesiod sings, "but either dead earlier or born later! For now it is a race of iron; and they will never cease from toil and misery by day or night, in constant distress, and the gods will give them harsh troubles."

Perhaps, the Greeks mused, the world will end soon. Perhaps life is cyclical and a new Golden Age awaits. For Homer's audience perhaps Cyclops's lush and pristine island, Calypso's sensual hideaway, or the humane fairyland of King Alcinoos is preferable to the halls of drunkenness and pigsties of civilized Ithaca. Such apocalyptic visions are central to the Judeo-Christian vision of life as well, are they not? The Greeks gave us progress, and then warned us that it might degenerate and become no progress at all. Science and learning exact a price as they lead us further from the womb of nature. It is one of the great slanders against classical antiquity that the ancient Greeks (far better than we) did not realize the price to be paid for the march of progress, for the ordering of the world according to the dictates of reason rather than by emotion or faith. Remember, there was a reason why Sophocles called civilization's wonders *deina*, the ambiguous "terrible."

The Greeks and Romans were not all moral or intellectual supermen who always followed what they preached. They may have bequeathed to us a desire to be self-analytical and supplied us with the tools to accomplish this examination, but they did not always like the critique and often despised the critic. The price Western society has paid for its open invitation to criticism is steep: instability, wars, revolution, martyrs, cycles of pseudo-learning, refutation, and still more intellectual trends, false knowledge, and fads. Every time a Westerner goes to war, seeks to discover a new continent, or worries about atoms, the world should beware. Constant discussion, controversy, creating and demolishing in search of a better way are central to our free markets, constitutional governments, and individual rights, but they are also expensive and bothersome—and sometimes deadly. The ancients who started this marketplace of ideas were as burdened by it as we are. Herodotus, like us, sometimes tired of the Western hubbub and often saw things in the East he rather liked.

Even the Athenians, who tolerated so much, had their limits. Anaxagoras, the first philosopher to live in Athens, and Protagoras, the sly Sophist, were driven out of town. Socrates, the greatest searcher of them all, preferred the imposed death sentence to exile. Thucydides' forced expulsion may account for his magnificent history. There were political reasons why Archilochus, Xenophon, and Herodotus did not always live or die where they were born. The Roman Ovid offended Augustus with his politically incorrect verse and was banished to the Black Sea for the last decade of his life. Petronius, Seneca, and Lucan were all snuffed out for being a little too talented and outspoken to suit Nero. Euripides' drama was the most challenging to traditional conceptions of the gods, myths, rulers, policies, and drama itself. Year after year his plays were chosen for competition—an honor in itself— yet year after year his plays came in second or third. He won only four times in his lifetime, earned a reputation for misogyny, was perhaps charged with impiety, and, frustrated by his reception in Athens, finally spent the last two years of his life in barbarous and regal Macedonia (where, rumor had it, he was torn to shreds by the royal hounds). Like Socrates, Euripides' genius was ridiculed by Aristophanes to the apparent applause of most of his peers. Aristotle and Plato each put his life in danger by advising Greeks who had no belly for their message or reputation, and both had heard quite enough of the sophistic denial of an "elusive referentiality" or "truth." And both free thinkers in their own writings reflect displeasure with critics: both would have been unwanted renegades in their own utopias, had the regimes of the *Republic* or *Politics* ever become flesh.

Over time, after painful scrutiny (sometimes over millennia), some ideas are junked as peripheral or wrong: slavery, for example, the second-class political status of women, or decisive warfare itself, as it now seems. New ideas, even new people from outside can also be incorporated, although again this may take a very long time and be done for the wrong reasons. The evil emperor Caracalla, for instance, hungry for increased tax revenues, first proclaimed the rights of universal citizenship for all free men in the Roman Empire—regardless of race, ethnicity, language, or place of birth. The Greeks and Romans learned much about astronomy, art, architecture, and social custom from other nations. They absorbed foreign religious ideas as well, intolerant primarily of the intolerant (such as the Christians). But most alien to the classical spirit is the suppression of argument, the rejection of self-criticism, or the idea that incorporating the ideas of others diminishes oneself.

The Beast is always there among the Greeks, but there were usually enough Greeks who recognized it as such—the worse for tyrants, autocrats, and reactionaries. These critics and skeptics, not the numerous toadies and sycophants, defined the ethical and moral landscape of literary expression, and so they condemned any and all for the next 2,500 years who would accept society as it was, rather than for what it might be. The greatest of Roman poets—Virgil, Horace, and Ovid—often make us uneasy. Few now read a Valerius Maximus, who dedicated his pretentious collection of hackneyed adages to the emperor Tiberius—and for good reason.

A final irony? The very tools which today's critics in the university use to dismantle Western culture and to deny the Greeks their progeny are themselves inevitably Western. No postmodernist goes on the attack against the "elitist construction of science" without resorting to a rational argument based on evidence, data, illustration, and logic—the entire Greek manner of formal invective and philosophical refutation. To craft his clever sabbatical request or grant proposal, the deconstructionist anti-Western classicist does not (as we should expect) quote God, footnote the president, insert the chairman's sayings, claim a drug-inspired supernatural revelation, break into religious chants, hand out cassettes, begin dancing, or warn openly of mayhem to come for disbelievers. No multiculturalist thinks his academic freedom is an oppressive idea, the concept of a university separate from the church and government a burdensome notion, or their presentation of research and opinion in journals peer-reviewed and free from state censorship "hegemonic," "patriarchal," "sexist," or "racist."

Radical feminists may decry the linear and positivist approach of

Western rationalism, but when they fly to speak about such oppressions, they assume that the same tyrannical manner of mathematical and technological inquiry ensures the jet's engines are running and its navigational instrumentation functional. Indeed, the entire architecture on which the university censor sits is Western to the core, from the library to the curriculum, from the elaborate process of acquisition, retention, tenure, and promotion of faculty to the conference room lights that go on with a flick.

The truth is that there is no workable alternative to the Greek method of wrestling with the Beast, to the relentless modes of dissent, induction, empiricism, and formal argumentation. The free critic (yet another Greek word) exists only in the West. Even today he is not easily found as an indigenous species in the Orient, the Arab world, or in Africa or South America. Native censors of Islamic justice, Chinese totalitarianism, African tyranny, and Latin American dictatorship are usually safely ensconced in Europe, Australia, or North America—the adherents of the Greek legacy. They are most often found in academia or journalism, always protected and subsidized by the very culture they have in the past despised.

Salman Rushdie and Edward Said have attacked the West from England and America, not so frequently from the tolerant enclaves of their beloved motherlands, drawing on a Western tradition of polemic, invective, satire, and allegory in their work. The temple and mosque of the non-West are not quite as hospitable to the big mouth as the parlor and campus of the West. Professor Wills's assertion that "We learn that 'the West' is an admittedly brilliant derivative of the East" seems lost on the contemporary intellectual—if only we examine where and how he lives and not what he says. One may write favorably about the sense of indigenous community under Khomeini, national fervor spawned by Saddam Hussein, Palestinian rights, religious awakening in Algeria, free health care from Castro, but one usually does so now from a tasteful and computerized study in Palo Alto,

Cambridge, or New Haven, rarely for long in Teheran, Baghdad, or Havana.

It is no surprise that in the last half century there have been hundreds of symposia, conferences, and public discussions of Hiroshima in America—almost all critical of U.S. policy—and few Japanese-sponsored counterparts devoted to a careful anatomy of Pearl Harbor or such atrocities in Asia as the Rape of Nanking. No public or private review of the Gulf War was published in Iraq after the deaths of tens of thousands, and we omitted the postmortem rallies and "victory" parades. Yet hundreds of books and articles criticizing our conduct of the war reached the American public when we lost but a few dozen soldiers. Anyone who knew of the Greek tradition would understand why that is so. To deny this tradition, to expose the Beast without examining the Greeks' incessant battle with the creature, is to dismiss the real value of studying our past.

V. Trend, Jargon, and the Strange Cycle of Self-Promotion

So the topics chosen by classicists for research and emphasis over the past twenty years often resulted in a one-sided and negative offensive against the very Greeks they were studying. Far too few classicists stood up to fight back, to talk about both sides of the Beast, to refute this simplistic dismissal that was palatable to contemporaries in the university but intellectually dishonest. Multiculturalism, then, rarely in any fair fashion presents the aggregate of Greek wisdom—and history will not be kind to the present multiculturalist classicists who knew better.

But classics suffered from more than just having its defenders join the enemies of the Hellenic tradition. At the same time that generation of academics was fashioning careers by feeding the Beast, a new way of *talking and writing* about texts and culture swept through the academy. Perhaps more deadly for the Greeks than the new revisionism was the very *way* these topics were approached—the creation of an angry and ultimately *elitist* vocabulary, tone, and attitude. In short, classicists, who publish so much, could no longer write; classicists worried about the Other had no intention of writing for the Other.

A "new" theory-oriented cohort arose in classics, adding a vacuous jargon and sophistic superstructure on top of the multiculturalist perspective. Everything became a text; truth was a construct and the Greeks could become *anything* you wanted. Not only were topics of research to be rigidly anti-Hellenic, now even the language and tone went against the tenets of Greek clarity and candor. Forget what the Greeks actually said and did; new rules were enlisted to prove what they did not say.

In classics, champions of radical egalitarianism not only openly acknowledge but actually *boast* that there is something superior about subspecialized and encoded research. The very *distance* of the forms of expression from ordinary human language makes it valuable. We promote and venerate—whether cynically, indifferently, or ignorantly—those who do the Greeks the most harm. Books in classics are praised in professional journals for their small-mindedness and pedantry; this is referred to as "densely argued" or "close readings." They are hailed for their bad prose; this is called "challenging." They are lauded for their jargon-filled phrases; this is termed "methodologically sophisticated." The contemporary prejudice against big ideas ("assumptions" and "assertions") and jargon-free writing ("middle-tone approach") ensures that no one outside a tiny cadre of subspecialists will read Homer. Of course, this new language and tone are not merely embarrassingly elitist; they are also absolutely fatal to the creation of any new interest in the Greeks themselves.

For example, a very positive review of a recent book on Homer's *Odyssey*[22] informs us that, owing to its "complexity" and the author's "exposition and organization" being "less clear than they might be," even specialists will have to read the book "at least twice for full comprehension." "Non-Classicists are unlikely to finish the book."[23] Should the fuzzy exposition and cloudy organization have been fixed before publication? No, because it does not seem to matter: the book receives high marks in an influential journal. The review seems to praise it while confessing that few can finish reading it.

We could document the cant-laden nature of much recent scholarship. Our criticism here, however, is not directed so much at the sterility of these trends but at the motives of those scholars who adopt them: self-promotion, whose apparent long-term goal is the avoidance of classroom teaching and the corny—and rather difficult—goal of convincing others of the value and beauty of the Greeks. The most serious crisis in classics—and the university as a whole—is not what academics *say* but what they *do* and do *not* do.

In the June 1995 issue of the *American Philological Association Newsletter* (the official voice of "classics"), classicists are told to mobilize against the proposed dismantling of the National Endowment for Humanities, the lifeblood of their grants, years off, conferences, and travel. They are advised how to reach congressmen "who believe agencies serve [a] rich elite" by *disguising* their true creed. In "Tips on Letter Writing," classicists are told, *"Use simple language.* Critics have often charged that NEH money supports elitist scholars. Thus it is important not to use technical words or high theory.... Observers believe that the 104th Congress is populist-minded. In demonstrating to your representatives the impact of NEH in your district, highlight traditionally populist concerns such as equal access and participation by the many, not the few" (emphasis theirs). Professor Konstan's "pose of middle-class populism" may not be so bad after all.

No classics professor, then, is to write like a classics professor ("technical words" or "high theory") to his hayseed ("populist-minded") congressman. Instead, apparently, connect affirmative action to populism and beat them at their own game. Instead of worry-ing over the charge of "elitist scholars" (largely true), why not advise Congress that the NEH is not a bad idea if it is the only chance for hundreds of draft horses to have one year of their lives free to gather their lifelong thoughts and write something that somebody might read, a crap shoot where there is sometimes a chance that something of value might emerge? Why not admit that Congress is not "believed" to be populist by "observers," but is populist inasmuch as a *vast* ma-jority of the electorate swept them into office through a popular vote—something the student of democracy surely can grasp? And why the need to instruct the stewards of Homer to *"use simple language"*?

What is behind this new research and writing that has been so fatal to classics? Corruption mostly—would-be revolutionaries in theory who indeed were for the most part quite traditional, careerist, and elitist. The 1980s and early 1990s were years of profit-making in America for student and professor alike. In the 1980s the more ambi-tious students boasted without conscious shame that immediately upon graduation they intended to become insurance salesmen, bond brokers, investment bankers, and other facilitating middle-men—Hesiod's old bribe-swallowers of the city. Classes, departments, and entire divisions within universities evolved to satisfy new customers. Had not Socrates and Jesus long ago railed against the money-chang-ers? But now student and teacher in the university joined whole-heartedly, with the zeal of converts, in the worship of the Golden Calf.

Yet the Greeks always questioned the relationship between virtue and currency, commerce and citizenship, and sought to impart an unashamedly impractical moral economy wherever they might. But in the eighties, classics (and, indeed, all of the academy) was rein-vented as a place of reduced teaching loads, extended leaves, think-tank hopping, conferences, endowed chairs, grants, and petty power politics—often decorated with a patina of trendy leftist ideology or neoconservative scorn as the volatile financial situation and funding source prompted.

Few argued, as their forebears had, that a classical education could be "useful" in some larger, Greek sense—skills such as reading, writing, thinking logically; qualities such as perseverance, pride in accomplishment, self-restraint; values such as egalitarianism, rational debate, demand for truth. Classics was now strangely led by individuals who saw their field as but another stepladder by which to enter the realm of a professional elite. Classicists—ironically and hypocritically—joined their cohorts throughout the university in transforming the professoriate into the "profscam" now so familiar to us all. These are tough charges, but a sampling of the behavior of our leading classicists supports them.

Classicist David Halperin, writing in a recent book, informs us that his career did not suffer from a lawsuit brought by one of his colleagues claiming that Halperin had demanded that MIT interview a job candidate because he was in love with him, and that Halperin had harassed undergraduates. Although the lawsuit was settled out of court, Halperin lists the signs of his success in the case: "I continued to get grants. My lecture invitations did not diminish; in fact, my lecture fee increased.... And MIT offered me two years of leave at a generous level of financial support, along with a research budget whose magnitude I shall probably not see the likes of again."[24] Time off from teaching in the form of grants, employment at think tanks, visiting professorships, and attendance at conferences to write works like *Saint Foucault* ("As far as I'm concerned, the guy was a f***ing saint"[6]) is the sign of the greatest success in classics; little is said about his students or the status of classical languages, literature, and culture at MIT.

The motives behind such un-Greek behavior are clear. One apparently does not reach our top universities by a lifetime of exploring Greek wisdom with undergraduates, explaining the Greeks to the general public, or tutoring the untraditional: talk always to a tiny elite few about the underprivileged but under no circumstances live, teach, marry, or go to school among them. And somehow reaching an elite university, not teaching America about the Greeks, has become the goal of most of our philhellenes. Teaching well or writing accessibly about classical antiquity counts little toward tenure, promotion, and career advancement in classics. They are, in fact, privately considered to be black marks on one's career; the stale odor of "popularizer" can never be fully expunged from the writer's *curriculum vitae*. Schliemann, Evans, and Ventris—none of them a classicist—suggest that this was not always true in our profession. It has often fallen to the "amateurs," then, the David Denbys of the world—who, upon returning to college in his forties to read the *Iliad*, wrote passionately of its beauty and its stark, existential challenge in *The New Yorker*—to pass on the flame.

In the academy, however, the university career, the pro forma title of academic "classicist" now defines a person as a student of the Greeks. Consider the recent sworn court testimony of the well-known classicist Martha Nussbaum. In an effort to belittle the authority of another Greek scholar, David Cohen, Professor Nussbaum argued that "Cohen...is not a classicist. He has never been employed by a department of classics, and is not a member of the American Philological Association.... He is a professor in a department of rhetoric, with a degree in law."[25] Whether one is knowledgeable about the Greeks is now defined by membership in a professional organization—whose candor we have just examined. Whether one knows or does not know the language of the Greeks depends on teaching in a department of classics. But again, are such protestations true—and are they always sincere? Shortly after testifying that one's classical credentials are to be equated with the locus of appointment, classicist Nussbaum herself took a more lucrative job at the University of Chicago—teaching in the schools of law and divinity.

Rarely in these budget-cutting days do we find a public confession of the true priorities of our field as forthright, for example, as the recent protestations of one Ivy League professor, David Konstan, at one time the president of the American Philological Association. Professor Konstan sincerely insists that the real "problem" in classics is "that small-minded deans and college presidents and legislators (with the collaboration of a certain number of faculty members) at more and more colleges and universities are trying to increase teaching loads and take away time from the research...."[26] He insists classicists should "fight for more research time" in order to publish on "women's roles or slavery or sexuality in antiquity" and that we must "demand respect for such work and the time it requires" (33). Many classicists at major universities actually believe this: professors of Greek and Latin are suffering from too little academic publication like *Sappho Is Burning* and too much teaching, too few journal articles like "Standing by the Stathmos" and too many students. Fifty more paid leaves to produce ten more books like *Penelope's Renown* might yet revive our discipline. More university presses to handle the dividends that accrue from less teaching might yet bring us "respect for such work and the time it requires."

Most academics, unlike Professor Konstan, usually have enough savvy to avoid complaining *publicly* that their lecturing to one or two large classes a year and conducting a graduate seminar or two on their esoteric research entitle them to such generous booty from either public coffers or the pockets of indebted parents and students—especially when so many of their junior colleagues are eager for, but out of, work. There is no doubt that they have demanded (and obtained) "time" for such research, but the quest for "respect" adds insult to injury.

The odd cycle of self-promotion—release time from teaching yields another obscure article which ensures a grant which earns more release time from teaching so that the article can be republished as a book chapter that few will be taught and fewer will read—requires the sacrifice of broad scholarship and teaching. The ambitious classicist must find something strikingly novel to write, something *startling* upon which to build a resumé of things published, not classes taught. But the aspiring researcher in classics *can rarely find much of anything spectacular to do anymore.* We can take only tiny, nearly invisible steps, not ostentatious leaps. These are important steps—progress in any field comes in increments—but there is nothing here to offer the self-promoter a splashy entrance on the road to success, though this is now required in the new corporate ideology of the university. There is little here, really, on which to build a grand career *that will liberate one from the classroom*—no new gene, nonpolluting gas, or cold fission.

Under our current values, all that is now left to the careerist classicist is to play the theoretical game, to reinvent the Greeks and Romans each year, to "gender" Homer in the fall, to unmask his ideology in the spring. To do something else, something actually important, to put stone and text together, to combine papyrus and coin, to make sense of some noble, big idea for the carpenter, teacher, and dentist, would require an eighteenth- or nineteenth-century scholar like Gibbon, Mommsen, or Grote. They would be people of action, of wide reading, of passion and prejudice—"assumers" and "generalizers," in other words, who, like Homer, rarely nod, have a life outside the campus, and certainly have not been ground out by modern American doctoral programs. Indeed, most classicists now suspect that those who argue for big ideas are advocating "nothing but pop phraseology for moral platitudes," as Professor Konstan once again intones.[28]

So irrelevancy, incoherence, and professional self-promotion have become blood brothers in a perverse kind of suicide pact: the more esoteric the research, the more cryptically it is expressed, the less meaning it has for anyone outside a clique—the better for one's career. Again, what a strange cycle! Tenure, promotions, leaves, salary, visiting lectureships, positions on editorial boards, prestige—these are the petty recompense for their wholesale destruction of Greek wisdom. We have lost sight of any real intellectual or educational goal—to explore, to understand, to explain, to disseminate, and, yes, to proselytize, to *convert*. Peewee gladiators in our own tiny and self-determined research arenas, we have now finally lost the interest of even the most blood-thirsty spectators.

VI. Opportunities Lost

The damage to the Greeks is not, as we have seen, just a question of commission, of offering Greeks who have been leveled, deliberately dumbed down and miscast, no different and surely no better than the Pharaohs, palaces, and serfs. Nor is the crime merely one of doing research that is not needed, unreadable, and antithetical to the ethos of the classical world. There is also a (in some sense) worse sin of omission. The industry of publication comes at a price: for every silly or needless article and book written, hundreds of students are not taught at all, and little is written to remind the reader of the role the Greeks could play in our own lives. Meanwhile we, the silent of classics, followed a very small cadre into an oblivion where no one can read what we write, understand what we say, or feel at home with our presence—and all for a few pieces of silver.

Instead of teaching the corporation the egalitarian ethos of the Greeks, we in the university were taught by corporate America, with disastrous consequences. Our administrators ("officers," no longer scholars) now justify their enormous raises on the rationale of running a "business" (no longer a university) with a "payroll" (salaried professors) in the millions, of supervising a "physical plant" and real estate (no longer the gym, library, or open field) worth millions, and offering a "product" in high demand by its "consumers" (so much for degrees and students). Much could have been learned in the 1980s from the Greeks, and much misery of our winner-take-all craze avoided. Much of the structure of the classical city-state was egalitar-

ian. Even the Greeks' earlier and more hierarchical oligarchy and
timocracy were essentially communitarian. The focus of ancient philosophers was not whether there should be equality of some kind but
how far it should extend. Kings, tyrants, aristocrats, and dictators are
the enemies of Greek political science. "Not for me are the things of
rich Gyges," Archilochus sings, "no love I have of great tyranny."

There was decentralization in the *polis* as well, assignment by committee from the Board of Generals, from temple construction to the
organization of tragic festivals. Those misfits who were power-grab-
bers and headline-stealers were ridiculed and attacked. Miltiades was
criticized for taking credit for Marathon. The noble general
Epameinondas's fellow commanders even set up a stele demanding
equal credit for their own role in the victory at Leuctra. The Greeks
conceded that brinkmanship and megalomania might bring some
results in the short term, but knew they inevitably become self-destructive. The ambition of the Athenian showboat Alcibiades remains
the textbook example. The careers of two of the most familiar figures
from classical antiquity, Alexander and Caesar, are notably unclassical;
both were in part responsible for the decline of the ancient egalitarian state. Alexander, a half-civilized Macedonian, had a brilliant but
brief career. When he died at thirty-three, alcoholic, diseased, and poi-
soned, his "empire" was quickly divided and weakened. Caesar was
butchered for setting himself above the ruling class, a lesson well
learned by Augustus. The successful establishment of the Principate
depended a good deal upon at least the illusion of a governing class
of equals.

Even business, where we might think the Greeks have the least
value and relevance, could have learned from a glance at the past. The
bitter experiences of buy-outs, golden parachutes, takeovers, layoffs,
down-sizings, closures, individual short-term success at the expense
of the company and the community—the entire miasma of the
present—could have been predicted by investing some energy in West-

ern culture, if leading classicists had stepped forth in public and in print and in the classroom with the necessary lessons. The Greeks made the first and ultimate critique of the present philistinism, the most persuasive cry for moderation and the reign of *to meson* (the middle). The Greeks already mapped the paths to individual success and the creation of a stable society: joint decision-making, no astronomical payoffs for an undeserving elite, constant audit and accountability, duties to the community, noblesse oblige toward the less fortunate (what the Greeks called *charis*).

How odd that so many of this last generation of academics adopted instead the ethics of the corporate state and created a careerism fatal to undergraduate teaching and broad scholarship. As we have seen, they were proud to label themselves almost everything but undergraduate teachers of Greek and Latin. In the process we lost both the student and the general reader, Homer's only links to the world outside classics. The crucial issue turned out to be a matter of character—of actions matching thoughts, of behavior rather than words, in believing in absolute, rather than relative, standards of conduct—as the Greeks, had the academy remembered them, would immediately have pointed out. If you want to learn why our lawyers, doctors, politicians, journalists, and corporate magnates equate the accumulation of data with character, inherited power with justice, titles and suits with dignity, and capital with talent, why they all know nothing of Greek wisdom, of deed matching word; if you want to know why college tuition has increased at over twice the rate of inflation—then one must look to what they have and have not been taught at America's universities. Is it any wonder, then, that our children no longer know what democracy, free speech, ethics, and Western culture are, much less where they came from and how they are to be preserved? Is it any wonder that Homer is dead?

Greek wisdom—which requires word to match deed—puts a burden on classics professors in a way unknown, say, to the instructor of postwar French literature or most academics in general. After all, we should expect something of the field to rub off on the experts, expect that they would enact in their lives what they admired in their books. Let comparative literature professors living in upscale communities drive imported cars and cry for "diversity." Let anthropologists put their kids in private schools and blather on about "the cultural mosaic" in our public schools. Let Marxist sociologists who spot "exploitation" have Latin American nannies and rely on poorly paid TAs. Let biologists with down parkas and four-wheel-drive Jeep Grand Cherokees decry global warming from old-growth redwood decks. Let English professors talk of egalitarianism and "community" as they negotiate reduced teaching loads and private perks. Let deconstructionists say there are no facts as they circulate their own detailed resumés and write blurbs for each other's books. But let not the classicist do so without remorse.

Thucydides writes of the mob because he was exiled by the mob. Socrates talks of courage and duty because he tried to save the rear guard of a defeated army. Plato writes of reckless democrat deckhands on the sinking ship of state because they killed Socrates and nearly himself. Do not believe historians who now say that their craft is faceless abstraction, dealing only with races, genders, classes, statuses, or ideas, the inevitable laws of the animal kingdom, or the endless processes of acquisition and consumption, of anonymous death and renewal. (Did not more than one Greek say, "Not finely roofed houses, nor the well-built walls, nor even canals or dockyards make the *polis*, but rather men of the type able to meet the job at hand"?) People, then, matter.

It is not primarily what classicists *say*, but what they *do*, that has destroyed formal Greek learning. Like Louis XIV, philologists and theorists alike have bragged these past two decades that *les classics c'est moi*. But old Mme. de Pompadour had their true behavior better pegged: *Après nous le déluge*. The real damage of the university clerks was in an attitude sown by the old and now reaped by a new—most likely the last—generation of classicists. Their classics by intent was to have little to do with Greek, nothing to do with the formation of character or the time-honored rebuke of current fad, was not to be an eccentric but nonetheless noble calling of the old breed, a lifelong vocation kept distant from lucre and status—in the past decade was not even to be *taught* by the successful classicist. At the moment when heroic and innovative efforts were needed in the university, this last generation of custodians of Greece and Rome adopted the ethics of the winner-take-all mogul it claimed to despise. Those who did not, kept silent.

Instead, like finance and law, the study of Greek in the past twenty years became a profession, a tiny world—but a world of sorts nonetheless—of jets, conferences, publicity, jargon, and perks. Knowledge of Homer was to be little more than a way of talking like an on-the-move professor, a manner of living like an in-the-know professor, an embrace of the attitude of a cutting-edge professor—but was no longer a cherished idea of the Greeks that one believed in and lived by, much less a burden to be shouldered and passed on. A few classicists now talk the talk of "teaching undergraduates" and of the need "to promote high-school Latin," but more often their own behavior indicts them. Their real genes show up in each new generation of graduate students who arrive at their new teaching posts with not a care other than to be somewhere other than where they are. No wonder the panicked elite university now is dreaming up all sorts of incentives to match the grandee with a few undergraduates.

If classics is ever to have a real revival, we must end what the therapists call "denial." Almost automatically academics now cry in unison, "But I teach!" "Classics has never been better!" "The parameters of research are exploding!" "Why are you saying these hurtful and damaging things about us?" "Why are you writing this screed, this polemic, this diatribe, this jeremiad, this harangue, this bombast, this broadside?" This from a generation that knows retiring faculty are more often now *not* replaced; that sections of introductory Latin are *not* increasing; that Greek programs are *not* being newly instituted; that classics departments themselves are dying, *not* springing up; that more is being published while *less* is being read; that as teaching loads diminish per individual classicist, new jobs for others are *not* being commensurably created.

The death of the Greeks and Romans means an erasure of an entire way of looking at the world, a way diametrically opposite to the new gods that now drive America: therapeutics, moral relativism, blind allegiance to progress, and the glorification of material culture. The loss of classical learning and the classical spirit as an antidote to the toxin of popular culture has been grievous to America, and it can be sensed in the rise of almost everything antithetical to Greek ideas and values: the erosion of the written and spoken word; the rise of commitments, both oral and written, that are not binding; the search for material and sensual gratification in place of spiritual growth and sacrifice; the growing conformity of urban life at the expense of the individual and the ethos of individualism; ahistoricism and a complete surrender to the present; the demise of the middle class. When Garry Wills claims that the "concept of a serene core of cultural values at the center of Western civilization is entirely false" (40), he simplifies and misrepresents the debate (has any contemporary scholar claimed the core was "serene"?). Certainly the classical worlds have been variously interpreted by different cultures at different times through the last two millennia, but to conclude from this comforting bromide that there was no real "core" to Greek culture itself, no set of values accessible even now to readers of Greek or of importance to all of us today, is simply a lazy nod to postmodernist hypocrisy.

CHAPTER 8

༄

BRUCE S. THORNTON

THE TWILIGHT OF
THE PROFESSORS

The problems with classics that the preceding essays have explored
have a wider context: the utilitarian assault on liberal education
in America that has been going on for nearly the entire twentieth
century. The idea that a university education should serve some
immediately practical end—whether training technicians for government and industry or transforming consciousness to promote
various social causes—is dangerous for the academy. Liberal education, rather, should be the cultivation of critical consciousness
and the passing on of the cultural tradition embodying what
Matthew Arnold called "the best that is known and thought in
the world."

In addition to the utilitarian imperative, the transformation
of academe into a site of careerist advancement has also compromised liberal education. Ambition and the thirst for profit have
been with us always, yet the postwar university, bloated with government money and immune to accountability, has made intellectual work a juicy plum for the lupine opportunist and peripatetic prof-on-the-make. Ideas then become important for their
cash value, not their truth or coherence. Clearly the ascendancy
of postmodernist thought—the incoherence and sloppiness of

which have been repeatedly demonstrated in the preceding essays—has to be understood in terms of the value this ideology has in the academic marketplace.

The erosion of the intellectual's public responsibility is the theme of the following essay. And though the temptation to dismiss the Lilliputian antics of academic pedants is understandable, we should all be concerned. The betrayal of the intellectual's Socratic mission to seek truth and expose cant, and to pass on to future citizens and leaders the same habits of independent thought, creates a climate in which flourish what Sir Thomas Browne called "subtler devisors"—spin-doctors who turn lies into truth, gratifying wishes into facts, and freedom into the worst kind of servitude: the slavery of the mind to false knowledge.

⌒

T HE traditional ideal of the professor—a vaguely eccentric, impractical seeker of truth always teetering, like the Greek philosopher Thales, on the brink of some well or other—has all but disappeared. Though obviously a caricature, this stereotype at least captured the essence of what a professor should be: someone whose life is passionately consumed with the pursuit of ideas, knowledge, and truth as goods worthy in themselves, apart from any practical benefits, someone who is equally passionately dedicated to speaking that truth through writing and teaching. Such a creature will be an irritant to the rest of society and stand apart from its dominant values. After all, this pursuit of truth necessarily is critical and often dissenting, for the other institutions of society too often are comfortable with a false knowledge that, though emotionally and economically gratifying, nonetheless has pernicious long-term effects. Like Socrates, then, the true professor *should* be annoying and disquieting, for he continually questions the received wisdom with which his fellows insulate their lives.

As I say, this type of professor has nearly disappeared. These days *homo academicus* is no longer a descendant of Thales and Socrates, but instead springs from the loins of Mammon. There are many causes for his disappearance, the most obvious being the politicization of the professoriate that has sacrificed the pursuit of ideas and truth on the altar of various supposedly liberating ideologies the professor now fancies himself to serve. Seventy years ago, Julien Benda wrote a book whose title still accurately describes and judges this phenomenon: *The Betrayal of the Intellectuals* (*La trahison des clercs*). In Benda's day nationalism was the ideology that intellectuals served at the expense of their duty "to urge their fellow beings to other religions than the religion of the material."[1] Today a strange amalgam of therapeutic leftist politics and postmodern antirationalism has become the false god to which many academic intellectuals have sacrificed their calling.

Anyone still in doubt that the professoriate, particularly in the humanities and social sciences, can be politically characterized in this way should pick at random a recently published scholarly book or article and examine the political and philosophical assumptions it betrays. Consider, for example, the following statement about the significance for us of Sophocles' *Ajax,* from a recent "cutting edge" collection of essays purporting to demonstrate the efficacy of postmodern theory for the study of classics:

> But I think we too in our culture need to come to grips with our deep emotional investments in our own John Waynes [and other] figures whose essential brutality, moral obtuseness, and gender-based emotional blockage we are constantly invited to forgive.... And why? Perhaps because we are dimly aware that, as a society, our privileges derive from the genocide of Native Americans, from the crushing of Japan, the devastation of Korea and Vietnam, and—not least—from the systematic brutal repression of the criminal element at home effected for us by our military and detective heroes.[2]

The astonishing historical ignorance of these sentences, their reductive, trite psychologizing, their unearned assumption of moral superiority, sadly are all too typical of most academic writing, where this same multiculturalist myth of history as therapeutic melodrama—in which wicked Caucasian Westerners brutalize and oppress peace-loving "peoples of color"—is told and retold with the robotic fervor of airport cult-solicitors.

The pervasiveness of these attitudes in the university is so obvi-ous one wonders why anybody bothers to deny it anymore. Not just in scholarly writing or the class syllabus but in every document most universities generate, in every event they sponsor, in every program they tout and fund, the mantras of multiculturalism are chanted as talismanic charms to ward off accusations of Eurocentric elitism and hegemonic pretensions. What is lost in this eager adherence to a ques-tionable ideology, of course, is the sense of the university's mission to encourage "the free play of the mind on all subjects," as Matthew Arnold put it, and to foster the "instinct prompting [the mind] to try to know the best that is known and thought in the world, irrespec-tively of practice, politics, and everything of the kind; and to value knowledge and thought as they approach this best, without the in-trusion of any other considerations whatever."[3] These days what is taught is driven instead by "identity politics": that is, whatever grati-fies the sensibilities, esteem, and prejudices of various state-certified victims and their self-selected tribunes, who profit in institutional power from their presumed representation of the "oppressed" and "exploited."

The net result is an illiberalism diametrically opposed to the lib-eral education to which professors supposedly are dedicated, and an antihumanism that challenges the fundamental assumptions of mod-ern democracy and its bedrock of human rights inherent in rational, autonomous individuals alone. Here too Benda was prophetic: he saw in the traitorous intellectuals of his day—many of whom, remember, would go on to contribute to the fascist and Communist barbarity of the thirties and forties—a scorn for universalism, a fetishizing of "liberationist" practicality over spiritual concerns, and an idolatry of ethnic particularism and "cultural" specificity all similar to the modern multiculturalist ideology.[4]

But our clerks today are afflicted as well by something equally destructive of liberal education: the juvenile epistemic, ethical, ontological, and linguistic nihilism of postmodernism and poststructuralism. That postmodernism and multiculturalism are essentially self-canceling and fundamentally irreconcilable makes no difference to the poorly educated and inadequately trained academics who dominate the humanities and social sciences and who, as E. P. Thompson noted years ago, suffer from an "amateurish intellectual preparation [that] disarms them before manifest absurdities and elementary philosophical blunders."[5]

Yet we would be mistaken to attribute the decline of the professor merely to a sixties-inspired fall into politics and the *morbus Gallicus* of postmodern theory. The charge that "tenured radicals" have corrupted the university from within in order to promote a leftist agenda, while partially true, obscures the larger developments in education that have brought us to this pass. And it provides the politically correct professors with a flattering foundation-myth about their daring "rebellion" against the "establishment." Rather than rebels, the politicized professors are "company men," as Camille Paglia puts it, "Rosencrantz and Guildensterns, privileged opportunists who rode the wave of fashion."[6] They have eagerly assimilated themselves to the bureaucratized university and its hierarchical systems of rewards and pelf, and it is here that we must look to find the deeper reasons for the professor's decline—in the decades-long transformation of the university from a haven of truth-seekers dispensing liberal education into a utilitarian industry, a profit-making trainer of technicians.

For most of this century the university has had to defend liberal education against the utilitarian bias.[7] But the opportunities for acquiring money and prestige from a traditionally impecunious profession accelerated with the rapid growth of higher education driven by postwar prosperity, the G.I. Bill, the peculiar American doctrine of higher education as an entitlement for everybody, and the perception that American students were falling behind our Cold War and economic rivals. This growth led to the creation of institutions structured on corporate bureaucratic models with their division of labor and administrative hierarchies and unions. And it was all financed by vast infusions of federal money via grants to students and universities alike, with the result that by the early nineties 60 percent of the budget for all of higher education, both public and private, came from the federal government.[8]

The postwar explosion of university growth had disastrous effects on the quality of the professoriate. To meet expanding demand, professors had to be manufactured very quickly to staff the new "colleges" and "universities" being created by Oz-like fiat out of old normal schools and state colleges. The result was creeping mediocrity, as standards for students and professors alike had to be debased to accommodate the vast numbers of both. As Martin Anderson has pointed out, the qualities that make for a genuine academic intellectual are rare—at least as rare as the qualities that make for a National Basketball Association player.[9] Imagine what would happen to the quality of play in the NBA if we suddenly expanded the number of teams from thirty to three thousand and guaranteed even mediocre players not just jobs but starting roles for life, and you can understand what has happened to higher education in the last fifty years.

Meanwhile, the sheer abundance of money and the proliferation of opportunities for grabbing it transformed the university into just another venue of opportunism and self-aggrandizement. The "absent-minded professor" was increasingly replaced by the lupine educrat, who thought not in terms of the impractical development of the individual student's critical consciousness and cultural literacy, but in terms of power, prestige, institutional expansion, and money—obsessions almost always destructive to the nonutilitarian, quirky, eccentric values of liberal education.

Along with the new class of education administrators, however, faculty have been just as aggressive in nosing up to the rich trough subsidized by the federal government and plutocrat philanthropies. Many have become what Robert Nisbet has called "the academic capitalist, the professorial entrepreneur, the new man of power."[10] Charles J. Sykes calls him "Academic Man, this strange mutation of 20th-century academia who has the pretensions of an ecclesiastic, the artfulness of a witch doctor, and the soul of a bureaucrat."[11] Rather than being committed to the life of the mind, to speaking the truth as he knows it, the Academic Capitalist is dedicated instead to career advancement and the acquisition of ever greater perks, status, and money in the form of cushier appointments at more prestigious universities, reduced teaching loads, grants from government and robber-baron trust funds, consulting contracts with industry, and sinecures at institutes and think tanks. This goal occupies his time and energy, leaving little of either for the classroom. And it shapes his research, which now must be what Nisbet calls "conspicuous research,"[12] significant not for quality but for quantity, driven not by the demands of truth and new knowledge but by the prejudices, ideologies, and dogmas of those determining who gets published, who gets hired, who gets promoted, who gets tenured, who gets to go to conferences and "network" for better jobs, who gets invited to think tanks and institutes and centers, and who gets the grants and fellowships. Conformism is more rewarded than originality, and intellectual fad and fashion are more important than truth. Rather than a reproach to a utilitarian, materialist society, the professor has become just another opportunist on the make, hungry for material rewards.

Given the ubiquity of academic capitalism, the conservative specter of ex-sixties radicals or postmodern subversives undermining the university from within misses the point. They *are* subversive, but not of the reigning values and orthodoxies of the amoral, philistine corporate marketplace into which they have smoothly assimilated themselves. After all, ethical relativism, epistemic nihilism, the therapeutic imperative, and the multicultural expansion of consumer choices are all not just compatible with, but essential to, the new global economic order.[13] Rather, careerist "tenured radicals" are subversive of the old-fashioned values of liberal education, of the life of the mind and critical consciousness, neither of which are immediately practical or profitable, and both of which are the deadliest enemies of what George Orwell called the "smelly little orthodoxies." Nothing could be further from critical consciousness than the slavish worship of authority displayed by your typical postmodernist academic, a habit of mind inculcated from the very first day of graduate school and evident in his deference to second-rate French windbags like Jacques Derrida or Michel Foucault.

Thus the motley crew of Marxists, squishy leftists, radical feminists, deconstructionists, social constructionists, multiculturalists, and other postmodernist warriors against patriarchal corporate hegemony are really nothing more than the court jesters of consumer capitalism, their antics tolerated because they are themselves implicated in the system's careerist values and rewards as much as their conservative brethren. They are the devotees of Mammon, who is the real god beneath the patina of leftist politics and postmodern cant. Unsuited, most of them, to the life of the mind and the genuine professor's devotion to ideas and truth, and crippled by mediocre training and trivial overspecialization, their mediocrity nonetheless is rewarded by a hierarchical bureaucracy that values conformity, process, and petty prestige over substance. Is it any wonder that they embrace incoherent ideas, write so poorly, and are incapable of engaging a nonspecialist audience and firing it with enthusiasm for their subject matter and its importance?

If I am correct about the state of the professoriate, then indeed the light is dimming, and night quickly approaches. Whether it comes from the multicultural Left and its desire to transform students into "new men" with the politically correct values, or whether it comes from the economic Right and its need for more technicians to man the new world order, the utilitarian imperative today is ever more powerful and confident. Even as we speak, institutions across the land, mouthing the shibboleths of cost-effectiveness and better "customer" service, are looking to technology—e-mail, videocassettes, television— as the way to "deliver product" to their "consumers" eager for job training and career advancement. The virtual university of the future will have no need for the old-fashioned professor, that quirky, trouble-some, impassioned seeker of truth, the Socratic gadfly who speaks that truth to power and strips away its illusions; who believes, like Socrates, that "the unexamined life is no life worthy of a human be-ing" no matter how materially prosperous it is; who believes passion-ately that critical consciousness is the best guarantor of the individual's freedom and autonomy. What dark consequences will follow the silencing of his dissenting voice, we can only imagine.

EPILOGUE

ᔓ

JOHN HEATH

NOT THE UNABOMBER

FINKING is serious business, even when done for the most noble of reasons against those who may well be guilty of serious crimes. We label informers with ugly words like snitches, rats, and stoolies—they are not our heroes (as Caesar famously noted, he loved the treason but hated the traitor). The Athenians called them "sycophants," a term applied especially to those who manipulated the legal system for their own personal gain by accusing their fellow citizens of complicity in trumped-up civil crimes. Aristophanes, the comic playwright, often humiliated them on stage, much to his audience's delight. After one of these episodes, a sycophant tries in vain to defend himself:

> SYCOPHANT: O gods above, should such things be endured?
>   That they should hurl abuse at *me!* What shame
>   For a decent, patriotic [*philopolis* = lover of his *polis*] man to suffer!
> JUST MAN: A patriot, *you*, and decent!
> SYC: Yes, like no other.
> JM: Then let me ask you something.
> SYC: Ask what you like.

JM: D'you live by farming land?

SYC: You think I'm mad?

JM: Then trading overseas?

SYC (slyly): I sometimes claim so [in order to enjoy the legal privileges accorded merchants].

JM: Well, did you learn a craft?

SYC: No, certainly not.

JM: Then how have you managed to live without a job?

SYC (self-importantly): I *oversee* all public and private business.

JS: But what gives *you* the right?

SYC: I'm free to do it.

JM: How dare you claim you're decent, you petty crook,
        When you're loathed for doing what's no concern of yours?

SYC: It is no concern of mine, you bird-brained fool,
        To serve my very own city with all my might?...
        ...Well *that's* just who I am.
        Which proves the city's business depends on me.

JM: Well, if that's so, the city's in rotten hands.

                              (*Wealth* 898-912, 918-20, trans. Halliwell)

Indeed, ratting out innocent (and even guilty) colleagues, friends,
and acquaintances remains so odious—and keeping one's silence is
considered so honorable—that Oliver North was nearly elected a U.S.
Senator, while much of liberal Hollywood was outraged at the honor-
ary Academy Award recently given to Elia Kazan, who gave *accurate*
information concerning the Communist memberships of his colleagues. A recent front-page article in the local paper with the head-
line "Turn On, Tune Out, Turn In: Files show LSD guru snitched on
others" details how Timothy Leary "quietly cooperated with the FBI
in 1974 and informed on a radical leftist group in hopes of winning
his freedom from prison" (*Mercury News,* July 1, 1999, 1A). Somehow
it's always news to learn that the self-proclaimed radical Left uses the
same cowardly techniques of self-preservation it so often (and rightly)
decried in the 1950s.

So, to compare big things with the very small, what in the world could have been in the mind of Professor Judith Hallett, a self-proclaimed liberal, feminist, and progressive scholar from the University of Maryland—a woman whom I had neither met nor even seen in person (and have not to this day)—when she announced to the world through the Internet in the spring of 1999 that in 1994 she had given my name, and that of my friend Victor Davis Hanson, to the FBI in connection with their hunt for the Unabomber, a man whom she herself characterized as a "deranged killer"?

The answer I have come up with is perhaps as strange as Hallett's actions themselves—as the FBI profilers note, to catch a lunatic one must sometimes think like a lunatic. The editorial in the *Wall Street Journal* (May 28, 1999, W11) about this entire wacky episode pointed in the right direction: it is mostly about petty academic vengeance. But the FBI hotline is an unusually heavy and remarkably original weapon in such skirmishes, and the zaniness is deeper and more twisted even than it appears. In short, I believe Professor Hallett made up the entire call to the FBI. Why, you may wonder, would a well-established scholar humiliate herself by admitting publicly to an ethically irresponsible act that she in fact had never committed? First, the story.

The "Unabomber Maneuver," as it is now called, has a long gestation that can mostly be ignored. It is enough to say for now that in 1997 Victor Davis Hanson and I published a long essay in the journal *Arion* (reprinted in this volume as "*Who Killed Homer?*: The Prequel") on the nature and causes of the decline of classical studies (we suggested that we classicists were to blame), followed up in spring 1998 with the publication of a book—*Who Killed Homer?* (*WKH?*)—on the same theme. Both the essay and book argue for the necessity of studying the Greeks as the originators of the blueprint of Western civilization. Professor Hallett made it clear in various public *fora* that she felt her subspecialties (feminism and theory) and friends had been made the goats of our argument and she resented it. Over the next year members of the classics "List" (an electronic chat room found at classics@u.washington.edu), led by a handful of "progressives" who for the most part identified with Professor Hallett's pain, took turns critiquing and criticizing our argument in *WKH?* This was often not a particularly scholarly effort (see below), but it provided an opportunity for sensitive academics to vent about our "hurtful" message. During one of these various discussions, the following passage from *WKH?* became the topic of concern:

> The only hope for this survival [of classical studies] rests with an imaginative and sympathetic Classics teacher who can each hour, each minute demonstrate some connection between third-declension nouns and Socrates' last speech, and then again between Socrates' last speech and the students' own lives. But to do all that requires imagination, a broad education, empathy for the suffering of others—more, then, than the mastery of Greek philology: knowledge of grammar without being a grammarian, cognizance of theory without being a theorist, familiarity with the academic landscape without being an academic. Rarely are any rotund and aproned Aunt Beas now to be found in Classics, smiling professors scurrying across the floor with cookies and Cokes, wiping brows and squeezing hands at the rear of the class, now fainting, now huffing, "Come on back, kids, it's not so bad, stay in Greek and have a slice of pie over irregular comparative adjectives." Even to hungry undergraduates, three hours a night in the library is too much to pay for dessert. Classicists can no longer huddle to the rear in the surf as waves of their greenhorn Greek and Latin 1A-ers are machine-gunned in the sand. If we are going to lose Greek, let us do so with burly, cigar-chomping professors, red-eyed from overload classes, wounds oozing from bureaucratic combat, chests bristling with local teaching medals and complimentary Rotary pens from free lecturing, barking orders and dragging dozens of bodies forward as they brave administrative gunfire, oblivious to the incoming rounds from ethnic studies and contemporary cinema. (*WKH?* 170-1)

Professor David Lupher from the University of Puget Sound, a frequent contributor to the List and critic of *WKH?*, was distressed by our language. He took our tongue-in-cheek depiction of classics professors braving the onslaught of postmodernity literally, apparently thinking we actually imagined students being gunned down by berserk sharpshooters from special interest programs on campus. When someone else on the List later tried to suggest that the passage was written as a "humorous caricature," Professor Lupher invoked W. H. Auden's war poetry and decried our "bombastic" prose. Such overdramatic responses to criticism of the academy are common fare in this era of light teaching-loads and plenty of free time, and usually make little impression on either friend or foe. But this time Professor Lupher had unwittingly hit the jackpot.

A few classicists joined in a loose deliberation of the passage from *WKH?*, a desultory discussion that danced whimsically from one topic to another as such chat room ventilations often do. On Tuesday, May 11, 1999, one member of the List tired momentarily of the banter and tried to steer the conversation into slightly deeper waters:

> All or most wistful silliness aside, have there been many cinematic depictions of classicists? Indiana Jones springs easily to mind (and actually seems to almost fit the silly portrait I drew above). Are there others? Should there be?

The import of these questions was not lost on List members. Professor Mark Williams of Calvin College did not have an answer to the weighty ethical issue at hand—*should* there be more classicists in the movies indeed!—but he had some information he wanted to share:

> There are two delightful French films that feature a husband-wife duo, one of whom is a detective and the other a professor of Greek. The twist is that the prof. is the husband, the detective the woman. I believe that the titles of the films came over into English as *Dear Detective* and *Jupiter's Thigh*. Can't remember the name of the actor who portrayed the Greek prof. but it was the same guy who gave the marvellous lead performance in *La Vie et Rein D'autre*.

If there's anything more enticing than a good game of cultural trivia, it is the chance to pounce on a wounded player. Professor Hallett did

not miss a beat: "It's Philippe Noiret (of *Cinema Paradiso* and *Il Postino*)."
Professor Williams, having met his match, quickly apologized for his
lapse, explaining that his brain had "plainly turned into mush here on
the day before classes end." One might reasonably wonder how much
time a professor feeling the crunch of his classes really ought to spend
on the Internet pondering such issues, but the question had evoked a
torrent of loosely connected thoughts from Professor Hallett and there
was no stopping her now:

> Arnold Moss (1920-1989) graduated Phi Beta Kapp from CCNY with
> a major in Latin and Greek, and played numerous evil types on the
> screen.
>
> Then there's the episode of Rumpole of the Bailey—"Rumpole
> and the Right to Silence." In it a classics professor, trying to save
> his department at Gunster U., is the murderer (of the Vice-Chancel-
> lor), and gives it away to Rumpole by quoting Catullus (as well as
> spouting Cicero at the murderous moment).
>
> My Latin prose comp students this semester put the passage
> featuring the Catullus quote into Ciceronian Latin. I gave a copy of
> the best effort to the author, (Sir) John Mortimer, when he spoke
> here in Washington a few months ago (and shared an amusing an-
> ecdote about his classical education at Harrow to explain his switch
> from the Communist to the Labour Party). He just wrote us a won-
> derful note, expressing his pleasure that "the classics are still being
> taught so well in America."

So far, so bad—such self-laudatory episodes and name-dropping are
often the *raison d'etre* for anecdotal meandering on the List—but
things quickly turned from the uninspiring to the ludicrous. Unwill-
ing and no doubt unable to counter Professor Hallett's blast, Professor Williams retreated to one of the original points of discussion of
the passage from *WKH?*: "Just out of curiosity, have H&H ever been
shot at? That bit about cigar-chomping makes me wonder."

To this odd question (later termed "very pertinent" by Professor
Lupher) Judith Hallett gave a reply so weird, so unexpected even in

this chat room from hell, that it earned her a starring role in an editorial in the *Wall Street Journal*:

> Their names were given to the FBI during the nationwide effort to find the Unabomber, at a time when he was thought to be in his early 40's and based in northern California.

Poor Professor Williams must not have known what to make of this—who would have?—for it took a while for someone else, a classicist in Japan in fact, to ask the obvious question: "Now what can this factoid possibly mean as cited here?" Indeed, the history of this passive, anonymous technique of defamation in the twentieth century is known to all and should have sent shivers up the spines of Professor Hallett's progressive friends. How could Professor Hallett possibly have access to still-sealed FBI files on the case? But this was only the beginning of her amazing pronouncements, as her passive accusation turned into an even more spooky admission:

> [1] Actually, it's a confession, not a factoid. It was I who phoned the FBI hot line, to say that while I didn't suspect either of any bombings, I thought that both might have leads as to the bomber's identity since they shared views and a similar mode of exposition.

> [2] And it's no secret: I have discussed my decision to do so (both before and after I did it) with several colleagues, including people on this list. [*Nota Bene!*] At the time I was working on Heath's contributions to that 1995 *CW* issue we kindly agreed to center on his prequel-to-*WKH*?-essay, and I was struck by many similarities between his/and VH's message and style, and those of the Unabomber's manifesto (as well as a physical resemblance: the drawing of what he was supposed to look like depicted a handsome blonde male in a hooded sweatshirt with a strikingly sculpted chin).

> [3] As everyone is aware, though, the FBI was wrong about the location and age of the Unabomber. Here I was trying to be a patriotic American and there they were wasting my time.

It would be unfair to examine Professor Hallett's reasoning(?) at this point, for over the next few days she felt compelled, mostly prompted by questions from a few incredulous List members, to try to explain her actions. The following paragraphs are the bulk of that attempt. Every relevant passage I could find has been included—the only important elements intentionally excluded are the prompts or questions to which she is replying, and those have been supplied in brackets when it has been deemed necessary for clarity. Here, then, are Judith Hallett's reasons for siccing the FBI—or so she claims—on Victor Davis Hanson and me in 1994. These passages are listed in rough chronological order; the numbering of paragraphs is for convenience of later reference—often a single e-mail message is divided into several separate paragraphs. This extensive quotation is not just an effort to be "fair"—such a concept is completely alien to Professor Hallett's style of academic kidney-punching. The following series of responses, justifications, rationalizations, and misrepresentations represents the state of discussion within the academy about the nature and function of education itself. In short, this sophistic and erratic rambling presents an accurate (if remarkably distilled) picture of the general level of intellectual honesty and moral integrity on today's campus, as a brief examination of the List's response to Professor Hallett will reveal. But first to Professor Hallett herself:

> [4] As it happens, both Hanson and Heath have attacked me viciously in print and other venues. And perhaps this has sullied my reputation, if this quaint term is an accurate way to describe discrediting someone's commitment to being fair and truthful.
>
> [5] I associated their views with his [the Unabomber's], which is a different matter. I share views with some pretty scary people, and I'm sure you do too. I made this association in response to someone who inquired if they had ever been subject to shooting. To judge from the list response, my call to the FBI is judged more heinous behaviour. I expected as much.

[6] Here's why I brought this up. The question was raised: Are H&H's views inflammatory enough, sufficiently offensive to drive those they insult and misrepresent to take up firearms against them? No, but only because those they insult and misrepresent (e.g. feminists, gays, Latinists) aren't firearms users, and will express their negative reactions to these views in other ways. I discerned affinities between these views and those of the Unabomber, and was willing to share my opinion with the FBI, while making it clear that I didn't think either was the Unabomber. Others simply ignore them, or dismiss them as scholars and serious, productive thinkers. If H and H cared about their reputations, by the way, they would not engage in such abusive personal attacks on other individuals. Someone may well sue them some day.

[7] But let me explain why I gave their names to the FBI several years ago, and why I mentioned this on the list. After the publication of the Unabomber's manifesto, the FBI were desperately seeking leads as to the Unabomber's identity so as to prevent further losses of human life (a matter more serious than tarnishing scholarly reputations). They wanted information about highly educated people in northern California who expressed views similar to those in the manifesto. At the time I was working with JH, a northern California academic who—along with a northern California academic collaborator VDH—voiced some of the same views. Whether or not these two men actually knew the author of the manifesto, these similarities seemed worth investigating: maybe they knew other people in common.

[8] The major reason I thought it reasonable to contact the FBI is that, thirty years ago now, I was not only contacted by them but harassed and hounded (my neighbors were harassed and hounded by them as well) when my name turned up in the address book of a classics graduate student named Jane Alpert (Swarthmore '67) who had bombed the Chase Manhattan bank. Jane worked as a classics editor at Cambridge Press in NY and she and I had met, had lunch etc. several times in connection with the new Cambridge Latin series which she was promoting and I was "testing". I had abolutely no idea of her political views but that did not stop the FBI from

investigating me, and indeed making it difficult for me to obtain
employment for several years: she had engaged in destructive, dangerous conduct (for which she ultimately was imprisoned) and I
was acquainted with her.

[9] [It was relevant that the writing style and/or views expressed by
H&H reminded me of the Unabomber manifesto] Because I had a
previous encounter with the FBI myself, and was familiar with what
they defined as helpful information that might be valuable to them
rather than have them beating down my door, interrogating me in
a hostile way, following me for days on end, bothering my neighbors (and badly frightening two of them, musicians who had fled
both Hitler and Stalin, by going through—and leaving in total dis-
array—the music in their studio on the grounds that it was in "alien"
foreign languages). The views these two men shared with the
Unabomber as well as the other resemblances to the FBI profile
were much better evidence, to me at least, that there might be some
connection worth pursuing than my name (or Martin Ostwald's, or
Helen North's) in Jane's address book.

[10] [How could H&H and the Unabomber have influenced each
other—a writing seminar?] I wouldn't trivialize the opportunities
for acquiring/articulating shared views with a dismissive academic
term like that. Perhaps they had heard or given talks expressing
these views at which the Unabomber had been present; perhaps they
had read or written materials with which he was also familiar. Certainly they had more in common with him—world-view-wise—than
I did with Jane Alpert. You should remember, too, that the FBI was
trying to determine the Unabomber's identity from his "academic"
writing. To do that required precisely those philological skills that
classicists have been praised for applying in military intelligence on
this list of late.

[11] [Why was it relevant that the drawing of the Unabomber reminded you of H&H if you didn't think either was the Unabomber?]
But the FBI's informants may have thought one of them was the
Unabomber, however wrongly. As it turns out, there was a good deal
of wrong information in their call for help. Again, I had dealt with
the FBI before, heard their justification for treating me as they did

and worked on the principle that any information that could be willingly furnished would be helpful.

[12] [The FBI was wasting *your* time?] Apparently so. They evidently chose to de-emphasize (accurate) suggestions that the Unabomber was in his 50's and NOT in northern California because they thought they would cast a wider net and elicit more helpful information in this way.

[13] I am pretty certain he [VDH] and John Heath know I gave the FBI their names in this connection already, because I told the FBI NOT to keep my identity a secret if they did in fact contact either of them. And I have shared this information with a great number of people. My interaction with the FBI in this endeavor is pertinent because Hanson should, in the interests of fair disclosure, acknowledge that I voluntarily went to a law enforcement agency and likened his and his collaborator's views to that of a deranged killer when he is asked to assess my work and my life.

[14] [I] hope you now understand the background to all of this. Obviously I took a risk by doing what I did, and admitting as much, but I don't regret any of it a bit.

[15] Over four years ago, at a time when—in my capacity as editor—I was working with John Heath on his CW article and response to responses to that article, I answered the public requests by the FBI for assistance in their effort to identify a deranged terrorist by suggesting that they contact Heath and his collaborator Hanson as leads, consultants who might be able to help them. I gave my name and told the FBI to feel free to tell Heath and Hanson that I had provided their names. I emphasized that I did not think either was the Unabomber, but that they shared provocative views with him, taught at the university level in the region where the FBI claimed he was located and frequented academic circles, were about the same age that the FBI said he was, and shared physical features with their published sketch of what they thought he looked like.

[16] I am reluctant to do so [provide a detailed explanation and justification for what I did] because several list members have already misconstrued my on-list remarks about my own painful experience

with the FBI of the 1960's. What I obviously failed to make sufficiently clear was tha[t] then, as in 1994, the FBI were trying to keep
a domestic terrorist with academic connections from causing further harm to the public. Then, however, the FBI chose to spy on
and harass those who might help. Many protests, including my own,
led to their adoption of new procedures: sharing valuable information with the public, enlisting aid through a hotline, and on this
hotline conducting themselves with far more openness and accountability than obtain in many job searches and tenure/promotion reviews in academia.

I felt comfortable with these new procedures (indeed far more
comfortable than I have when consulted or volunteering references
in any number of academic job searches and tenure/promotion reviews), which was one of my reasons for making use of this hotline.
Another is that the lives of my—of our—colleagues in science/tech
fields, not to mention those of their families, students and staff,
were in serious danger as long as the Unabomber remained at large.
Although I never actually witnessed anyone else phone the
Unabomber hotline, it is my impression that many in the scientific
community also provided them with leads of various sorts, mostly
fellow academics with northern California connections.

[17] But I am also reluctant to provide more information to the list
on why I decided to help the FBI in this instance because I'm not
sure how much I can share publicly about my other interactions
with them, and the CIA, and other law-enforcement and intelligence
gathering organizations. Here in the Washington area there are a
great many present and prospective employees of these organizations, as well as people who require security clearance by these organizations to perform other jobs. I get many, many calls from their
representatives about past and present students, colleagues, neighbors, people in my carpools. In every case, my name has been provided to these representatives not by the person on whom information is sought, but because someone else identified me as a "lead". I
haven't been all that impressed by the CIA, but—again—the folks
from the FBI conduct themselves as professionally as (sometimes
more so than) fellow academics who call upon me to assist in hiring and promoting.

[18] Anyhow, it would seem as though many listmembers from different parts of our country and the world don't have as many opportunities to interact with the FBI. Which explains why so many seem to assume that any interaction which involves providing the FBI with other people's names is tantamount to "turning these people in" as potential criminals, "sic(c)ing the FBI on them."

But I don't think I can discuss FBI interactions any further.

Michael [professor at UC Berkeley to whom this letter is a reply], if you have any evidence that I phoned the FBI to "turn" Heath and Hanson in, that I claimed they were the Unabomber (rather than they might, without realizing it, know the Unabomber), please provide it. If not, please retract your statement.

[19] Although I prefer to ignore the taunts of bullies, I will clarify matters misrepresented in another recent posting tomorrow. Suffice it to say that there is no way a call I made in 1994 can be explained by a review written several years later. Such biographical criticism is totally irresponsible.

[20] I have just received a telephone call from Joseph Bottum, Books and Arts Editor of the *Standard* here in Washington [and eventual author of the editorial in the *Wall Street Journal*].... I need the advice of the list as to what I do next. Do we want this "discussion" covered in the media? I would prefer that we keep it to ourselves.

Before explaining my reasons for believing that Professor Hallett never really called the FBI at all—or has such a muddled recollection of her actions that nothing of use can be deduced from her justifications—it is worth noting what the chat room's reaction was to this series of confessions, for this too supplies a telling sample of the level of fortitude in the modern university. Ninety-nine percent of the thousand or so members said nothing. Many e-mailed Professor Hanson and me personally (neither of us subscribes to the List) to ask if we knew anything about it (we didn't), but they didn't care to step into the tar pit publicly. A handful of members expressed their shock at the nuttiness of Professor Hallett's actions, but even here some were careful to align themselves politically with her. Professor Jeffrey S.

Carnes of Syracuse University, for example, who considers Hallett "a political ally, a friend, a fellow feminist," admitted that "impeccable liberal (or leftist) credentials do not justify ratting personal enemies out to the FBI (or to Ken Starr—not very pleased with Christopher Hitchens, either) on the shakiest of grounds." Torn between what he acknowledged to be the "bizarre" behavior of his political ally and his dislike of the politically incorrect *WKH?*, he carefully prefaced his concern over Hallett's "curious distance from reality" by reassuring List members that "I and many of my friends refer to them [Hanson and Heath] with such technical terms as 'f***ing a**holes' and 'bitter, envious pricks'—but of course that's the sort of thing about which one can only speculate..." After all, as Professor Carnes noted in his own confession, "[I] don't know them personally." Cogent words indeed from someone who has never met us and who objects to what he believes are our "ad hominem" criticisms in *WKH?*

Professor Carnes's reasoned eloquence need not be taken as representative of the entire List—rumors have it that he later apologized for his language if not for his twisted logic—but it does suggest the kind of miasmatic environment in which actions like Professor Hallett's are engendered and nourished. Once again we see that it is only through the imposition of some sort of external scrutiny that universities and "scholars" will ever be held accountable to the community. Despite confessed pride in her actions—"Obviously I took a risk by doing what I did, and admitting as much, but I don't regret any of it a bit" [# 14]—Professor Hallett also seemed to be vaguely aware of how this might look if someone actually lifted up the classics couch and looked about with a flashlight: "Do we want this 'discussion' covered in the media? I would prefer that we keep it to ourselves" [#20].

But under any scrutiny, Professor Hallett's confession simply doesn't hold up. She may have called the FBI, but it could not have possibly happened the way she describes it or for the reasons she now adduces. Professor Hallett says that she made the call to the FBI when she was editing my contributions to a 1995 edition of *Classical World*—this, according to her, included both my original article and the rebuttal [#2, #15]. She also claims that this call was made in 1994 [#16, #19]. She had certainly seen my original article in 1994, which I submitted to *CW* at the beginning of 1993. But I did not submit the first version of my rebuttal until June of 1995. Thus the best that we can say is that Professor Hallett has confused the time frame, and she based her call to the FBI only on my original *CW* article.

But Professor Hallett also says repeatedly that she based her belief about my connections with the Unabomber on the shared views and mode of exposition between my writings and those found in the Unabomber's manifesto: for example, "At the time I was working on Heath's contributions to that 1995 *CW* issue we kindly agreed to center on his prequel-to-*WKH?*-essay, and I was struck by many similarities between his/and VH's message and style, and those of the Unabomber's manifesto..." [#2; cf. #1, #6, #7, #9, #15]. This is a remarkable claim, considering that I turned in the final copy of my *CW* article in August of 1994 (and that of my rebuttal in July of 1995—but again, she must not be referring to this) and she insists that she made her call in 1994, but the Unabomber's manifesto was *not* published in the *Washington Post* until September of 1995! Professor Hallett purportedly told the FBI my writing and views were similar to the Unabomber's *an entire year before anyone else had read it.* How could this be? If I were to apply Professor Hallett's paranoid logic to the situation, I would have to conclude that Professor Hallett was editing the Unabomber's prepublished work at the same time she was working on mine.

Even more unsettling, Professor Hallett insists that she turned in both me and my "collaborator," Victor Davis Hanson [#2, #7, #15]. The overwhelming obstacle to believing this statement is that Victor Davis Hanson and I did *not* publish anything together until fall of

1997, *a year and half after Theodore Kaczynski had been arrested.* I had *no* collaborator on either *CW* piece. True, I thanked Professor Hanson in a footnote for one observation—but I also thanked Professor Hallett twice for her help, and indeed I rewrote the original article four times under her careful scrutiny. If anyone deserves to be called my collaborator in 1994, it is certainly she. In fact, now that I think about it, it was Editor Hallett who overturned two negative referee reports and encouraged me to rewrite the article; it was Editor Hallett who refused to accept my withdrawal of the paper in early 1994; it was Editor Hallett who sent me seven single-spaced pages of comments to be incorporated into the paper (they weren't); it was Editor Hallett who made it the centerpiece of an entire edition of *CW*.

Now as to her primary defense, that she believed we (that is, I) shared similar views and mode of exposition with the Unabomber, I have demonstrated above that unless Professor Hallett had a copy of the manifesto a year *before* anyone else, such a charge cannot stand. But it is a charge nevertheless that she makes repeatedly [#1, #6, #7, #9, #10, #15] without once making the slightest effort to demonstrate its validity. Even her single specific objection to my (our) argument— that we attack "feminists, gays, and Latinists"—is completely erroneous. I leave it to any reader to compare my article (reprinted in this volume as "Self-Promotion and the 'Crisis' in Classics") with the antitechnology scribblings of the manifesto. My paper, in any of its versions, says nothing about culture, either ancient or modern—in fact, it says virtually nothing about Latinists and absolutely zilch about gays—but concentrates almost entirely on the role self-promoting classicists have played in the undermining of the study of the Greeks and the Romans. It criticizes some feminist scholarship, but praises some as well. I think every reader, whether classicist or not, will find Professor Hallett's self-proclaimed philological skills—"You should remember, too, that the FBI was trying to determine the Unabomber's identity from his 'academic' writing. To do that required precisely those philological skills that classicists have been praised for applying in military intelligence on this list of late" [#10]—have failed her on this occasion. As one respondent on the List observed, "I too read the manifesto, and only someone whose stylistic sensitivities had been occluded by hatred or inability could find any similarity." Bruce Thornton has pointed out to me that it was the noted *leftist,* Kirkpatrick Sale, who wrote a semi-approving piece on the manifesto in *The Nation* (Sept. 25, 1995, 305-9): the Unabomber's Romantic faith in "wild nature" (in which he includes human nature) is exactly the opposite of what we praise about the Greeks (see "*Who Killed Homer? The Prequel*") and ultimately comes much closer to the oft-professed liberal leanings of Professor Hallett than anything I (or Professor Hanson) have ever published.

Professor Hallett also makes a good deal out of the FBI profile [#2, #11, #15], a copy of which I was able to download from the Internet. She is right that the Unabomber was originally profiled as a white man in his late thirties or forties who "normally mails the bombs out of Northern California" and was "familiar with university life." Again, we are playing Professor Hallett's impossible game of the Unabomber Maneuver, but we need to examine all of her justifications. The profile also says that the Unabomber is a "recluse"; Professor Hallett could have asked our wives, families, friends, colleagues, and neighbors to find out just how antisocial we are. He "has low self-esteem, most likely has had problems dealing with women"; Professor Hallett could surely have called our wives and asked. "He is a neat dresser with a meticulously organized life"; she *really* should have called our wives about this. "If he does have a relationship, it would be with a younger woman." Our wives would definitely be glad to hear this. "5'10 - 6' tall Weight 165"; well, I haven't been that short or weighed that little since high school. "Reddish-blonde hair, a thin mustache and a ruddy complexion"; alas, I've never had any red in my hair, although it does take on a fiery tinge when the sun sets behind it. I haven't had a mustache since my sophomore year in college, and it wasn't thin. Ruddy? I've always thought of myself more as swarthy, although I go pale in the California winters.

Now Professor Hallett got tripped up here. By saying that one of the reasons she thought I (we) might be the Unabomber was because I (we) looked like the sketch, she definitely implied that she was turning us in *as* the Unabomber, not merely having possible connections with him (unless she thinks people who hang out with deranged killers all look alike). When pressed, she retreated to the fallibility of the FBI's informants, not her own: "But the FBI's informants may have thought one of them was the Unabomber, however wrongly. As it turns out, there was a good deal of wrong information in their call for help" [#11]. Nice try, but the profile she relied on is very explicit about the origin of the sketch: "The suspect seen moving the bomb in the February 20, 1987, Salt Lake City bombing is the one seen in the sketches of the Unabomber. The description given at the time was..." and thus follows as given above. Professor Hallett, who says she based her tale to the FBI at least partially on this profile, must surely have read that sentence. If she did in fact call the FBI, then she knew that her suggestion that I (we) looked like the Unabomber meant that I (we) had been seen with the bomb. Is she suggesting that the informant saw Mr. Kaczynski running around with a bomb in Salt Lake City and then accidentally instead gave a description of a classics professor in Santa Clara to the FBI sketch artist? If she did not trust the informant's information for whatever purpose, then she had no reason to base her phone call on any resemblance, however imaginary. (Professor Hanson and I disagree, by the way, on how we should respond to Professor Hallett's implication that either of us is—as the possible Unabomber—"a handsome blonde male...with a strikingly sculpted chin," [#2] her own words not found in the FBI profile. Desperate for any approbation, I am flattered; Professor Hanson finds it positively creepy.)

If, as I think I have shown fairly conclusively, Professor Hallett could not have given the FBI our names in 1994 in connection with the Unabomber and his manifesto, at least not in the manner or for the reasons she has subsequently supplied, what *did* she do? I seriously doubt she ever called the FBI about me—indeed, when I finished working on the *CW* article in 1995 I thought that we were still on good professional terms. I had no reason to believe otherwise (see my introduction to "Self Promotion"). Although we disagreed on the role of feminism in academia, and I had expressed frustration with the editorial process, our exchanges were always cordial and I assume she opened my letters and manuscripts without flinching. She is clearly now trying to pose as a good patriot [#3, #7, #16]—another easy refuge for scoundrels, as Aristophanes' sycophant reveals—but her discussion of her relationship with the FBI is caught up in a past history of harassment [#8, #9] and spy novel mystery (e.g., her role as consultant, about which she is not at liberty to speak, to the CIA, #17, #18) which she describes so vividly that it appears she was more interested in hounding us than in saving human life. Why would she want to do that?

Well, she wouldn't have wanted to do that, not in 1994 or 1995. But she would now. In the past two years Victor Davis Hanson and I have caused her some embarrassment, and if you read her explanations of how she claims to have acted in 1994 it is easy to see that they only make sense in a post-*WKH?* context. Professor Hanson and I have in fact been collaborators since 1997; we have in fact argued that the scholarship of her subspecialties has led to the decline in interest in the ancient worlds and a denial of what is true and wonderful, as well as dangerous, about the Greeks and the Western paradigm; we have in fact angered her and a handful of "leading" classicists by suggesting in our populist argument that their ideological agendas are elitist and self-promoting. We mention her in a footnote in *WKH?*, and several of her friends had their work held up to badly needed public scrutiny. More than this, Professor Hallett has invested much of her time and energy the past few years trying to promulgate a "new" approach to scholarship called the "personal voice." She organized panels at the annual meeting of classicists for several years and found a publisher for the papers. The book she ultimately co-edited was panned almost everywhere, but the most devastatingly accurate and unanswerable review was that of my "collaborator," Victor Davis Hanson (which appears in this volume as chapter 4). First published in 1998, "Too Much Ego in Your Cosmos" mercifully snuffed out and buried "personal voice" scholarship in classics. Oh, there will be a few more agonistic twitches, but these efforts are now impossible to take seriously, like trying to watch an airport disaster movie after seeing the parodic *Airplane*. Professor Hallett's dream of converting scholarship into whiny accounts of personal trauma was mothballed as soon as it saw the light of day, the *Spruce Goose* of modern theory.

My suggestion, then, is that in 1999 Professor Hallett invented her 1994 call to the FBI and made a public announcement of it on the Internet solely to earn a little vengeance—and to salvage her fast-sinking efforts to promote the "personal voice." Everyone—even her political allies—has been appalled at the sloppiness of her efforts. Vengeance has a long and deep tradition—there is scarcely a Greek text that does not deal with it—so it is doubly embarrassing for a classicist to fail so miserably. She gives the game away in several of her answers to the legitimate question: Okay, so you called the FBI in 1994. That's dirty water under the bridge. Why do you bring it up now in 1999?

> Here's why I brought this up. The question was raised: Are H&H's views inflammatory enough, sufficiently offensive to drive those they insult and misrepresent to take up firearms against them? No, but only because those they insult and misrepresent (e.g. feminists, gays, Latinists) aren't firearms users, and will express their negative reactions to these views in other ways. I discerned affinities between

these views and those of the Unabomber, and was willing to share my opinion with the FBI, while making it clear that I didn't think either was the Unabomber. Others simply ignore them, or dismiss them as scholars and serious, productive thinkers. If H and H cared about their reputations, by the way, they would not engage in such abusive personal attacks on other individuals. Someone may well sue them some day. [#6; cf. #5]

Hallett's dudgeon makes her misread the entire thread of the discussion on the list. The question was *not* "Are H&H's views inflammatory enough, sufficiently offensive to drive those they insult and misrepresent to take up firearms against them?" but "Just out of curiosity, have H&H ever been shot at? That bit about cigar-chomping makes me wonder." A weird question, to be sure, and hardly relevant to the topic at hand, but if it means anything it must be a question about whether we are veterans or have served in some form of police duty (thus the curiosity about the cigar-chomping caricature). Hallett thinks that our discussion of the state of classics in *WKH?*—and no doubt in Hanson's review as well—is so painful that classicists would think of shooting us! Again, we do lament the current state of feminist scholarship in classics in our recent writings, but say nothing about gays or Latinists in particular. Moreover, as one respondent on the List noted, the "notion that feminists, gays and 'Latinists' [sic, whoever they are] do not use firearms is false. Visit any firing range; you will see lots of the first two, especially the first. Can't say about the last. Maybe the genus should speak up." But more importantly, how out of touch with reality must one be even to imagine shooting someone because he or she disagrees with your approach to Euripides' *Medea*? Talk about your deranged killers. This is academic vindictiveness at its wackiest, sort of a "Clytemnestra meets Garp."

Hallett is simply out to slur in any fashion possible, a car-struck dog snapping wildly but impotently at its invisible attackers. Note her suggestion that the ever-present and never identifiable "others" ignore and dismiss us, a wish that the mere fact of our seemingly eternal presence as a topic of discussion on her beloved List immediately refutes. She never substantiates a single charge. As the same respondent (who has published a lengthy review of *WKH?* and thus knows the book well) countered:

> The repeated charges that H&H have engaged in abusive, inflammatory and offensive attacks on others, kai dh kai [especially] on Judith Hallett, is nonsense. But if she is going to make it repeatedly without the slightest factual basis, then I for one request proof. JH tends to construe all criticism of her work, or the work of her allies, as misrepresented, inflammatory, offensive and personal. Apparently personal voice criticism predisposes some to read rational critique, including very biting but reasoned critique, in a childishly personal way. I have learned from JH and her fellow feminists, but that does not mean I must hang up my personal assessment of logic and evidence when approaching a kind of holy grail.

Professor Hallett's true motivations were in fact more explicitly revealed early on in the discussion: "As it happens, both Hanson and Heath have attacked me viciously in print and other venues. And perhaps this has sullied my reputation, if this quaint term is an accurate way to describe discrediting someone's commitment to being fair and truthful" [#4]. Again, this is untrue. We have criticized her scholarship and that of some other feminists and personal voice allies in print, but the adverb reflects her own paranoia. (Theodore Kaczynski's words upon being sentenced to four consecutive life terms plus thirty years were that he would respond to "the many falsehoods that have been propagated about me.") We have never "attacked" Professor Hallett in any venue—until her "confession" we have had no reason ever to mention her name in any public arena—but it is clear she believes we have and is out to get even. In fact, she admitted as much recently in the *Chronicle of Higher Education* (July 2, 1999, A13) in defense of her claim to have called the FBI ("I felt I did something that was reasonable and patriotic"): "They have an absolute right to speak that way"—but "you can't have it both ways. If you don't want to be careful, considerate, and cautious with your colleagues, you can't expect to be treated that way in return." So it's personal. Catch the amazing logic here: because we criticize her scholarship, it is perfectly "reasonable," indeed to be "expected," that she would try to link us to a national manhunt for a homicidal terrorist. She seems not to have noticed that such a personal response makes no sense in the context of my article in 1994-95 in which neither she nor Professor Hanson was featured and which she herself insisted on publishing.

So her vengeance, I think, came not in the form of a call to the FBI but in the fabrication of that call in 1999 after the appearance of *WKH?* and especially of "Too Much Ego in Your Cosmos." And this brings us to the final touch that even the staid *Wall Street Journal* had to admit "deserves a high place in the annals of academic infighting." This Unabomber Maneuver explains, so Professor Hallett now insists, just why Hanson's review of her book was so negative:

> I am pretty certain he [VDH] and John Heath know I gave the FBI their names in this connection already, because I told the FBI NOT to keep my identity a secret if they did in fact contact either of them. And I have shared this information with a great number of people. My interaction with the FBI in this endeavor is pertinent because Hanson should, in the interests of fair disclosure, acknowledge that I voluntarily went to a law enforcement agency and likened his and his collaborator's views to that of a deranged killer when he is asked to assess my work and my life.

This is an insanely brilliant, if transparent and botched, effort to save her reputation. No one should believe the devastating review of her book in 1998, she now insists, because the reviewer, Professor Hanson, was just getting back at her for turning him in to the authorities in 1994! *And she turned him in on the basis of similarities between a collaborative publication that did not exist and a manifesto that had not been pub-*

lished! If Professor Hallett did by some distant chance actually go to the FBI at some point, they certainly would never have believed such ridiculous charges, much less have contacted either one of us. Hallett's egocentrism perhaps reaches its apex here: "As everyone is aware, though, the FBI was wrong about the location and age of the Unabomber. Here I was trying to be a patriotic American and there they were wasting my time" [#3]. They were wasting *her* time! Her implication of a commonality of opinion held by many—she has "shared this information with a great number of people" (cf. #2: "And it's no secret: I have discussed my decision to do so...with several colleagues, including people on this list")—is another classic technique of defamation, for it is completely unverifiable. She *may* have discussed with colleagues the possibility of calling the FBI. But did she in fact call? There is no evidence that she did, and we know for a fact that we never heard about it until she fessed up on the Internet in May of 1999.

What then, is the larger significance of this sordid and embarrassing episode? Has the academy really sunk so far below the horizon of reality that it will tolerate, even reward, a professor who confesses to a petty and despicable act she may not even have committed—an act that if actually performed would have wasted valuable time in the national pursuit of a genuine threat to American lives—solely to attempt to mitigate a negative review of a book that should never have been written? Is today's professor really so isolated from the community outside the university walls that a dispute over the value of a certain kind of scholarship warrants—with the silence and thus apparent blessing of one's peers—the summoning of the FBI? What happened to the good old days of academic testiness, when one scholar could be satisfied with simply snubbing her enemy, refusing to invite him to a conference, setting her former graduate student upon him in a book review, spreading gossip in late-night phone calls? It was all so simple once, as Stephen Leacock observed many years ago: "I have known two professors of Greek who ceased speaking to one another because of divergent views on the pluperfect subjunctive." Or is all this just the act of one distraught pariah whose actions are not condoned even by her sympathizers?

The sad answer to these questions is that yes, the modern academy seems to have lost its collective mind, or at least its courage. As of this writing (August 1999), Professor Hallett remains a vibrant and frequent contributor to the on-line Classics List, a full professor in her publicly funded university, a director of the American Philological Association, and president of the Classical Association of the Atlantic States. Perhaps most fittingly, she also retains her appointed position as chair of Outreach, a new committee of the national classics association that is responsible for bringing classics to the people.

She is off to a good start. The *Wall Street Journal* has a circulation of nearly two million, and the *Chronicle of Higher Education* is read by most who run our universities. If you think that I am being hard on the profession, play this game: imagine what the response would have been if I, or Professor Hanson, had given Professor Hallett's name to the FBI under identical circumstances and then boasted of it on the Internet. The squeals would have been loud enough to rouse Homer himself. Almost. Ultimately, this episode reveals as much about the skewed ideology of the academy as about anything else. But that is not news.

The one unfortunate aspect of all of this is that the national attention on Hallett's looniness merely confirms in the minds of influential people across the country that the humanities, not just the professors, are as irrelevant as the antihumanist dinosaurs who spout theory and waste national resources. The humanities are in trouble, but these are difficulties that can be fixed by the promotion of a populist agenda in curriculum and behavior. There are good reasons, crucial reasons for studying the ancient worlds, but all of that gets lost when the chair of Outreach of the national association of classicists gets on the hotline or jumps on the Internet. As the *Wall Street Journal* editorial concluded of her Unabomber Maneuver: "That's the way to defend, once and for all, the high-minded, classical profession of Greek and Latin." Oh, and Professor Lupher? I think that was tongue-in-cheek.

NOTES

Introduction

1. David Konstan (1999 president of the American Philogical Association) in *Classical World* 89.1 (1995) 32-33; quoted in *Who Killed Homer?*, 148, 151, 161.

1. Cultivating Sophistry

1. Martha C. Nussbaum. *Cultivating Humanity: A Classical Defense of Reform in Liberal Education* (Cambridge, Mass. and London 1997). For the whole story of Nussbaum's testimony in the Colorado Amendment 2 case, see John Finnis, "Shameless Acts in Colorado: Abuse of Scholarship in Constitutional Cases," *Academic Questions* (Fall 1994), and Robert P. George, "'Shameless Acts' Revisited," *Academic Questions* (Winter 1995-96).
2. In addition to the "conservative" studies by Roger Kimball and Dinesh D'Souza, see especially the essays collected in *Partisan Review*, 60.4 (1993); Robert Hughes, *Culture of Complaint* (Oxford 1993), 83-151; Russell Jacoby, *Dogmatic Wisdom* (New York 1994), passim.
3. David Theo Goldberg, "Introduction: Multicultural Conditions," in *Multiculturalism: A Critical Reader,* ed. David Theo Goldberg (Cambridge, Mass. 1994), 7. This collection, most of the essays in which are riddled with postmodern and/or leftist assumptions, should disabuse anyone inclined to believe Nussbaum's assertion that multiculturalism is actually an expression of Enlightenment liberalism.
4. Peter McLaren, "White Terror and Oppositional Agency: Towards a Critical Multiculturalism," (note 3), 51.
5. *Dogmatic Wisdom,* 157-58.
6. "Critical Multiculturalism," (note 3), 123.

7.   Note 3, 82; rpt from (nota bene!) *Multiculturalism and the "Politics of Recognition"* (Princeton, N.J. 1992).

8.   Taylor, 85.

9.   *The Defeat of the Mind* (1987), trans. Judith Friedlander (New York 1995), 79.

10.   See Finkielkraut, *The Defeat of the Mind,* and Arthur Herman, *The Idea of Decline in Western History* (New York 1997), 364–99. Cf. 388: "So while the multicultural revolution in America is unmistakably a revolution on the Left, its dominant images of change still come from the earlier revolution on the Right. Vital Kultur will reemerge from the ruins of Civilization as new multicultural identities replace the old."

11.   Allan Bloom, "Western Civ," 1988; rpt. in *Giants and Dwarfs: Essays 1960–1990* (New York 1990), 26.

12.   I say "partially" because very few students of any race are being introduced to the Western tradition anymore, since education is driven by social engineering and job-training imperatives—that unsavory alliance of Democratic therapeutic mush with Republican corporate pork.

13.   Nussbaum's complaint about the dearth of minority students at the tony universities where she has worked strikes me as rank hypocrisy. After all, if she's genuinely concerned about minority students, then she should teach someplace where there are minority students. Is it a coincidence that such places tend not to be that useful for furthering academic ambitions?

14.   In Isaiah Berlin, "Joseph de Maistre and the Origins of Fascism," *The Crooked Timber of Humanity,* ed. Henry Hardy (New York 1991), 100.

15.   A point made by Victor Hanson and John Heath on page 256.

16.   See Balkrishna Govind Gokhale, *Asoka Maurya* (New York 1966), 109. Nussbaum's attempt to deal with the question of Western influence (140) is little more than a lame tu quoque argument. No one argues that the Greeks, for example, weren't influenced by other Mediterranean cultures. It's what they did with those influences that is important. As Hanson and Heath ask, "from what part of the East did the West brilliantly derive democracy, free inquiry, the idea of a middle class, political freedom, literature apart from religion, citizen militias, words like 'parody,' 'cynicism,' and 'skepticism,' and a language of abstraction and rationalism?" In *Who Killed Homer?* 117.

17.   Jacques Ellul, *The Betrayal of the West,* trans. Matthew J. O'Connell (New York 1978), 21.

18.   The falseness of the widely accepted view that the presixties literary establishment fostered an exclusive, monolithic canon reflecting the professors' own race and class is pointed out in terms of American literature by Richard B. Schwartz, *After the Death of Literature* (Carbondale, Ill. 1997), 3–6.

19.   The idea that the presixties professoriate was somehow "conservative" is another self-serving myth of contemporary academics who define themselves as sixties-style progressives. As Robert Nisbet pointed out, "among faculties at least in this country [1945–60] was a period of constantly growing political commitment, political zeal, and political ideology. Not only was the faculty of the 1950s much stronger in these qualities than had been the faculty of the 1930s, there was also...far greater readiness to extend this commitment, zeal, and ideology, drawn from national and international politics, to the traditional academic matters that faculty members dealt with." In *The Degradation of*

the Academic Dogma: The University in America, 1945–70 (New York and London 1971), 141–42.

20. "The Function of Criticism at the Present Time," in *Selected Prose,* ed. P. J. Keating (Harmondsworth 1970), 141, 155.

21. George Payne, "Education and Cultural Pluralism," in *Our Racial and National Minorities,* ed. F. J. Brown and J. S. Roucek (New York 1937), 762.

22. William E. Vickery and Stewart G. Cole, *Intercultural Education in American Schools* (New York 1943), ix, xiv.

23. Note 22, 13.

24. Note 22, 35.

25. Paglia describes the course in "East and West: An Experiment in Multiculturalism," in *Sex, Art, and American Culture* (New York 1992). Quotes on 136, 139.

26. "The Democratization of the University," 1969; rpt. in *Giants and Dwarfs,* 374.

27. *The Closing of the American Mind* (New York 1987), 21.

28. Bloom (note 27), 253.

29. Bloom (note 27), 36.

30. Bloom (note 27), 36.

31. "The Crisis of Liberal Education," 1966; rpt. in *Giants and Dwarfs,* 359.

32. Bloom (note 27), 249.

33. "Western Civ," 1988; rpt. in *Giants and Dwarfs,* 29.

34. "The Crisis of Liberal Education," 359.

35. Bloom (note 27), 267, 268, 272, 312.

36. *The Defeat of the Mind,* 105.

37. Nussbaum tries to answer the charge of politicization by indulging the either-or fallacy: "It is frequently claimed that it is inappropriate to approach literature with a 'political agenda.' Yet it is hard to justify such a claim without embracing an extreme kind of aesthetic formalism that is sterile and unappealing" (89). But of course there are alternatives other than "aesthetic formalism" to a "political agenda." And as John Ellis notes, it is the crudity of the "political agenda" that is the problem, not the recognition of politics as one aspect of literature: "What they [race-gender-class critics] do to politics is in fact analogous to what they do to literature: just as they narrow the content of literature to politics, they also reduce the content of politics to oppression and victimology. Thus they not only reduce all of literature to one issue but handle even that issue reductively." In *Literature Lost: Social Agendas and the Corruption of the Humanities* (New Haven, Conn. and London 1997), 63.

38. Remember that Texaco spent $115 million on diversity training because on a tape it sounded like an executive had used a racial epithet. See Hanna Rosin, "Cultural Revolution at Texaco," *The New Republic,* 218.5 (2 February, 1998), 15–18.

39. A stroll through any college bookstore will demonstrate the triumph of multiculturalism in the curriculum. I just reviewed the syllabuses for a couple of philosophy courses at my school: One, an Introduction to Philosophy course, has the following primary texts assigned, with one day on each: Socrates/Plato, Buddha, Video: *The Razor's Edge, Bhagavad-Gita, Eagle Man,* Marx and Engels, Martin Luther King, and Paulo Freire. The other course, entitled Self, Religion, and Society, spends two class periods on Plato and ten on

I...*Rigoberta Menchú*, that psalter of the Sandalista.

40. *The Revolt of the Elites and the Betrayal of Democracy* (New York 1995), 6.

41. Finkielkraut (note 9), 112.

42. See *Closing*, 246–56. Nussbaum's false analogy works by distorting Socrates as well. Her statement that "he regards democracy as the best of the available forms of government, though not above criticism" (26) isn't even a half-truth. She doesn't discriminate, for example, between Athenian democracy and what a modern nonspecialist will understand by the feel-good term "democracy." Cf. Thomas C. Brickhouse and Nicholas D. Smith, *Plato's Socrates* (Oxford 1994), 157–66, who survey all the evidence and conclude: "The sort of political structure Socrates favors—if it can be called a structure at all—is in a way oligarchic and in a way democratic...because each decision would require a different 'few,' a great many people, from all walks of life, will be called upon to make decisions for the state," (165). That's a far cry from Athenian democracy, which assumed all citizens were all the time capable of running the state, an idea Socrates derided.

2. Socrates Redux: Classics in the Multicultural University?

1. Martha C. Nussbaum. *Cultivating Humanity: A Classical Defense of Reform in Liberal Education* (Cambridge, Mass. and London 1997).

2. See her remarks quoted by Robert P. George, "'Shameless Acts' revisited," *Academic Questions* (Winter 1995-96) 40 n. 41.

3. See John Finnis, "'Shameless Acts' in Colorado: Abuse of scholarship in constitutional cases," *Academic Questions* (Fall 1994), especially 19-35.

3. More Quarreling in the Muses' Birdcage

1. John M. Ellis, *Literature Lost: Social Agendas and the Corruption of the Humanities* (New Haven, Conn. and London 1997), and Alvin Kernan, ed., *What Happened to the Humanities?* (Princeton, N.J. 1997).

2. *The Killing of History: How Literary Critics and Social Theorists Are Murdering Our Past* (New York 1996), 12.

3. It should be noted at the outset that the essay by Francis Oakley in *WHTTH?* stands as an exception to the general tone of despair. Here, as in many other similar articles penned in the shadow of his book (*Community of Learning* [New York 1992]), Oakley, former president of Williams College, presents a benign apologia for the current state of the liberal arts. A similarly unconvincing attempt to defend the status quo is Martha Nussbaum's *Cultivating Humanity: A Classical Defense of Reform in Liberal Education*; see chapters one and two. I examine Oakley's methodology below.

4. University presses are famously liberal. While Bloom, D'Souza, Paglia, Kimball, Lefkowitz, and most other critics of the New Humanities are published by New York presses (perhaps because someone other than a handful of academics might be interested in their arguments), the university presses have been the prime sponsors of revisionist work, both its metadisciplinary scholarship and its self-defense (e.g., *The Politics of Liberal Education*, published by Duke U.P., 1992). In a recent article in *The Nation*, Phil Pochoda—himself editorial director

of University Press of New England—laments that no "alternative radical political theory has emerged [since the collapse of Marxist scholarship]...that might frame responses to the right-wing assaults on civil liberties in general and on women, racial and ethnic minorities, and labor in particular" ("Universities Press On," December 29, 1997, 14). He does not specify what these assaults might be. Apparently it does not occur to Pochoda that Marxist academic scholarship has had to try to change its spots because the theory was proven to be intellectually untenable in light of events in the real world. Are we really supposed to long for another errant vision of human nature in order to keep his university press in business?

5.   See the amusing and thoughtful essay by Mark Edmundson, "On the Uses of a Liberal Education I. As Lite Entertainment," *Harper's Magazine* (September 1997) 39–49.

6.   See the discussion of A. Kernan, 5.

7.   J. Engell and A. Dangerfield, "The Market-Model University: Humanities in the Age of Money," *Harvard Magazine* (May–June 1998) 48–55, 111. They find the primary cause of this deterioration in the increasing importance of money (that is, the promise, knowledge, and source of money) in education. I have recently been accused of being selective in my choice of statistics in a separate but related discussion of the decline in classical studies. I suppose it depends whether one, to paraphrase Chesterton, uses statistics as a drunkard uses a lamppost, for support rather than for illumination. I'll leave it to others to decide who is tipsy. But even Professor Nussbaum, who works so hard to defend the New Humanities, concedes that the "shortage of jobs in the humanities and social sciences has led to hardships; many have left the professions they love" (note 3), 3.

8.   *San Francisco Chronicle*, Monday, Jan. 26, 1998, D4.

9.   Pochoda (note 4), 11–16. University presses alone still turn out over 160 books each week; J. Shapiro, "There Has to Be an Easier Way to Find Worthy Scholarly Books," *The Chronicle of Higher Education*, Jan. 30, 1998, B9. On the opacity of modern scholarly writing, see the discussion of Windschuttle (note 1), p. 6 with footnote 6. Clear writing, after all, according to Derrida, is the sign of a reactionary. As usual, the French themselves have been among the first to reject the antihumanism of their own theory. See especially L. Ferry and A. Renaut, *French Philosophy of the Sixties: An Essay on Antihumanism*, trans. Mary S. Cattani (Amherst, Mass. 1990).

10.   *The New York Times*, Monday, Jan. 12, 1998, A14.

11.   Note 7, 50.

12.   Stuart Hall, "Cultural Studies and its Theoretical Legacies," in L. Grossberg, C. Nelson, and P. Treichler, eds., *Cultural Studies* (New York 1992), 285, quoted in Windschuttle (note 2), 9.

13.   *WHTTH?*, 90. Of course, some graduate departments are notoriously one-sided. Ellis observes in a footnote that in the literature department at UC Santa Cruz a bitter conflict has split the faculty. On one side are the race-gender-class scholars who teach classic texts to denounce them; on the other side are the race-gender-class scholars who have dumped the classics and teach the "literature of the downtrodden" (254 n.8).

14.   *WHTTH?*, 156. Francis Oakley (*WHTTH?*, 63–83) is the only contributor who

finds minimal influence of the New Humanities on the current curriculum. He argues that the change in the humanities over the past twenty-five years is primarily in the increased number of courses offered, all for the better since the increasingly diverse student body now has interdisciplinary, globalized, and multicultural options in addition to more traditional fare. He reaches this conclusion by comparing course listings and descriptions of courses found in catalogues at a select group of institutions for the years 1969-1970 and 1994-1995. The naivete in this approach is as frightening as it is revealing: how many college presidents know what is going on in the classrooms of their own institutions? The model of thoughtful analysis of education by former presidents of universities set by Clark Kerr has given way to memoirs like that of Donald Kennedy of Stanford. Kennedy suggests that those in higher education have not adequately justified to the public why they deserve its trust. Could this be at least in part because the public has learned that government funds for research turn out to have been spent on the enlargement of the university president's bed? I take it that the title of his book, *Academic Duty,* is not intentionally ironic.

Using Oakley's approach, one might conclude, for example, from the recent introduction of a U.S. History core requirement at Santa Clara University, that we were experiencing a wave of Western culture nostalgia on campus, some primordial civic desire to have students explore the grand experiment of their country's constitution. Only upon closer examination—the kind not available in course listings and descriptions—would one discover that of the fifty-nine courses meeting the requirement only two specifically cover the ideas of the Founding Fathers. On the other hand, twenty-nine explicitly deal with minority, feminist, and multicultural issues, and many others (e.g., American Novel II, The American West) frequently focus almost exclusively on the Other.

Titles of courses and programs are notoriously deceptive. There is no humanities requirement at Santa Clara University. Yet liberal arts students (the vast majority of our undergraduates) must take a very traditional three-quarter survey of Western culture in one of five humanistic disciplines—art, literature, history, philosophy, or music/theater—along with three courses in religious studies, one ethics course, three writing classes, and a variety of other general education requirements (such as two world culture courses) that can be fulfilled in the humanities. On the other hand, a glance at the catalogue of our neighbor up the road, Stanford, reveals an official Introduction to Humanities sequence that satisfies an area requirement. But there students are introduced to the humanities by one of two courses, meta-humanities really, either "Why Read It?" or "The Word and the World: Conversations Across Time and Space," the latter of which teaches how the "two-faced" texts "are concerned with both power's legitimation and its usurpation. These texts generate authority structures and authority figures, yet their own authority has regularly been called into question" (*Guide to Choosing Area One Courses* 1997-98, 15). Oakley's approach cannot distinguish these two sequences.

More importantly, Oakley's methodology can tell us nothing at all about the most important issue of all, that is, how these humanities courses are being taught. Shakespeare's appearance in a curriculum is no sign that things have not changed. Denis Donoghue quotes Terry Eagleton's analysis of Macbeth:

> To any unprejudiced reader—which would seem to exclude Shakespeare himself, his contemporary audiences and almost all literary critics—it is surely clear that positive value in Macbeth lies with the three witches. The witches are the heroines of the piece, however little the play itself recognizes the fact, and however much the critics may have set out to defame them. It is they who, by releasing ambitious thoughts in Macbeth, expose a reverence for hierarchical social order for what it is, as the pious self-deception of a society based on routine oppression and incessant warfare. The witches are exiles from that violent order, inhabiting their own sisterly community on its shadowy border-lands, refusing all truck with its tribal bickerings and military honors. (quoted in *WHTTH?*, 129-30)

Like it or hate it, most would agree that this is not the same Shakespeare we studied thirty years ago. Topics and methodologies have changed.

15. Whereas the elite research universities (accepting students in the top eighth of their high school class) have tended to be placed in upscale locales—La Jolla, Berkeley, Santa Cruz, Westwood, Santa Barbara (we are not so uncivilized out here as to expect renowned gender, race, and class scholars to live with the oppressed)—the Cal State system (accepting students in the top third of their high school class) have gone directly to the people—Bakersfield, Chico, Fullerton, Fresno, San Jose, Turlock, Hayward, and so on. Teaching loads at the research universities are generally from three to six; at the Cal States, eight (with no doctoral programs).

16. These quotations are taken from the University Learning Requirements as listed at the CSUMB website.

17. Literary Analysis Through Global Narratives; Literature, Film, and Culture; Auto/biographias; Ethnicity, Gender, Creative Writing: Writer as Witness; Women's Literature: Re-Writing the Script/Taking Action; American Ethnic Literature and Cultures; Latina Life Stories in Comparative Context; Multicultural Poetry: Verse, Voice, and Video; Literary and Visual Witness Narratives: Poetry, Prose, Pictures and Empowerment; World Mythological Literature; Multicultural Children's Literature; Japanese Literature in Translation; Survey of Jazz; Survey of World Music; Music for Children; Chicano Literature; Auto/Biographias: Oral Narrative and Life Writing in Spanish; The Chicano Novel; Latina Life Stories; La Literatura Mexicana; La Narrativa Hispanoamericana Contemporanea; Latin American Women Writers; La Literatura Afro-Latina; Introduction to Teledramatic Arts and Technology; World Film History: Film Festivals; World Theater History; Script Analysis: Deconstructing the Screenplay; Diverse Histories in Contemporary Art; Ways of Seeing: Seminar on Philosophy and Ethical Thinking in Public Art.

18. C. Irving, "No Bard by the Bay," *The California Higher Education Policy Center,* Vol. 5.1 (Winter 1997), News.

19. Quoted in Irving (note 18).

20. "On the Uses of a Liberal Education II. As a Weapon in the Hands of the Restless Poor," E. Shorris, *Harper's Magazine,* Sept. 1997, 53.

21. Shorris (note 20), 59.

22. "A Short History of Liberal Guilt," *Critical Inquiry* 22 no. 2 (1966), 370, quoted in Bromwich, *WHTTH?*, 235.

23. One classicist, for example, writing not about Penelope in particular but about the archetype of the "helpful princess," for some reason even confesses to us that like "many women, I have found myself performing the role of the helpful princess too often. I read the 'ruthless' story very differently thirty years after I first encountered it..." J. de Luce, "Reading and re-reading the helpful princess," in *Compromising Traditions: The Personal Voice in Classical Scholarship*, J. P. Hallet and T. Van Nortwick, eds. (London and New York 1997), 26.

24. Can we doubt the crumbling state of humanities when this same antihumanist Professor Fish, apparently considered for a Dean of Humanities position here in California, decides to stay on in order to develop "something like The Duke Institute for the Study of the Humanities and Social Thought"? *The Chronicle of Higher Education,* April 25, 1997, A10.

25. See Margaret Talbot, "Being White," *The New York Times Magazine,* Nov. 30, 1997, 116–19.

26. Irving (note 18). In 1983, N. J. Smelser, "California: A Multisegment System," 127–28 in A. Levine, ed., *Higher Learning in America:* 1980–2000 (Baltimore and London 1983/94), suggested that the California campuses would have to meet the needs of a diverse public in one of three ways: 1) "The program of assimilation of racially, ethnically, and culturally diverse groups to the existing values and roles of higher education...continuing traditional patterns of liberal education and occupational and professional training, with students being socialized in these patterns, accommodating to them, and preparing themselves for participation in the institutions of the larger society." 2) "The program of altering the traditional missions of higher liberal education...to some mission that gives greater recognition to 'nonmainstream' groups." 3) "The program of converting campuses into a microcosm of the pluralistic polity, with racial, ethnic, cultural, gender, and other groups competing..." Although the planning commission favored the first option, it is clearly the last that has been seized upon.

27. Irving (note 17); R. Ferrier, "Is This Really What We Want?" *Ventura Star,* Thursday, April 3, 1997.

28. This and the following quotations come from the Tenth Campus Academic Planning Committee Summary of Recommendations.

29. *WHTTH?,* 224. The core of Western culture and the humanities continues to be diluted at colleges and universities throughout the country; see, for example, the discussion of the "Brooklyn Connections" program at Brooklyn College, *The Chronicle of Higher Education,* August 8, 1997, A12.

30. Note 2, 4–5.

31. Sabin discusses two collaborative teaching ventures that she believes may point a way out of the impasse (*WHTTH?,* 96–101).

32. January 4, 1998, 33.

33. December 22, 1997, 96.

34. Quoted in C. J. Lucas, *Crisis in the Academy: Rethinking Higher Education in America* (New York 1996), 75.

35. Lucas (note 34), 172. Business executives were very interested in hiring liberally educated generalists, citing their excellent reading, writing, and oral communication abilities; foreign language proficiency and understanding of foreign cultures; critical judgment and problem-solving skills; flexibility in dealing with people, taking on new tasks, and switching gears quickly; and a highly

developed sense of personal responsibility and ethics. In theory, at least.

36. It is unclear whether Professor Ricks helps or hurts his cause by then delivering the keynote address this January at the humanities symposium on Dylan—Bob Dylan—organized by a humanities doctoral student at Stanford.

37. Jacques Barzun made a similar argument several years ago in "A Future for the Liberal Arts, If...," *Academic Questions* 7 (Fall 1994), 74–76.

38. *The New York Times,* Monday, Jan. 12, 1988, A14.

39. Here I mean good old vocationalism, not the philosophical pragmatism of Dewey and Rorty now advanced by Bruce Kimball, in which a sensible modernist awareness of fallibility can quickly devolve into political multiculturalism and the radical relativism of postmodernism; see *The Condition of American Liberal Education: Pragmatism and a Changing Tradition,* R. Orrill, ed. (New York 1995).

40. See the strange boast of G. M. Fredrickson, "America's Caste System: Will It Change?" *New York Review of Books* (Oct. 23, 1997), 75 n. 13. As noted in the rejoinder by S. and A. Thernstrom, this episode also reveals the complete lack of diversity—or cowardice of the minority—in the modern academy: "Those who march behind the banner of diversity regard diversity of opinion on this subject as heretical." *New York Review of Books* (Nov. 20, 1997), 65. Not a single member of the faculty voted the same as the majority of Californians? Clearly the elite academics out here are living in another world.

41. Irving (note 18).

42. *Alexander to Actium* (Berkeley, Calif. 1990). The lampoon is found at Athen. 1.22d. The translation is an adaptation of Green's, 87.

43. Menand, *WHTTH?*, 213. Determining contact hours is virtually impossible beyond the notoriously unreliable self-reporting. According to the 1993 National Survey of Postsecondary Faculty by the National Center for Education Statistics (U.S. Department of Education), the mean for hours spent each week in class by faculty at research universities was 6.9.

44. Cited in *The Chronicle of Higher Education,* April 24, 1998, A12.

45. J. Amberg, "Higher (-Priced) Education," *The American Scholar* 58 (1989) 572, cited in R. M. Huber, *How Professors Play the Cat Guarding the Cream* (Fairfax, Va. 1992), 193.

46. Higher Education Research Institute, cited in Lucas (note 34), 170. This was true even though at the same time another study revealed that 67 percent of all liberal arts faculty reported that they had never published a book, 38 percent had never published in a professional journal, and 49 percent were not engaged in research that was expected to lead to publication (cited in Lucas, 192).

47. "I'm History," *The American Scholar* (Winter 1998), 16.

4. "Too Much Ego in Your Cosmos"

1. Judith P. Hallett and Thomas Van Nortwick (eds.), *Compromising Traditions: The Personal Voice in Classical Scholarship* (London and New York 1997), vii + 196 pages, cloth.

2. "I would prefer to be wrong with Plato than to be right with people such as these." Cicero, Tusculan Disputations, 1.17.39.

3. "May all perish who should ever do these things again." Homer, *Odyssey,* 1.47.

5. The Enemy Is Us: The "Betrayal of the Postmodern Clerks"

1.   See page 205.

2.   A point made as well by Jeanne N. O'Neill, "Rethinking the Cursus Honorum," *The Classical Journal* 91.3 (1996), 297–307. See also Victor Davis Hanson, *The Other Greeks: The Family Farm and the Agrarian Roots of Western Civilization* (New York 1995), 414–19.

3.   Even those in the profession aware of the problem look for its solution in changes in pedagogical technique or in better marketing, rather than making a case for the value of classics for society at large. See for example, Kenneth F. Kitchell, Jr., Edward Phinney, Susan Shelmerdine, and Marilyn Skinner, "Greek 2000—Crisis, Challenge, Deadline," *The Classical Journal* 91.4 (1996), 393–420.

4.   Obviously another article could be written about the pedantic bean-counting of some traditional philologists, which also does little to promote understanding of classics beyond the profession. But traditional philologists at least can fall back on the legitimate claim that no matter how technical and abstruse their work, it contributes a few bricks to the edifice of knowledge. The poststructuralist by definition cannot make that claim, since by his lights there is no "knowledge" or "facts," only "interpretation" (actually, "misinterpretation"). Thus those "interpretations" have to find some other justification, and usually some liberationist goal is offered as legitimizing the poststructuralist "project." Hence it is fair to judge their activity in terms of its impact beyond the profession.

5.   Martin Classical Lectures, New Series Vol. 1 (Princeton, N.J. 1990). Subsequent references parenthetical.

6.   For a critical discussion see Luc Ferry and Alain Renaut, *French Philosophy of the Sixties: An Essay on Antihumanism* (1985); trans. Mary H. S. Cattani (Amherst, Mass. 1990), 26–32, 64–67, 97–121, 208–227. Despite the breathless enthusiasm of some literary critics for what they think is a "cutting-edge" postmodern idea like the "death of the subject," delivered by Foucault descending from Paris like Moses from Sinai, the attack on the subject is an old idea. Cf. Isaiah Berlin, in an essay on the tradition of historical determinism delivered over forty years ago: "Individuals remain 'abstract' precisely because they are mere 'elements' or 'aspects,' 'moments' artificially abstracted for ad hoc purposes, and literally without reality (or, at any rate, 'historical' or 'philosophical' or 'real' being) apart from the whole of which they form a part...." In "Historical Inevitability," 1953; rpt. *Four Essays on Liberty* (Oxford 1969), 41–117.

7.   *The Fate of the Self: German Writers and French Theory* (New York 1986), 50.

8.   "Limited Inc: abc," *Glyph* 2 (1977), 162–254.

9.   See for example, Derrida's defense of Paul de Man, "Like the Sound of the Sea Deep Within a Shell: Paul de Man's War," *Critical Inquiry* 14 (1988), 590–652.

10. As David Hirsch has pointed out, "[t]he quintessence of Nazism was precisely an assault on the concept of the existence of the self carried to its logical extreme." In *The Deconstruction of Literature: Criticism after Auschwitz* (London 1991), 95. Cf. also 165: "Purveyors of postmodern ideologies must consider whether it is possible to diminish human beings in theory, without, at the same time, making individual human lives worthless in the real world."

11. Charles A. Moser points out, "it is not surprising that Yale's Paul de Man, a pillar of deconstruction, should have been an adherent of Fascism in his native Belgium during the war years: he always believed in the political definition of meaning," "Literary Theory, The University, and Society," *Modern Age* 34.2 (1992), 121. For the whole de Man affair and the reaction of de Man's defenders see Hirsch, 69-117.

12. Peradotto's conceit of institutional intransigence noted as well by Jenny Strauss Clay in *Classical Philology* 82 (1992), 161.

13. Since none of the books under consideration here alert the reader to the nearly twenty-five years of critical examination of poststructuralist ideas, I will provide here a brief bibliography. In addition to Hirsch's and Ferry and Renaut's books mentioned above, and Merquior's in the next note, see Rene Wellek, "The Attack on Literature," *The American Scholar* 42 (1972), 27-42, rpt. in *The Attack on Literature and Other Essays* (Chapel Hill, N.C. 1982), 3-18; M. H. Abrams, "The Deconstructive Angel," *Critical Inquiry* 3 (1977), 423-38, rpt. *Doing Things with Texts: Essays in Criticism and Critical Theory*, ed. Michael Fischer (New York and London 1989), 237-52; "How to Do Things with Texts," *Partisan Review* 46 (1979), 566-88, rpt. in *Attack,* 269-96; "Construing and Deconstruing," *Romanticism and Contemporary Criticism,* ed. Morris Eaves and Michael Fischer (Ithaca 1986), rpt. in *Attack,* 297-332; Terry Eagleton, *Literary Theory: An Introduction* (Minneapolis 1983), 127-50; Frederick Crews, "Deconstructing a Discipline" (1979), rpt. in *Skeptical Engagements* (Oxford 1986), 115-20; "Criticism without Constraint" (1982), rpt. in *Skeptical,* 122-36; "The Grand Academy of Theory" (1986), rpt. in *Skeptical,* 159-78; Alan Mcgill, *Prophets of Extremity: Nietzsche, Heidegger, Foucault, Derrida* (Berkeley, Calif. and Los Angeles 1985); Cedric Watts, "Bottom's Children: the Fallacies of Structuralist, Post-Structuralist, and Deconstructionist Literary Theory," in *Reconstructing Literature,* ed. Laurence Lerner (Totowa, N.J. 1983), 20-35; Tzvetan Todorov, "All Against Humanity," *Times Literary Supplement* no. 4,305 (October 4, 1985), 1093-94; John Searle, "The World Turned Upside Down," *New York Review of Books* 30.10 (October 27, 1983), 74-79; Robert Scholes, *Textual Power: Literary Theory and the Teaching of English* (New Haven, Conn. 1985); John Ellis, *Against Deconstruction* (Princeton, N.J. 1989).

14. In *From Prague to Paris: A Critique of Structuralist and Post-Structuralist Thought* (London 1986), 227.

15. A very brief refutation can be found in John Searle, "Is There a Crisis in Higher Education?" *Partisan Review* 60.4 (1993), 703-4. See also Paul R. Gross and Norman Levitt, *Higher Superstition: The Academic Left and its Quarrel with Science* (Baltimore and London 1994), esp. 42-70. More technically, Susan Haack, *Evidence and Inquiry: Toward Reconstruction in Epistemology* (Oxford 1993). Even intellectuals sympathetic to postmodernism have begun to see that epistemic nihilism leads to the dead-end of political quietism. See Reed Way Dasenbrock, "We've Done It to Ourselves: The Critique of Truth and the Attack on Theory," in *PC Wars: Politics and Theory in the Academy,* ed. Jeffrey Williams (New York and London 1995), 172-83.

16. Hirsch, *Deconstructing Literature,* 18-19.

17. The reader should see, for example, J. G. Merquior, *Foucault* (London 1985), 56-76.

18. As Crews notes, "The same license to subscribe to a theory without actually believing what it says also permits the ideologically committed to combine two

or more doctrines which look to be seriously incompatible," "The Grand Academy of Theory," *Skeptical Engagements* (note 13), 172.

19. *Beyond Deconstruction: The Uses and Abuses of Literary Theory* (Oxford 1985), 205.

20. "All Against Humanity" (note 13), 1093.

21. Rpt. in *Writing and Difference,* trans. Alan Bass (Chicago 1978), 278–93.

22. Terry Eagleton, *Literary Theory*, 134. Cf. also Merquior (note 14), 195: "The Derridean radicalization of the principle of difference entails two broad strategies:...dropping once and for all the 'kaleidoscope' idea that structure is an identical ground, a core beneath the multiple surfaces" and "sticking more than ever to the 'mantic' severance of signifier from signified."

23. Merquior (note 14), 191. See also Howard Felperin, "Beyond Theory," (note 19), 205.

24. Peradotto's reading of Bakhtin oversimplifies into a crude dichotomy the political dimension of "centrifugal" and "centripetal" forces, as is evident in Peradotto's feminist reading of Circe's protest against letting Odysseus return home. Bakhtin, rather, is after much bigger philosophical game—the symbiotic and dialectic relationship of order and disorder. See Gary Saul Morson and Caryl Emerson, *Mikhail Bakhtin: Creation of a Prosaics* (Palo Alto, Calif. 1990), 30–31.

25. Cf. Merquior, on the appeal of structuralist jargon: "First the sacralization of Method and the lavish use of jargon seem to have become staple defense mechanisms to the soft-brained humanities, increasingly corroded by inner doubts about their cognitive validity in our science-shaped world," (note 14), 212.

26. *Innovations of Antiquity,* ed. Ralph Hexter and Daniel Selden (London and New York 1992). Subsequent references parenthetical.

27. Frank Lentricchia, *After the New Criticism* (Chicago 1980), 185, 186. The charge that American deconstructionists water down Derrida is made by traditionalists as well. Cf. M. H. Abrams: "Critical followers of Derrida have...assimilated deconstruction to their pre-existing critical assumptions and procedures. The result has been in various degrees to domesticate, naturalize, and nationalize Derrida's subversiveness-without-limit, by accommodating it to a closer reading of individual works," in "Construing and Deconstruing," *Doing Things with Texts* (note 13), 314.

28. Hirsch (note 10), 47.

29. Cf. Ferry and Renaut: "[I]t seems there is nothing intelligible or sayable in the contents of Derrida's work that is not, purely and simply, a recapitulation of the Heideggerian problematics of ontological difference," (note 6), 124. For Heidegger's Nazism see Hirsch, *The Deconstruction of Literature* (note 10), passim; Victor Farias, *Heidegger and Nazism,* ed. Joseph Margolis and Tom Rockmore, trans. Paul Barrell and Gabriel R. Ricci (Philadelphia 1989).

30. Harold Fromm, "Academic Capitalism and Literary Value," in *Academic Capitalism and Literary Value* (Athens, Ga. 1991), 212. Fromm's essay is a brilliant explosion of the sorts of pretensions Hexter and Selden's collection displays and an exposure of their origins in academic careerism.

31. See page 217.

32. "Bottom's Children" (note 13), 31–32. Ferry and Renault point out that "*the cult of paradox and the insistent demand for complexity if not, in fact, for a rejection of*

clarity" are a stylistic feature of French philosophy of the sixties (note 6), 12; emphases in original.

33. *Pluto's Republic* (Oxford and New York 1982), 50.

34. Heath and I both owe this point to Victor Davis Hanson.

35. "Politics and the English Language," 1946; rpt. in *A Collection of Essays* (New York 1953), 170. If, as I suspect, the real reason for this collection's existence is academic careerism, the following remarks of Orwell are especially pertinent: "The great enemy of clear language is insincerity. When there is a gap between one's real and one's declared aims, one turns as it were instinctively to long words and exhausted idioms, like a cuttlefish squirting out ink," 167.

36. Orwell (note 35), 159. Emphases in original.

37. Charles Segal, *Tragedy and Civilization: An Interpretation of Sophocles* (Cambridge, Mass. 1981), 14, 15.

38. Thomas Docherty, *Postmodernism/Postmarxism* (London 1990), 2.

39. Eagleton (note 13), 134. Emphases in original.

40. "Deconstruction Reconstructed," in *Beyond Deconstruction* (note 19), 119.

41. See for example, *The Pursuit of Signs* (London 1981), 41; or *On Deconstruction* (Ithaca, N.Y. 1982), 86.

42. "Deconstruction Reconstructed," 130.

43. Note 14, 228.

44. Denys Page, *Sappho and Alcaeus: An Introduction to the Study of Ancient Lesbian Poetry* (1955; rpt. Oxford 1979), 28 n.2.

45. Cf. Frederick Crews: "Such servility constitutes an ironic counterpart of positivism—a heaping up, not of factual nuggets, but of movement slogans treated as fact." In "The Grand Academy of Theory" (note 13), 172.

46. Ferguson suspects she may be out of fashion, as evidenced by her claim in the notes that "Were I writing [the essay] today, I would no doubt attempt a more historicizing mode of analysis than did the author of what you are about to read" (87). She prints this essay anyway because it looks at Augustine "from a theoretical premise still relatively unusual in scholarly studies of Augustine" (89). In other words, "I may be out of style, but I'm still ahead of the traditionalists." Ferguson's apology confirms further that she thinks Derrida discovered some permanent truth about language and meaning.

47. John Ellis (note 13), 36–37. I quote Ellis's definition because he formulates it after close examination of the vague and sometimes incoherent definitions of Derrida himself and his explicators (29–36).

48. Ellis (note 13), 37–38.

49. Ellis (note 13), 57. My necessarily brief summary of Ellis's argument does not do justice to its thorough destruction of Derrida's position. See 45–57.

50. Ellis (note 13), 55, 56.

51. This, however, is not Derrida's problem but his epigones'. As Allan Megill reminds us, "To attempt to isolate a Derridean position or articulate a Derridean thesis is to misunderstand the character of Derrida's enterprise," *Prophets of Extremity* (note 13), 260. A criticism like Ellis's becomes necessary when eager disciples, mostly Americans conditioned by graduate school to avoid original thinking and defer to intellectual authority, demand a positive doctrine or discovered truth which they can then use to elevate their own feeble ideas. Given the financial rewards and celebrity resulting from this phenomenon, one

cannot blame Derrida for going along for the ride.

52. As pointed out by Norman Furman, "Deconstruction, de Man, and the Resistance to Evidence: David Lachman's *Signs of the Times,*" *Academic Questions* 5.3 (1992), 38.

53. For example, in *Problems of Dostoevsky's Poetics,* ed. and trans. Caryl Emerson (Minneapolis 1984).

54. René Girard, *Deceit, Desire, and the Novel: Self and Other in Literary Structure,* trans. Yvonne Freccero (Baltimore 1965); Patricia Meyer Spacks, *Desire and Truth: Functions of Plot in Eighteenth-Century English Novels* (Chicago 1990).

55. Karl Popper's phrase quoted in W. K. C. Guthrie, *The History of Greek Philosophy: 5, The Later Plato and the Academy* (Cambridge 1978), 268. See 262-69 for an overview of the varying interpretations of the "receptacle." See also George S. Claghorn, *Aristotle's Criticism of Plato's "Timaeus"* (The Hague 1954), 5-19.

56. See Guthrie (note 55), 265 n. 5. Bergren could have strengthened her case considerably by referring to the arguments for "spatiality" of Anne Freire Ashbaugh, *Plato's Theory of Explanation: A Study of the Cosmological Account in the Timaeus* (Albany, N. Y. 1988), 96-136.

57. For exposure of the silliness of deconstructive architecture, see Roger Kimball, *Tenured Radicals: How Politics Has Corrupted Our Higher Education* (New York 1991), 116-41.

58. But Bergren herself lists in n. 67 all the various Platonic uses of *dêmiourgos,* none of which include "architect." Thus in the same note she has to make a feeble attempt to argue for this meaning:

> The particular craft of architecture is indicated here in the *Timaeus* by the use with the *dêmiourgos* of verbs of building: *tektainô* (cf. *tektôn* "builder," and *architektôn* "architect") and construction: *sun*—"together, with" + *histémi* "make stand, set up." The *Timaeus* is not the only dialogue in which a *dêmiourgos* figures as architect of the cosmos: see also *Republic* 507c, 530a4b4, *Politics* 270a5, 273bl. (295, n.67)

The smoke-screen of etymology cannot hide the fact that the *dêmiourgos* more usually means "craftsman" or "artificer," in other words, one who designs *and* executes, not, like a modern architect, one who merely designs: "[T]he word [*dêmiourgos*] reminds us that a craftsman works in a given material and to a pattern or form, either before his eyes or reflected in his mind," (Guthrie [note 56], 254). Nor do verbs of building or construction necessarily imply an architect—they more accurately refer to a carpenter, who does the actual building and constructing, and who may or may not be also involved in the design. Finally, the references to the *Republic* and the *Politics* do not support Bergren's case one bit, despite the dishonest phrase "figures as architect of the cosmos," which implies that in those dialogues the word *dêmiourgos* more obviously means architect. But of course it does not—it means exactly what it means in the *Timaeus,* "artificer," "craftsman," "technician."

59. See Carl N. Degler, *In Search of Human Nature: The Decline and Revival of Darwinism in American Social Thought* (Oxford 1991). Degler shows that disciplines such as psychology and anthropology dominated thinking about human nature in the earlier part of the century, but have had to come to terms with advances in the hard sciences that have shifted emphasis back to nature

and biology. Moreover, Degler traces the way the political ideologies of individual researchers tilted their thinking in one direction or the other.

60. E. P. Thompson has explained how such intellectually shaky ideas as radical constructionism could gain so much credence among intellectuals with liberationist pretensions. Speaking of Althusserian-inspired skepticism about the "subject" and the possibility of empirical knowledge, Thompson writes:

> This particular freak...has now lodged itself firmly in a particular social *couche,* the bourgeois *lumpen-intelligentsia*: aspirant intellectuals, whose amateurish intellectual preparation disarms them before manifest absurdities and elementary philosophical blunders, and whose innocence in intellectual *practice* leaves them paralysed in the first web of scholastic argument which they encounter; and *bourgeois,* because while many of them would *like* to be "revolutionaries," they are themselves the products of a particular "conjuncture" which has broken the circuits between intellectuality and practical experience...and hence they are able to perform *imaginary* revolutionary psycho-dramas (in which each outbids the other in adopting ferocious verbal postures) while in fact falling back upon a very old tradition of bourgeois élitism.... *The Poverty of Theory* (New York 1978), 3.

Many other commentators have noted that the philosophical semi-literacy of literary critics has contributed to their enthusiastic endorsement of questionable ideas. Cf. Merquior: "Normally illiterate in philosophy, the latter [literary critics] are increasingly colonized by theoretical literary criticism in a frantic search for a *weltanschauliche* pedigree.... For deconstruction is acclaimed in philosophically unskilled quarters precisely because it got rid of argumentative rigour while providing the pathos of an apocalyptic *Weltanschauung.* The first thing liberated by the Liberation of the Signifier movement is the right to wild philosophizing," (note 14), 218, cf. also 246, 256.

61. Bergren obviously never learned Sam Spade's dictum that "the cheaper the crook, the gaudier the patter" applies to academics as well as gunsels.

62. Lentricchia (note 27), 186.

63. Ed. by Barbara Goff (Austin, Tex. 1996). Subsequent references parenthetical.

64. I am reminded of Hirsch's comment that "[l]iterary theorists play philosophers' games with minimal skills, and they dabble in philosophical discourses they do not necessarily control," *The Deconstruction of Literature* (note 10), 67.

65. In *Beyond Deconstruction* (note 19), 19.

66. Half-truth because the "object of historical inquiry" is very often *not* textual. It is rather something like ancient bones or pottery shards or ruins. But of course, "all the world's a text" is another unexamined poststructuralist credo.

67. In "The Grand Academy of Theory" (note 13), 164.

68. Note 14, 253.

69. Note 6, 18–19. See also Hirsch (note 10), 255–68.

70. "Deconstructing a Discipline" (note 13), 118.

71. *Decadence and Renewal in the Higher Learning: An Episodic History of American University and College Since 1953* (South Bend, Ind. 1978), 177.

72. "Literary Politics and Blue-Chip High-Mindedness," in *Academic Capitalism and Literary Value* (Athens, Ga. and London 1991), 177. Many others, of course, have made the same point, including Camille Paglia in *Arion.*

73. "America's Professoriate: Politicized, Yet Apolitical," *Chronicle of Higher Education* 42.31 (April 12, 1996), B2.

74. *The Degradation of the Academic Dogma: The University in America, 1945–1970* (New York and London 1971), 75: "conspicuous research" on 109, emphasis omitted. See also the remarks of Jacques Barzun, "The University as the Beloved Republic," 1966; rpt. in *Begin Here: The Forgotten Conditions of Teaching and Learning,* ed. Morris Philipson (Chicago and London 1991), 160: "We keep speaking of a company of scholars, but what we have in our new Babylons of higher learning is a scrimmage of self-seeking individuals and teams, the rugged age of gilded research. This commercial outlook, reinforcing professionalism, explains the absence of original ideas in almost every field of learning and will insure the continuance of that dearth for as long as the boom lasts."

75. Frederick Crews, "Criticism Without Constraint" (note 13), 129. This problem of course is even more acute in classics, which unlike modern literatures has a finite number of texts, and which lacks the popular literature English criticism can exploit to keep itself going.

76. In "The Shame of the Graduate Schools," 1966; rpt. in *Arion,* third series 2.2 & 3 (spring and fall, 1992), 174.

77. In *The Theory of Education in the United States* (New York 1932), 52, 53. See the defense of the character-forming power of classics by E. Christian Kopff, "The Classics and the Traditional Liberal Arts Curriculum," *Modern Age* 34.2 (1992), 136–42.

6. Self-Promotion and the "Crisis" in Classics

1. Lanham, Md., New York, and London 1989; hereafter cited as *Crisis.*

2. Martin Bernal begins his essay, for example, by simply noting that his only quarrel with the title of the book "is with the final question mark" ("Classics in Crisis: An Outsider's View In," *Crisis* 67–74, quotation on p. 67).

3. Lewis Sussman, "The Research, Publication, Advancement Triangle and the Teaching of Classical Civilization Courses: A Modest Proposal," *Crisis* 107–15, refers to the two groups as the CGRDs (Comprehensive Graduate Research Departments) and all the rest (ATRs). Edward Phinney, "The Classics in American Education," *Crisis* 77–87 (esp. 77), draws the line in this two-tier system between high school and university/college teachers. There is no doubt that much important work has been done and needs to be done in helping to build the classical curriculum in the high schools, but my argument here concerns the structure of classics at the college/university level and will not examine this other division.

4. K. Galinsky, "Classics beyond Crisis," *CW* 84.6 (1991) 441–53, quotation on p. 453; reprinted in Galinsky, *Classical and Modern Interactions* (Austin, Tex. 1992) 154–70.

5. See, for example, the factional debate between Richard Thomas, who would define himself as a traditional classical philologist, and two feminist classicists, Judith Hallett and Barbara McManus, over the APA elections in *Lingua Franca* ("Thomas Unbound," 2.3 [Feb./March 1992] 3, 54; "Classical Feminism," 2.5 [June/July 1992] 53). The press itself has a role in all this, choosing to emphasize

this debate over any other issue, no doubt at least partially because it is a "better sell." Thus it is all the more important for classicists to make a serious effort to redirect the discussion.

6. Some of what I have to say would be appropriate to a discussion of *any* discipline in the humanities. My belief is that classics is particularly vulnerable at this moment, but is also especially valuable. The strengths of the field have been obscured by the posturing of a few histrionic elitists for their own benefit.

7. "The Training of Classicists," *Crisis* 89-98, quotation on 89.

8. Very good on this issue, in addition to Henderson, is Ronald Mellor's discussion of the increasing irrelevance of a classical graduate education to undergraduate teaching: "Classics and the Teaching of Greek and Roman Civilization," *Crisis* 99-105.

9. Henderson (above, n.7) 92.

10. Or worse; see the remarks by Sherill L. Spaar, "*Veni, Vidi, Spem Abieci*: A Report from the Provinces," *Crisis* 155-62.

11. Henderson (above, n.7) 93.

12. The APA teaching award can be a mixed blessing. Dennis G. Glew, in addition to noting the likelihood that this award too must become a vehicle for self-promotion, asks, "Is it not a kind of bone being tossed to the little dogs who usually lose out in the scramble for the meat?" ("Some Reflections on Teaching Classics Alone," *Crisis* 163-87, quotation on 166).

13. "Arthur Darby Nock: 1902-1963," *CO* 70.1 (1992) 8-9, quotation on 8. Nock's insufferable behavior might be excused given the truly *tremendous* contribution he made to our understanding of the ancient world (and with the hopes that someone else at Harvard bothered to teach undergraduates on occasion). But how many of us have his excuse? Far fewer than could make the claim, I fear.

14. R. J. Ball, *The Classical Papers of Gilbert Highet* (New York 1983), 6. Calder himself, some twenty years before his encomium of Nock's pedagogy, wrote approvingly of (the still living) Highet, "For me Professor Highet will always represent the peaceful coexistence of popularization and specialization." ("Gilbert Highet, Anthon Professor of Latin, Emeritus," *CW* 66.7 (1973) 385-87, quotation on 387). What I am really contrasting here, of course, is the *image* of these two scholars conjured up by their devoted students. Whether Nock was *always* so callous or Highet so generous may be left up to their colleagues and students to debate.

15. I thank Judith Hallett for sharing with me her paper summarizing the status of feminists in classics: "*Ubi fuimus? Quo vadimus?*: Feminist Challenges and the Profession of Classics," delivered at the conference on Feminism and Classics, University of Cincinnati (Nov. 5, 1992). Feminists are not alone in laying claim to a more inclusive vision, for this is a standard call of the left. See, for example, David Konstan's suggestions that "this resurgent version of the Old Humanities is often openly hostile to the ideals of radical egalitarianism that mark the New Humanities" ("What Is New in the New Approaches to Classical Literature," *Crisis* 45-49, quotation on 48). Such egalitarianism is theoretical—all cultures and systems of values must be given equal consideration. But are the "New Humanities" demonstrably more open to the "Old Humanities" than the Old are to the New? Comments made by each extreme about the other would seem to suggest we have far to go.

16. I take these different "feminisms" from the discussions of J. Birkeland,

"Ecofeminism: Linking Theory and Practice," and L. Gruen, "Dismantling Oppression: An Analysis of the Connection Between Women and Animals," in G. Gaard (ed.), *Ecofeminism: Women, Animals, Nature* (Philadelphia 1993), 17 and 25, respectively.

17. The connection between theories and the life of theorists has always been problematic. Political scientists who advocate Marxism or socialism in their publications live in big houses in the most exclusive neighborhoods of Palo Alto and La Jolla—I know one in Florida who boasted for weeks that his front lawn had won a neighborhood prize for "best-groomed." Even if feminism in some of its forms can be shown to be communitarian, does this mean that feminist scholars will necessarily live that life?

18. The recent controversial APA elections were generally read as a "victory" for the Right over the Left, but they can just as easily be seen as a continued control by the top over the rest. The ironies multiply to the point of absurdity when Richard Thomas, accurately termed an "elitist" by the feminist contingent, attempts to call our attention to the fact that both female candidates "teach at elitist East coast colleges" ([above, n.5] 54).

19. See Henderson's discussion of "serious" and "unserious" students ([above, n.7] 93) and Sussman's (above, n.3) analogy of the major and minor leagues.

20. Galinsky (above, n.4) 445.

21. Galinsky apparently attempts to defuse any charges of possible elitism (after proudly listing his elitist credentials) by referring to his years on "the assembly line" during his college days ([above, n.4] 442). And Ronald Reagan was president of a union.

22. Galinsky (above, n.4) 448. Some, on ideological grounds, may object to Galinsky's use of a Western economic model, but the better objection would be that anyone who argues for *any* general education requirement—and I know very few who do not—believes in some form of education protectionism. Indeed, many of us who have taught at liberal arts colleges chose that environment because *by definition* the students' curricular choices are limited to areas we believe to be *more important than others*; see Hallett (above, n.15) 5–7 for a good critique of Galinsky's ideas.

23. Galinsky, "The Challenge of Teaching the Ancient World," in D. M. Astolfi (ed.), *Teaching the Ancient World* (Chico, Calif. 1983) 3.

24. David Halperin, "Normalizing Greek Desire," *Crisis* 257–72.

25. Charles Segal, *Orpheus: The Myth of the Poet* (Baltimore and London 1989). And to be fair to all sides (examples are too easy to find), one can point to a recent book on Pindar by Mary Lefkowitz, the *bête noire* of feminist classicists, every single chapter of which has appeared over the past thirty years.

26. Martin Bernal, for example, (above, n.2) 72 comments on the "advent of the Reagan Administration and the ideologies of the Far Right that it put into power over academia." David Halperin also discusses the 1980s, "when much of Western Europe and America seems to have sunk into a reactionary torpor, embracing with a hollow and cynical enthusiasm the comforts of conventional pieties and rushing to rediscover the demagogic possibilities of a self-serving obscurantism" (*One Hundred Years of Homosexuality* [New York 1990] 8). Surely the "reactionary" right is not the only side to have discovered "the demagogic possibilities of a self-serving obscurantism." Camille Paglia rightly notes that

the "French invasion of the Seventies had nothing to do with leftism or genuine politics but everything to do with good old-fashioned American capitalism, which liberal academics pretend to scorn" ("Junk Bonds and Corporate Raiders: Academe in the Hour of the Wolf," *Arion* 3rd ser. 1.2 [1991] 139–212, quotation on 185). For Paglia's own part in the debate, the words of Mary Lefkowitz (in general quite favorable) fit closely with my argument: "I can't help noticing that she too is a product of the American academic world: quick to schematize, eager to promote herself, ready to jump on a theoretical bandwagon" ("Madonna's Intellectual," *The Public Interest* [Winter 1993] 93–97, quotation on 97). George H. Douglas also uses the analogy of what I term Reagademics in his discussion of the failure of the American university system to free itself from the Germanic graduate model: "What we have is a 'trickle-down' style of undergraduate education. Undergraduates get the drippings or leavings of the table from graduate schools. No idea that has ever taken hold in the American university has been more harmful and destructive than this one" (*Chronicle of Higher Education* 39.27 [March 10, 1993] B6).

27. Henderson (above, n.7) 90 notes that the sciences have overcome this dichotomy in such figures as Richard Feynman and Stephen Hawking (and I might add Stephen Jay Gould and Richard Dawkins). Mellor (above, n.8) 103 observes that both British and French classical scholars write general works about the ancient world apparently without ruining their careers.

28. Ralph Hexter and Daniel Selden, *Innovations of Antiquity* (New York and London 1992), xx.

29. More revealingly, the sentiment is merely a rehashing of archetypal remarks from the founding fathers of the Left, who themselves are the direct descendants of the Sophists; see D. Roochnik, *The Tragedy of Reason* (New York 1990). Note, for example, Marcel Detienne's review of the ways classicists of the twentieth century had kept the study of Greek mythology to themselves (and away from anthropologists) in his "Myth of 'Honeyed Orpheus'," in R. L. Gordon (ed.), *Myth, Religion and Society* (Cambridge 1981) 95 (originally published as "Orphée au miel" in 1971):

> But most effective of all was their third method, the handing over of mythical narrative to literary history. Ever since, classical scholars have used the written status of classical mythology to justify their prior claim to it, and until quite recently they did no more than select from it the elements compatible with the dominant ideology of the bourgeois society whose interests and aims so-called "classical" philology has always so faithfully served.

For a thorough discussion of the ironies of this introduction to a series of remarkably familiar and "tempered" articles, see Bruce Thornton's analysis in chapter five of this volume. Victor Davis Hanson has pointed out to me that Daniel Selden can, in fact, when it serves his own purposes, praise "accommodating" prose, as in his blurb for Jack Winkler's *The Constraints of Desire*: "Winkler writes with a *precision and liveliness that are rare within the field*...consistently *clear, logical, and persuasive,* and one needs no Greek to follow his discussion" (first emphasis in blurb itself, second emphasis mine). Similar criticisms of clear prose from the ideological Left can be found in other fields of the humanities. In a *Chronicle* article examining the debate on accessible language in the feminist journal *Signs,* for example, the historian Joan Scott lumps together "simple language" and "personal experience," which "to me suggest a kind of anti-intellectualism" (*Chronicle of Higher Education* 39.27 [March 10, 1993] A12).

30. This discussion takes place not only in such purely academic publications as the *Chronicle of Higher Education* but in the popular press as well. Camille Paglia's *Sex, Art and American Culture* (New York 1992), the first essay of which is a reprint of her *Arion* review of Winkler, Halperin, and the state of classics, was a bestseller for many weeks.

31. For comments and bibliography on the demise of deconstruction, see Thornton (above, n.29).

32. See the indirect quotation from Amy Richlin in the article in the *Chronicle of Higher Education* cited at the beginning of this paper.

33. One should celebrate the efforts of Barbara McManus, for example, to gather members of small classics programs in various formats at the recent APA meetings; see her comments in the *APA Newsletter* 15.6 (1992) 19-20. Thanks may also be owed for the decision of the latest editor of the *Biographical Dictionary of North American Classicists* (Greenwood Press 1993) to include "a third group, less distinguished, the laborers in the vineyard who kept classics alive in the small or more remote institutions of our country and achieved at least regional distinction for their work" (Ward W. Briggs, Jr., "Prolegomena to the Study of the History of Classical Scholarship in the United States," *CB* 68.1 [1992] 7-12, quotation on 9). At least there is no attempt here to disguise who stomps on the grapes and who enjoys the vintage.

34. "Keynote Address to the Conference on Teaching the Ancient World," *Crisis* 39-43, quotation on 42. Lowell Edmunds presents a more realistic picture of the difficulties involved in attempting any change: "What is actually elitist in the situation I have described is not the two-tier system itself but the attitude of the upper toward the lower tier" ("Introduction," *Crisis* ix-xxviii, quotation on xiv). But it is also the members of the "lower tier," all of whom are products of the "upper tier," who are accomplices in perpetuating the myth of graduate faculty as the ideal of the profession. Could the entire discipline have an inferiority complex? This would account for both the arrogance of the elites and the complicity of the rest.

35. Judith Hallett draws my attention to the promising efforts to "sketch an agenda for reform of graduate education" organized at the APA in December 1993, by the Department of Classical Studies of the University of Pennsylvania. This is an ongoing project, with results to be presented over the next few years.

36. A series of articles and letters in the *Chronicle of Higher Education* debating the relationship between teaching and research revealed the tensions quite clearly. Surprisingly neither side argued that teaching and research should not be combined (as I remember, one Stanford science faculty insisted, "If they want to teach, let them go to Williams"). Even Bryan Barnett's "Teaching and Research Are Inescapably Incompatible" (38.39 [June 3, 1992] A40), which provoked the discussion, based the dichotomy primarily on the realities of publication requirements, not on an educational *desideratum*. The resulting letters (June 10, June 17, June 24, July 8) and the more formal response by Robert McCaughey, "Why Research and Teaching Can Coexist," 38.48 (Aug. 5, 1992)

A36, reflect the ideal of the teacher-scholar which is becoming more and more difficult to realize.

37. Sussman (above, n.3) 114-15. This sort of exchange program could be started immediately in parts of the country where Ph.D.-granting institutions are located near undergraduate colleges and universities. The graduate program might serve as a regional nexus for the faculty exchange (somewhat on the southern California model).

38. The protestations to such a plan, or similarly conceived consortia, ring very hollow. If, as is often the case, a young Ph.D. one year out of graduate school can conduct a graduate seminar (even though he or she has no record of peer review on the research), certainly a teacher-scholar with a record of publication on a topic, and a record of excellent teaching, can perform in a similar, if not superior fashion. The real problem might very well be the reverse. Would a graduate researcher be able to teach effectively a forty-student undergraduate course with students of average ability?

39. I have quite intentionally not attempted to define "good" teaching. There are many ways to be effective, rigorous, and inspiring in the classroom.

40. "After Smashing the Wedgwood," *American Scholar* 58 (1989) 531-41, quotation on 537.

41. See, for example, John Leo's review of this "Gong Show" in *U.S. News and World Report* (Jan. 18, 1993), 25. I found it both interesting and foreboding that this review ended with the comments of Professor Feroza Jussawalla, who "passionately supports multicultural studies." She worries about intimidation and censorship in the MLA (in this case, from the Left) and "calls for freedom from both the old 'scholarly humanist elites' and the new 'elitist hegemonic Marxists'." The titles of the silly papers given each year at the MLA may present a skewed view of the priorities of all its members, but this has been encouraged and sponsored by its leadership. Is classics *that* far behind? Wasn't there a cry for the APA to become more like the MLA in at least one of the candidates' statements last year?

42. See the comments of Francis R. Bliss, "The APA and the Regional Associations," *TAPA* 123 (1993) 411-13, with the reply by Jerry Clack (413-16), on the dismissal of regional organizations by the "big-wigs and careerists."

43. E. Christian Kopff, "Home Thoughts on British and American Classicists," *Crisis* 317-20, quotation on 319. For a quite different, but equally impassioned, view of the role of foreigners in American academics, see Thomas Figueira's "The Prospects for Ancient History," *Crisis* 369-81. The issue is not completely irrelevant to my argument. If undergraduate teaching and the training of undergraduate teachers should really become a high priority, one would have to make a very good case for hiring a classicist with absolutely no experience in our undergraduate world and no demonstrable ability to perform either of the desired tasks; see James W. Halporn, "Foreign Scholars and American Classical Education," *Crisis* 305-315 (esp. 313-14). One has to question the thinking behind the hiring of foreign scholars at any time, but especially to head a department—some can barely speak English!

44. This paper began life as a frenetic and restive infant. The editors and referees recommended a nearly two-year course of surgical procedures and heavy medication. As a result of these efforts, for which I am genuinely grateful, it is

now much better behaved and perhaps ready for company. I must admit, however, that I miss some of its youthful obstreperousness.

7. *Who Killed Homer?*: The Prequel

1. For discussions of the FBI and the so-called "Unabomber Maneuver," see John Heath's epilogue in this volume. Hours before going to press, James Clark, the director of the University of California Press, made a sudden list of non-negotiable demands aimed at eliminating our criticism of prominent classicists in the paperback edition of *Who Killed Homer?* that was scheduled for publication in Spring 2001—after a mysterious delay of nearly two years. For an account of the strange paperback odyssey of *Who Killed Homer?* with the University of California Press, see the Afterword in the new edition by Encounter (San Francisco 2001).

2. *New York Times Magazine,* Sunday, February 16 (1997), 38, 40, 42. Wills is not alone, of course, in his contention that classics is flourishing as never before. Some classicists agree. These cheerful souls base their optimism on a few heavily enrolled courses at those institutions where students can, for example, satisfy their "Gender Studies" requirement by taking a course in "Women in Antiquity." Professor Judith Hallett of the University of Maryland, for example, claims that "[t]he study of classics thrives in the United States—though not necessarily in the form of undergraduate classics majors. Many students, though concentrating in other subjects, fill their requirements for a liberal arts degree by studying ancient languages, classical texts-in-translation, and other aspects of Greco-Roman civilization." *Lingua Franca* Sept./Oct. (1995), 62–63. As we will make clear, a handful of courses like these is not indicative of the health of classics in America but rather provides the last narrow foothold for an academic discipline on the university curriculum, the final justification for jobs of a final generation of classicists.

3. These and the following numbers come from *L'Année Philologique,* the official bibliographical guide to scholarship on the classical worlds. 1992 is the most recent year available—the bibliography itself cannot keep up with the volume of publication and is years behind. The 16,168 publications do not include the thousands of book reviews published in professional journals.

4. Jean Susorvey Wellington, *Dictionary of Bibliographic Abbreviations Found in the Scholarship of Classical Studies and Related Disciplines* (Westpoint, Conn. 1983), xi.

5. Keith Stanley, *The Shield of Homer: Narrative Structure in the Iliad* (Princeton, N.J. 1993).

6. Celia McGee, in her supplementary article to Wills's, claims without documentation that enrollment in Latin courses at the college and graduate school level increased twenty-five percent between 1992 and 1994 ("The Classic Moment: Signs that B.C. is P.C." *The New York Times Magazine,* Sunday, February 16 [1997], 41). In reality, the numbers provided by the MLA tell a different story: Latin enrollments actually declined a further 8 per cent between 1990 and 1995; see *CAMWS Newsletter* 6.2 (1996), 7. The desperate attempts of supporters of the phantom "multicultural Greeks and Romans" to document their success hang on equally insubstantial evidence. McGee cites the publication of new translations of Greek authors (hardly a new phenomenon and unrelated to most

recent scholarship), art exhibits (even less novel), and the Disney movie *Hercules*. The appearance of Hercules in an animated feature film has as much connection to classical studies as the success of *The Little Mermaid* had to the study of marine biology.

7. Marilyn Skinner et al., "Greek 2000—Crisis, Challenge, Deadline," *The Classical Journal* 91.4 (1996), 406.

8. For these statistics on the demise of classics, we have drawn from *Classics: A Discipline and Profession in Crisis?* edited by Phyllis Culham and Lowell Edmunds (Lanham, Md. 1989), and David Damrosch, "Can Classics Die?" *Lingua Franca* Sept./Oct. (1995), 61–66. Despite the question mark in these titles, the consensus is that our ship is indeed sinking—even as the doomed point fingers at one another before we drown. The most recent data are particularly distressing. While Latin enrollments at the *pre-college* level have increased during the past few years (Latin is studied in fewer than 2 percent of America's high schools), the number of students taking Latin and Greek continues to decline as a percentage of the total *university* population. That is, colleges and universities fail to sustain students' incipient interest in the classical world. See Richard A. LaFleur, "*Latina Resurgens*: Classical Language Enrollments in American Schools and Colleges," *Classical Outlook* 74.4 (1997), 125–30.

9. *Classical World* 65.8–9 (1972), 258.

10. D. Konstan, *Classical World*, 89.1 (1995), 33.

11. James O'Donnel, *Lingua Franca* Sept./Oct. (1995), 62.

12. Ian Morris, ed., *Classical Greece: Ancient Histories and Modern Archaeologies* (Cambridge 1994), 3.

13. Tina Passman, "Out of the Closet and into the Field: Matriculture, the Lesbian Perspective, and Feminist Classics," *Feminist Theory and the Classics*, N.S. Rabinowitz and A. Richlin, eds. (New York and London 1993), 181.

14. M. Bernal, *Black Athena: The Afroasiatic Roots of Classical Civilization, Vol. 1: The Fabrication of Ancient Greece 1785–1985* (New Brunswick, N.J. 1987), 2, 5.

15. Page Dubois, *Sappho Is Burning* (Chicago 1995), 147.

16. Eva C. Keuls, *The Reign of the Phallus: Sexual Politics in Ancient Athens* (New York 1985), 1.

17. V. J. Wohl, "Standing by the Stathmos: The Creation of Sexual Ideology in the *Odyssey*," *Arethusa* 26 (1993), 44.

18. I. E. Holmberg, "The *Odyssey* and Female Subjectivity," *Helios* 22.2 (Fall 1995), 120.

19. N. S. Rabinowitz, "Introduction," *Feminist Theory and the Classics* (note 12), 16.

20. "Black Feminist Thought and Classics: Re-membering, Re-claiming, Re-empowering," *Feminist Theory and the Classics* (note 12), 29.

21. Barbara Goff, "Introduction" in *History, Tragedy, Theory* (Austin, Tex. 1996), 20.

22. Marilyn A. Katz, *Penelope's Renown: Meaning and Indeterminacy in the Odyssey*, Princeton 1991.

23. Review by L. E. Doherty, *Classical Journal* 89 (1994), 205.

24. *Saint Foucault* (Oxford 1995), 12.

25. Quoted in *Academic Questions* 7.4 (1994), 33.

26. *Classical World* 89.1 (1995), 32.

27. *Classical Outlook* 70 (1992), 8.

28. *Classical World* 89.1 (1995), 33.

8. The Twilight of the Professors

1. *The Treason of the Intellectuals,* trans. Richard Aldington (New York, 1928), xi.

2. Peter W. Rose, "Historicizing Sophocles' *Ajax,*" in *History, Tragedy, Theory: Dialogues on Athenian Drama,* ed. Barbara Goff (Austin, Tex. 1996), 75.

3. "The Function of Criticism at the Present Time," in *Selected Prose,* ed. P.J. Keating (Harmondsworth, 1970), 141–42.

4. Benda, 79, 103, 117.

5. *The Poverty of Theory* (New York, 1978), 3.

6. In "Junk Bonds and Corporate Raiders: Academe in the Hour of the Wolf," 1991; rpt. in *Sex, Art, and American Culture* (New York 1992), 210.

7. For a brief history see Russell Jacoby, *Dogmatic Wisdom: How the Culture Wars Divert Education and Distract America* (New York 1994), 92–119.

8. See George Roche, *The Fall of the Ivory Tower: Government Funding and the Bankrupting of American Higher Education* (Washington, D.C. 1994), 72.

9. See *Impostors in the Temple* (New York 1992), 32.

10. *The Degradation of the Academic Dogma: The University in America, 1945–1970* (New York and London 1971), 75.

11. *Proscam: Professors and the Demise of Higher Education* (Washington, D.C. 1988), 4–5.

12. Nisbet, 109. Emphases omitted.

13. Radical multiculturalists understand this: cf. David Theo Goldberg, who identifies a "corporate multiculturalism" that is really the ideology "of a centrist academy and multinational corporations that take themselves to be committed to the broad tenets of philosophical liberalism." In "Introduction: Multicultural Conditions," *Multiculturalism: A Critical Reader,* ed. David Theo Goldberg (Cambridge, Mass. 1994), 7.

INDEX

and multiculturalism, 7

chôra, Bergren's definition of, 172

Choral Works, 172-173

classical criticism, 126

   History, Tragedy, Theory: Dialogues on Athenian Drama, 177

classical literature

   and contemporary customs, 266

   criticism of, 264

Classical World, 195-203, 323

classics majors, and GRE scores in humanities, 249

Classics: A Discipline and Profession in Crisis?, 203

Cleopatra, ethnicity of, 275

clerks, 303

Clinton, Bill, 104, 130

close reading, 75

The Closing of the American Mind

   and freedom of the mind, 23

   and need for Socratic education, 24

   and required courses in non-Western cultures, 22

Clouds , simplistic reading of, 31-32

Cohen, David, 289

Colorado's Amendment Two, 48

compassion, and academic Left, 37

Compromising Traditions, 93, 122, 132

   and anti-British themes, 117-118

   contradictions and, 108-121

   criticism of, 106

   diversity in authorship and, 109-110

   flaws of, 94-95

   and language of the personal voice, 116

   as metaphor of academia, 95

Connor, W.R., and adversarial models, 223

Constraints of Desire, 158

Corngold, Stanley, 141

corporate multiculturalism, 5

countermovements, and traditional modes of scholarship, 64

Crews, Frederick

   and glut of research, 189

   and theoreticism, 181

Culler, Jonathan, 161

Cullham, Phyllis, 203

cultural pluralism, definition of, 19

cultural relativism, 11-13

   and rejection of moral relativism, 43-44

   and Western history, 17-18

culture wars, 42, 50

curricular reform, 250

curriculum development, 223-224

D

Dangerfield, Anthony, and vital signs of humanities, 62-63

D'Arms, John, grants and, 89

Davis, Angela, 65

de Luce, Judith, 108

   and personal voice theory, 126-127

de Maistre, Joseph, and Enlightenment universalism, 11-12

de Man, Paul, 73, 142, 154

   and opposition to deconstructionism, 75

deconstructionism

   critics of, 154

   detractors of, 178

   domestication of, 161

Denby, David, 85, 289

ABOUT THE AUTHORS

VICTOR DAVIS HANSON is a professor of Greek and Director of the Classics Program at the California State University in Fresno. He has authored or edited a number of books, including *The Other Greeks* (1995), *Fields Without Dreams: Defending the Agrarian Ideal* (1996), *Who Killed Homer? The Demise of Classical Education and the Recovery of Greek Wisdom* (with John Heath, 1998), *The Soul of Battle* (1999), and *The Land Was Everything* (2000). In 1992 he was named the most outstanding undergraduate teacher of classics in the nation.

JOHN HEATH is Associate Professor of Classics at Santa Clara University. His books include *Actaeon, the Unmannerly Intruder* (1992) and *Who Killed Homer? The Demise of Classical Education and the Recovery of Greek Wisdom* (with Victor Davis Hanson, 1998).

BRUCE S. THORNTON is Professor of Classics and Humanities in the Department of Foreign Languages at the California State University in Fresno. His books include *Eros: The Myth of Ancient Greek Sexuality* (1997), *Plagues of the Mind: The New Epidemic of False Knowledge* (1999), and *Greek Ways: How the Greeks Created Western Civilization* (2000).